Murder on Trial

Murder on Trial

1620–2002

EDITED BY

Robert Asher,
Lawrence B. Goodheart,
and
Alan Rogers

State University of New York Press

Published by
State University of New York Press, Albany

Printed in the United States of America

For information, address the State University of New York Press,
90 State Street, Suite 700, Albany, NY 12207

Production by Diane Ganeles
Marketing by Anne M. Valentine

Library of Congress Cataloging-in-Publication Data

Murder on trial : 1620–2002 / edited by Robert Asher, Lawrence B. Goodheart,
and Alan Rogers
    p. cm.
    Includes bibliographical references and index.
    ISBN 0-7914-6377-X (hardcopy : alk. paper) — ISBN 0-7914-6378-8 (pbk. :
alk. paper)
    1. Murder—United States—History.   2. Homicide—United States—History.
I. Asher, Robert.   II. Goodheart, Lawrence B., 1944–   III. Rogers, Alan, 1936–

HV6524.M876 2005
345.73'02523'09—dc22   2004009619

10 9 8 7 6 5 4 3 2 1

To Bruce Fraser and the Connecticut Humanities Council

Contents

Gender and Class Norms

Acknowledgments

The editors would like to thank the Connecticut Humanities Council for funding the 2001 conference on Murder in New England, Wethersfield Historical Society, Wethersfield, Connecticut. This volume, whose scope reaches beyond New England, is based on long versions of many of the papers first delivered at that conference. We would also like to thank Beth De Wolfe for her astute advice.

Introduction

1

Adjudicating Homicide:
The Legal Framework and Social Norms

Robert Asher,
Lawrence B. Goodheart,
and
Alan Rogers

Mark Twain once asked, "If the desire to kill and the opportunity to kill came always together, who would escape hanging?" The great humorist was entertaining. But he was too glib. The essays in this volume indicate that throughout the history of England's North American colonies and the United States, legal decisions about the guilt of people accused of murder and the proper punishment of those convicted of murder have not followed automatically any set of principles and procedures. People, with all their human prejudices, create murder jurisprudence—the social rules that govern the arrest, trial, and punishment of humans accused of homicide, i.e., the killing of a human being.

Between colonial and present times, the dominant English-speaking inhabitants in the area that became the United States have altered significantly the rules of criminal homicide, providing increasing numbers of constitutional and judicially constructed safeguards to those accused of homicide and to convicted murderers. Changing community ideas about insanity, the development of children, gender roles, and racism have affected the law.

The essays in *Murder on Trial* analyze the effects of changing social norms on the development and application of the legal frameworks used to determine the motives and the ability to distinguish between right and wrong of people who are accused of a homicide. Especially after 1930, fewer white Americans—but not all—accepted the notion that racial and ethnic minorities were biologically and morally inferior. But the application of the law of

3

murder has always been uneven. Human rivalries and biases always have led prosecutors, judges, and jurors to side with or against accused murderers because of the latter's class, gender, race, or perceived mental competency.

I

Due process—fair and reasonable rules consistently applied—is the means by which governmental power is restrained and a criminal defendant's rights are safeguarded. The development of procedural fairness has long distinguished Anglo-American jurisprudence, but the concept that liberty and rights could not exist without due process of law only gradually became a part of our constitutional heritage. Supreme Court Justice Felix Frankfurter celebrated this dynamic process in 1945. "The history of American freedom," Frankfurter wrote in *Malinski v. New York*, "is, in no small measure, the history of procedure."[1]

State and federal bills of rights lay out a due process framework for criminal defendants. The Fourth, Fifth, Sixth and Eighth Amendments of the United States Bill of Rights protect the accused against unreasonable searches and self-incrimination, guarantee a public jury trial, representation by counsel, and the right to confront witnesses. The Eighth Amendment prohibits cruel and unusual punishment. These federal rights did not extend to state criminal proceedings until a series of Supreme Court rulings in the 1960s incorporated the Bill of Rights through the Fourteenth Amendment's due process clause. Together with habeas corpus, the legal term for the procedure by which a judge probes the legality of a defendant's imprisonment, the Court's rulings and changing political and social attitudes shaped the development of defendants' rights primarily by curbing governmental power. Common law rules and constitutional rights also are meant to buffer the defendant from the racial, ethnic, gender and class biases that might taint criminal proceedings. Anglo-American due process has been justly celebrated for its success in minimizing the impact of social attitudes on the law, but it is by nature an imperfect system. The proper administration of justice, Professor David Fellman observes, "depends upon the temper of the community, the nature of its prejudices and values, the character of its scapegoats, the state of the economy, the quality of its bench and bar, its educational system, and related non-legal factors."[2]

Seventeenth-century English colonists carried to North America a remarkably sophisticated legal system that they regularly modified to fit local conditions and their particular value systems. The Puritans mixed English common law and biblical injunctions to create a simplified law code that laymen could understand. Although the *Massachusetts Body of Liberties* (1641) contained harsh punishment for moral crimes, it included far fewer capital crimes and extended greater procedural protection to the accused than did English law. In England hundreds of crimes were punishable by death. By contrast, Massachusetts listed only a dozen crimes and Connecticut just fourteen crimes for which death was the penalty. A capital defendant in the Bay Colony also had greater legal protection than did a defendant in England. A colonist facing murder charges had a right to some of the following: knowledge of the charges, indictment by a grand jury, a jury trial, the assistance of counsel, challenge of potential jurors, cross-examination of witnesses, and, from an early date, at least a limited right to appeal a guilty verdict. Significant as these procedural rights were, they were neither absolute nor unalloyed. Judges often pressured defendants to confess, warning them that nothing could be hidden from an all-knowing God; lawyers who might have buffered their clients from this kind of treatment were few and far between.[3]

New England colonists assumed their form of criminal justice was superior to Indian legal systems. For Indians justice was defined by the victim's clan and the perpetrator's clan and did not involve the intervention of an impersonal state. The blood feud was the centerpiece of Indian law, although it did not inevitably involve bloodshed. A murder victim's clan might negotiate a settlement, including the payment of valuable goods to compensate for their loss. In this way peace and social harmony were restored. However, the colonists tarred the blood feud as "barbaric" and smugly insisted all New England residents must be subject to English law. New England colonial courts made some adjustments when an Indian defendant stood trial. Interpreters explained the process to the accused Indian and Christian Indians were added to capital juries in Massachusetts. We also know not all Indian capital defendants were found guilty, nor were whites charged with murdering an Indian necessarily freed. Except in wartime, all New England defendants were presumed innocent until proved guilty.[4]

The opposite was true in seventeenth-century Virginia. All free white criminal defendants were assumed guilty as charged until proved innocent. They were not entitled to a lawyer. The accused might opt for a jury trial, but since they had little knowledge of the offense with which they were charged and could not call witnesses on their behalf, it was not a popular choice. The General Court in Williamsburg heard all capital cases, but a defendant had no greater rights in that court than in the lower courts. Servants and slaves were denied even this rudimentary form of justice.[5]

The American Revolution transformed the values that underlay criminal due process, though the pace of change varied from state to state. The Anglo-American claim that rights were linked to liberty and that governmental power had to be limited to preserve freedom had ancient roots, but following the Revolution all American citizens claimed greater individual rights than they had had as English subjects, and state and federal constitutions expressly articulated those rights. The results of this change were striking. Trial juries provide a good example. In England, social class was the primary consideration in forming a jury of peers, but in the new American republic every propertied white adult man was eligible to sit in judgment of any defendant, a practice Americans celebrated as the most important barrier to arbitrary government.[6]

Jurors in murder trials, lawyers, and legislators in the early American republic were enormously influenced by a book published by Italian nobleman, Cesare Beccaria. Although some American patriots worried that the traditional fragility of a republic necessitated a death penalty in order to maintain order, others such as Benjamin Rush of Pennsylvania and Attorney General James Sullivan of Massachusetts denounced capital punishment as monarchical and touted the benefits of Beccaria's enlightened approach to punishment. Translated into English in the 1770s, Beccaria's *Essay on Crimes and Punishments* blasted capital punishment as unsuited to a republic. First, he argued no one could surrender to the state the right over his or her own life; therefore, the state had no right to take a life. Second, Beccaria insisted that the death penalty was not a deterrent to murder. The most hardened criminals "can look upon death with intrepidity and firmness." What they loathe is lengthy imprisonment at hard labor. Therefore, imprisonment is a greater deterrent to crime than death, but it is less cruel. "If all the miserable moments in the life of a slave were collected into one point," Beccaria argued, imprisonment "would be a more cruel punishment than any other; but these are scattered through his whole life, whilst the pain of death exerts all its force in a moment." For this reason, a reasonable person "considers the sum of all [a prisoner's] wretched moments" as worse than death. However, the prisoner, "who by the misery of the present, is prevented from thinking of the future," thinks his punishment to be less severe than death. Third, Beccaria believed executions corrupted a society. The barbarous spectacle of a public execution coarsened the spectators, deterred no one, and probably encouraged violent behavior.

The immediate result of Beccaria's argument was that five states abolished the death penalty for all crimes other than murder. In 1790, for example, Pennsylvania abolished the death penalty for robbery and burglary and four years later became the first state to divide murder into degrees. Only "wilful, deliberate, or premeditated killing" carried the death penalty. By 1846 a dozen states had enacted similar statutes.[7]

As these early nineteenth-century reforms suggest, the trial and punishment of murderers was a state matter. According to the United States Supreme Court's decision in *Barron v. Baltimore* (1833), the Bill of Rights limited only the federal government. This fact shaped the campaign strategy of moral reformers, who focused not on the reform of criminal trial procedures but on the abolition of capital punishment. Reformers who sought to abolish the death penalty stressed religion's regard for human life and the long-term social and political benefits of abolition. New Yorker John L. O'Sullivan, for example, argued that the New Testament repudiated the Old Testament argument of retribution, and he predicted that the practical as well as the political and social benefits of abolition would be profound. A jury would be more likely to convict a capital defendant if there was no death penalty, and abolition would be a giant stride toward ending violence and tyranny throughout American life, according to O'Sullivan. Although proponents of capital punishment successfully blocked abolition in New York, a coalition of clergymen and middle-class professionals in Michigan and Rhode Island did succeed in ending the death penalty. In New York, Massachusetts, and Pennsylvania, reformers settled for moving executions behind prison walls. The Northern crusade against slavery and the Civil War sapped the effort to abolish the death penalty.[8]

In the aftermath of the Civil War, however, changes in federal criminal procedure enacted to bolster the goals of the Thirteenth, Fourteenth, and Fifteenth Amendments powerfully influenced the rights that states extended to the accused. To buttress African-Americans' freedom, Congress enacted laws permitting a criminal defendant to testify in his or her own behalf and armed federal prosecutors with the right to use peremptory challenges—a strike of a potential juror for which no justification was required. Because it signaled equality before the law, the *New York Times* believed allowing a black criminal defendant to tell his or her own story was even more important than extending to African-Americans the right to vote. Shortly after Congress enacted the law, most states followed suit by extending the right to testify to all state criminal defendants. To further protect African-American criminal defendants from prejudiced whites, states also followed Congress's lead by empowering state prosecutors, as well as defendants, to use peremptory challenges. Ironically, what seemed at the time to be part of a solution to protect African-American criminal defendants against racially prejudiced jurors became, in the hands of racist prosecutors, an *obstacle* to achieving race-neutral juries.[9]

By the 1880s the effort to implement a color-blind Constitution had collapsed. One result was the growth of "strange fruit," the extralegal lynching and the often unjust execution of black criminal defendants throughout the Southern states. The former was made possible by the unchecked rise of racial animosity and the latter by a string of Supreme Court decisions limiting the Fourteenth Amendment's due process and equal protection clauses as they applied to state criminal proceedings. In 1880, for example, the Supreme Court heard two cases involving black men convicted of murder by all-white juries. The Court distinguished the cases in a way that rationalized racially discriminatory jury selection practices. It found that a West Virginia statute restricting jury service to white males violated the Fourteenth Amendment's equal protection clause, but it permitted to stand a Virginia practice of achieving the same discriminatory result. Southern states were quick to pick up the Court's broad hint about how best to exclude blacks from jury service. For more than a century, the vast majority of criminal juries in the South were all-white.[10]

The jurisdictional wall between state and federal criminal proceedings began to crumble when the Supreme Court heard two cases involving the so-called Scottsboro Boys, nine young black men charged with raping two white women riding on a freight train in the spring of 1931. In *Powell v. Alabama* (1932) the Court ruled for the first time that the Fourteenth Amendment's due process clause included the right to a fair trial and, therefore, required state courts to appoint counsel for indigent defendants in all capital cases. The Scottsboro Boys were retried and again sentenced to death. One of the defendants, Clarence Norris, appealed his conviction, arguing that African-Americans had been excluded from both the grand jury that indicted him and the trial jury that found him guilty of rape. Previously, the Court had rebuffed every challenge to discriminatory jury practices, but in *Norris v. Alabama* (1935) it held that "long continued, unvarying and wholesale exclusion" of black people from juries was a violation of the Fourteenth Amendment's equal protection clause. Eventually, the Scottsboro Boys were freed, but not until they had served years in jail for a crime they did not commit. Although the Court's decisions placed the burden on the defendant of proving the lack of effective assistance of counsel and the systemic exclusion of eligible black jurors, the rulings signaled the beginning of the so-called due process revolution.[11]

In the three decades following these decisions, the Court struggled to determine what procedural rights included in the due process clause should be applied to state criminal proceedings. The chief obstacle to nationalizing the Bill of Rights was the absence of a theoretical framework. Most judges held to the belief that the federal structure gave states exclusive control over state criminal matters. Still, *Scottsboro* had opened the way for exceptions. The year following *Norris*, for example, the Court reversed the convictions of three black Mississippi tenant farmers who had been sentenced to death for the murder of a white planter chiefly on the basis of their coerced confessions. During the trial, police officers freely admitted beating the defendants with a metal-studded leather belt and repeatedly placing a rope around the neck of one of the men and hanging him above the ground until he lost consciousness. At trial, the defendants repudiated their "confessions." In *Brown v. Mississippi* (1936), Chief Justice Charles Evans Hughes conceded that the Fifth Amendment's prohibition against compulsory self-incrimination did not apply to the states, but he insisted that a state could not "substitute trial by ordeal" for the fair trial standard guaranteed by the Fourteenth Amendment.[12]

Although the Court's intervention in a handful of cases had saved men's lives, its effectiveness was limited, because the "fair trial" standard was not spelled out. Indeed, as late as 1937 the Court announced that the Fourteenth Amendment did not incorporate the right to trial by jury. According to Justice Felix Frankfurter, all the Court could do was decide on a case-by-case basis if the fundamental rights of the accused had been violated. Justice Hugo L. Black, a former Alabama Klan member appointed to the Court by President Franklin Roosevelt in 1937, offered an alternative strategy. Black argued that the framers of the Fourteenth Amendment had intended to incorporate the Bill of Rights into the due process clause and to apply those rights to the states. Throughout the 1940s and 1950s Black and Frankfurter jousted over which interpretation of the Fourteenth Amendment and the Bill of Rights should determine the law of the land.[13]

The interpretive logjam was broken under the leadership of Chief Justice Earl Warren. In 1955, the year after his appointment to the Court, Warren published an essay in which he rejected judicial restraint in favor of an active, evolving interpretation of the Constitution, particularly the Bill of Rights. The pursuit of justice, Warren wrote, implied a continual revision of what rights meant, a process of creating "a document that will not have exactly the same meaning it had when we received it from our fathers," but one that would be improved because it was "burnished by growing use." Beginning in 1961, when it ruled in *Mapp v. Ohio* that the Fourteenth Amendment applied to the states the Fourth Amendment's prohibition of unreasonable searches, the Warren Court rapidly dismantled the wall separating the Fourteenth Amendment from the Bill of Rights.[14]

In 1963 the Court abandoned the fair trial interpretation. Clarence Earl Gideon, a fifty-four-year-old Florida drifter who had spent nearly seventeen years behind bars, was convinced that he had a constitutional right to an attorney to defend him against a charge of breaking and entering a poolroom with intent to commit petty larceny. The Florida trial judge told Gideon that the court appointed counsel only in capital cases, and the Florida Supreme Court rejected his appeal. But the United States Supreme Court agreed with Gideon. Writing for a unanimous Court, Justice Black insisted the Court was returning to its old precedent in *Powell v. Alabama,* in which the Court had held that a defendant "who is too poor to hire a lawyer cannot be assured a fair trial unless counsel is provided for him." Although Black's opinion used the fair trial language, the decision represented a victory for the nationalization of the Bill of Rights.[15]

The year following *Gideon*, the Court incorporated the Fifth Amendment's protection against self-incrimination into the Fourteenth Amendment. By vote of 5–4, in *Malloy v. Hogan* (1964), the Court overturned a half-century-old precedent holding that states were not bound by the Fifth Amendment. The

Court's decision was foreshadowed by a line of cases, including *Brown v. Mississippi* (1936), that overturned state convictions based on confessions obtained by improper methods. The time had come, Justice William Brennan wrote in *Malloy*, to recognize "that the American system of criminal prosecution is accusatorial, not inquisitorial. . . ." Two years later, in *Miranda v. Arizona* (1966) the Court extended the Fifth Amendment privilege to persons taken into police custody.[16]

To 1966 there had been little public comment about the Court's foray into state criminal justice, but *Miranda* ignited a firestorm of criticism. Across the country, district attorneys, police officers, and politicians lashed out at the Court's decision extending the Fifth Amendment's protection against self-incrimination to questioning initiated by police after a person has been taken into custody. Prior to *Miranda*, state courts had decided on a case-by-case basis if a suspect's confession had been voluntary, that is, given without fear or favor. Ernesto Miranda's confession to rape and kidnapping would have passed the voluntariness standard, but writing for a 5–4 majority Chief Justice Earl Warren rejected trickery, intimidation, and the lies police too often used to secure a suspect's confession. To replace those reprehensible techniques, Warren spelled out the now-familiar fourfold warning police must give to a suspect before he or she is subject to "custodial interrogation." Suspects must be told they have a right to remain silent and that anything they say can and will be used against them. The police also must inform suspects of their right to talk with an attorney before being questioned and to have an attorney present when being questioned. Suspects must be told that if they cannot afford an attorney, one will be provided. Finally, suspects must knowingly and effectively waive their rights before any questioning may begin. Despite the exaggerated response from police and prosecutors—a Boston-area district attorney predicted innocent people would be murdered and their killers set free—studies have since demonstrated that most suspects waive their rights to remain silent, and the police get their confession.[17]

The Warren Court's due process revolution reached a divisive climax in *Witherspoon v. Illinois* (1968). Following a nineteenth century practice a state criminal court could challenge a potential juror for cause or a prosecutor could use a peremptory challenge if he believed the juror held an opinion about capital punishment that would prevent him (for several decades after passage of the Nineteenth Amendment women in many states were excluded from jury service) from finding the defendant guilty of murder. By this means the court or a prosecutor eliminated jurors who had qualms about the death penalty. Lawyers referred to this process as "death qualifying" a capital jury. A death-qualified jury in Illinois convicted William Witherspoon of murder in 1960. On appeal before the Supreme Court, Witherspoon claimed the Illinois procedure deprived him of his Sixth Amendment right to a fair trial by an impartial jury. Writing for the majority, Justice Potter Stewart concluded that dismissing a juror opposed to the death penalty made the jury unconstitutionally prone to return a death sentence. The state might legitimately exclude jurors who would automatically vote against the death penalty, but it could not eliminate those who merely voiced general objections or expressed conscientious or religious scruples about sentencing a defendant to death. Just prior to the Court's *Witherspoon* decision, the U.S. Congress enacted legislation designed to end the practices that had for a century perpetuated the all-white jury in the South. The Jury Selection Act (1968) required federal jurors to be chosen randomly and to represent a cross-section of the community. In *Taylor v. Louisiana* (1975) the Supreme Court extended the Jury Selection Act's provisions to state criminal proceedings. Many observers thought *Witherspoon* and the Jury Selection Act signaled the beginning of the end of capital punishment.[18]

In fact, unknown to outsiders, the Court had decided in the spring of 1971 to select a handful of capital cases for review with an eye toward resolving the death penalty issue "once and for all." As preparation of the death penalty cases was well under way, the composition of the Court changed dramatically. During his first two years in office President Richard M. Nixon, whose "law-and-order" campaign promised dramatic changes at the Court, appointed Warren Burger and Harry Blackmun, as chief justice and associate justice, respectively. Just as the fall term was about to begin, Justices Hugo Black and John Marshall Harlan resigned. Nixon appointed William Rehnquist, an Arizona conservative, and Lewis Powell, an outspoken critic of the Warren Court, to fill the vacancies. On January 17, 1972, this Nixon Court heard oral argument in *Furman v. Georgia*.[19]

William Furman, a twenty-six-year-old black man with a sixth-grade education, had been convicted of shooting to death a Savannah, Georgia, homeowner during a late night break-in. The police responded quickly and found Furman hiding in nearby woods. He still had the murder weapon. A court-appointed attorney represented Furman. The trial lasted just one day. Although Furman testified the shooting was accidental, he was sentenced to death because the murder had occurred during the commission of a felony, the break-in. The Georgia supreme court affirmed the conviction, but stayed Furman's execution pending an appeal to the United States Supreme Court. The National Association for the Advancement of Colored People, Legal Defense Fund, which had recently made a commitment to a campaign against capital punishment, represented Furman before the Court. Anthony Amsterdam, a University of Pennsylvania law professor, centered his argument on the conviction that "evolving standards of decency" had made the death penalty cruel and unusual. The death penalty persisted in America, Armstrong insisted, solely because juries imposed it rarely and against the outcasts of society. "The short of the matter," he concluded, "is that when a penalty is so barbaric that it can gain public acceptance only by being rarely, arbitrarily, and discriminatorily enforced, it plainly affronts the general standards of decency of the society."[20]

The Court handed down *Furman* on the very last day of its 1972 term. By a 5–4 vote, the Court struck down the death penalty as contrary to the Eighth Amendment's prohibition against cruel and unusual punishment. Each of the nine justices wrote a separate opinion, a splintering that had not occurred since the early nineteenth century. The majority was split on the key issue: was the death penalty inherently unconstitutional, or was the process simply flawed? Justices Brennan and Thurgood Marshall concluded the death penalty was cruel and unusual, plainly unconstitutional. Brennan condemned capital punishment as degrading to human dignity, arbitrarily severe, and unnecessary. Marshall agreed, adding that it was offensive to contemporary values. Justice William O. Douglas rejected the "evolving standards of decency" argument and focused primarily on the way in which the penalty was disproportionately applied to the poor and disadvantaged. To many observers' surprise, Justices Potter Stewart and Byron White cast their votes with the majority. By his own account Stewart had spent sleepless nights wondering why some men sat on death row while thousands of others convicted of rape and murder had received jail sentences. For this reason, he thought the death penalty cruel and unusual in the same way that being struck by lightning was cruel and unusual. Unlike Stewart, White found nothing repugnant about capital punishment, but like his colleague, he could not fathom how a punishment imposed with great infrequency for the most atrocious crimes could be a deterrent.[21]

Although they also wrote separately, the dissenters struck common themes. Each accused the majority of privileging their personal views, rather than deferring to legislative judgment or finding a specific constitutional violation in the death penalty statute before the Court. The dissenters also pointed to opinion polls showing widespread public support for the death penalty, thereby undermining the "evolving standards of decency" argument. Finally, Chief Justice Burger's dissent recognized the narrow common base on which the majority opinion rested, and he invited states to write new death penalty laws that would provide specific standards for capital sentencing.[22]

Four years later, in *Gregg v. Georgia* (1976), the death penalty was before the Court again. By a 7–2 vote the Court embraced a procedure designed to minimize arbitrariness and affirmed the constitutionality of the death penalty. A capital trial was to be bifurcated. The jury deliberated first to determine the defendant's guilt or innocence and then, if the defendant was found guilty, to determine the sentence. In the sentencing phase the jury considered evidence showing aggravating and mitigating circumstances. Jurors had to agree on at least one aggravating circumstance (a prior capital felony conviction, a jailbreak, etc.) before it could impose the death penalty. The statute also required consideration of mitigating factors such as a defendant's youth and his or her emotional state at the time of the murder, among others. And, the state supreme court had to review all death cases to determine whether the sentence was "excessive or disproportionate to the penalty imposed in similar cases."[23]

Gregg did not end the controversy over the death penalty, but whatever hope the abolitionists had was shattered a decade later in *Lockhart v. McCree* (1986) and *McCleskey v. Kemp* (1987). Lockhart argued that eliminating jurors who were philosophically opposed to the death penalty produced a jury unconstitutionally biased toward convicting a defendant. For a slim majority, Justice William Rehnquist rejected the argument. Even if the death qualification process tended to skew juries toward convictions at the guilt stage, Rehnquist wrote, that bias did not violate a defendant's right to an impartial jury. Warren McCleskey's plea fared no better with the Court. A black man convicted of the 1978 shooting death of a white Atlanta police officer, McCleskey argued that the Georgia death penalty was implemented in a racially discriminatory manner in violation of the Eighth and Fourteenth Amendments. He produced a massive statistical study showing that the odds of a death sentence for someone accused of killing a white person were four times higher than the odds of a death sentence for someone charged with murdering a black person. Justice Lewis Powell wrote for a bare majority who rejected McCleskey's data. The Georgia study did not prove race was a significant factor in McCleskey's trial, but merely showed a "discrepancy that appears to correlate with race." To be of legal, as opposed to social science, value, Powell wrote, McCleskey must show that specific decision-makers in his case acted with discriminatory purpose. In a bitter dissent, Justice William Brennan argued that the Court rejected McCleskey's claim about pervasive racism within the justice system "at our peril." We "remain imprisoned by the past so long as we deny its influence on the present," Brennan warned.[24]

In 1986 the Court revisited the use of racially discriminatory peremptory challenges, the preferred means since the Jury Selection Act of achieving an all-white jury. Three decades after *Norris v. Alabama* (1935) held the systematic exclusion of African Americans from jury pools a violation of the equal protection clause of the Fourteenth Amendment, Robert Swain, a black man convicted of raping a white woman, was sentenced to death by an all-white Alabama jury. Swain argued the equal protection clause prohibited prosecutors from using their peremptory challenges to remove all the would-be black jurors. Speaking for the majority, Justice White insisted a prosecutor was entitled to the presumption he or she was using the state's peremptory challenges to obtain a fair and impartial jury. Moreover, there was no equal protection argument, since members of any group were vulnerable to peremptory exclusion "whether they be Negroes, Catholics, accountants, or those with blue eyes." White did recognize some danger, but he set an extraordinarily high evidentiary bar. In order to show an unconstitutional use of peremptory challenges, a defendant must provide evidence that "in case after case, whatever the circumstances, no Negroes ever served on petit juries."[25]

Swain allowed prosecutors throughout the country to continue using peremptory challenges to achieve an all-white jury. From 1965 to 1986, several cases reached the Court in which the evidence supported a black defendant's claim that prosecutors had used peremptory challenges to eliminate all black would-be jurors. In the face of this growing body of data, the Court finally overruled *Swain*, holding in *Batson v. Kentucky* (1986) that using race as the reason for striking a potential juror was contrary to the equal protection clause of the Fourteenth Amendment. According to *Batson*, a prima facie case of discrimination exists whenever a prosecutor's use of peremptory challenges creates a racial pattern. The burden is then on the prosecutor to convince the judge that he or she struck black potential jurors for nonracial reasons. Although *Batson*'s rules seem tightly drawn, prosecutors have continued to use racially motivated peremptory challenges by relying upon indulgent or biased judges.[26]

We are more than forty years from the beginning of the modern due process revolution, and nearly thirty years have passed since the Court upheld the constitutionality of capital punishment. The Rehnquist Court has chipped away at the protections extended to the accused and has taken steps to speed up the executions of men on death row. Murder trials are still plagued with serious procedural errors. In 2002 and 2003 several state governors released all convicted prisoners on death row in their states because the governors had seen evidence of large numbers of jury verdicts that were tainted by violations of the rules of due process established by statute law and Supreme Court decisions.

II

Human societies have always distinguished between justifiable homicide (in self-defense, whether in peacetime or during war) and criminal homicide. The preceding section has detailed the way statute law and judge-made law defining criminal homicide have changed in English-speaking North America during the last four centuries. Murder prosecutions have been influenced greatly by such changes. Murder jurisprudence has also been affected by the existence of powerful social norms that influenced the way juries, judges, prosecutors, and lawmakers viewed persons accused of criminal homicide. From the seventeenth century on, English settlers and their descendants subjugated the indigenous people and imposed their culture on the vanquished in a pattern that, in one way or another, would be replicated across the North American continent as the English dealt with African Americans and Hispanics.

In seventeenth-century New England, a dual pattern of legal culture existed. Where English sovereignty reigned, whites and Native Americans were subject to English jurisdiction. From the earliest contacts along the eastern coast of North America, the English denied the legitimacy of Native American legal traditions, which the English regarded as heathen (i.e., non-Christian) and barbaric. Outside the pale of European settlement, tribal law prevailed for Native Americans. Justice in matters of murder for Native Americans was based on consanguinity and clan retribution, while for the colonists the criminal law was coextensive with state jurisdiction and was guided by the laws passed by each colonial legislature. Depending on circumstances and political expediency, Native Americans who killed one another might be subject to either jurisdiction.[27] As John Navin demonstrates, initially the English settlers and the eastern Indians were pragmatic, working out behavioral norms as they interacted, albeit against a background of cultural suspicion, political negotiation, and the need to mainain order. Certainly the need for law and order and self-interest combined when Plymouth authorities executed Thomas Peach in 1638 for the murder of a Narragansett, and peace was preserved a year later, when, thanks to the damning testimony of his tribesmen, Connecticut officials executed Nepaupuck for murdering Abraham Finch. The same commitment to peace motivated the weak United Colonies government to defer to Uncas, allowing him to execute a Mohegan suspected of plotting against the powerful Connecticut sachem.

However, by the 1670s immigration had swelled the English population of southern New England; and Native Americans had been hit by a plague in the 1630s that had drastically reduced their numbers. The government of Plymouth Colony was aggressively pressuring the Wampanoags to sell more land to the English. The Wampanoags, led by King Philip, did not want to give any English permanent title to Indian land. Tensions mounted. In 1675, when three Wampanoag Indians were charged with the murder of John Sassamon (who might have died of natural causes), the trial took place in an highly charged atmosphere. The Plymouth colonists did not give the Wampanoags the rights that were specified in the 1641 Charter of Liberties, which had been promulgated by the Massachusetts Bay Colony and was adopted by the Plymouth Colony. The Wampanoags on trial for the murder of Sassamon did not have a "lawyer" (we do not know if they asked for a lawyer and were turned down). In all other capital cases in the Massachusetts Bay Colony, accused Indians always had a lawyer. Most importantly, the Wampanoags were convicted on the basis of the testimony of one witnesses, not the two witnesses stipulated by the Charter of Liberties. Concluding that the English could not be trusted, King Philip declared war in an attempt to roll back English power.

From the beginning, the Plymouth and Massachusetts Bay colonists had insisted that accused white murderers of Native Americans be tried only in colonial courts. (There were cases in which colonists prevented Indians accused of murder from receiving a trial: in Marblehead, Massachusetts, enraged women in 1677 murdered and mutilated two captive Indians rather than let the judicial process unfold.) Native Americans and African Americans were allowed to testify against whites accused of crimes. But because colonists did not fully trust nonwhites, whom they regarded as inferior, such testimony was generally held valid only it was accompanied by corroborating evidence.[28] Although the colonial statutes were silent on the subject of jury composition, there is no record of an Indian being chosen as a juror for the trial of a white person. (In some instances, especially on the frontier and despite abundant evidence, local juries of whites refused to convict whites accused of murdering Indians.)[29] By contrast, Indians were allowed to serve on juries trying Indians, as long as white jurors outnumbered substantially the number of Indians.

Overall, Native Americans accused of murdering whites were less likely to receive reduced sentences for manslaughter than were Indians who murdered Indians. (Native American women accused of infanticide, however, were as likely as English and African America women to win acquittal or a reduced sentence.) As Nancy Steenburg's essay suggests, when judges and jurors dealt with murders committed by children whose age placed them on the cusp of adulthood, so that it was hard to determine if they understood that murder was wrong, Native American/Black children and Irish children were less likely to receive a break than were children of English/Protestant stock.

For more than two centuries, the paradox of slavery and freedom persisted in the colonies and the United States. Especially in the South, slaves accused of murder were either punished by their masters without trials or were tried by all-white juries. White masters accused of murdering their slaves rarely were convicted of this capital crime. Frederick Douglass relates the story of a slave owner's wife, Mrs. Hicks, who beat to death the fifteen-year-old cousin of Douglass's wife: "There was a warrant issued for her arrest, but it was never served. Thus she escaped not only punishment, but even the pain of being arraigned before a court for her horrid crime."[30]

The Civil War eradicated slavery, but during 1865–66 black codes and vagrancy laws in the South continued to subjugate four million freedpeople. African Americans were repeatedly denied the right to vote, the right to contract—without landowner coercion—the right to testify against whites in court, and the right to serve on juries. With laws designed to subjugate blacks enforced by sheriffs and judges who wanted to profit from the labor of blacks, legal intimidation and unpunished landowner violence, including murder, severely oppressed the freed slaves.

In opposition to the racist policies of President Andrew Johnson and Southern white landowners, Republicans implemented Reconstruction. To secure basic civil rights for the former slaves, Congress passed and the states ratified the Thirteenth (1865), Fourteenth (1868) and Fifteenth (1870) Amendments. The first definitively ended slavery everywhere in the United States. The second held that no state could "deprive any person of life, liberty, or property, without due process of law; nor deny to any person within its jurisdiction the equal protection of the laws." And the last post–Civil War amendment barred discrimination in voting based on "race, color, or previous condition of servitude." (Giving the former slaves the vote would prevent the reemergence of slavery and maintain the hegemony of the Republican Party.) With their right to vote protected, many freedman found they were treated relatively fairly by judges (often white Republicans elected by both black and white voters) when the freedmen went to court to collect full wages or crop payments from parsimonious white landowners.

The veneration for private property, pervasive racist attitudes, and the tradition of states' rights barred any redistribution of wealth or financial compensation to the former slaves for the exploitation they had endured at the hands of their masters. There was no hoped-for "forty acres and a mule." Often trapped in sharecropping and debt peonage, the freedpeople had little economic wherewithal with which to protect their basic freedoms in a hostile environment. (In the 1880s some Southern African Americans were able to migrate to better jobs or to Arkansas and Oklahoma, where many purchased cheap land.) Northern public opinion during the 1870s turned more to other problems besides the incomplete civil rights revolution of Reconstruction: economic downturns, labor unrest, political corruption, monetary policy, and the rise of big business. As part of the Compromise of 1877 that led to the election of the Republican Rutherford B. Hayes, the last federal troops were withdrawn from the solidly Democratic South. Southern whites then intensified their use of illegal force to prevent African Americans from exercising their civil rights, and especially the right to vote. When Congress responded with civil rights statutes, the U.S. Supreme Court, in the 1873 *Slaughterhouse* cases, narrowly interpreted the protections to African Americans and restricted the ability of the federal government to intervene at the state level to preserve the civil liberties of African Americans. Then, in *Hutardo v. California* (1884), the Court ruled that Fifth Amendment rights to due process during criminal trials (and civil actions) were not protected by the Fourteenth Amendment.

Racial attitudes hardened during the 1890s. White domination was assured, but its structure had not been firmly fixed since the end of slavery. Black men still voted in significant numbers in some parts of the upper South and competed with whites for jobs. In the early 1890s the Populist movement in the South urged a class alliance of hard-pressed black and white farmers against the white elites who controlled the Democratic Party. When white elites intimidated or bribed blacks to vote against the Populist candidates, white agrarian radicals backed the disenfranchisement of blacks by means of literacy tests, poll taxes, and grandfather clauses. The Supreme Court upheld the legality of these legal instruments. On the social side, Jim Crow segregation, sanctioned in cases such as *Plessey v. Ferguson* (1896), legitimated racial apartheid, an outcome most attractive to poor whites.

Without federal protection for the civil liberties of blacks, white violence, ranging from public whipping to murder, went unpunished, whether conducted on a small scale or on a large scale, as in Wilmington, North Carolina, in 1898 when elite whites launched genocidal attacks against blacks who had helped to elect radical officials to positions in the city's government. After 1880, especially in cotton-producing areas and the "black belt," of the lower South, the lynching of blacks accused by whites of murder, assault, rape and insubordination intensified. Lynching was summary punishment and ignored the normal due process of law (indictment, jury trial, appeal). Although lynching subsided in the 1920s, blacks accused of murder (and other crimes) did not receive proper due process in the South. The historian W. Fitzhugh Brundage writes that the justice blacks accused of raping white women received in Southern courts entailed a "disregard for evidence and a ferocity only a step removed from the so-called justice imposed by mobs."[31] Since blacks rarely were allowed on juries in the South until the civil rights era of the 1960s, black men and women accused of murder could hardly expect to receive impartial justice, and especially when blacks were accused of murdering whites. The Supreme Court did not begin to address this issue until 1986.

In the 1890s an average of two African Americans were lynched per week in the South. But economic and racial polarization proceeded unevenly. Virginia never had a strong white or white-black agrarian radical movement. In 1895 many blacks still voted in Virginia. Thus, in chapter three, "Jim Crow Justice, *the Richmond Planet,* and the Murder of Lucy Pollard," Michael Trotti shows that in a racially charged ax murder case in 1895 that took place near Richmond, Virginia, many state militiamen as well as prominent whites supported a color-blind adherence to the rule of law. A black man was convicted and hanged for the brutal killing of a white woman. He accused three black women of the actual murder. Pressure from the African American community and the actions of various white officials, however, led to their acquittal. Paternalistic reluctance to execute these humble women acted in their favor, especially because the testimony against them seemed patently contrived. Fearful of mob violence, the governor, at the sheriff's insistence, employed a sufficient force of militia to maintain order. Whites and blacks served on the first juries in the case, and both races contributed money to the defense of the accused black women. Furthermore, prominent white lawyers eventually took up the cause of the defendants, and state militiamen filed affidavits charging the state's leading witness with inconsistent statements. The state's attorney dropped two of the cases, and the appeals courts overturned some of the guilty verdicts. Despite a racially biased criminal justice system, especially involving the adjudication of murder, many white Virginians concluded that an obvious miscarriage of justice—especially in a capital case—was a threat to all. As the white-owned *Richmond Times* editorialized, "If they are to be judicially murdered under the present progamme, the life of none of us is safe."[32]

In Atlanta, Georgia, in 1913 Leo Frank was charged with the murder of fourteen-year-old Mary Phagan, an employee in the mill he managed. At trial, the prosecutor stressed Frank's Jewishness and implied that he "engaged in sexual acts with his nose."[33] A white mob eventually lynched Frank while he was in jail awaiting the outcome of his appeal of his murder conviction. In May 1920, in the middle of a period of intense fear of the activities of immigrant revolutionaries, Nicola Sacco and Bartolomeo Vanzetti, Italian immigrants who were militant anarchists and frequently carried revolvers, were charged with payroll robbery and the murder of two payroll guards in Braintree, Massachusetts. The prosecutor in this case (Frederick Katzman) decided early on that anarchists must have carried out the robbery. The eyewitnesses to the robbery initially were unsure of their identification of the two robbers; but at trial, under pressure from Katzman, several witnesses went on to proclaim the certainty of their identifications. Documents first made available in the 1970s also suggest that Katzman initiated or condoned evidence tampering, substituting a bullet that was not actually found at the murder site for one that had been found there to buttress his case that the murder weapon had been a gun Sacco had stolen during an earlier robbery.[34]

Since World War II racial and ethnic biases in the United States have declined or have been muted. But racial prejudice is still virulent in many communities. The 1988 Philadelphia murder trial of Mumia Abu-Jamal took place in a city that had been racially polarized since the 1960s. As Dave Lindorff's essay notes, a judge and a prosecutor, both of whom appear to have been racially biased, perpetrated and condoned procedural irregularities during Abu-Jamal's murder trial, thereby contributing to a guilty verdict and a jury vote for the death penalty. Like the celebrity murder trial of O. J. Simpson during the mid-1990s, the case of Mumia Abu-Jamal raises important issues that transcend the final verdict of guilt or innocence. An extraordinary expansion of civil liberties accompanied the civil rights revolution of the 1950s–60s, which was in effect a second Reconstruction a full century after the Civil War.

The aftermath of the Holocaust and other atrocities during World War II made clear that systematic oppression of African Americans in the United States was, in the words of the Swedish sociologist Gunnar Myrdal, the "American dilemma." Employing a wide variety of tactics, ranging from civil disobedience to urban rioting, the civil rights movement forced a series of state laws, federal statutes, and Supreme Court rulings to affirm adherence to due process and equal protection of the law at the local and national level. The effort was to confront the gross violations of the criminal law that had disproportionately been borne by African Americans, who presently constitute close to one-half of the nation's prison population, the largest in the world. Yet persistent racial bias and unequal distribution of wealth in the larger society continues to unbalance the scales of justice. Policing, procedures, and personnel, if not the law itself (notably drug laws), continue to be stacked against African Americans, particularly poor black men with limited formal education. Technological advances in criminology, such as DNA testing, show that alarming numbers of (largely African American) inmates on death row were wrongly convicted of murder. Despite the civil rights revolution of the 1950s–60s, the legacy of slavery, sharecropping, and segregation has left America, in the words of the Kerner Commission in 1968, two societies—one black, one white, separate and unequal. Indeed, the U.S. Department of Justice reported in 2003 that black men have nearly a one in three chance of being incarcerated during their lifetime.

When Malcolm X pointedly told Northern, black audiences in 1964, "South? Don't talk of the South! When you are south of the Canadian border, you are South," he might well have had Philadelphia in mind.[35] By 1970 the population of the city was 40 percent black, and the west side was a notoriously rundown ghetto. Frank Rizzo, the police chief and later mayor of Philadelphia built his political career on white dislike of blacks, which was particularly vocal in the Italian American south side. His harassment of the Black Panthers during the late 1960s and early 1970s and encouragement of police brutality made him the Northern equivalent of Eugene "Bull" Connor, the infamous commissioner of public safety in Birmingham, Alabama. The zeal of Rizzo's 1978 raid on MOVE, a militant black group, was exceeded only by the actions of Wilson Goode, the city's first African American mayor. Intimidated by militant white officials, Goode permitted the police in 1983 to launch a Vietnam-style attack with helicopters, antitank weapons, and firebombs on the defiant MOVE that killed eleven men, women, and children and burned down a whole city block.

In this context, Dave Lindorff's essay, "Justice Denied: Race and the 1982 Murder Trial of Mumia Abu-Jamal," deals with the conviction of a former Black Panther for the murder of a Philadelphia policeman in 1981. While in prison on a death sentence, Abu-Jamal's case has garnered international attention. He has indicted the way in which the dominant white culture mistreats young black men and the way in which racism corrupts the justice system. Abu-Jamal also sees prison and capital punishment as products of bias permeating the law. Without question, race played a significant part at his trial. Prosecutors challenged for cause twenty potential black jurors because they expressed reservations about capital punishment. Despite the Supreme Court's ruling in *Batson v. Kentucky* (1986) prohibiting race-based peremptory challenges, the Philadelphia prosecutor used that means to strike at least ten black potential jurors. And the trial judge did not challenge the prosecutor's actions.[36]

Abu-Jamal has been spared execution because a federal appeals court judge has found that the trial judge's sentencing instructions to the jury misrepresented the options jurors had to indicate they believed there were mitigating circumstances that justified a sentence of less than death for Abu Jamal. In addition, in February 2003 the Supreme Court in the *Miller-El* decision ruled 8–1 that a black death row inmate in Texas must be granted a hearing on a claim that the prosecution improperly excluded blacks from his jury. The *Miller-El* decision may well lead Abu-Jamal to appeal his trial verdict. Academic studies have shown that Philadelphia prosecutors from 1978 to 1986 excluded blacks from juries at a rate more than twice that of whites. It is, of course, naïve to believe that racial bias has been driven from the courtroom, especially when a radical black man is on trial.[37]

III

Throughout the history of colonial settlement and the creation of the United States of America, people who were mentally ill were treated with special sympathy by the courts. By 1700, a belief had emerged in England and the English colonies that when the mentally ill committed crimes, their punishment should be mitigated, because their mental illness prevented them from knowing they had acted wrongly.

According to the legal concept of *mens rea*, a person can be held responsible for a criminal act only if he or she has some degree of critical understanding of such actions. Without sufficient mental competency, some degree of rational volition, an individual cannot be found culpable. This tradition was well established in English law even when John Locke wrote the *Second Treatise on Government* in 1690. Locke observed, "But if, through defects that may happen out of the ordinary course of nature, any one comes not to such a degree of reason, wherein he might be supposed capable of knowing the law, and so living within the rules of it, he is never capable of being a free man, he is never let loose to the disposure of his own will (because he knows no bounds to it, has not understanding, its proper guide) but is continued under the tuition and government of others, all the time his own understanding is incapable of that charge." The English philosopher and physician cited the case of children and the insane, among others, who were not legally accountable.[38]

Reflecting English seventeenth-century law, age differentiated the legal standing of youth in the North American colonies. It was presumed that children under age seven simply could not be criminals and should never be tried. Children who were between eight and fourteen years old were presumed innocent of illegality unless persuasive evidence proved otherwise. Youth who were fourteen and older were considered adults and subject to the full force of the law. In the New England colonies in the seventeenth century, juvenile murder fell under a mix of ecclesiastical and secular laws. Ecclesiastical and secular laws were initially mixed in matters of murder, with biblical injunctions calling for retribution for murder. Despite the scriptural imperative, by the eighteenth century colonists in practice set different standards for children and adults. Enlightenment concepts of the innocence of children led to an emphasis on nurturing mothers, moral education, and beneficial environments. By the mid-nineteenth century, as popular thought increasingly differentiated between adolescents and adults, reform schools to separate "youthful" offenders from hardened adults (both had formerly been jailed in the same prisons) were opened in a number of Northern states. Separate juvenile courts were established in the early twentieth century.

Based on meticulous archival research, Nancy H. Steenburg's essay, "Murder and Minors: Changing Standards in the Criminal Law of Connecticut, 1650-1853," shows how cultural norms affected juvenile justice cases, which are hard to track down for the early period. Youngsters tried for murder were treated leniently when they were under the age of discretion—age fourteen. At fourteen, children were assumed to be able to understand the difference between good and evil, and thus were capable of forming criminal intent. A glaring exception occurred with a nonwhite child in 1786. Twelve-year-old Hanna Occuish, of Pequot-African ancestry, was found guilty of murder and hanged, despite testimony that she had not been raised to understand Christian and European-American values. Indeed, racial bias and anti-Irish sentiment appears to have contributed to unduly harsh sentences in many murder trials involving youths. By the 1830s antebellum reformers advocated differential treatment for children who were convicted of crimes; they were incarcerated in separate cells from adult convicts and then placed in juvenile reform schools.

The essays on the insanity defense by Lawrence B. Goodheart and Alan Rogers also illustrate the complexities of the law when dealing with capital defendants. The principle in English jurisprudence that the insane were not criminally responsible for homicide was well established in the New World. In seventeenth-century Connecticut, Harvard-educated Gershom Bulkeley rendered such an opinion in defending a deranged mother of filicide: "If she were not compos mentis at the time of the fact it is no felony and consequently no willful or malicious murder; and if she be known to be a lunatic, though she have her lucid intervals, there need be very good and satisfactory proof that she was compos mentis, for the law favors life."[39] During the nineteenth century, Enlightenment rationalism led many educated Americans to consider mental illness a medical matter. The influential McNaughten rule, based on an English murder case in 1843, defined the legal basis of insanity in a manner not unlike Bulkeley's. If a defendant at the time of the crime could not tell the difference between right and wrong, he or she was legally insane and thus not criminally culpable. Furthermore, American physicians like Isaac Ray argued that a condition of moral insanity existed: a mania or irresistible impulse might compel one to murder, even though other aspects of cognition appeared entirely normal. The new doctrines of forensic psychiatry, however, contradicted the social norms of individual self-control and personal responsibility that were so important to emerging middle-class culture.

In "Murder and Madness: The Ambiguity of Moral Insanity in Nineteenth-Century Connecticut," Lawrence B. Goodheart explores the controversial matter of legal insanity in Connecticut, a pioneer in the treatment, not punishment, of the insane. The resolution of a brutal ax murder case in 1835 showed, asylum doctors thought, the complementary relationship between medicine and the law. Although the building blocks for a new understanding between science and jurisprudence seemed to be in place, a workable accord between psychiatry, the law, and the public was not achieved by the end of the century, as many had expected. In 1876, after nearly fifty years of experience with the insanity defense, the Connecticut Supreme Court expressed its frustration: "Unsoundness of mind is a fact which is not susceptible of proof." In fact, the Massachusetts Supreme Judicial Court (MSJC) worked on this definitional problem for another one hundred fifty years before achieving what it regarded as a workable relationship with psychiatry and a defendant's pleas of not guilty by reason of insanity.

Alan Rogers's essay, "'This troublesome issue': Murder and the Insanity Defense in Massachusetts, 1844–2000," tracks the MSJC's long, torturous path to a new era in the relationship between murder, malice, and a defendant's mental state. The MSJC was the first court of last resort to adopt modern rules on criminal responsibility by welding together a cognitive and an emotional test, but the law continued to hold psychiatry at arm's length, and the public remained skeptical. Spurred by reformers and several high-profile cases, the MSJC experimented with new rules extending greater protection to capital defendants making an insanity defense. Advances in biological psychiatry, particularly successes in treatment of mental illness with psychotropic drugs, and research indicating that mental illness was an organic disease, not a moral failure, contributed importantly to that resolution. The Massachusetts court took a major step toward bringing psychiatry and the law into theoretical harmony by recognizing the impact of permanent diminished mental capacity on a murder defendant's ability to act with malice.

Texas and other states had followed the MSJC rulings with legislation in the 1970s that held that even if a murderer knew he or she had committed a wrongful act, a demonstrable mental illness made the murderer "incapable of conforming his conduct" to social norms and the murderer should not be convicted of a homicide. But the 1982 acquittal on the grounds of insanity of John Hinckley Jr, who in 1981 had tried unsuccessfully to assassinate President Ronald Reagan, created a backlash against the insanity defense in many states. In 1983 the Texas legislature reverted the law to a standard very close to the McNaughten rule. Thus, in 2001, when Andrea Yates, a diagnosed schizophrenic, drowned her children in the bathtub of her home, she was convicted of capital murder in March 2002. The prosecution had acknowledged her mental illness, but under the 1983 Texas law she could not plead that she was unable to behave in accordance with social norms.[41]

IV

New ideas about mental illness were not the only fresh intellectual currents in the mid-nineteenth century. After 1800, many women and men, especially the affluent, altered their views about gender roles. The notion that middle-class and elite women should receive more than a basic education led to the founding of scores of private female academies. Women educated in such schools often took paid and volunteer jobs in institutions that were outside the home, especially schools and charities. In the late 1840s a limited number of American women launched a voluble movement for equal civil rights for women. The first women's rights movement was especially successful in getting states to allow married women to control their own property. In the years after the Civil War, small numbers of women moved into elite professions like medicine and law. But most middle- and low-income women still embraced the traditional notion that a woman's place was in the home, nurturing her family.

Certain additional aspects of gender roles were in flux in the mid-nineteenth century, particularly notions about fatherhood and views about women's honor. After 1850, male parenting increasingly was seen as a trait of manhood. Male parenting would improve the morality of the nation's children. The upheaval of the Civil War reinforced this domestic paradigm. Thomas Wier had placed his children among the Shakers in order to protect them while he served in the Union army; when he returned from the war he sought to reclaim his rightful role as guardian of his children's moral development. Caleb Dyer, head of the Shaker community, refused to release Wier's children; enraged, Wier shot Dyer.

Elizabeth A. De Wolfe shows that the trial defense used by Wier's attorneys stressed his alleged temporary insanity, brought on by the effects of war and the loss of his children. But Wier was convicted. However, Wier's wife, and eventually his daughter, waged a public campaign for his pardon, and received a great deal of support after arguing that because a father's nurturing of his children was so important, Wier should be forgiven for murdering Dyer, who had headed a community whose rigid rules fragmented families and prevented fathers from parenting their children. New Hampshire's governor freed Wier in 1880.

A 1879 New Haven murder trial reveals the persistence of this new view of fatherhood. Formidable forensic evidence suggested that Rev. Hebert Hayden had poisoned a lower-class, pregnant woman who had written a note stating she was his mistress. The defense questioned the technical evidence and then stressed the respectable, middle-class character of Hayden and his family, noting his role as a father: "You are to settle whether those bright little children shall have a father whose name they cannot mention but with a blush of shame. You, gentlemen, are to say whether that devoted father . . . shall be sent from this courthouse disgraced. . . ."[41]

Laura-Eve Moss's analysis of the acquittal of George W. Cole for the murder of L. Harris Hiscock, his willing wife's adulterer, indicates that in the mid-nineteenth century many jurors held to the age-old belief that a man could not be blamed if, in a fit of rage after discovering adultery, he tried to vindicate his honor and his wife's honor by murdering the adulterer. But this belief may have been amplified, in the thinking of juries, by the emergent notion that a *temporarily* insane person, driven to such insanity by justifiable anger over being dishonored, should not be punished for the ensuing violent assault. Since jurors rarely explained their deliberations, it is hard to know if the temporary insanity defense was taken seriously or was a rationalization for exonerating a man who the jurors felt had an "ancient" right to avenge his honor.

But most newspaper reaction to the Cole murder trials and his subsequent acquittal was critical. Editorial writers propounded a new paradigm of women's and men's honor. First, women were increasingly portrayed as having a strong sense of honor, comparable to a man's. Second, influenced by evangelical religion, many editors argued that Cole should have practiced dignity, not vengeance, doing all he could to protect his wife's honor by shielding her from publicity and disgrace. While the jury did not accept this argument, most editorial writers did.

While some people's ideas of gender roles changed in the nineteenth century, the age-old belief in the virtues of an ordered home and the moral superiority of a middle-class or upper class home persisted. For example, in the 1879 New Haven trial of Rev. Hayden, the defense compared the honor of his good wife, who dressed properly and was dignified, with the coarse speech and appearance of the sister of the house servant whom Hayden was accused of ravishing and killing.

> You are to settle whether that woman henceforth is to be a widow with the stinging disgrace that her husband was a murderer. . . . That loving old mother . . . waits upon your lips for the decision which shall either make her happy . . . or make her remaining days ten-fold more wretched. . . . So do your duty with that group that their hearts shall not be broken.

After eleven of the twelve New Haven jurors voted to acquit (the twelfth, a farmer, voted for a manslaughter conviction), one juror commented: "How can we convict a man with a beautiful wife like that?"[42]

After 1880, scientific racism, based on distortions of Charles Darwin's writings, influenced many Americans, who concluded that the evolutionary process had led to the creation of many distinct human races, each of which had evolved at different rates. The descendants of immigrants from Northern European countries—England, Scotland, Ireland, Germany and the Scandinavian countries—believed they were members of the most highly evolved, superior races. Americans of Northern European stock believed that immigrants from Southern and Eastern Europe, who arrived in large numbers after 1880, were members of backward, less evolved races that were both highly immoral and intellectually inferior to the descendants of Northern European races.

The most famous murder of the nineteenth century was the August 4, 1892 axe slaying of Andrew and Abby Borden in Fall River, Massachusetts. Lizzie, Mr. Borden's daughter, was charged with his murder. (Abby Borden was Lizzie's stepmother). Lizzie Borden was tried and acquitted. Ten months after the murder of Lizzie Borden's parents, Bertha Manchester, a young Fall River, Massachusetts woman, was killed by a brutal axe attack. The Fall River police quickly arrested José Correira, a Portuguese immigrant and manual laborer, even though there was evidence that Bertha's father appeared unconcerned about his daughter's demise. Correira, who was subsequently convicted and imprisoned, fit the stereotype of the "savage" criminal who belonged to an "inferior" race.

The acquittal of Lizzie Borden for the axe murders of her parents was influenced by luck and by the skillful manipulation of cultural symbols. Borden benefited from a decision by the trial judge that inconsistent statements she had made at the coroner's inquest could not be introduced by the prosecution during her trial. Tiffany Bidler Johnson demonstrates (chapter 10) that Lizzie Borden and her attorneys showed jurors photographs of the interiors of her parents' home to suggest that a young adult raised in cultured, neat, comfortable physical environment could not possibly commit a brutal crime. In his closing arguments, one of Borden's attorneys emphasized the brutal nature of the axe murders to suggest to the jury that a woman of middle class status and Northern European origins could not possibly commit such savage deeds. This line of reasoning resonated with newspaper reports of the arrest of José Correira for the murder of Bertha Manchester, accounts that appeared just as Lizzie Borden's trial was about to start. The existence of an alleged axe murderer who was a common laborer and a member of an "inferior" race emphasized the point that Borden's defense was trying to establish: Lizzie was a properly socialized, middle class woman; only a member of the lower orders of society was capable of committing a savage axe murder.

V

The essays in this collection show that the careful investigation of murder reveals much about the crime and the society in which the crime occurred. Homicide focuses attention on the victim, the defendant, their general characteristics—race, ethnicity, mental competency, gender, and age—and society's perception of the larger cultural context of the crime. At trial, these characteristics, as well as a society's fundamental values manifested in the legal rules by which a court seeks to protect the rights of a capital defendant, are highlighted. In short, murder and its adjudication often reveal the core values of a society.

This anthology points to a fundamental tension in American legal history between the ideal of justice—equality under law, protection of the rights of the accused, and humaneness—and deep and enduring social biases and economic inequalities. Ideally, the criminal justice system neutralizes bias and makes possible a defendant's fair treatment before the law. Since World War II there has been a significant expansion of personal freedom and legal protection, especially for the most vulnerable economic and racial groups in American society. Yet, despite reforms and changes over time, the wealthy, powerful, and dominant ethnic and racial groups remain most likely to tilt the scales of justice in their favor.

It would be, however, too fatalistic to spotlight only the negative aspects of the American legal system. This collection of essays shows that the law of murder has been made more equitable and humane over the course of American history. The framers of the Constitution believed an active and informed citizenry was necessary to maintain a republic and the rule of law. So there is reason to believe that pursuit of justice will be improved even more if the public supports the ideal of having the legal protections of the Constitution and federal and state laws tendered, fairly and equitably, to *all* inhabitants of our country.

Notes

1. *Malinski v. New York*, 324 U.S. 401, 414 (1945).

2. David Fellman, *The Defendant's Rights Today* (Madison, Wisc.: University of Wisconsin Press 1976), 11.

3. Max Farrand, ed., *The Laws and Liberties of Massachusetts* (Cambridge, Mass.: Harvard University Press, 1929). Lawrence H. Gipson, "The Criminal Codes of Connecticut," *Journal of Criminal Law* 6 (1915): 177, 182

4. Yasuhide Kawashima, *Igniting King Philips' War: The John Sassamon Murder Trial* (Lawrence, Kans.: University of Kansas Press 2001), 66–73.

5. Warren Billings, "Pleading, Procedure, and Practice: The Meaning of Due Process of Law in Seventeenth Century Virginia," *Journal of Southern History* 47 (1981): 569.

6. William E. Nelson, *The Americanization of the Common Law: The Impact of Legal Change on Massachusetts Society, 1760–1830* (Cambridge, Mass.: Harvard University Press, 1975).

7. Cesare Beccaria, *An Essay on Crimes and Punishments* (Palo Alto, Calif., 1953), 97, 99, 101–104.

8. *Barron v. Baltimore*, 32 U.S. 243 (1833); Louis P. Masur, *Rites of Execution: Capital Punishment and the Transformation of American Culture, 1776–1865* (New York: Oxford University Press, 1985), 142–44. Alan Rogers, " 'Under Sentence of Death': The Movement to Abolish Capital Punishment in Massachusetts, 1835–1849," *New England Quarterly* 66 (1993): 27–46.

9. *New York Times*, October 6, 1865; *Boston Daily Evening Transcript*, October 16, 1865; George Fisher, "The Jury's Rise as Lie Detector," *Yale Law Journal* 107 (1997): 575, 713.

10. *Strauder v. West Virginia*, 100 U.S. 303 (1880) and *Virginia v. Rives*, 100 U.S. 313 (1880); Jeffrey Abramson, *We the Jury* (New York: Basic Books, 1994).

11. *Powell v. Alabama*, 287 U.S. 45 (1932); *Norris v. Alabama*, 294 U.S. 587 (1935); Dan T. Carter, *Scottsboro: A Tragedy of the American South* (Baton Rouge: Louisiana State Uniersity Press, 1979).

12. *Brown v. Mississippi*, 297 U.S. 278 (1936). To avoid being lynched or sentenced to death again, Ed Brown and the other two defendants pleaded no contest to manslaughter and received prison terms.

13. *Palko v. Connecticut*, 302 U.S. 319 (1937) and *Sonzinsky v. U.S.*, 300 U.S. 506 (1937). William E. Leuchtenburg, *The Supreme Court Reborn: The Constitutional Revolution in the Age of Roosevelt* (New York: Oxford University Press, 1995), 251–57.

14. Earl Warren, "The Law and the Future," *Fortune* 51 (November 1955): 106, 226. *Mapp v. Ohio*, 367 U.S. 643 (1961).

15. *Gideon v. Wainwright*, 372 U.S. 335 (1963). At his retrial Gideon had a lawyer, and a jury acquitted him.

16. *Malloy v. Hogan*, 378 U.S. 1, 7 (1964).

17. *Miranda v. Arizona*, 384 U.S. 436 (1066).

18. William Oberer, "Does Disqualification of Jurors for Scruples against Capital Punishment Constitute Denial of a Fair Trial?" *Texas Law Review* 39 (1961): 545; *Witherspoon v. Illinois*, 391 U.S. 510 (1968); *Taylor v. Louisiana*, 419 U.S. 522 (1975).

19. Lee Epstein and Joseph F. Kobylka, *The Supreme Court and Legal Change* (Chapel Hill, NC: University of North Carolina Press: 1992), 70, 75.

20. Ibid., 71–75. *New York Times*, January 18, 1972.

21. *Furman v. Georgia*, 408 U.S. 238 (1972).

22. Ibid.

23. *Gregg v. Georgia*, 428 U.S. 153 (1976). The Court found the death penalty for rape unconstitutional in *Coker v. Georgia*, 433 U.S. 584 (1977).

24. *Lockhart v. McCree*, 476 U.S. 162 (1986). *McCleskey v. Kemp*, 481 U.S. 279 (1987). More appeals were brought on behalf of McCleskey, all of which failed. He was executed September 25, 1991.

25. *Swain v. Alabama*, 380 U.S. 202, 222 (1965).

26. *Batson v. Kentucky*, 476 U.S. 79 (1986); Randall Kennedy, *Race, Crime and the Law* (New York: Pantheon Books, 1997), chap. 6.

27. Lawrence M. Friedman, *Crime and Punishment in American History* (New York: Basic Books, 1993), 1–15; Roger Lane, *Murder in America* (Columbus: Ohio State University Press, 1997), 46.

28. Kawashima, *Puritan Justice: White Man's Law in Massachusetts, 1630–1763* (Middletown, Conn.: Wesleyan University Press, 1986).

29. Kawashima, *Igniting King Philips' War*; Kawashima, *Puritan Justice*, 129–131.

30. The cousin had been watching Mrs. Hicks's baby and had fallen asleep from fatigue. When the crying baby awakened Mrs. Hicks, she was so enraged that she grabbed a stick and beat the young woman to death. *Narrative of the Life of Frederick Douglass, An American Slave* (New York: Signet Books, 1968), 41–42.

31. W. Fitzhugh Brundage, *Lynching in the New South: Georgia and Virginia, 1880–1930* (Urbana: University of Illinois Press, 1993), 71.

32. Historians have noted that beginning in the eighteenth century, English jurisprudence in capital cases stressed strict adherence to legal procedures. If a person's life was to be taken, the law had to be followed to the letter. Without adherence to the processes stipulated by the law in capital cases, in which the punishment was the most severe possible—death—all law would come into disrepute. Douglas Hay, "Property, Authority and the Criminal Law," in *Albion's Fatal Tree: Crime and Society in Eighteenth Century England,* ed. Douglas Hay, et al. (New York: Pantheon, 1975), 17–64.

33. Nancy MacLean "Gender, Sexuality, and the Politics of Lynching: The Leo Frank Case Revisited," in *Under Sentence of Death: Lynching in the South,* ed. W. Fitzhugh Brundage, (Chapel Hill: University of North Carolina Press, 1997), 169.

34. William Young and David E. Kaiser, *Post Mortem: New Evidence in the Case of Sacco and Vanzetti* (Amherst: University of Massachusetts Press, 1985).

35. Malcolm X, "The Ballot or The Bullet," 1964.

36. Lindorff's article details other procedural biases of the trial judge, who played the race card in his own way. Compare Judge Albert Sabo's behavior with the Rhode Island Supreme Court, sitting as a trial court, in the 1844 murder trial of two Irish brothers, John and William Gordon, known to be sympathetic to Dorr's Rebellion. After the conviction of the first brother, the all-Protestant Supreme Court, despite its distaste for the Irish, acceded to a defense request to delay his sentencing so that if the trial of the second brother provided new evidence that exonerated the first brother, his life could be spared. Charles Hoffmann and Tess Hoffmann, *Brotherly Love: Murder and the Politics of Prejudice in Nineteenth-Century Rhode Island* (Amherst: University of Massachusetts Press, 1993).

37. David P. Lindorff, "Rigged Justice," *In These Times,* April 14, 2003, 4–5.

38. John Locke, *Second Treatise of Government* (Indianapolis: Hackett, 1980), 33–34.

39. Quoted in Walter R. Steiner, "The Reverend Gershom Bulkeley, of Connecticut, An Eminent Clerical Physician," *Johns Hopkins Hospital Bulletin* 27 (1906): 47–52.

40. *New York Times,* March 13, 1902.

41. Virginia A. McConnell, *Arsenic under the Elms: Murder in Victorian New Haven* (Westport, Conn.: Praeger, 1999), 118–120.

42. Ibid.

Race

2

Cross-Cultural "Murther" and Retribution in Colonial New England

John J. Navin

In the early seventeenth century, prospective colonists described New England as a wilderness "devoid of all civil inhabitants." Colonial leaders knew that maintaining order within their nascent settlements would be a formidable task. The prospect of extending their jurisdiction to include the "savage people, who are cruel, barbarous and most treacherous" was deemed well nigh impossible at the outset.[1] Over time that attitude changed, so much so that within threescore years, English legal imperialism was an established fact in southern New England, notwithstanding the many injustices it bred. During that transitional period, murders and attempts at retribution that involved Native Americans contributed significantly to the establishment of English hegemony. These killings and the responses they provoked thrust indigenous peoples into the compass of English adjudication and initiated armed conflicts that hastened the decline of Native American autonomy and power.[2] The very nature of murder accusations between 1620 and 1680, the principals involved, and the manner in which those deaths were avenged underscored the cultural conflicts between the English and their Native American neighbors.

I

In the wake of a murder in colonial New England, the effort to set things right frequently pitted indigenous tradition against imported law. Even in the wilds of North America, Europeans regarded murder as an offense against the state, one that required a harsh, legally proscribed response. This differed

33

markedly from Native American tradition, a set of binding social customs based upon the principles of blood feud and clan responsibility.[3] In the Indian world, a murder victim's male kin were compelled to seek revenge or they would lose face.[4] Retaliatory killings were common, though Indians in the Northeast sometimes employed an honorable means of bloodless appeasement. The practice of materially compensating the victim's kin, sometimes called "covering the grave" or "wiping away the tears," ended the matter without further violence. English law, codified and impersonal, was less flexible and not nearly so forgiving.

In his seminal work *Puritan Justice and the Indian,* the historian Yasuhide Kawashima observes, "Indian law was based upon kinship and consanguinity, while English criminal law was based upon territoriality."[5] The former was grounded in the principle that the law of the individual's tribe took precedence over local law or custom, which meant that clan-based retributive justice superseded political boundaries. Conversely, European tradition held that "the law of the place of action rules"—each crime occurred within the jurisdiction of a specific political entity whose laws applied and whose duty it was to punish the offender.[6] These incongruities between Native American tradition and English law became most prominent during the emotionally charged period that followed a deadly assault, a circumstance that only exacerbated New England's racial divide.

II

In the 1620s, Plymouth colonists were anxious to establish a basis for peaceful coexistence with nearby tribes whose numerical superiority was viewed as the gravest threat to their fledgling plantation.[7] The men of Plymouth forged treaties with neighboring sachems such as Massasoit, who agreed that "if any of his did hurt to any of ours, he should send the offender, that we might punish him."[8] Despite their vulnerability, the newcomers claimed the right to exact punishment on any lawbreaker who victimized an English settler, regardless of race. This marked the inception of English extraterritoriality—the "extension of jurisdiction by a state beyond its own borders"— in seventeenth-century New England.[9] That the colonists should seek immunity from indigenous custom was understandable; the fact that they planned to discipline certain Native American offenders was audacious. Plymouth's founders intended to exercise both sovereignty and jurisdiction not merely within their fledgling community and dubious patent, but even outside the bounds of both. This went beyond extraterritoriality: it presaged a type of dominion usually reserved for conquerors. It was a bold but shortsighted approach, for complications ensuing from intertribal rivalries surfaced almost immediately. When Plymouth's leaders were wrongly informed that Squanto, their friend and translator, had been murdered by a "petty sachem" named Corbitant, they dispatched ten men to "be avenged on him." The error was discovered in time, but the English did not depart from Corbitant's camp until they made it clear that, "if hereafter he should make any insurrection . . . or offer violence to Squanto, Hobomok, or any of Massasoit's subjects, we would revenge it upon him, to the overthrow of him and his."[10] In colonial New England, retribution sometimes entailed but clearly did not require due process of law.

Ironically, one of the first murders in New England that involved both races may have been a deadly charade. In the summer of 1622, sixty "lusty men," mostly servants sent by the merchant-entrepreneur Thomas Weston of London, established a new plantation called Wessagusset, just north of Plymouth.[11] Poorly supplied and lacking effective leadership, they soon faced starvation. After trading their clothing and other goods to their Indian neighbors for corn, some resorted to thievery. In *New English Canaan,* Thomas Morton claims that in February 1623, following the theft of "a capp full of corne" by an "able bodied man" of Wessagusset, the Indian owner demanded satisfaction. The fearful colonists concluded that the only way "to appease the salvage [*sic*]" was to hang the culprit in their midst, but rather than execute someone who "being younge and stronge [was] fit for resistance against an enemy, which might come unexpected," they decided to put the thief's clothes on someone who was "old and impotent" and "let the sick person be hanged in the other's steede [stead]." Accordingly, an older, ailing colonist, innocent of any crime, was "fast bound in jest, and then hanged."[12]

Plymouth's settlers appear to have been less prone to be intimidated than to intimidate. Soon after the Wessagusset incident, their militia ambushed and killed seven Indians suspected of plotting an attack on both plantations. The fact that the colony's leaders deemed a preemptive strike both lawful and necessary points to the distinction in their minds between murder, in which a man killed another "feloniouslie . . . with a premeditated and malicious mind," and homicide, which was "tolerated in necessary defence of a Man's selfe, goods, &c." Regarding the latter, English law required a man being pursued to "flee as farr as he can" before taking another's life; Plymouth's inhabitants apparently reasoned that they had nowhere to flee and were justified in using deadly force to prevent the anticipated attack.[13] Following the ambush, Myles Standish, captain of the Plymouth militia, decapitated the ringleader, Wittuwamat, and mounted his head on the Plymouth blockhouse as a "warning and terror" to other Native Americans. Thereafter, the English were known as "Wotowequenage," which signified "stabbers" or "cutthroats."[14] According to one colonist's account, Wittuwamat had deemed it necessary to exterminate all Englishmen in one bold stroke, since he knew that any survivors "would never leave the death of our countrymen unrevenged."[15] Nor would Wittuwamat's countrymen, as it turned out. Following the ambush, three unsuspecting Englishmen who had abandoned the plantation at Wessagusset to live among the Indians were summarily executed.[16]

In 1630 Governor John Winthrop and several thousand of his fellow Puritans crossed the Atlantic and established the seed towns of Massachusetts Bay Colony. The "Great Migration" of the 1630s dramatically altered the racial balance in southern New England, adding more than twenty thousand English settlers during the same period that disease, warfare, and relocation were reducing the Native American population. Even before undertaking their perilous voyage, the Puritans announced their intention to "civilize" and convert the region's "savages." Scripture seemed to offer these itinerant Christians ample encouragement, promising Winthrop and his companions "the heathen for thine inheritance, and the uttermost parts of the earth for thy possession."[17]

Although the leaders of the "Bay Colony" were slow to sign any formal treaties with nearby tribes, they did make it clear that any colonist who wronged their Native American neighbors "in the least kinde" would be punished, and that it was expected that justice would be dispensed by sachems and their tribal councils with equal alacrity if the situation were reversed.[18] The naïveté of that approach became evident in 1634 when Native American disdain for English attempts at retribution laid the groundwork for New England's first interracial war. After Pequots violated their treaty with New Amsterdam officials by slaying other Indians who came to trade furs, the Dutch captured and murdered their grand sachem, Tatobem, despite the payment of a substantial ransom by his followers. Outraged, the Pequot retaliated by assaulting and killing everyone aboard a trading vessel on the Connecticut River. Unfortunately for the Pequots, the vessel and its crew were not Dutch, but English, thus bringing the Connecticut Colony and the Massachusetts Bay Colony into the fray.

John Stone, captain of the vessel, was not entirely blameless, for he had seized several Pequots to serve as river guides, inadvertently placing himself and his crew in the midst of an escalating conflict. Stone had been banished from Massachusetts and was under sentence of death in Plymouth, but the "cruell murthers" committed by a "barbarous and bloudy people called Peaquods" somehow elevated him and his crew to the status of "indeared friends."[19] Bay Colony officials warned that unless the Pequot murderers were brought to justice, they would "revenge the blood of our countrimen as occasion shall serve."[20] Notably, English authorities did not demand that punishment be meted out by the appropriate sachem; rather, Bay Colony officials wanted to see justice done within their own judicial framework and by their own hands.

The Pequots' failure to deliver up Stone's killers contributed to their undoing, but the more immediate cause of New England's first interracial war—one that nearly extinguished the Pequots as a tribal entity—was the murder of John Oldham, an English trader with close ties to the Puritan leadership. In July 1636, Native Americans boarded his vessel in Narragansett Bay, ostensibly to trade; shortly thereafter they were discovered dismembering Oldham's corpse.[21] His gruesome demise, the unavenged murders of Stone and his crew, and continuing Pequot intransigence prompted a vindictive frenzy among the English. In May 1637 colonial militia, supported by their Indian allies, surrounded a fortified Pequot encampment at Mystic, Connecticut, and shot or burned alive some seven hundred inhabitants, most of whom were unarmed.[22] The bloodbath was justified in English eyes, no matter how many defenseless men, women, and children went to the grave. As far as the colonists were concerned, the extermination of a murderous people represented the "necessary execution of Justice," fully tolerated by the laws of England. According to the Puritan Edward Johnson, the slaughter at Mystic was simply "the Lord intending to have these murtherers know he would looke out of the cloudy pillar upon them."[23] In a setting where governors and assistants, frequently advised by clergy, also served as judges, a declaration of war was tantamount to a court order, and militiamen were merely executing the court's will. When the "slaughter of a Man" was "commanded" by the court, it was homicide, not murder; when lawbreakers were "putt to death by an officer appointed thereto . . . this is rather called Judgment."[24] Thus, when the victorious English bound thirty captive Pequot males and threw them into the sea, the soldiers felt vindicated.[25] Their violence was sanctioned by God and King, or at least by their New England representatives. English law and Mosaic law went hand in hand: predatory and insolent behavior had to be punished; "wild men" had to be civilized and converted, or rendered harmless; conspirators and murderers had to be brought to justice. Native Americans might not understand this logic, but they could be forced to submit to it.

The Hartford Treaty of 1638, which documented English ascendancy in southern New England, required the Narragansetts and Mohegans to appeal to colonial magistrates rather than seek revenge if one tribe wronged the other. It also called on the sachems of both tribes to bring any remaining Pequot "murtherers" to justice by "take[ing] off their heads."[26] Anxious to endear himself to the victors, Uncas, leader of the Mohegans, promised to uphold English law and to protect English colonists, saying: "Command me any difficult thing, I will do it. . . . If any man shall kill an Englishman, I will put him to death, were he never so dear to me."[27] Uncas's pledge to avenge the deaths of people whose laws strictly forbade personal acts of revenge merely underscored the incompatibility of English law and Native American tradition. Such a course of action would put him outside the scope of clan revenge and in violation of English legal procedure. Neither the Mohegan sachem nor anyone else on either side of New England's cultural divide could meld two conflicting bodies of precedent.

Elsewhere in 1638, English justice was put to the test in a landmark murder trial. When four men from Plymouth Colony robbed and fatally wounded a Native American in Rhode Island, the victim's Narragansett kin demanded retribution. Massachusetts authorities recommended that Thomas Peach, the alleged ringleader, be handed over to the Narragansett sachem for execution, since the crime occurred outside English jurisdiction. This was not so much in deference to the Native American tradition of clan revenge as it was a reaffirmation of political bounds and claims of sovereignty within specified patents. Instead of heeding the advice of Bay Colony Puritans, the autonomous Rhode Island authorities opted to deliver Peach and his companions to Plymouth officials who promised that the Indians "should see justice done upon the offenders."[28] In Boston, Governor John Winthrop reversed course and voiced his support, noting, "The whole country here were interested in the case, and would expect to have justice done."[29] It was, after all, a chance for English law to nudge Indian custom one step closer to the brink of irrelevance.

Before the trial, one defendant escaped and made his way to Maine, but the other three were indicted for "murther & robbing by the heigh way."[30] Peach, a veteran of the Pequot War, claimed that his victim "had killed many of them [English]." However, even though colonial authorities might tolerate outright slaughter in the course of a war, they refused to condone what they considered unsanctioned violence, even against "savages." Consequently, Peach and his fellow perpetrators were sentenced to death. According to Governor William Bradford of Plymouth, "some of the rude and ignorant sort murmured that any English should be put to death for the Indians." But Rhode Island's founding father, Roger Williams, warned that the victim's "friends and kindred were ready to rise in arms" if the crime went unpunished. A number of Native Americans, including relatives of the victim, were present in September 1638 when the execution of the three murderers "gave them and all the country good satisfaction."[31]

III

The 1640s saw various New England tribes submit to English rule; they agreed, "to bee governed & protected . . . according to their just lawes & order, so farr as wee shalbee made capable of understanding them."[32] Even though the "Body of Liberties" published in the Bay Colony in 1641 stated that "Every person within this Jurisdiction, whether Inhabitant or forreiner shall enjoy the same justice and law," colonial leaders showed little inclination to track down and prosecute Native Americans for murders that did not involve whites, especially if the victim and assailant hailed from the same tribe or if the incident took place in a remote location.[33] Conversely, governors and magistrates were zealous in their efforts to punish Indians who slew colonists, even if it meant coercing tribal leaders or crossing political boundaries. After a "giant-like Indian" in Dutch territory killed Thomas Farrington of Connecticut, Captain Gardner persuaded Waiandance, the Long Island sachem, to execute the felon.[34]

Ordinarily, colonial leaders preferred to exact retribution within their own legal system. However, despite their increasing strength and compass, the English often found themselves unable to apprehend Native American murderers without the cooperation of their Indian allies. In October 1639 an Indian named Nepaupuck was indicted for the murder of one Abraham Finch. Thanks to the courtroom testimony of "Quillipeck Sagamour and his Indians," Nepaupuck's head was "cutt off . . . and pitched upon a pole in the market place."[35] When another Englishman was "cruelly murdered" in May 1644, the subsequent trial and execution came only after a Potatuck Indian delivered the culprit, a Native American named Busheage, to Connecticut authorities.[36] Still, even when Indian assistance was required in the apprehension of an alleged murderer, extraterritoriality, not consanguinity, ultimately determined the course of justice. Indians in the Northeast gradually came to understand that they had less to fear from the relatives of a murdered colonist than they did from the system of constables, courts, statutes, juries, judges, and militia that demanded conformity to English law on an ever-broadening scale.

In areas of southern New England where Native Americans remained most numerous, colonial leaders had to temper the application of English law with good sense. Rhode Island authorities decreed in 1640 that, "if any Indian shall be unruly . . . he shall receive his punishment according to Law." However, in deference to their powerful Narragansett neighbors, the Rhode Islanders also proclaimed "for any matters of great weight . . . Miantanomy . . . is to come and see the Tryal."[37] Miantonomi, the Narragansett sachem, was described by one Englishman as a "potent Prince" whose followers numbered in the thousands.[38] In May 1643, rumors that he was conspiring with other sachems for a joint assault on English settlements prompted the leaders of Connecticut, Massachusetts, Plymouth, and New Haven to establish a confederation known as "The United Colonies of New England." Thereafter they would cooperate for "offence and defence, mutuall advice, and succour upon all occasions."[39] No sooner had United Colonies commissioners been appointed by their respective colonies than they found themselves in the midst of a serious intertribal dispute. Uncas, the Mohegan leader, accused Miantonomi, whom he had taken prisoner, of hiring an Indian to assassinate him. Rather than avenge himself personally (as he had promised to do should an Englishman be slain), Uncas turned the Narragansett sachem over to the United Colonies. Judging that "it would not be safe to set him at liberty, neither had we sufficient ground for us to put him to death," the commissioners decided to return the prisoner to his Mohegan rival for punishment. The records show that "Uncus was advised to take away the life of Myantenomo," but "within his own jurisdiction, not in the English plantations." The English even sent representatives to "see the execution for our more full satisfaccion." Uncas left the session with the condemned sachem in tow and, between Hartford and Windsor, Uncas's brother "clave his head with an hatchet."[40]

Miantonomi's assassination not only exposed the arbitrary nature of English justice, it also shed light on the awkward interplay of English law and Native American tradition, as the former gradually took precedence over the latter. Unsure of their legal position but certain in their motives, the Commissioners elected to appease their ally by sanctioning the execution of his rival. They also denied Miantonomi's clan any chance of avenging his death by instructing the authorities at Hartford to "furnish Uncas with a competent strength of English to defend him against any present fury or assault."[41] When the Narragansetts sought permission to "make war upon Onkus in revenge," the sachems "marvelled why we should be against it," according to Winthrop.[42] Like many other New England tribes, the Narragansetts had formerly pledged to "give over ourselves, peoples, lands, rights, inheritances, and possessions" to that "worthy and royal Prince, Charles . . . upon condition of His Majesties' royal protection."[43] It had not taken long for Miantonomi's followers to discover that the English allocated "protection" on the basis of expediency, not pact.

IV

In the eyes of New England colonists, the taking of an Englishman's life by a Native American was never justified. There was a clear double standard at work. Even during pitched battles or fighting to defend their village, Indians were acting outside the law—otherwise the English would not be engaging them in combat, or so their thinking went. Thus, colonial militia went to war against "murtherers," not enemy soldiers. As the Pequot War demonstrated, the actions of a few might invite retaliation against the many. Their inherent racism allowed colonial courts and militia to extend complicity for a crime down to the youngest member of an offending tribe. Colonial statutes might promise equanimity to Native Americans, but experience proved otherwise.[44]

The distinction between murder and warfare was far less precise when it came to intertribal killings, at least insofar as the English were concerned. Some took the form of isolated slayings; others involved deadly, large-scale raids. English authorities were hard-pressed to put an end to either. In June 1645 Roger Williams reported that "the flame of war rageth next door to us . . . Narragansetts and Mohegans, with their respective confederates, have deeply implunged themselves into barbarous slaughters."[45] The United Colonies dispatched three hundred troops to force the combatants to sign treaties in which they promised not to wage war on each other "till they have liberty and allowance from the Comissionrs." They also promised to deliver up "any Peacott [Pequot] or other . . . who hath in tyme of peace murthered any of the English."[46] However, the treaties did little to curtail the violence.

During the same period, English efforts to convert New England's "heathens" to Christianity complicated white-Indian relations and added a new and divisive element to tribal politics, both internal and external. The Massachusetts General Court declared in 1644 that the "natives (amongst whome wcc live, & whoe have submitted themselves to this government) should come to ye good knowledge of God." The conversion of some but not all members of various tribes drove a wedge into their society and pushed a significant number of Native Americans into a cultural no-man's land where they found themselves ostracized by members of both races. The establishment of "Praying Towns" in Massachusetts Bay Colony beginning in 1652 only exacerbated these tensions. No longer did conversion alone separate "praying Indians" from the rest; soon their manner of dress, their mode of living, and ultimately their place of residence marked them as Native Americans on the English path of acculturation, but not assimilation.

For a time, it appeared that New England's indigenous peoples had more to fear from each other than from the English. Most murders in the 1650s were internecine, not interracial. In May 1654 Captain John Mason informed the governor of Massachusetts Bay Colony that "the Quinabaug Indians whoe are under yor protection have lately plundered a towne belonging to Onkos."[47] Uncas reportedly had "much adoe to keepe his men from revenge" and looked to the English for "due sattisfacon . . . otherwise he must be enforced to right himselfe." That same year, Ninigret, the Niantic sachem, and his followers "fell upon the long Iland Indians" and "kild many of them & took others Captives, & yt without any Just pvocation given by them." Colonial authorities could hardly ignore Ninigret's insolence in killing an Indian couple "living upon the land of the English," but they were unwilling or unable to prosecute the sachem for murder, since he had "hired & drawn downe many forraigne Indians Armed wth guns pistols & swords to the terror of the English and Indians thereabouts."[48] In May 1659, the minister John Eliot reported to Bay Colony authorities that Uncas and his Mohegan followers from Connecticut had invaded central Massachusetts and murdered eight unarmed Nipmuck Indians. In addition, he had taken captive twenty-four Nipmuck women and children.[49] A strong but troublesome ally to the English,

Uncas's cooperation and deference had waned as he consolidated power. Eliot cautioned Puritan leaders, "All the Indians of the country, wait to see the issue of this matter."[50] This posed a dilemma. Massachusetts was reluctant to initiate hostile action against a powerful sachem in a neighboring colony, yet Bay Colony authorities were certainly not going to defer to the Native American tradition of clan revenge. Such a decision would undermine their efforts to bring all Indians in their jurisdiction into a state of dependency. Once again, expediency, not justice, appears to have won the day. Uncas escaped unscathed, a circumstance that may have encouraged his son to assault the "defenceless town" of Quabaconk two years later.

Notwithstanding their inability to halt the violence among the native population, retribution remained a top priority for English authorities whenever a colonist was murdered, especially if the assailant was an Indian. After Shinnecocks killed a white woman in Southampton, their sachem refused to deliver the suspects for trial. Colonial leaders responded by threatening to destroy the entire Shinnecock village. The accused were soon in English hands, in English courts, and on English gallows.[51] When Native Americans committed a "most horrid murder" at Farmington, the Connecticut magistrates ordered that three tribal leaders be "kept as pledges in the prison till the murtherers & accessories are brought forth to triall & judgmt." They encouraged local settlers to apprehend any person "that may justly bee suspected to bee guilty" and enjoined nearby sachems to surrender any "accessory to that bloody act." The English announced that tribes or individuals who sheltered the suspects would be regarded "as our enimyes."[52] In fairness to colonial authorities, it should be pointed out that they occasionally displayed vigor in their efforts to prosecute whites who had murdered Indians. However, such slayings were rare, except in times of war when Englishmen generally enjoyed immunity from charges of murder. Even in times of peace, Englishmen serving on juries were likely to grant their fellow colonists considerable latitude in claims of (justifiable) homicide, which the law "tolerated in necessary defence of a Man's selfe, goods, & c."[53] However, the relative paucity of murders of Indians by whites suggests that colonists felt constrained not only by their own laws, but also by their continuing fear of reprisal by Native Americans.

In October 1664, the General Assembly at Hartford strengthened its efforts to curb intertribal warfare in southern New England:

> Whereas ... the Natives about us notwithstanding all counsel and
> advice to the contrary ... have and still doe proceed to commit
> murther and kill one another wthin the English plantations and upon
> the English land, and take no course that justice be executed upon
> such malefactors ... this Court doth order that for the future what-
> ever Indian or Indians shall willfully and violently fall upon any

other Indian or Indians wthin this Colony upon the English land and murther him, he shall be put to death; and if the Indians doe not execution upon such a murtherer or murtherers forthwith, the next civill officer . . . shall forthwith cause him or them to be apprehended . . . for a tryall [at] the next Court of Assistants.[54]

The seeming deference to the Native American tradition of clan revenge reflects the precariousness of English settlements in that region. Well into the seventeenth century, Connecticut remained thinly populated by colonists and heavily populated by Native Americans.[55] This explains why that colony's magistrates depended first and foremost on Indians for "execution upon . . . a murtherer or murtherers" in their jurisdiction, unless whites were involved. It also explains their reluctance to prosecute Indians for murders that did not occur "upon the English land." Of course, if the outcome satisfied the ambitions or sense of justice of colonial authorities, Native American traditions became far more palatable.

Even the powerful Massachusetts Bay Colony used extreme caution when dealing with sizeable Native American tribes that had not pledged submission to the English. When five heavily armed Mohawks or Maquas were seized near Boston in 1665, Puritan officials had to risk inciting a bloody war or permit alleged murderers to go free. Following their arrest, the five "stout and lusty" warriors told the Court "they came not hither, with an intent to do the least wrong to the English, but to avenge themselves of the Indians, their enemies."[56] According to Indian Superintendent Daniel Gookin, the Maquas were "so great a terrour to all the Indians" that the appearance of four or five in the woods "would frighten them from their habitations." Local tribes pressured the English "not to let them escape, but to put them to death, or, at least, to deliver the Maquas to them to be put to death." They claimed, "Maquas are unto us, as wolves are to your sheep. . . . They secretly seize upon us and our children, wherever they meet us, and destroy us." Despite the entreaties of their Indian allies, the magistrates concluded it was "not suitable to the Christian profession, to begin a war with a people, that had not killed or slain any Englishmen." They released the five Maquas with a written warning to their sachems "to forbid any of that people, for the future, to kill and destroy any of the Indians under our protection, that lived about forty miles from us on every side." It is telling that the Indians under the Bay Colony's protection were described as those "which they might distinguish from other Indians, by their short hair, and wearing English fashioned apparel."[57]

The favoritism shown to Christianized Indians, none of whom appear to have been charged with murder prior to 1675, and the growing pressure to join their ranks did not sit well with traditional Native Americans. When Roger Williams prepared to visit London, Narragansett leaders asked him "to present their Peticion to ye high Sachims of England yt [that] they might not be forced from their Religion." The sachems claimed that they were "dayly visited with Threatnings by Indians yt came from about ye Masachusets yt if they would not pray, they should be destroyed by War."[58] Another indignant sachem was Metacomet, called "King Philip" by the English. He assumed leadership of the Pokanokets in 1662 when his brother Wamsutta died unexpectedly during a visit to Massachusetts Bay Colony. Philip maintained that the English had poisoned Wamsutta, but he had no proof.[59] After Plymouth Colony settlers encroached on his homeland to establish the town of Swansea in 1667, Philip was rumored to be in league with the Dutch and French against the English.[60] Ninigret, the Niantic sachem, was also suspected of plotting against the colonists. His confederates reportedly included the Montauks, the Wampanaogs, the surviving Pequots, and the fearsome Mohawks, as well as the French in Nova Scotia and certain Quakers.[61] Although Philip and Ninigret denied the allegations and remained free, trouble was clearly afoot in southern New England.

V

Despite the palpable tension between the races, murders of whites by Indians and vice versa remained isolated events in the early 1670s. One notable exception involved the son of Matoonas, a Nipmuck sachem, who killed a colonist near Boston in 1671. After being convicted for the crime, he was "hanged, and afterwards beheaded, and his head set upon a pole, where it was to be seen six years after."[62] During this period, intertribal rivalries continued to spawn deadly encounters, sporadically provoking English intervention. In 1673 the Rhode Island General Assembly, which preferred to avoid involvement in such matters, obliged local Narragansett and Niantic sachems by agreeing to choose six Indians to serve as jurors in a murder trial in which the assailant and victim were both Native Americans.[63] Conversely, the Connecticut General Court, anxious to prosecute an Indian for slaying a Pequot girl, was frustrated by a lack of interracial cooperation. When the alleged murderer escaped and "fled to Ninicraft," the Narragansett sachem refused to hand him over to the English, "pretending his own right to be the proper judge himself."[64]

Galvanized by Rhode Island's initiative and Connecticut's difficulties, other New England colonies made alterations in their respective legal systems. In June 1674 the Plymouth General Court declared that Indians could testify without swearing an oath as required by English common law. Instead, Native American testimony could be valued according to the "Judgment and Conscience" of the hearers.[65] In another significant departure from tradition, both Plymouth and Massachusetts began to allow the use of praying Indians as jurors. This set the stage for a momentous trial, one instigated by the growing rift between Christian and non-Christian Indians. It did much to precipitate the second interracial war in New England, this one more deadly than the first.

Plymouth Colony's second landmark cross-cultural trial was occasioned by the murder of John Sassamon, a praying Indian who had incurred the wrath of King Philip, the Pokanoket leader. A member of the Massachusett tribe, Sassamon had attended Harvard College, served as assistant to the minister John Eliot, and may have spied for Massachusetts authorities.[66] According to John Easton's "Relacion of the Indyan Warre," Sassamon served for a time as scribe and witness to treaties for Philip. While serving that important role, Sassamon took advantage of Philip's illiteracy and secretly named himself heir to much of the sachem's land while recording his will.[67] Philip somehow discovered the ruse but may have forgiven Sassamon, who was married to his niece.[68] However, in late 1674 Sassamon committed a far more serious offense by implicating the Pokanoket sachem in a plot against the English. Shortly thereafter, the former scribe's body was discovered under the ice in Plymouth Colony's Assawompsett pond.

Sassamon's death was initially accounted an accident. However, when a praying Indian named Patuckson claimed that he had seen three Pokanokets murder Sassamon and conceal his body beneath the ice, the inference that Philip had ordered his execution could hardly be avoided. In fact, when Sassamon had made his fateful visit to Plymouth to expose Philip's efforts to organize a pan-Indian assault on the English, he informed Governor Josiah Winslow that the sachem might have him killed if he discovered his treachery.[69] In June 1675, the Plymouth court charged three of Philip's followers, all non-Christians, with the crime. In an effort to appear impartial, the Plymouth magistrates allowed the jury of twelve Englishmen to consult with six of the "most indifferentest, gravest, and sage Indians" in their deliberations.[70] Although the Body of Liberties drawn up by the Bay Colony required a minimum of two witnesses for a murder conviction, one eyewitness apparently sufficed in a Plymouth courtroom, at least in this instance.[71] The panel of English jurors and "sage Indians," all of whom current scholars deem to have been Christians, heard Patuckson's damning testimony. The three defendants were found guilty and sentenced to death. One received a temporary reprieve when the gallows rope broke, but he was shot a month later, supposedly after confessing to the murders and implicating Philip.[72]

In a recent work entitled *Igniting King Philip's War: The John Sassamon Murder Trial*, the historian Yasuhide Kawashima argues that the Sassamon trial was orchestrated by Plymouth authorities, who readily undermined their own legal principles in order to force King Philip and the Wampanoags to conform. According to Kawashima, the trial violated existing treaties between Plymouth and the Wampanoags, who claimed the right to handle the matter based on the principle of personality.[73] However, existing treaties that had been signed (under pressure) by Philip and various Pokanoket leaders who preceded him gave the English full jurisdiction in the Sassamon case, because the alleged crime took place within the bounds of Plymouth Colony.[74] Had Plymouth's leaders allowed Philip to try the accused murderers, or even allowed outside arbitrators to settle the matter as the Quaker deputy governor of Rhode Island suggested, they would have been forfeiting their claim of "territoriality" and reversing the process of legal imperialism that they had advanced very deliberately, case by case and treaty by treaty, for decades.[75]

Kawashima contends that although the guilty verdict had "the appearance of fairness, impartiality, and complete justice," the process was severely flawed: there were no decisive proofs of assassination, the defendants should have had legal counsel, the jury was not composed of the defendants' peers, the testimony of one witness should have been deemed insufficient, and the witness may have acted out of self-interest. In the end the charge of murder remained unsubstantiated, and the botched execution of the defendant Wampapaquan entitled him to a reprieve.[76] Although Kawashima does fairly expose certain injustices that took place, there is no evidence that the accused murderers asked for and were denied the right to legal counsel. The definition of "peers" in the English concept of trial by jury of peers originally referred to persons living in the same locality as the accused. By the seventeenth century there was considerable ambiguity in English practice in respect to the constitution of juries. Less defensible was the decision of the Plymouth authorities to ignore the provision in the Body of Liberties (which Plymouth Colony largely adopted after it was promulgated by the Bay Colony in 1641) calling for two witnesses in capital cases. Justice was poorly served, but the decision that was made should hardly startle modern scholars—the management of the case to Plymouth Colony's perceived advantage was consistent with the general trend exhibited by colonial leaders away from legal coexistence with southern New England's Native Americans, a trend rooted in the devastation of the Pequots nearly four decades earlier.[77]

Following the execution of the three Pokanoket defendants, Philip lashed out against a judicial process that relied on the testimony of Christian Indians who "wer in everi thing more mischievous, only dissemblers." He claimed, "[I}f 20 of there [h] onest Indians testefied that a Englishman had dun them rong, it was as nothing, and if but one of ther worst Indians testified against ani Indian or ther king when it plesed the English that was sufitiant." John Easton, the Quaker deputy governor of Rhode Island, privately substantiated Philip's claims, noting, "We knew it to be true."[78] But few of Easton's contemporaries sympathized with the Pokanoket leader: he and many of his followers remained on the wrong side of the Christian-heathen divide, and on the undesirable side of a widening double standard. A prominent Boston merchant wrote to a friend in London that Sassamon had been sent to preach to the Pokanokets, "but King Philip (Heathen-like) instead of receiving the Gospel, would immediately have killed this Sosomon, but by the Perswasion of some about him did not do it." Instead, three of Philip's men, "not liking his [Sassamon's] Discourse, immediately Murthered him after a most Barbarous Manner," for which they "were found and apprehended, and after a fair Trial were all Hanged."[79]

Tensions had soared on the eve of the Sassamon trial; John Easton wrote, "[T]he English wear afraid and Philop was afraid and both increased in arems." After the execution of his followers, Philip lamented that "all English agred against them." The fragile trust that had prevented the resumption of interracial war for nearly four decades had finally disintegrated, since "the English dear not trust the indians promises nether the indians to the Englishes promises." Philip now understood that his tribe's affiliation with Plymouth Colony was not sufficient protection against English intrusiveness, greed, and subterfuge. According to the disgruntled sachem, not only had the Plymouth settlers encroached on his homeland, but also the Bay Colony's efforts to convert Native Americans had undermined his power: "the English made them not subject to ther kings, and by ther lying to rong their kings."[80] According to one colonist, from the time of his men's execution, Philip "studied to be Revenged on the English, judging that the English Authority have Nothing to do to Hang any of his Indians for killing another."[81] Another observed, "[T]he English wear jelous that ther was a genarall plot of all Indians against English and the Indians wear in like maner jelous of the english."[82]

The murder of John Sassamon and the subsequent trial and executions set the stage for an orgy of violence known as "King Philip's War." By today's standards the conflict more closely resembled a series of violent, interconnected assaults than a clash of armies. Not surprisingly, the war began in much that fashion. In June 1675 a young colonist mortally wounded a Pokanoket Indian who was plundering a house in the Plymouth Colony town of Swansea. "The next day," said one account, "the lad that shot the indian and his father and fief [five] English more wear killed so the war begun with philop."[83] The fast-growing conflict soon pitted the New England colonists against a Native American confederacy that included Wampanoags (of which Philip's Pokanoket were a subgroup), Nipmucks, Massachusetts, Pocumtucks, and some Narragansetts.

Rumors of atrocities committed by Native Americans appalled the English and propelled them to action. A Boston resident reported, "[T]he Indians continued daily to commit many Acts of Hostility . . . killing many People after a most Barbarous Manner; as skinning them all over alive."[84]

Mary Rowlandson, the wife of a Bay Colony minister, wrote: "[T]hese murtherous wretches went on, burning, and destroying before them." Many colonists ceased to regard Native Americans in human terms. In the narrative of her captivity, Rowlandson described her captors as "wolves," "hellhounds" and "ravenous bears."[85] Rev. Solomon Stoddard advised the governor of Massachusetts that Indians "are to be looked upon as thieves and murderers . . . they act like wolves and are to be dealt withal as wolves." He recommended that the English "hunt Indians with dogs, as they do bears." Bay Colony soldiers collected thirty shillings per head for all enemies killed or taken, a policy originally employed to extinguish New England's population of wolves. The General Court eventually offered a bounty for Indian scalps, irrespective of sex or age.[86] The disparaging terms used to describe Native Americans and the portrayal of their actions as "massacres," "murthers," or worse helped the colonists justify their actions in their own minds and in the eyes of other "civilized" people. Historian Jill Lepore argues that "the language of cruelty and savagery was the vocabulary Puritans adapted" to distinguish between themselves and their Indian enemies.[87] As Lepore points out, the colonial historian William Hubbard titled his 1676 account of King Philip's War a "narrative" because the "Massacres, [and] barbarous inhumane Outrages" he described did not, in his opinion, deserve the "Name of a War."[88]

Native Americans sometimes faced impromptu trials when they were captured. Captain Henchman reported that during his expedition near Pawtucket Falls, a number of Indian captives were judged: "Eleven persons we had in all, two of whom by council we put to death."[89] But in the field, most executions proceeded without any pretense of due process. An English expedition near Hatfield seized a squaw who was "ordered to be torn in peeces by Doggs, and she was soe dealt withal."[90] When Captain Benjamin Church captured Tatoson, he refused to grant him quarter "because of his inhuman murders and barbarities," and the sachem was put to death.[91] The 150 English soldiers who assaulted the Indian settlement at Hadley in May 1676 were not interested in taking prisoners or conducting impromptu hearings; they simply killed the inhabitants in their wigwams or shot them as they attempted to flee across the river.[92] Some of the most appalling executions were of Native American women and children who were intercepted as they fled toward New York, where Governor Andros had offered them safe haven.[93] When Connecticut militia captured 171 Narragansett Indians in a Rhode Island swamp in July 1676, they killed all of the men and 92 of the women and children. Their commander's expeditionary orders had been to "kill and destroy them, according to the utmost power God shall give you."[94]

Even when Native Americans were afforded due process, public sentiment remained strongly against them. When Bay Colony magistrates declared twelve of thirteen Indians on trial not guilty of murder, those acquitted had to be spirited away under cover of darkness before a lynch mob arrived at the courthouse.[95] In 1676 a Massachusetts soldier accused of murdering an inoffensive Christian Indian was acquitted, despite the judges' strong disagreement with the jury's verdict. One month later two men went on trial for the murder of praying Indians at Wamesit; they too were found innocent, "to the great grief and trouble" of the magistrates and ministers.[96] As the war against Philip and his allies progressed, Plymouth courts sold hundreds of Indians into slavery, reserving the gallows for "any of them [who] should appeer to have had a hand in any horred murder of any of the English."[97] The Bay Colony also culled out the more notorious prisoners and made Boston Common the site of numerous executions. About thirty Native Americans were hanged there in August 1676, and fifteen or more were hanged or shot the following month.[98] One was Matoonas, whose son had been executed for murdering a colonist five years earlier. According to Increase Mather, the Nipmuck chief "had given it out that he would be avenged of us for his son's death."[99] Having upheld tradition and obtained blood revenge, the sachem forfeited his life to the state.

Like their English counterparts, Native American combatants killed armed soldiers and defenseless civilians with equal relish. They took some captives for purposes of ransom, slew others out of sheer malice, and fought with the fury of a people that had endured many wrongs. But the conflict did not pit all Indians against all colonists—New England wars were endlessly complicated matters. Philip, the Pokanoket leader, was eager to settle the score with members of his own race who in his eyes had become traitors and minions of the English. He issued word that certain praying Indians should be brought to him "that he might put them to some tormenting death."[100] Such killings would indeed be "cross-cultural" affairs, for the very bone of contention between Philip and the Christian Indians he so despised was the injection of toxic English culture into the bloodstream of Native American tradition. Yet the sachem had to worry about certain non-Christian Indians as well, for the war only served to exacerbate New England's many intertribal rivalries. The Nipmuck Wabaquassucks held some of Philip's company captive for a time and showed the English six scalps to prove it.[101] Mohegan warriors served as scouts for Connecticut troops during their overland expeditions. When Sagamore John and his 180 followers sought clemency in Boston, he delivered a fellow Nipmuck sachem into English hands and carried out the sachem's execution on Boston Common.[102] Similarly, after Captain Church's company took Tatoson captive, he was dispatched by one of Church's Indian allies.

Ultimately, Philip's uprising proved a disastrous failure, because certain New England tribes remained faithful to the English and the powerful Mohawks or Maquas elected to oppose the Pokanoket sachem and his confederates rather than join their cause. The war's final irony was the death of Philip on

August 12, 1676, at the hands of one of his own men, whose brother may have been killed for suggesting surrender.[103] Overall, between six hundred and eight hundred English soldiers and civilians had fallen. Three thousand Native Americans may have perished in combat, and several thousand more are believed to have died from exposure and disease or been sold into slavery.[104]

Not surprisingly, the staggering death toll prompted a widespread thirst for vengeance. Increase Mather noted that, "a sort of a Peace was patched up, which Left a Body of Indians, not only with Horrible Murders Unrevenged, but also in the possession of no little part of the Countrey."[105] Revenge was also on the minds of many Englishmen, but once the military contest was decided, colony leaders were not about to open the floodgates and let their charges engage in wanton killing sprees. Five days before the death of "King Philip," four colonists from towns that had suffered Indian attacks brutally murdered six Native American women and children who were picking berries on Hurtleberry Hill. The victims, Christian Indians from a nearby praying town, had been "shot through, others their brains beat out with hatchets." Despite their claim that the killings were legally warranted, the four Englishmen were tried for murder, found guilty, and sentenced to death. Two were eventually pardoned, but Stephen Goble was hanged on September 14, 1676, and his uncle met the same fate one week later on Boston Common. The latter paid the price for his crime alongside three Indians who had been convicted of "imbru[ing] their hands in English blood."[106] Despite the recent carnage, despite the enmity, despite the new sense of English hegemony, justice resurfaced following the Hurtleberry Hill massacre—more precisely, justice as interpreted and administered within the tradition of English common law.

VI

The decisive English victory in King Philip's War eradicated any pretense of legal coexistence between Indians and colonists in southern New England. Independent tribal government all but disappeared, and the law increasingly became a means for whites to exploit Native Americans.[107] After 1676, virtually all "murthers" in the region fell within the scope of English jurisdiction. As in the past, the pursuit of malefactors continued to accentuate English bigotry and Native American intractability. With the advent of English legal imperialism, institutional law established its ascendancy over the Indian tradition of clan-based retribution. Territoriality, not consanguinity, had prevailed. But soon enough, the battle between whites and Indians and their clashing notions of justice would be renewed on the northern boundaries of English settlement. As conflicts raged in Maine and on the periphery of Massachusetts Bay Colony, individual acts of vengeance would again become commonplace.

Ironically, while colonial militia struggled to subdue northern tribes, forcing them to observe English law rather than ancient traditions such as "blood revenge," some colonists seemed to be moving in the opposite direction.[108] In July 1677, Indians in Maine seized a number of English fishing vessels, prompting rumors that the crews had been murdered. When a ketch sailed into Marblehead harbor with two Native Americans in bonds, women poured out of the meetinghouse and down to the docks. According to a crewman on the ketch, "[W]hen they saw the Indians, they demanded why we kept them alive and why we had not killed them." The captors intended to take the Indians to the authorities for criminal prosecution, but "with stones, billets of wood, and what else they might, [the women] made an end of these Indians." The crewman deposed that "we found them with their heads off and gone, and their flesh in a manner pulled from their bones." Rather than let the English court system administer justice, the women of Marblehead took things into their own hands, claiming that "if there had been forty of the best Indians in the country here, they would have killed them all, though they should be hanged for it."[109] Evidently the notion that retribution was sometimes a personal matter, not an institutional one, had not been extinguished, and was not confined to New England's indigenous population.

Notes

1. William Bradford, *Of Plymouth Plantation, 1620–1647*, ed. Francis Murphy (Boston, 1856; reprint, New York: Random House, 1981), 26.

2. In an article on the "diplomacy of murder" in upper Canada after the American Revolution, Alan Taylor has drawn the distinction between "intercultural" murders and "intracultural" murders, pointing out that colonial authorities regarded the latter incidents as "far more trouble than they were worth." I do not disagree with that fundamental assessment, but I try to show that such murders were not easily disregarded, and trouble indeed resulted. See Alan Taylor, "Covering the Grave: The Diplomacy of Murder in Upper Canada, 1783–1826," paper presented to the Massachusetts Historical Society Early American Seminar, September 21, 2000.

3. Yasuhide Kawashima, *Puritan Justice and the Indian: White Man's Law in Massachusetts, 1630–1763* (Middletown, Conn.: Wesleyan University Press, 1986), 5.

4. Daniel Gookin, the Indian superintendent in the Bay Colony, wrote, "These Indians . . . are very revengeful, and will not be unmindful to take vengeance upon such as have injured them or their kindred, when they have opportunity, although it be a long time after the offence was committed. If any murther, or other great wrong upon any of their relations or kindred, be committed, all of that stock and consanguinity look upon

themselves to revenge that wrong, or murder, unless the business be taken up by the payment of wompompeague, or other satisfaction, which their custom admits, to satisfy for all wrongs, yea for life itself." Daniel Gookin, "Historical Collections of the Indians in New England," *Massachusetts Historical Society Collections*, 1, (1792): 149.

5. Kawashima, *Puritan Justice and the Indian*, 177.

6. Ibid., 7.

7. The Native American population dropped precipitously during the small-pox epidemics of 1616–17, 1633–34 and 1639–40, particularly between Cape Anne and Cape Cod, where mortality may have approached 90 percent or more. Still, Native Americans remained numerically superior in southern New England until the 1640s. See Gary Nash, *Red, White and Black: The Peoples of Early America* (Englewood Cliffs, N.J.: Prentice-Hall, 1982), 76; and Lyle Koehler, "Red-White Power Relations and Justice in the Courts of Seventeenth-Century New England," *American Indian Culture and Research Journal* 3, no. 4 (1979): 8.

8. Edward Winslow, *A Journal of the Pilgrims at Plymouth* ("Mourt's Relation"), ed. Dwight Heath (London, 1622; reprint, New York: Corinth Books, 1963), 56.

9. Kawashima, *Puritan Justice and the Indian*, 225–27. Kawashima posits three overlapping stages in the development of English law in North America: extra-territoriality, legal coexistence, and legal imperialism. As the text implies, such paradigms falter in the wake of Native American and English pragmatism—customs are always flexible, whether societies are governed by tradition or statute law. Nonetheless, Kawashima is accurate in his assessment of the overall trend of white-Indian relations in colonial New England.

10. Winslow, 74–75.

11. Ibid., 121.

12. Thomas Morton, *New English Canaan* (Amsterdam, 1637; reprint, New York: Da Capo Press, 1969), 108–10.

13. John Russell Bartlett, ed., *Records of the Colony of Rhode Island and Providence Plantations, in New England*, vol. 1, *1636 to 1663* (Providence, R.I.: A. C. Greene and Bros., 1856), 163–72. This legal distinction between murder and homicide was spelled out in the acts and orders passed at the General Court of Election at Portsmouth, Rhode Island, on May 19–21, 1647. They are representative of the interpretations used elsewhere in New England in the seventeenth century, all of which were based on the laws of England.

14. Morton, 112. Ironically, three Indians who intended to appease the wrath of the English governor with tribute set out by boat for Plymouth but were drowned. See Alexander Young, ed., *Chronicles of the Pilgrim Fathers of the Colony of Plymouth, 1602–1625* (Boston, 1841; reprint, New York: Da Capo Press, 1971), 345 (Winslow's Relation").

15. "Winslow's Relation," quoted in Samuel Gardner Drake, *History of the Early Discovery of America and Landing of the Pilgrims with a Biography of the Indians of North America*, 11th ed. (Boston: L. P. Crown and Company, 1854), 96.

16. Both William Bradford and Thomas Morton comment on the retaliatory slayings, though neither offers any specifics. The historian Francis Jennings argues that the Native Americans did not grasp the difference between the Englishmen of the two colonies, implying that they might not have executed the three Wessagusset men had they made the distinction. Francis Jennings, *The Invasion of America: Indians, Colonialism, and the Cant of Conquest* (Chapel Hill: University of North Carolina Press, 1975), 186–87.

17. Ps. 72: 9, King James Version.

18. Nathaniel B. Shurtleff, ed., *Records of the Governor and the Company of the Massachusetts Bay in New England* (Boston, 1853–54), 1: 399, cited in Koehler, 3.

19. Jennings, 189–90; [Edward] Johnson's Wonder-Working Providence, 1628–1651, in J. Franklin Jameson, ed., *Original Narratives of Early American History* (New York: Barnes & Noble, 1910), 147.

20. Leift Lion Gardiner, "Leift Lion Gardner His Relation of the Pequot Werres," *Massachusetts Historical Society Collections*, 3rd ser. 3, (1833): 131.

21. Historians have variously speculated that John Oldham was murdered by West Niantics, tributaries of the Pequots, or by tributaries of their rivals, the Narragansetts. See Alfred Cave, "Who Killed John Stone? A Note on the Origins of the Pequot War," *William and Mary Quarterly*, 3rd ser., 49, no. 3 (July 1992): 509–21; Jennings, 194, 208; Drake, 168.

22. Charles Orr, ed., *History of the Pequot War: The Contemporary Accounts of Mason, Underhill, Vincent, and Gardiner* (Cleveland, 1897), 42–43.

23. "[Edward] Johnson's Wonder-Working Providence," in Jameson, ed., *Original Narratives*, 168–70.

24. Bartlett, 1: 163–72.

25. William Hubbard, *A Narrative of the Troubles with the Indians in New-England, from the first planting thereof in the year 1607. to this present year 1677. But chiefly of the late Troubles in the two last years, 1675. and 1676. To which is added a Discourse about the Warre with the Pequods In the year 1637* (Boston, 1677), reprinted in *The History of the Indian Wars in New England from the First Settlement to the Termination of the War with King Philip, in 1677*, ed. Samuel Gardner Drake, vol. 1 (Roxbury, Mass., 1865; reprint, New York: Kraus Reprint Co., 1969), 127.

26. Drake, *History of the Indian Wars*, 125.

27. James Kendall Hosmer, ed., *Winthrop's Journal "History of New England" 1630–1649*, 1 (New York: Scribner, 1908), 271.

28. Bradford, 336.

29. Hosmer, 273.

30. Nathaniel B. Shurtleff, ed., *Records of the Colony of New Plymouth in New England, Court Orders*, vol. 1, *1633–1640* (Boston, 1855; reprint, New York AMS Press, 1968), 96.

31. Bradford, 337.

32. *Records of the Governor and the Company of the Massachusetts Bay in New England,* 2:40, 55, cited in James Drake, "Symbol of a Failed Strategy: The Sassamon Trial, Political Culture, and the Outbreak of King Philip's War," *American Indian Culture and Research Journal* 19 no. 2 (1995): 120. Drake posits that whites and Indians in the Northeast were searching for compatibility and accommodation, and that such compatibility enabled Native Americans to "form a semiseparate 'parapolitical' entity within the English polity to protect their own sovereignty." Ibid., 116–17.

33. Edwin Powers, ed. *Crime and Punishment in Early Massachusetts, 1620–1692: A Documentary History* (Boston: Beacon Press, 1966), 533–48.

34. Drake, *A History of the Early Discovery,* 138.

35. Charles Hoadly, ed., *Records of the Colony and Plantation of New Haven, from 1638 to 1649* (Hartford, Conn.: Case, Tiffany and Co., 1857), 23–24.

36. Ibid., 135 Bartlett, 1:107–8..

37. Bartlett, 1:163–72.

38. "[Edward] Johnson's Wonder-Working Providence," in Jameson, ed., *Original Narratives,* 220. In the early 1640s, when there were about 21,000 colonists in New England, there were at least 30,000 Indians living around Narragansett Bay alone; the most numerous of these were the Narragansetts.

39. David Pulsifer, ed., *Records of the Colony of New Plymouth in New England*, vol. 9 (Boston, 1859; reprint, New York: AMS Press, 1968), 3–4.

40. Richard Dunn et. al., eds., *The Journal of John Winthrop, 1630–1649* (Cambridge, Mass.: Harvard University Press, 1996), 472–73; Pulsifer; 9:14–15.

41. Pulsifer, 9:15.

42. Dunn et al., 509.

43. Bartlett, 1: 134–35.

44. Combatants typically justify their own actions and condemn those of their enemies by employing a "moral vocabulary of warfare," according to Michael Walzer. Michael Walzer, *Just and Unjust Wars: A Moral Argument with Historical Illustrations* (New York: Basic Books, 1977), 16. In her study of King Philip's War, Jill Lepore argues that "acts of war generate acts of narration, and that both types of acts are often joined in a common purpose: defining the geographical, political, cultural,

and sometimes racial and national boundaries between peoples." Jill Lepore, *The Name of War: King Philip's War and the Origins of American Identity* (New York: Alfred A. Knopf, 1998), x.

45. Roger Williams to John Winthrop, June 25, 1645, in *The Correspondence of Roger Williams*, ed. Glenn LaFantasie, vol. 1 (Hanover, N.H.: University Press of New England, 1988), 225.

46. Pulsifer, 9:46–48.

47. David Pulsifer, ed., *Records of the Colony of New Plymouth in New England,* 10 (Boston, 1859; reprint New York: AMS Press, 1968), 429–30.

48. Pulsifer, 10:436.

49. "Letter of John Eliot, May 12, 1659," in Drake, *History of The Early Discovery* 144–45.

50. Ibid.

51. John A. Strong, "The Imposition of Colonial Jurisdiction over the Montauk Indians of Long Island," *Ethnohistory* 41, no. 4 (Fall, 1994): 564–65.

52. J. Hammond Trumbull, ed., *Public Records of the Colony of Connecticut Prior to the Union with New Haven Colony, May 1665* (Hartford, Conn., 1850), 294.

53. Powers, 533–48.

54. Trumbull, 117.

55. According to Lyle Koehler, Connecticut still had 10,000 Indians in or near the colony in the 1660s. Citing Cook's research, he says they included 5,000 Narragansetts, 3,000 Wappingers and River Indians, and 1,700 Pocumtucks. Another 2,500 Mahicans could also be added to the total. Koehler says this is why treatment of Indians in Connecticut "remained more equitable." See Koehler, 15, 28; and Sherburne F. Cook, *The Indian Population of New England in the Seventeenth Century* (Berkeley: University of California Press, 1976), 49, 53, 58, 60–84.

56. Massachusetts Historical Society Collections, 1 (1792): 162–65. When the magistrates chastised their prisoners, saying it was "more like wolves than men, to travel and wander so far from home, merely to kill and destroy men, women and children," the Maquas replied that "It was their trade of life: they were bred up by their ancestors, to act in this manner towards their enemies."

57. Ibid., 165.

58. Pulsifer, 10:438–42.

59. [John Easton], "A Relacion of the Indyan Warre, By Mr. Easton, Of Roade Isld., 1675," Charles H. Lincoln, ed., *Narratives of the Indian Wars, 1675–1699* (New York: Barnes & Noble, 1913), 11.

60. Jennings, 292–93; Eric Shultz and Michael Tougias, *King Philip's War* (Woodstock, Vt.: Countryman Press, 1999), 24.

61. Eva Butler, Indian Notebooks no. 58, Old Mystic, Conn., Indian and Colonial Research Center; Connecticut State Archives, n.d., 1:18, cited in John A. Strong, "Imposition of Colonial Jurisdiction," *Ethnohistory* 41 (Fall 1994): 577–78.

62. Drake, *History of the Early Discovery*, 263.

63. Koehler, 17.

64. Pulsifer, 10:389.

65. David Pulsifer, ed., *Records of the Colony of New Plymouth in New England,* 11, "Laws 1623–1682" (Boston, 1861; reprint New York: AMS Press, 1968), 236.

66. Jennings, 294–95.

67. "John Easton's Relacion," Lincoln, 7.

68. Yasuhide Kawashima, *Igniting King Philip's War: The John Sassamon Murder Trial* (Lawrence: University Press of Kansas, 2001), 80–81.

69. Drake, "Symbol of a Failed Strategy," 128. Several scholars have pointed to Sassamon's attempt to bridge two conflicting cultures as the cause of his sudden demise. Yet Sassamon's duplicity in his dealings with Philip and his repeated warnings to the English of Indian conspiracies were more likely the immediate causes of his death than his literacy or his advanced assimilation. Other praying Indians, including some who were literate, were far less notorious in Philip's eyes than the ambitious informant who ended up under the ice. The historian Jill Lepore believes "Sassamon's literacy was mysterious, potent, and dangerous"; learning to read and write English were "among the very last steps on the path to cultural conversion." She argues that because of his literacy, Sassamon's very "Indianness" was called into question and his life thereby endangered. Lepore, 42–43. A more recent work claims that Sassamon's adoption of English ways, including literacy, and his efforts to tutor other Indians in Christian worship and morals were steps on his path of assimilation, a course that "infuriated and frightened native leaders who wished to protect Indian ways against the inroads of colonial customs and beliefs." Kawashima, *Igniting King Philip's War*, x.

70. Nathaniel B. Shurtleff, ed., *Records of the Colony of New Plymouth in New England,* Court Orders: 1668–1678 (Boston, 1856: reprint New York: AMS Press, 1968), 168.

71. Kawashima, *Puritan Justice and the Indian*, 130–31. The Massachusetts Body of Liberties established general legal principles adhered to by neighboring colonies in most cases; this deviation from the norm—i.e., that a murder conviction required the testimony of two witnesses—seems to represent just one of many triumphs of pragmatism over principle in colonial New England.

72. "John Easton's Relacion," Lincoln, 8.

73. Kawashima, *Igniting King Philip's War*, 124, 102.

74. In 1671 Philip was summoned twice by Plymouth authorities to account for his actions. In April he was suspected of plotting an uprising against the English, and in September he was charged with having "broken his couenant made with our collonie." On September 29, 1671, he was compelled to agree to a document professing the Pokanokets' subjection to "his majesty the Kinge of England, &c, and the gouvernment of New Plymouth, and to theire lawes." See Drake, "Symbol of a Failed Strategy," 126–27.

75. John Easton met with Philip and urged impartial arbitration by an Indian chief and Governor Edmund Andros of New York. The Massachusetts Bay Colony and the Plymouth Colony rejected the proposal. See Kawashima, *Puritan Justice and the Indian,* 232–33.

76. Kawashima, *Igniting King Philip's War,* 124.

77. The treaty signed in Hartford by Miantonomi and Uncas on September 21, 1638, established a firm precedent for English intervention in Native American affairs—an option the colonial authorities exercised with considerable discretion, but invariably when a colonist was involved as perpetrator or victim. By the 1660s the English included in their legal fold tribes who had subjected themselves by treaty and Indians who had become Christians.

78. Lincoln, 110.

79. "The Present State of New-England with Respect to the Indian War" (London, 1675) in Lincoln, 24–25.

80. Lincoln, 8–16.

81. Ibid., "The Present State of New-England," Lincoln, 25.

82. Lincoln, 8–16.

83. Ibid., 12.

84. "The Present State of New England," Lincoln 30.

85. "Narrative of the Captivity of Mrs. Mary Rowlandson, 1682," Lincoln, 118.

86. "Letter from Reverend Soloman Stoddard to Governor Joseph Dudley, October 22, 1703," in *New England Historical and Genealogical Register,* XXIV, 269–70.

87. Lepore, xiv.

88. Hubbard, 1: 15–16.

89. Robert B. Caverly, *Heroism of Hannah Duston Together with The Indian Wars of New England* (Boston: B. B. Russell & Co., 1875), 277.

90. Daniel Gookin, "Christian Indians," quoted in James Truslow Adams, *The Founding of New England,* vol. 1 (Boston: Little, Brown & Co., 1927), 357.

91. Adams, 1: 247.

92. Jennings, 319.

93. Shultz and Tougias, 4–5.

94. Jennings, 319–21.

95. Alan Rogers, "Murder and Due Process in Colonial Massachusetts," *Supreme Judicial Court Historical Society Journal* 2 (1996): 10.

96. Daniel Gookin, "An Historical Account of the Doings and Sufferings of the Christian Indians in New England, in the Years 1675, 1676, 1677" (1677), *Archaeologia Americana, Transactions and Collections of the American Antiquarian Society* 2 (1836): 475–83, quoted, in Jenny Hale Pulsipher, "Massacre at Hurtleberry Hill: Christian Indians and English Authority in Metacom's War," *William and Mary Quarterly*, 3rd ser., 3, no. 3 (July 1996): 481.

97. Pulsifer, 11: 242–43.

98. Shultz and Tougias, 109.

99. Drake, *History of the Early Discovery of America,* 263–64.

100. Daniel Gookin, "History of the Praying Indians," cited in Drake, *History of the Early Discovery of America,* 272.

101. Jenny Hale Pulsipher, "'The Overture of This New-Albion World': King Philip's War and the Transformation of New England" (diss., Brandeis University, 1999), 173.

102. Increase Mather, *A Brief History of the Warr with the Indians in Newe-England* (Boston: printed by John Foster, 1676), reprinted in *So Dreadful a Judgement: Puritan Responses to King Philip's War, 1676–1677,* ed. Richard Slotkin and James Folsom (Middletown, Conn.: Wesleyan University Press, 1978), 135.

103. Shultz and Tougias, 69–70.

104. Ibid., 4–5; Sherburne Cook, "Interracial Warfare and Population Decline among the New England Indians," *Ethnohistory* 20 (Winter 1973):15–21.

105. Mather, "Decennium Luctuosum: An History of Remarkable Occurrences in the Long War, which New-England hath had with the Indian Salvages, from the year 1688, to the year 1698" (Boston, 1699), reprinted in Lincoln, 184.

106. John Noble, ed., *Records of the Court of Assistants of the Colony of Massachusetts Bay, 1630–1692,* vol. 1, (Boston: published by the County of Suffolk, 1901), 71; Pulsipher, "Massacre at Hurtleberry Hill," 459–86.

107. Kawashima, *Puritan Justice and the Indian,* 233–34; James Ronda, "Red and White at the Bench: Indians and the Law in Plymouth Colony, 1620–1691," *Essex Institute Historical Collections* 110, no. 3 (July 1974): 214.

108. The historian Yasuhide Kawashima's tendency to downplay the degree to which local circumstances affected the shift from legal coexistence to legal imperialism

has already been noted (see note 9 above). More significant, perhaps, is this movement of colonists toward a policy of individual retaliation, which Kawashima's research exposes, but about which he says little, at least insofar as the colonial period is concerned. As the line of settlement spread northward and into the interior, colonial authorities were less well able to offer adequate protection to settlers on the frontier and less capable of controlling whatever violence they offered fellow colonists or neighboring Indians. As Alan Rogers noted, from 1677 to 1692 juries tended increasingly to return a verdict of manslaughter rather than murder. Rogers, "Murder and Due Process in Colonial Massachusetts," 14–15. The outbreak of wars involving the French and their Native American allies only exacerbated the frontier tensions and gave settlers a freer hand in disposing of nearby Indians. In 1717 John Keniston shot an Indian on his boat on the Piscataqua River and was found not guilty "despite overwhelming evidence including the testimony of his own relatives." Paul Hughes, " 'Moved and Instigated by the Devil': John Keniston and the Murder of Honnick in 1717," *Historical New Hampshire* 53 (1998); 90–100. In 1750, John Alby and five others were apprehended for the murder of a Penobscot Indian; the jury declared the men not guilty "to the great surprise of the Court." Five years later, James Cargill of Bristol was charged with the murder of two friendly Penobscots; he was tried and released despite the weight of evidence against him. Kawashima, *Puritan Justice and the Indian*, 132, 153. In 1816, long after the Indians of southern New England had been subdued and contained, John Neptune, a Native American in Maine, spoke on behalf of a fellow Indian on trial, saying, "You know your people do my Indians great deal wrong. They abuse them very much—yes they murder them; then they walk right off—nobody touches them." Drake, *History of the Early Discovery of America*, 321. The evidence suggests that clan-based retaliation as practiced by Native Americans in the colonial period was succeeded by a haphazard, unjustified, racially based pattern of violence exhibited by unruly white frontiersmen.

109. James Axtell, "The Vengeful Women of Marblehead: Robert Roule's Deposition of 1677," *William and Mary Quarterly*, 3rd ser., 31 (October 1974): 647–52.

3

Jim Crow Justice, the *Richmond Planet*, and the Murder of Lucy Pollard

Michael Ayers Trotti

Thus grew up a double system of justice . . .

—W. E. B. Du Bois[1]

On 14 June 1895, an aging white farmer, Edward Pollard, returned from his fields to find the body his wife, Lucy, outside their home in Lunenburg County, Virginia, southwest of Richmond. She had been hewn repeatedly with an ax, and more than eight hundred dollars was missing from the Pollard home. Found with two twenty-dollar bills, a black man from North Carolina, Solomon Marable, was charged with the crime, and he confessed to his involvement as an accessory. He implicated three local black women—Mary Abernathy and Pokey and Mary Barnes—as the actual murderers. "Feelings were high" in Lunenburg and the surrounding counties, and lynchings appeared imminent. The local sheriff spirited the four defendants out of the neighborhood, assigning a deputy to guide them on a trek on foot through the night to the Petersburg jail to the north.[2]

In the following eighteen months, this case would become a sensation in Virginia's African American community and, to a lesser extent, among whites. Solomon Marable would be tried twice, convicted both times, and hanged for his part in the crime. This part of the story was predictable in end-of-the-century Virginia. Pokey and the two Marys—who came to be known collectively as the Lunenburg women—had a much more interesting, complex, and telling path to tread, one that indicates that in 1895 racial lines and feeling in Virginia were not as rigid as they would become after 1900.

The saga of the Lunenburg women fits a model of the best-case (although still inequitable) scenario for blacks facing southern justice in the Jim Crow era. They resided in Virginia rather than in the still more prejudicial Deep South. Lunenburg County was 60 percent black, and in 1895 this population was not yet fully humbled by disfranchisement.[3] Indeed, black as well as white citizens sat on their juries in the first series of trials. The defendants were women, and what chivalry whites could muster for black womanhood softened the hardest edges of Virginia's judicial system. The case attracted a great deal of attention and raised questions of the legitimacy of the entire criminal justice system, which led a few prominent white lawyers to intervene to help protect the rights of the accused.

It is a measure of endemic Southern racism that the Lunenburg women were repeatedly convicted in the Virginia courts. It was only a series of unusual actions by both blacks and whites in Virginia that saved the women from the gallows. The Lunenberg case was a rare success for blacks facing white justice in the South, but its exceptional nature merely throws into stark relief the racist nature of Southern justice in the era of Jim Crow.

From 1880 to 1920, African Americans in the South experienced not only segregation and disfranchisement, but also lynching, race riots, and milder forms of intimidation. Violence and prejudicial justice were the most pressing issues confronting Southern African Americans in this period. White crimes against the race were so common as to be a steady drumbeat in the black press for decades. The ubiquity of white crimes also meant that individual crimes against blacks rarely became notable sensations in the African American press; they were simply too commonplace. But the most haunting cases in the black community involved strong evidence of the innocence of black defendants, as with the Lunenburg case. Such cases raised a larger question: would prejudicial white courts be able to acquit?

This essay places the Lunenburg murder case in the wider context of justice and race in Virginia, evaluating the perspective of one of the South's most prominent black editor-activists. John Mitchell, the editor of an African American weekly, the *Richmond Planet*, covered the case closely, and his newspaper provides a rare source in the historical record of the era of lynching: a Southern black condemnation of Southern injustice.[4]

John R. Mitchell Jr. was born near Richmond, Virginia, in the midst of the Civil War. In his childhood, Mitchell obtained the sort of education that had been denied most African Americans, graduating with distinction from Richmond's Colored Normal School in 1881. For the next two years, he taught in Fredericksburg, then briefly in Richmond, where he began his newspaper career as a weekly reporter for the African American paper the *New York Globe*.[5] In 1884, he took over the editorial post at the newly founded *Richmond Planet*, and remained in that position for the next forty-five years.

Little in John Mitchell's early history marked him as a radical. But in the 1880s and 1890s, he was as strident and vocal in opposition to lynching and white supremacy as any editor in the nation. He "has the reputation of being the bravest Afro-American editor in the country," in large part due to his "uncompromising war on lynching and all other forms of lawlessness," wrote the *Colored American Magazine* in 1902.[6]

John Mitchell lies in between the poles of W. E. B. Du Bois's assertive philosophy and Booker T. Washington's quieter path to raise the race, and Mitchell's years editing the *Planet* (1884-1929) nicely coincide with the pinnacle of the black press's influence. Mitchell could be aggressive; but he could also counsel caution, emphasizing business development and social peace. Mitchell confronted tidal forces—black people's postslavery yearning for equality and a repressive, white-run South tending toward the retrograde. He was what some whites called a "new issue Negro," born to freedom's first generation. Unlike many other vocal defenders of his race in the era, however, he never moved to the North. His struggle would be to find a place for himself and his people within this white-dominated New South.

In the 1890s, John Mitchell sensationalized his stories of black innocence, highlighting the forces at battle in the black community: the rule of law, the prejudiced mobs and officials, the innocent victims, the protecting arms of the black community. The victims, along with the active public (including Mitchell himself, of course) were the heroes, fending off a system of white justice that was patently and persistently unjust. The clearest example of these themes was the 1895 Lunenburg murder case.

The Lunenburg Case

Solomon Marable, Mary Abernathy, Pokey Barnes, and Mary Barnes, arrested for murdering Lucy Pollard in June 1895, returned to Lunenburg County three weeks after the murder to face trials in the county court. So intense was the feeling against the prisoners that the sheriff asked for state militia to guard them upon their return to the county and during their trial. The governor ordered two companies, approximately eighty men, to guard the prisoners around the clock. Three days into the trials, the commanding officer perceived that a mob might attempt to take the prisoners despite these troops. Writing that he could "not with safety perform the duty required of me with the number of men now under my command," the major in charge asked for reinforcements of "one company of not less than thirty men with 2,000 rounds of ammunition. Matters are becoming complicated," he explained.[7] The complication was the local concern that the women might be acquitted, whereupon the county's whites would probably lynch them.[8] But with 120 armed militiamen encamped on the courthouse green, the threat of lynching was over.

This caution on the part of officials was probably due in good measure to the events in Roanoke two years before. In 1893, a black man, identified only by his "slouch hat," was imprisoned in that city for attacking and robbing a white woman. But before he could stand trial, a mob of thousands attacked the jail, someone fired a gun, and in the ensuing melee, eight men died. The prisoner was spirited out of town, but then, inexplicably, the officers returned and handed him over to the crowd, who promptly hanged him, then burned his body to char. These events horrified Virginia—particularly the loss of white lives in the gunfight. When elected the next year, Governor O'Ferrall made a concerted effort to stifle any further mob violence in the state. Lunenburg's angry crowds seemed to threaten this resolution, and the state responded in strength.[9]

Every year in the postbellum South, scores of arrested blacks were brutally murdered by mobs. In fact, the 1890s saw 1,540 extralegal hangings, 1,108 of which were of blacks. The first decade of the 1900s experienced 895 lynchings (796 black), and in the 1910s the numbers dropped further to 621 (565 black).[10] This averages out to more than 6 blacks lynched in America every month for thirty years. The 1890s averaged more than 2 blacks lynched every week. Lynching was never as prominent in Virginia as the Deep South, but it followed the same pattern: 27 lynchings in the 1890s, falling to 13 and 3 in the following two decades.[11]

If many stories of black defendants ended early with the rope, Solomon Marable, Mary Abernathy, and Pokey Barnes withstood this threat of lynching, thanks to the militia. But that was only the first challenge confronting them; they all still faced the charge of first-degree murder, a capital offense.[12] The defendants had no money to hire lawyers; common custom was for the court to appoint an attorney to handle such cases. When pressed by the judge, J. B. Bell, a local lawyer present in the courtroom, "respectfully declined on the ground that he could not spare the time."[13] A former judge in the county, William Perry, submitted a motion for a change of venue on behalf of Mary Abernathy, stating that the local population was so prejudiced against all the accused women that the defendant feared for her life and did not believe she could get a fair trial. When that motion was denied, he retired from the case. No other lawyer agreed to take these defendants, and under Virginia law, the judge could not compel one to serve.[14] In the words of the Supreme Court of Appeals of Virginia:

> [I]f a prisoner is unable to employ counsel, the court may appoint some one to defend him, and it is a duty which counsel owes to his profession, to the court engaged in the trial, to the administration of

justice, and to humanity, not to withhold his aid, nor spare his best efforts in the defense. . . . *But we cannot presume that the trial court denied the prisoner her right to have counsel,* or failed if she were unable to employ counsel, to assign some one to aid her in her defense.[15]

Until the U.S. Supreme Court's decision in *Gideon v. Wainwright* (1963), state constitutional safeguards of the right to counsel were not interpreted to mean that a state or municipality had to secure counsel for indigent defendants. Without this protection, neither Solomon Marable nor the women accused by him had much of a chance to avoid conviction. Each defendant testified on his or her own behalf, and Pokey Barnes in particular attempted to bring witnesses and cross-examine those brought against her—but to no avail.

In succession, each defendant was tried without counsel, convicted, and sentenced to death. The three capital cases, along with the trial of Pokey Barnes's mother for second-degree murder, were completed in the space of seven days. This included one court day cut short to allow the women to attempt to find attorneys and another day spent trying to find a witness who could not be located.

Solomon Marable's trial took less that two days, and, on the strength of his confession as well as the money found in his possession, the jury deliberated only nine minutes before convicting him of first-degree murder. But only Marable's accusation implicated the women.[16] Their juries took much more time, and, two hours into deliberations in Mary Abernathy's trial, her jury reported that they could not agree. They were sent back to continue their discussions, and in fact deliberated the following morning. Importantly, this was precisely the moment when the threat of lynching arose and new troops were called for. The following morning, the jury found Mary guilty. Likewise, Pokey Barnes's jury could not agree when they first deliberated late in the evening, but they returned a guilty verdict the following day. The juries struggled more with the two women's cases, but ultimately found against them both. Again concerned for their safety after the convictions, the authorities removed the prisoners from the county once more, this time sending them back with the militia to Richmond.[17]

In the midst of these trials, Solomon Marable changed his story, then switched back, then reversed himself once again. He first said that he had been drafted by the local women simply to hold Mrs. Pollard while they robbed her house. The women then slew her with the ax, much to his horror, and paid him off with the two twenty-dollar bills. It was this story which sent the Lunenburg women to the gallows.[18]

But even early reports spoke of contradictions and changes in his story that drew Marable's accusations into question. During Mary Abernathy's trial, in fact, he made a number of conflicting statements and admitted to lying in court during his own trial.[19] Then, during the course of the trial against Pokey Barnes, Frank Cunningham, the captain of one of the militia companies, took Marable aside and assured him that, despite what he might have been told, the soldiers would not allow any lynch mob to take him, something Marable seemed to hold "in very great terror." He would hang for his crime, admitted Cunningham, and nothing would change that. But if Marable had any hope of avoiding eternal damnation, he continued, then he must tell the truth and go to his death without innocent blood on his hands. Marable then changed his statement, saying that a white man he had never seen before compelled him to grab Mrs. Pollard and then this man, whom he later identified as David Thompson, killed her. Marable made this admission to several parties and again in the trial of Barnes. But during this testimony, a confusing series of events occurred. A juror passed a note to the judge informing him that a white man in the audience was attempting to tamper with the witness, having winked and nodded at Marable. The judge cleared the courtroom, but Marable was apparently unnerved by the incident: he recanted his story of the white man and returned to his accusation of the women. After the convictions and the removal of the prisoners to Richmond, Marable again said that the women were innocent, and that a white man had done the deed and told him that if they were caught, he should implicate these women. After this series of oscillations in his charges, most observers concluded simply that Marable was, in the words of the *Richmond Times*, "a colossal liar" and his testimony was worthless.[20] Nevertheless, that testimony had convicted three women.

A month after the murder, the three blacks faced the imminent threat of the scaffold; their hangings were scheduled for late September. For most cases against poor blacks, that would be the end of the story: only their executions awaited them. In fact, the *Richmond Dispatch* made just such a prediction for the Lunenburg women. After charting the path of possible appeals, the *Dispatch* ended with realism: "It is, of course, quite unlikely that we shall see these cases take such a course: it would cost a great deal of money, and the accused are penniless."[21] So ended virtually all cases against poor blacks in the South in this era.

But the vacillating testimony of Marable raised a host of questions in the minds of many observers. The militiamen returned to their homes telling stories of untrustworthy testimony and witness tampering. Many of them felt that the lack of counsel for the defendants, coupled with widespread intimidation and inflamed passions that required the militia to be there, meant that these women had been unfairly condemned.[22] Three white lawyers—paid for by John Mitchell and by donations from around the state and nation—agreed to help the Lunenburg women. The first fortuitous action on behalf of the Lunenburg convicts was the strong action of the governor to stave off the threat of lynching; this support from prominent white lawyers was the second exceptional moment in the case.

These lawyers were among the most respected white attorneys in the Commonwealth. George D. Wise was the Commonwealth's attorney for the city of Richmond from 1870 to 1880, whereupon he served Richmond in the House of Representatives until 1895. Henry W. Flournoy was a judge in the city of Danville, also serving several terms as secretary of the Commonwealth as well as having a private practice. Captain A. B. Guigon, the youngest of the three, was the son of a long-serving and respected Richmond judge. He was an attorney mostly in private practice, although he also served as acting Commonwealth's attorney in Richmond from time to time.[23]

These lawyers earned the defendants a hearing before the Supreme Court of Virginia in November 1895. Virginia's highest tribunal ordered new trials for both women and for Solomon Marable as well, thus ending their first stay on death row. But the Court did not overturn their convictions because of the weakness of the cases against them. "The granting of a new trial by the Supreme Court of Appeals was an act of justice which will be readily recognized by right thinking people everywhere," the *Planet* crowed. But it added more ominously, "And yet the result of this prolonged contention was achieved upon technical grounds alone."[24] The records of the first trials of Barnes, Abernathy, and Marable did not show that their juries were committed to the care of the sheriff and thereby insulated from popular sentiment while sitting in judgment on these cases. The sheriff may or may not have adequately sequestered the jury; but in any event, the record of the case was at fault for not noting the fact, and that was enough for the Supreme Court to overturn their convictions. What is most surprising here is not this decision — appeals were regularly decided on procedural grounds — but that such a case against poor blacks ever made it to the state's highest court.[25]

The second set of trials began in March 1896 and ended in a telling split decision. A change of venue to neighboring Prince Edward County should have helped the defense by avoiding the passions of the excited Lunenburg population. As expected by all observers, Solomon Marable was again convicted, and he was executed in July of that year. The more engrossing and indeterminate part of the Lunenburg story involved the women, whom most believed were innocent or at least could not be convicted on Marable's word alone. John Mitchell's hyperbole that "they cannot be legally convicted" was echoed in a more moderate tone by much of the white press.[26] The *Richmond Times*, for instance, editorialized that these women "have had no trial, and that if they are to be judicially murdered under the present programme, the life of none of us is safe."[27] Nevertheless, these women had been convicted and sentenced to die the summer before.

In April 1896, the Prince Edward court retried Mary Abernathy for the murder of Lucy Pollard. With a formidable defense team in place, the case took more than a week, longer than all four of the first Lunenburg trials together. Also promising was the fact that the jury deliberated for some time before returning a verdict. But despite the weakness of the evidence against her, the jury again found her guilty of first-degree murder and sentenced her to the gallows for the second time. Surprising many, the jury's verdict was unanimous on the first ballot.[28] "This is no surprise to us," wrote editor Mitchell in the next issue of the *Planet*.

> When we learned that there had been no difficulty experienced in selecting a jury, and this too in a county where the people had been as much wrought up over the atrocious murder of Mrs. Lucy Jane Pollard as they were in Lunenburg county, we were confident as to what it meant.
>
> We knew so far as the jury was concerned that Mary Abernathy's fate was sealed.[29]

The verdict in the first trial cannot be surprising: without counsel and with feelings high in Lunenburg, Abernathy's conviction was almost assured. But this second trial is particularly interesting—here there was a change in venue, a strong defense team, public criticism of the earlier verdict, and a period of time elapsing that might cool heads. But the Prince Edward County jury was at least as forceful in its guilty verdict as had been the Lunenburg court.

Was justice in Virginia this prejudiced? John Mitchell thought so, and most blacks in the South would have joined him in his pessimism. From the police all the way to the gallows, the system of justice in the South was perceived by African Americans with a jaundiced eye. The racist behavior of Richmond police had upset the city's black community for some time. In 1867, a Richmond policeman had attempted to take a drunken and disorderly black man into custody. Within moments, several dozen neighbors surrounded the officers, pelting them with brickbats and loose cobbles from the road. Reinforcements held off the mob, but several participants were wounded and shots were fired on both sides.[30] No black sources survive to leave a record of this conflict from their perspective. Still, this rock battle confirms that, from the earliest moments of postwar Richmond, African Americans were thoroughly suspicious of the white institutions responsible for dispensing justice. Dozens of similar cases in later years testify to the endurance of this suspicion. In 1896, for instance, a young black girl demanded the release of her brother from two Richmond policemen. When they attempted to arrest her, a crowd of up to two hundred gathered, pelting the officers with stones until a patrol wagon with other officers arrived.[31]

African Americans in Richmond had much reason to be suspicious of the police, for racial prejudice is clearly evident in the historical record.[32] On a number of occasions, officers shot blacks on the street with little provocation.[33] The police routinely and prejudicially arrested blacks for little cause, often "on suspicion." In an unusually frank assessment in 1874, Richmond's mayor decried the "flagrant outrage" that was common practice up to that time of the police "arresting whole companies of colored people on general warrants," thereby making all of them pay for court costs.[34]

In addition, the law itself allowed room for prejudice to flourish. In the antebellum period, slaves had been punished with harsh, often corporal measures. Offenses classed as capital crimes were much more numerous for them, including not just violent crimes but those against property as well. Even free blacks faced harsher penalties when the crime involved assault on whites.[35] After the Civil War, overtly race-specific laws became unconstitutional, and Virginia revised its criminal statutes to comply. But the resulting criminal code reflected a continuing desire to differentiate in the law. The harsh penalties against slaves were not abandoned after the war; rather, the Commonwealth combined the white and black codes, widening a jury's options in regard to punishment for a number of crimes. Before the war, slaves faced death or transportation out of the state for burglary, for example, while whites faced a prison term. Beginning in 1866, anyone "guilty of burglary shall be punished with death, or in the discretion of the jury, by confinement in the penitentiary for not less than five nor more than eighteen years."[36] In all, three capital crimes—rape, robbery, and burglary—were grafted from the slave codes onto the new "color-blind" Virginia legal code. Whites and blacks faced the same statutes in the same courts of law before the same judges. But if the laws themselves were evenhanded, they also allowed juries to make as many distinctions—now informal rather than statuatory—in their verdicts as before the war. And, as the *Planet* emphasized, they made those distinctions regularly.

In the context of routine discrimination, it is not surprising that white juries provoked a good deal of contempt in the black community. Occasionally, judges in late nineteenth-century Virginia allowed blacks to sit on juries, but it was rare enough to be noted by the press as an unusual sight.[37] A visitor to Virginia in 1880 noted with shock "that blacks are here systematically excluded from the juries. This seems to be avowed, the excuse being, 'they have got votes, and we cannot give them everything.' In the United States Courts black are put on the juries, but not in the Virginian Courts."[38] By 1901, "a negro juryman is seldom seen in Virginia . . . [judges] have been deciding almost unanimously for several years that he has no place in the box."[39] One Alabama judge believed they had no place even observing trials. Speaking to the black onlookers, he said: "Now, you Negroes go home and stay there or you will get into trouble. This is a white man's country and a white man's court and you Negroes must keep to your places."[40]

How could Virginia exclude blacks from the jury box? In 1879, the U.S. Supreme Court affirmed that the Fourteenth Amendment to the Constitution and other federal legislation outlawed any and all official state action to discriminate against blacks in selecting jury pools and juries.[41] West Virginia, for example, passed a law specifically excluding blacks from juries, and the U.S. Supreme Court ruled it unconstitutional. In the same session, however, the Court vitiated this ruling by making it clear that it was limited to overtly racist statutes and actions of state officers. In other words, the Supreme Court banned discrimination in form, but not in practice. In *Virginia v. Rives*, the court decided that an all-white jury, grand jury, or even the wider jury pool did not, in itself, constitute evidence of discrimination.[42] A mixed jury was not, they held, essential to justice. A lily-white jury would constitute a violation of federal guarantees of equal protection only if it could be proven that a court *intentionally* excluded blacks; otherwise, the assumption would be that it was a fair selection. Since intention rarely can be proven, that was a high bar indeed. This set of decisions in 1880 prohibited statutory discrimination, but gave ample room for racial prejudice to flourish informally in the practice of selecting juries. In effect, these decisions helped to bar blacks from juries a generation before disfranchisement erected yet another barrier, for jurors in Virginia were drawn from eligible voters.[43]

Facing white juries, black defendants had little chance, even if other elements in the judicial system operated fairly. On more than one occasion, the *Planet* praised judges and Virginia's higher courts, saying that they adhered to the letter of the law as they should. Mitchell likewise applauded more than one governor for being "as generous as he is in the granting of pardons." In contrast, such articles typically continued, cases in lower courts and those given over to juries regularly rendered "remarkable evidence of [their] prejudiced character." In 1899, the paper prefaced the story of a jury's harsh decision by saying "we have never seen injustice of some of the decisions of juries more impressively emphasized, and the kind-heartedness of the judge more strikingly shown" than when a judge personally appealed to the governor to commute the jury's outrageous sentence.[44]

Interestingly, the Lunenburg juries (the first trials) each included blacks. Mary Abernathy had four black and eight white jurors, while both Solomon Marable and Pokey Barnes had ten white and two black jurors. The presence of these black jurors surely helped the cause of the defendants, and one rumor hinted that at least one of the black jurors delayed a decision by holding out (briefly) for acquittal. But given the racial climate in southern Virginia, an African American juror would be signing his own death warrant by disagreeing with the white majority in such a case. Importantly, no blacks served on any of the second set of trials in Prince Edward County.[45]

Though white juries were of particular concern, the *Richmond Planet* in the 1890s repeatedly emphasized the lack of fairness in the judicial system overall. Mitchell illustrated most effectively this injustice with well-chosen comparisons of white and black treatment. On dozens of occasions, editorials and features by Mitchell described how a black infraction drew the penalty of years in prison or even death, while a white man might be fined lightly for serious offenses. After reprinting the guarantee of equal protection under law in the Fourteenth Amendment to the Constitution, one such story, titled "No Justice in Virginia," described a white man's ten-dollar fine for killing a black man, contrasting it to the death penalty rendered a black man for committing highway robbery.[46] Mitchell regularly pointed out the disparity between the penalty of death typically imposed upon black murderers and the acquittals granted to white lynchers. In 1899, the *Planet* announced with banner headlines "A New Departure in Virginia Criminal Justice" when six white men were convicted of second-degree murder for lynching.[47] Yet, such a laudatory (and sarcastic) headline merely drew into deeper contrast the dozens of cases each year of white assaults on blacks that went lightly punished if at all, particularly since these convicted lynchers had killed not a black man but a white man who was "a discharged lunatic and almost an idiot."

Lynching, then, was a horror, but it was only the most blatant and violent wrong in a system of justice that persistently discriminated against blacks. The Constitution and the laws of the nation provided certain protections for all its citizens, and Mitchell's *Planet*, along with the broader black community, protested loudly when those protections were so regularly violated—by the police, the courts, and juries, as well as lynch mobs. Their activism on behalf of the Lunenburg women was merely one part of a broader effort to achieve justice for African Americans in Virginia. Here was a case against black women that was so clearly unfair, where the injustice was so blatant, that perhaps, for once, blacks might achieve the justice they sought.

After Mary Abernathy's second conviction—this time by a Prince Edward County jury—the court turned to the case against Pokey Barnes. She had a stronger alibi than Abernathy, leaving only a brief window of opportunity for her to have participated in the supposed conspiracy to murder Mrs. Pollard. On the fifth day of her trial, when the prosecution's testimony was completed, the Commonwealth's attorney for Prince Edward County, Asa Watkins, surprised everyone. He submitted a motion of nolle prosequi, in effect dropping the charges against Barnes. Watkins explained that the evidence failed to incriminate her:

> Now that all the evidence in the possession of the Commonwealth has been given in, I cannot believe that it is sufficient to justify the jury in bringing in a verdict of guilty. This murder has been fixed upon two persons, but so far, in my opinion, there has been nothing adduced to

connect this prisoner with these persons, nor have there been any evidences of a conspiracy between the prisoner and those persons.[48]

Freed immediately, Pokey Barnes quickly left the county for Richmond and a celebratory tour of Virginia's black churches. It is telling that she first returned to jail until her train arrived, and when on the train, her father hid her for fear that whites might yet accost them.[49]

Of the prosecuting lawyers, the Commonwealth's attorney was alone in his assessment of the weakness of the case against Barnes. As the attorney in charge of the case, Watkins had the authority to submit this motion, and he was careful to say that he had "reached this conclusion without consultation with any one," apparently inoculating his two fellow prosecuting attorneys from any popular backlash against the decision. One of the other attorneys, Judge Mann, while bowing to Watkins's authority, added that "as far as I am concerned, I wish to state that I believe as firmly in the guilt of Pokey Barnes as I do in my own existence."[50] It was yet another exceptional moment in their cases, particularly since the other attorneys were willing to continue the case and conviction by the jury appeared possible, if not probable, given all of the previous trials.

Mary Abernathy's lawyers again appealed her conviction, and after several more months on death row, her conviction was set aside by the circuit court in September 1896, as contrary to the evidence. Lawyers in this era regularly filed exceptions on the grounds that the verdict was contrary to the evidence—a sort of formulaic objection. But rarely did an appeals court judge remand a case to a court on those grounds. Again, this was an unusual action in favor of the defendant. Rather than attempting to prosecute her again on the same evidence, the Commonwealth once more dropped the charges, and Mary was free. Barnes and Abernathy had spent eleven and fifteen months in jail, respectively, but at last they had gained their liberty.

What of Mary Barnes, mother of Pokey, who was convicted of being an accessory to the crime? She served eighteen months of her ten-year sentence in the penitentiary before being freed in January 1897. In this case, it was the action of the governor, presented with a petition for her pardon, that freed her. In his pardon, Governor Charles O'Ferrall wrote that Solomon Marable's testimony, which was "the only testimony against her," was "absolutely unworthy of belief." He continued in a manner that surely gratified the black community. "The life or liberty of a citizen, however humble, is too sacred in the eyes of the law or of civilized man to be taken upon the testimony alone of a self-convicted perjurer and murderer. . . . Every mandate of justice and dictate of conscience require that the prisoner be restored to her liberty."[51]

John Mitchell and Black Solidarity against Injustice

Late nineteenth-century African Americans were understandably obsessed with the issues of crime and justice in the white-controlled world about them. "The most talked about subject of the period was clearly violence," according to one national study of the black press. "The number of lynchings was at a record high. Blacks did not take it without struggle. As much militancy as has been seen in black papers could be seen in some of the papers publishing toward the end of the century."[52] The *Richmond Planet* provides an example of this militancy in the late nineteenth century as John Mitchell Jr. made violence and justice the central themes of his columns.

The Lunenburg case was the most sensational of the era in Virginia, but it was not alone. It became so important to black Virginians, in fact, because the issue of justice was such a raw and painful wound already. Mitchell's voice throughout the Lunenburg case allows us to see the injustice of the system in stark relief against the ideals of fairness the nation claimed to promote. Dozens of stories in the *Planet* every year simply described the brutal injustice of whites, ending with a final sentence stating only "Lynch Law Must Go!", "the case speaks for itself," or "no comment is necessary."[53] The *Planet* first reported the Lunenburg murder in just this way. It was almost a commonplace: yet another crime, yet another black man to be hanged in Virginia. Only when Marable withdrew his confession implicating Abernathy and Barnes—and the women were nevertheless convicted—did the *Planet*'s coverage burst from this flat and cynical frame. The account of the militiamen gave even more support for the women. With this growing likelihood of their innocence, the Lunenburg case became a cause célèbre for the paper and the black community.[54]

For a year and a half, this case simmered on the pages of the *Planet*, with John Mitchell leading the charge to fund prominent white lawyers in an effort to save the women. Richmond's black paper described and illustrated every aspect of the Lunenburg case: the crime, the women and their pasts and families, their jail cells, the lawyers, courts, and public opinion. Between June 1895 and January 1897, the *Richmond Planet* published more than 120 articles or editorials on the case.[55] It became a staple of the front page, completely filling it almost a dozen times. But it was not just the *Planet* immersing itself in the Lunenburg case: the wider black community demonstrated its active support for the women. Hundreds of individuals and groups contributed thousands of dollars to support hiring the white lawyers.[56]

Throughout this sensation, the *Richmond Planet* emphasized the clear and obvious innocence of the women. They were of good character and family, the paper argued (with mixed evidence to draw upon). They had no convincing motive, and nothing to tie them to the crime but a false accusation later recanted. Mitchell did not investigate the women or mention anything that might sully their reputations, but rather invested them with the typecast roles of embattled heroines. Photographs of Mary Abernathy show her with her baby, born in jail, while other articles set the convicted women within the context of their families bemoaning their absence. "No one who has gazed upon the open countenance of poor Mary Abernathy and [the] mirth-loving face of Pokey Barnes," wrote Mitchell, "will doubt the innocence of these two people."[57] In turn, Mitchell castigated the whites of Lunenburg, officials and citizenry, for their prejudice and malevolence. Their conviction was "one of the most flagrant outrages perpetrated upon human beings," he thought. "Most of the people in Lunenburg County were grievously in error when in their blind fury they condemned" the prisoners to death. The whites were overcome by the "evil propensities" of prejudice and race hatred.[58] There was little distant or objective about these stories in the *Planet*; in keeping with bold late nineteenth-century journalistic standards, these articles were passionate, emotional, active, and sometimes shrill.

Convicted a number of times, Mary and Pokey were saved from the gallows by the pressure of the black community and the action of a number of white officials. John Mitchell, of course, was central to this effort, a driving force in the crusade to save the innocent women.[59] But even Mitchell admitted that others had aided the prisoners. Governor O'Ferrall answered the local sheriff's call for troops to protect the defendants from the Lunenburg mobs; otherwise these innocent women might have been lynched even before their first trials. These troops, in turn, rendered dispassionate evidence of their belief in the innocence of the women. Blacks and whites alike contributed money to the defense of the Lunenburg women, and three able lawyers successfully used the court system to challenge the juries' verdicts. The state's higher courts overturned several guilty verdicts, and the Commonwealth's attorney dropped the case against Pokey Barnes and later that against Mary Abernathy.

Without each of these actions, according to the *Planet*, a single spurious charge by Marable might have killed innocent women. That is how close they came, and how close all African Americans were to injustice in the courts of Virginia. The Lunenburg case was "an object lesson never to be forgotten," wrote Mitchell after Mary Abernathy was freed. He envisioned it as an example of "the relentlessness of prejudice" and "everlasting aggression of our people" as well as "the most phenomenal effort ever made for the saving of human lives."[60]

But what a sour object lesson it was. If accused of a violent crime, blacks in Virginia might be lynched. If they avoid lynching, they might face a court without the means to protect themselves. Even if they were somehow able to hire lawyers, they might still be convicted by white-dominated juries and hanged despite insubstantial evidence.

Sadly, the Lunenburg case was not the only sensational case involving black innocence in this era; this dynamic recurred on a number of occasions. In July 1893, for instance, a black man from Nansemond County, near Norfolk, was accused of burning a white neighbor's house and poisoning his horses. A white mob abducted, shot, and hanged Isaac Jenkins, leaving him for dead. None of his several wounds, however, was life-threatening, and the noose was improperly tied, slipping off as he struggled.[61] More than anything else, Mitchell leads the reader to marvel at Jenkins's luck to have survived the ordeal. But as important as his survival was the active nature of the whole incident: his efforts to save himself, but also the vigorous efforts on the part of Mitchell and the wider African American community to save him. Even in this successful case, his lynchers were never prosecuted, and Jenkins endured three jury trials, almost a year in jail, and permanent effects from the many wounds he received.[62]

In many other editorials in the late nineteenth century, Mitchell took this assertive and protective philosophy even further: African Americans had to defend themselves. If the ballot, the courts, and the Constitution could not guarantee the protection of home and family, then bullets would prove necessary.[63] John Mitchell and the black community in Richmond concluded that Virginia's judicial and law enforcement systems were enemies as often as defenders of their safety and well-being. After listing two dismissed cases of white-on-black murder in one of many editorials titled "No Justice for the Negro," Mitchell declared, "It is far better to hang for the killing of one of these worthless creatures than to be ourselves ushered to our Maker unprepared. We are sick at heart over the butchery of our people. Self-defense should be our watchword, and when this is heralded from one section of the country to the other, these murders will cease, and not until then."[64] If a lynch mob approached, Mitchell thought, the best remedy "is a 16-shot Winchester rifle in the hands of a Negro who has nerve enough to pull the trigger."[65] It was this sort of talk that earned Mitchell the title of Richmond's "fiery" editor:

> We are in favor of [a hardworking black man] firing upon all intruders and law breakers who would despoil his home, and we earnestly beseech our leading men to preach the dawn of the new day, and bring about a realization of our fondest hopes. . . .
>
> Colored men, buy shot-guns, purchase rifles. Use them with discretion, fire them with wisdom; but let every charge find a resting place in the bosom of some would-be murderer who regards neither God nor Mammon, and are [sic] anxious to shed human blood and to sacrifice innocent victims. Lynch law must go![66]

John Mitchell even acted out this assertive philosophy when a black man was lynched in Charlotte County in 1886. Mitchell argued that the lynchers deserved to die. After receiving an unsigned letter the next week stating that "if you poke that infernal head of yours in this county long enough for us to do it we will hang you higher than he was hung," Mitchell published the letter and his defiant response. Armed with two Smith and Wesson revolvers, he then traveled to the county. Detained briefly in jail but otherwise unharmed, this "fighting editor" from Richmond lived to tell of this moment of bravado.[67]

Mitchell never called for an uprising, noting that all the force of white America, state and federal, would crush any such effort.[68] Rather, he wrote that blacks must protect themselves when threatened, concluding that reasonable whites would concur with this sound American philosophy. It is an argument, then, not for lawlessness, but rather one upbraiding whites for *their* lawlessness and urging them to live up to the standard of justice that the law had enshrined. Radical only in the context of the era's racist violence, this philosophy was the natural conclusion of his broad-based indictment of Southern justice.

A small number of articles in the 1890s described just such moments of active resistance when bullets were used. These columns portrayed their black protagonists as neither brutes nor passive victims to be added to the litany of martyrs of vicious white violence. Instead, the accused blacks were strong and in control. "A Colored Man's Nerve Died, But Carries Two White Men with Him," read one headline. [69] Apparently in the midst of an argument over pay, this black man talked back to the white, who then responded by clubbing him on the head for his insolence. What made this story unusual was the fact that this beaten black man had a gun, and he used it with effect. A second white man—who did not even see or know about the original conflict, according to the witness—then rushed into the fray. Both men fired; both died. In this case, the framing of this letter to the *Planet* emphasized not the horror of violence, but rather the nerve of the black man to stand up against not one but two whites who threatened him: "He defends himself against threats to take his life because he demanded his whole pay."[70]

The whole field of crime and justice was charged for African Americans because of the tremendous gap between the promise of equality before the law and the violent and unfair reality facing black defendants. In response, many in the African American community joined John Mitchell's *Planet* in its crusade for justice. Making crime, violence, and justice central elements of its reporting, the *Planet* took an active role in trying to sustain the rights promised all Americans but so often denied to blacks. In 1895, Mitchell summed up this philosophy:

> We maintain that every official in this state is in honor bound to recognize the civil and political equality of all men before the law.

In dealing with a white man and a colored one they must treat the
two just as they would two white men or two colored ones when
the aforesaid gentlemen come to them with conflicting interests. . . .
We aver that severity in dealing with a Negro and leaning [le-
niency?] in dealing with a white man is in direct antagonism with
the oath of office and in violation of the guarantees of the Bill of
Rights of Virginia.[71]

In the twentieth century, however, sensationalized stories of black innocence were rare, as the *Planet* and the black middle class turned away from
their forceful stand against injustice and toward a focus upon self-sufficiency.
In 1914, when a white jury—after eighteen hours of deliberation—acquitted
the black defendant, John Clements, of attacking and raping a young white
woman, Mitchell celebrated the victory, but in a remarkably even tone. The
Planet made no mention of any tours of black churches, speeches, or fund-
raising. Far from sensationalizing this case of black innocence, Mitchell's
coverage of the Clement's trial was notably distant—it was chiefly comprised
of reprints from the white press. In fact, when white police officers shot and
killed a resisting suspect in the case (the rape victim later denied that this
man had been her attacker), Mitchell printed two strongly worded editorials
criticizing their fatal mistake. Yet this killing of an innocent black man was
but a side issue even in the *Planet*. At one point, Mitchell even called this
shooting merely a "blunder" and said that he was not asking for punishment
of the officer, that public contempt would be punishment enough. This is a
mild rebuke for shooting down an innocent man, and Mitchell was critical of
nothing else in the Clements case. The emotional and sensational responses
to injustice in the 1890s had faded to a more distanced observation by the
1910s. As strident as John Mitchell had been in support of Pokey Barnes and
Mary Abernathy in 1895, he had become more muted and hopeless in the face
of the power of white supremacy in the early twentieth century.[72]

Mitchell and the black community had succeeded in protecting the
Lunenburg women from both lynching and the injustice of Virginia's judicial
system. But countless others were not so well protected against lynchers,
were not tried with prominent white counsel, did not get the support of white
militiamen who raised the issue of the fairness of their trials, and did not have
their cases appealed, their convictions overturned, and their cases dropped. In
addition, the era in the South was trending toward the retrograde for African
Americans. Lynchings were at an all-time high, the South was in the process
of rewriting its state constitutions to allow for the disfranchisement and segregation of its poor and black populations, and in the next few years, race
riots would join the persistent threat of lynching as the white South cemented
its supremacy. If Mitchell had the sense in the 1890s that the nation could

treat its black citizens with fairness and give them their due, that belief was broken at the turn of the century. "We submit," wrote a dispirited Mitchell in 1901, "because we are powerless to do otherwise."[73] If other vocal editors and activists—W. E. B. Du Bois and Max Barber in Georgia, Jesse Duke in Alabama, Alex Manly in North Carolina, and Ida B. Wells in Tennessee[74]— abandoned the South for the more moderate North during this era's rising tide of white supremacy, John Mitchell and his *Planet* remained, but with their critical voices muted.

At the end of the Lunenburg ordeal, John Mitchell reflected that these trials amounted to "the most remarkable defenses ever made in the criminal annals of the Commonwealth."[75] Sadly, Mitchell was right. In the era of Jim Crow justice, it *was* remarkable and exceptional for innocent blacks to succeed in defending themselves against the judicial system of Virginia. After 1900 the outlook for justice for black people dimmed even further. And it would be more than half a century before Southern blacks began to enjoy some of the protections that the criminal justice system tendered to their white peers.

Notes

1. W. E. B. Du Bois, *The Souls of Black Folk: Essays and Sketches* (Chicago: A. C. McClurg and Co., 1903; reprint, New York: Norton, 1999), 113.

2. Descriptions of these events can be found in any of the Richmond papers in June and July of 1895. "Barnes v. Commonwealth," *Records and Briefs of the Supreme Court of Appeals of Virginia*, o. s., 68 (1895): 121.

3. Suzanne Lebsock, *A Murder in Virginia: Southern Justice on Trial* (New York: Norton, 2003), 59.

4. The historical scholarship generally mentions the Lunenburg case only rarely and in passing. But Suzanne Lebsock's new book—*A Murder in Virginia*— explores the case in depth and quite well. For more on John Mitchell's wider career, see another newly published book, Ann Field Alexander's, *Race Man: The Rise and Fall of the "Fighting Editor," John Mitchell, Jr.* (Charlottesville: University of Virginia Press, 2002). This essay was substantially complete before either of these volumes appeared, but its findings are consonant with and supported by both.

5. Interestingly for this study, Mitchell's first column for the *Globe* described the public hanging of a black woman for killing her husband. See Alexander, 24.

6. *Colored American Magazine* 4 (March 1902): 295–98. For similar assessments of Mitchell's activism, see I. Garland Penn, *Afro-American Press and Its Editors* (1891; reprint, New York: Arno Press, 1969), 183–87; *New York World*, 22 February, 1887, quoted in Penn, 183; William J. Simmons, *Men of Mark: Eminent, Progressive, and Rising* (1887; reprint, New York: Arno Press, 1968), 314–21.

7. J. H. Derbyshire to M. C. Cardozo, 16 July 1895, and Derbyshire to Col. H. C. Jones, 16 July 1895, in Correspondence of C. T. O'Ferrall, Executive Papers, Library of Virginia. See also "Barnes v. Commonwealth" *(Records and Briefs)*, 121–30; *Journal of the Senate of the Commonwealth of Virginia, 1895* (Richmond, Va.: J. H. O'Bannon, 1895), 115–21. The steps taken by the militia are also recorded in the *Report of the Adjutant-General of the State of Virginia* (Richmond, Va.: J. H. O'Bannon, 1895), 64–67.

8. *Richmond Times*, 17 July 1895.

9. Ann Field Alexander, " 'Like an Evil Wind': The Roanoke Riot of 1893 and the Lynching of Thomas Smith," *Virginia Magazine of History and Biography* 100 (1992): 173–206. Members of the militia in Lunenburg were approached concerning the possibility of releasing the prisoners to them, supposedly to extract a confession and discover where the missing money was. *Richmond Times*, 23 July 1885.

10. Margaret Werner Cahalan, *Historical Corrections Statistics of the United States, 1850–1984* Washington, D.C.: U.S. Department of Justice, Bureau of Justice Statistics, 1986), 11.

11. W. Fitzhugh Brundage, *Lynching in the New South: Georgia and Virginia, 1880–1930* (Urbana; University of Illinois Press, 1993), 263. In contrast, a Deep South state like Georgia had 116 lynchings in the 1890s, falling to 99 and rising again to 137 in the following two decades before a dramatic decline in the 1920s (to 41).

12. The fourth defendant, Mary Barnes, mother of Pokey, was with Mr. Pollard in his fields at the time of the murder. She could not be charged with first-degree murder, and the prosecuting attorneys indicted her for conspiring before the fact, a second-degree murder charge. She was found guilty and sentenced to ten years in prison.

13. *Richmond Times*, 13 July 1895.

14. "Barnes v. Commonwealth" *(Records and Briefs)*: 118; *Richmond Times* and *Richmond Dispatch*, 16 July 1895.

15. "Barnes v. Commonwealth," *Reports of Cases in the Supreme Court of Appeals of Virginia* 92 (1895): 803; italics added.

16. Observers frequently emphasized that the only evidence against the women was Marable's accusation, a point driven home in the governor's review of the case against Mary Barnes, Pokey's mother. The "several conflicting and contradictory statements" of Marable comprised the "only testimony against her." Charles O'Ferrall, "Communication from the Governor of Virginia Transmitting List of Pardons," senate document no. 4, *Journal of the Senate of the Commonwealth of Virginia,* 1897, 4.

17. *Journal of the Senate,* 1895; 117.

18. Reported in the *Richmond Dispatch,* 13 July 1895; and in the *Richmond Planet,* 20 July 1895.

19. *Richmond Times,* 16 and 17 July 1895.

20. "Affidavit of F. W. Cunningham" in "Barnes v. Commonwealth" *(Records and Briefs)*, 131–33. Also reported in the *Richmond Dispatch*, 20 July 1895; and the *Richmond Planet*, 27 July 1895. David Thompson was never seriously pursued as a suspect—he had an alibi.

21. *Richmond Dispatch*, 23 July 1895. The *Dispatch* was not alone in assuming nothing would be done for these poor blacks. Some of the evidence in the case was lost at this time, apparently because no one believed the items would ever be needed again. See Lebsock, 249–51.

22. Affidavits of several militiamen can be found in the *Records and Briefs of the Supreme Court*, o. s., 68 (1895): 131–37. In addition, some white newspapers reported their belief in the prisoners' innocence, although they could be ambivalent on this issue; see, for instance, the *Richmond Dispatch*, 23 July 1895.

23. *Richmond Planet*, 2 January 1897.

24. Ibid., 28 Dec. 1895.

25. "Barnes v. Commonwealth" *(Reports)*, 807. For the report on the decision, see *Richmond Times*, 13 December 1895. Rather than an ominous sign, ordering a new trial "on technical grounds" was actually the norm for the Virginia Supreme Court. In "The Virginia Supreme Court, Blacks and the Law," Samuel Pincus demonstrates that the state supreme court generally decided cases upon procedural rules and, less frequently, ordering new trials due to a lack of evidence for the charge. In this thorough study, Pincus finds that the Commonwealth's highest court, in notable contrast to its lower courts, was remarkably evenhanded toward blacks, reversing judgments even in interracial crimes and violations of antimiscegenation statutes, two hot-button issues for white Virginians. Samuel Norman Pincus, "The Virginia Supreme Court, Blacks, and the Law, 1870–1902" (diss., University of Virginia, 1978).

26. *Richmond Planet*, 18 April 1896.

27. *Richmond Times*, 20 Aug. 1895.

28. Ibid., 26 April 1896. The delay might simply have been practical—they started to deliberate late on a Saturday evening, and reconvened on Monday. They discussed the case on Sunday, but did not cast ballots until they reconvened on Monday morning.

29. *Richmond Planet*, 2 May 1896.

30. *Richmond Dispatch*, 13 May 1867.

31. Ibid., 13 Oct. 1896. To give a few other examples, other "riots" over police arrests were reported in the *Dispatch* of 26 June 1878, 3 Aug. 1887, 16 Jan. 1889, and 9 May 1867, the latter case followed up on the 27th.

32. The clearest expression of this comes from the work of Howard Rabinowitz; see particularly his "The Conflict between Blacks and the Police in the Urban South," in *Race, Ethnicity, and Urbanization: Selected Essays* (Columbia: University of Missouri Press, 1994), 167–80, and his chapter "Justice" in Rabinowitz, *1865–1880* (New York: Oxford University Press, 1978), *Race Relations in the Urban South*, 31–60. See

also the latter half of Edward Ayers, *Vengeance and Justice: Crime and Punishment in the 19th-Century American South* (New York: Oxford University Press, 1984). For a different explanation from the urban North, see Roger Lane, *Roots of Violence in Black Philadelphia, 1860–1900* (Cambridge, Mass.: Harvard University Press, 1986). Lane finds no convincing evidence of institutional racism in Philadelphia's policing and court systems. He explains racial disparities in crime and incarceration by pointing to the very different place of blacks in the modern, industrial, urban order: African Americans, in essence were forced to remain in a premodern role, and their crime rates reflect that place. In contrast in the South, racism was more overt.

33. *Richmond Planet,* 18 Oct. 1890. Other Southern black papers made similar complaints. For once instance, see Eugene J. Watts, "The Police in Atlanta, 1890–1905," *Journal of Southern History* 39 (1973): 172.

34. A. M. Keiley, *Fourth Annual Message of the Mayor of Richmond* (Richmond, Va.: Evening News Steam Presses, 1874), xiv.

35. *The Code of Virginia, 1849* (Richmond, Va.: William F. Ritchie, 1849), 723, 753–54. Other antebellum codes duplicate these distinctions. See Philip J. Schwarz, *Twice Condemned: Slaves and the Criminal Laws of Virginia, 1705–1865* (Baton Rouge: Louisiana State University Press, 1888); and idem. *Slave Laws in Virginia* (Athens: University of Georgia Press, 1996).

36. *Acts of the General Assembly of Virginia, Passed in 1865–6* (Richmond, Va.: Allegre and Goode, 1866), 90.

37. *Richmond Dispatch,* noting black members of jury: 11 Feb. 1883; the "novel sight" of an all-black jury in Manchester, Virginia: 7 July 1879.

38. George Campbell, *White and Black: The Outcome of a Visit to the United States* (London: Chatto and Windus, 1879), 300–301.

39. *Richmond Dispatch,* 7 July 1901.

40. Quoted in the *Richmond Planet,* 7 Aug. 1897.

41. "Strauder vs. West Virginia" 100 U.S. 306 (1880); "Ex Parte Virginia" 100 U.S. 339 (1880).

42. "Virginia vs. Rives" 100 *United States Reports* 313.

43. Not until the 1930s did the Supreme Court amend this ruling on race and jury selection. See Abraham L. Davis and Barbara Luck Graham, *The Supreme Court, Race, and Civil Rights* (Thousand Oaks, Calif.: Sage Publications, 1995), 18–25.

44. *Richmond Planet,* 27 July 1889, 28 Jan. 1899. See also 7 January 1911, when Mitchell again clearly pointed toward lower courts and juries as the problem: "[A]s a rule, [miscarriage of justice] is in the cases of magistrates and juries. Southern judges higher up have always been disposed to accord justice in keeping with the State laws."

45. *Richmond Planet,* 20 July 1895; *Richmond Dispatch,* 13–21 July 1895; Lebsock, 72, 85, 94, 210, 241.

46. *Richmond Planet*, 16 Sept. 1899; for another parallel among dozens: 21 Nov. 1896. One study of Georgia convicts found that blacks were sentenced to terms twice as long as whites. See Leon F. Litwack, *Trouble in Mind: Black Southerners in The Age of Jim Crow* (New York: Vintage Books, 1999), 252.

47. *Richmond Planet*, 8 July 1899. See also "Can Get Justice Here!" *Richmond Planet*, 1 Nov. 1902.

48. *Richmond Times*, 6 May 1896.

49. Lebsock, 262–63.

50. *Richmond Times*, 6 May 1896.

51. O'Ferrall, 4–5. See also *Richmond Planet*, 2 Jan. 1897.

52. Henry Vance Davis, "The Black Press: From Mission to Commercialism, 1827–1927" (diss., University of Michigan, 1990), 173.

53. To give two examples literally among dozens: *Richmond Planet*, 29 September 1894 and 21 November 1896.

54. The first sensational treatment—"Women Innocent"—was on July 27, a month after the *Planet* first reported the crime, six weeks after it took place. The earliest mention of the crime was in an editorial, when Mitchell simply argued that the courtroom was the place to decide such a case and no mob should be allowed to preempt such justice. *Richmond Planet*, 29 June 1895.
  In contrast to the *Planet*'s sensational treatment, Richmond's white papers were ambivalent about the case. The *Richmond Dispatch*, the city's largest daily, remained cautious. The *Dispatch* raised a number of questions about the strength of the case against the women, but it also persistently emphasized that the judge and jury "would hardly have found the women guilty upon Solomon's unsupported testimony" (23 July 1895). It believed that the full trial record would show more corroborative testimony than brief press reports from the trials implied. The *Richmond Times* was more critical, clearly arguing that Marable was unconvincing, that his testimony was all that convicted the women, and that justice demanded a new trial.

55. Because the *Planet* was a weekly, this averages exactly 1.5 articles or editorials for every issue in these eighteen months, and they were often quite lengthy. Some articles and editorials were short, but others, especially those reporting trial developments, could be as long as two full pages of the four-page *Planet*. For comparison, the *Richmond Dispatch* covered the case almost daily during the various trials and appeals, but these were, in general, short reports of the progress of the case. Between the discovery of the crime in June 1895 and Pokey Barnes's freedom eleven months later, the *Dispatch* printed eighty-two stories and editorials, a number comparable to the *Planet* for that period. Frequent editorials on the possibilities of the innocence of the Lunenburg women in the first few months of their coverage ended in September 1895; thereafter, the *Richmond Dispatch* covered this case strictly through reports, generally quite short ones. In the surprising turns in the story—the Supreme Court demanding new trials (13 December 1885), the nolle prosequi against Pokey (6

May 1886), Mary's (second) conviction remanded to the lower court (3 September 1886), and Mary attaining her freedom (22 September 1886) — the *Richmond Dispatch* printed stories reporting each development. But the paper published not a single editorial about any of these developments, and the last two turns in Mary's story merited only a single article each, and ones only half a column in length. The white response to this story of justice to blacks was therefore notably muted: the papers recorded what happened, but the matter was quickly dropped.

56. One of the prominent stories in the early months of this sensation was simply a list of all contributors, with the headline "Lunenburg Case — Shall We Save the Women?" See *Richmond Planet*, August–September 1895. This effort previews the actions of the NAACP in the 1920s and 1930s, when the organization both publicized particularly disturbing cases of injustice and funded legal teams to appeal convictions. See Mark Robert Schneider, *"We Return Fighting": The Civil Rights Movement in the Jazz Age* (Boston: Northeastern University Press, 2002).

57. *Richmond Planet*, 27 July 1895; 18 April, 2 May 1896.

58. Ibid., 27 July 1895, 16 May 1896.

59. The limit of John Mitchell's self-congratulation was perhaps reached when he printed a song written in his honor: "Let Us Rally 'Round John Mitchell" sung to the tune of "Hold the Fort," Ibid., 21 Sept. 1895.

60. Ibid., 17 Oct. 1896, 2 Jan. 1897.

61. *Richmond Dispatch*, 18 July 1893.

62. Another example of this sort of innocent-sensation is the case of Simon Walker, accused of killing a man in 1889 and sentenced to hang. The governor commuted Walker's sentence to a jail term at the last moment, due in part to efforts of the black community. No copies of the *Planet* exist for 1889, but Mitchell refers to this case in a self-congratulatory article at the end of the Lunenburg case, 24 Oct. 1896.

63. "There should be no more cowards among the negroes of the South, but that they would fight it out there with the ballot, or if necessary, with the bullet," said John Mitchell in a meeting of the Afro-American Press Association in Philadelphia in 1892. *Richmond State*, 28 September 1892.

64. *Richmond Planet*, 26 Feb. 1898.

65. Ibid., 8 Feb. 1890.

66. Ibid., 26 Feb. 1898.

67. *New York Freeman*, 29 May 1886, Alexander, 42. No copies of the *Planet* exist from this time, but this Northern black paper carried a treatment of the story, and many biographical source reference it. The lynching occurred in Charlotte County, but the threat came from a town just across the Prince Edward County line, leading several scholars to say that these events occurred there. W. Fitzhugh Brundage, " 'To Howl Loudly': John Mitchell Jr. and His Campaign Against Lynching in Virginia,"

Canadian Review of American Studies 22 (1991): 329. But Mitchell himself wrote that it was Charlotte County, and other biographical works from the 1890s as well as the original notice of the lynching in the *Richmond Dispatch* (7 May 1886) concur. See John Mitchell, "Shall the Wheels of Race Agitation Be Stopped?" *Colored American Magazine* 5 (1902): 386.

68. *Richmond Planet*, 27 August 1892; see also a similar story, 31 July 1897.

69. Ibid., 2 June 1894.

70. The *Planet* took a similar tone in several other instances. When a black man south of Lynchburg, Va., was shot three times, he was still able to beat off his attackers—who numbered fourteen—and make his escape into the dark woods about his house. The story's emphasis was not upon the crimes that he was charged with, the gruesome details of his wounds, nor even injustice. Instead, the article centered upon his will and effort. The first headline (of six) neatly summed up the central focus of the article: "Whipped Them All." Ibid., 12 June 1897. See also stories on 15 January 1893 and 31 July 1897.

What of cases where active black protagonists were clearly violating the law? In this the *Planet* is much more difficult to parse, in part because it rarely reported such stories at all. Occasionally, it introduced a black criminal in an ambivalent way that did not overtly praise him, but might lead the reader to do so. For instance, a brief story taken from an Alabama paper received the headline "His Deadly Aim—A Colored Man's Unerring Rifle Killed the Sheriff—Not Yet Captured." Like the headline, the entire article was full of ambiguity: he was a criminal, but the harshest language used against "Railroad Bill" was that he was "notorious," a man whose "record for the year is a bad one." Even these words could be interpreted as implying a nod and a wink. The central point of the article was how powerful and dangerous a man he was, not his crimes: "Several hundred men are scouring the swamp to-day. The outlaw will probably never be taken alive." This article appeared in the first week of Railroad Bill's fame: he foiled the authorities and robbed freight trains until he was shot down a year later. But his legend continued to grow until he became a part of the black folk pantheon of "bad men," each interpreted in much the same way as in this early *Planet* article: censure for their bad deeds mixed with a healthy dose of admiration. For more, see Lawrence W. Levine, *Black Culture and Black Consciousness: Afro-American Folk Thought from Slavery to Freedom* (New York: Oxford University Press, 1977), 410–11; John W. Roberts, " 'You Done Me Wrong': The Badman as Outlaw Hero," in *Trickster to Badman: The Black Folk Hero in Slavery and Freedom* (Philadelphia: University of Pennsylvania Press, 1989), 171–219.

These stories show that the *Planet*—and surely the wider African American community—found appealing these accounts of countervailing tendencies in the late nineteenth century. They longed for instances when the victim won and when the real culprit in their lives—a system of justice that was not just—received some semblance of retribution or at least was denied its prey.

71 *Richmond Planet*, 2 Feb. 1895.

72. Ibid., 7 Nov. 1914. The Clements case was covered by the *Planet* and the local white papers from 16 May to 7 November, 1914.

73. Ibid., 8 June 1901. In addition to becoming dispirited by the power of white supremacy, the "fiery" editor of the 1890s became a black businessman in the 1900s. The editor of the *Planet*—who had sounded like the antithesis of Booker T. Washington in the 1890s—founded a bank in Richmond in 1902, and by 1910 he often sounded like a Tuskegee man himself: "Colored men should be respectful in their demands. We can secure the support of the conservative contingent of the white folks by a discreet management of our cause, and will lose if we go beyond the bounds of reason." Ibid., 7 March 1908.

Mitchell saw a "revulsion of feeling" against blacks, and his solution was now mild-mannered and conservative: "Each man, woman, and child can most surely counteract its effect by being on their good behaviors." Ibid., 10 Oct. 1908. Instead of defending blacks against injustice, Mitchell was as likely to speak out against black criminals, who were "an incubus upon our prosperity and a dangling weight to the neck of all our fondest hopes." *Richmond Planet,* 16 Jan. 1909.

74. Jesse Duke was run out of Alabama, but he moved to another Southern state, Arkansas, and continued to publish a series of newspapers, although it is unclear if he remained outspoken. Manly, Wells, Du Bois, and Barber moved to the North. Allen W. Jones, "The Black Press in the 'New South': Jesse C. Duke's Struggle for Justice and Equality," *Journal of Negro History* 64 (1979): 215–28; Dominic J. Capeci, Jr. and Jack C. Knight, "Rechoning with Violence: W. E. B. Du Bois and the 1906 Atlanta Race Riot," *Journal of Southern History* 62 (1996): 727–66; David S. Cecelski and Timothy B. Tyson, eds., *Democracy Betrayed: The Wilmington Race Riot of 1898 and Its Aftermath* (Chapel Hill: University of North Carolina Press, 1998); Alfreda M. Duster, ed., *Crusade for Justice: The Autobiography of Ida B. Wells* (Chicago: Univeristy of Chicago Press, 1970), 47–59. Soon, Eugene N. Bright would be another editor forced to flee ahead of a mob. See Neil R. McMillen, *Dark Journey: Black Mississippians in the Age of Jim Crow* (Urbana: University of Illinois Press, 1989), 176.

75. *Richmond Planet,* 2 Jan. 1897.

4

Justice Denied:
Race and the 1982 Murder Trial
of Mumia Abu-Jamal

Dave Lindorff

From the moment that the first police squad car arrived at the bloody scene of a fatal shooting on the morning of December 9, 1981, in Philadelphia's Center City red-light district, it was clear that race and politics would be central issues in a murder case that would gain worldwide attention. Dead on the sidewalk with a bullet between the eyes was Daniel Faulkner, a promising young white police officer. Not far away, sprawled on the curb and gravely wounded by a bullet to the chest, was Mumia Abu-Jamal, a young black journalist who only weeks before had been hailed in a local monthly magazine as one of the key people to watch in Philadelphia.[1]

Over the years, this case has gained an astonishingly high profile, not just because of the issues it raises about the American legal system and capital punishment system, but because of the writing talents of the defendant. For two decades, from his cell in the supermax death row facility at State Correctional Institution–Greene in western Pennsylvania, Abu-Jamal has written essays and books that have provided a searing exposé of the inhuman conditions deliberately imposed on America's thousands of doomed death-row convicts, as well as of the broader scandal of the imprisoning of a generation of young black men. As his fame and notoriety as a prison journalist grew, so too did the campaign to have him executed, which has been spearheaded by the Fraternal Order of Police, a state and national trade union and political lobbying organization of police officers. When Albert Sabo, the judge who sat for Abu-Jamal's trial and his Post-Conviction Relief Act hearing died in the spring of 2002, his obituary in the *New York Times* was devoted entirely to his role in this case, despite his having presided over the death sentencing of over thirty other people.

The uncontroverted facts of the case do not indicate much about the specific actions of Abu-Jamal on that fateful December morning. At about 3:45 A.M., Faulkner, for unknown reasons, decided to stop a battered blue Volkswagen sedan driven by William Cook, the younger brother of Abu-Jamal. Faulkner radioed in from his cruiser that he was doing a routine stop, then within seconds, he got back on the radio and said to "send a wagon," indicating that he intended to make an arrest. In the short interval between that second call and the time police arrived, however, Faulkner had gotten into an altercation with Cook, in which he had hit Cook several times on the head with his police-issue metal flashlight, and had been shot dead, with one bullet entering his lower back and exiting his throat and a second entering his face and exploding in his skull. Abu-Jamal, who had been in a parking lot across the street filling out his passenger log in a taxicab he was driving, ended up gravely wounded himself, with a bullet to the chest later identified as having been fired by Faulkner's gun. What happened in those brief moments—the sequence of shots fired, and who fired them—remains unclear. No witness saw Abu-Jamal get shot, and there were conflicting accounts, often by the same witness, about how Faulkner had been shot.

There were other major questions about this case, too. Strangely, though the equipment for testing for gunpowder residues was in many of the police vehicles that were on the scene in minutes, no test was made of Abu-Jamal's hands to see if he had recently fired a gun. Nor was his gun tested to see if it had been recently fired. (If either or both of these routine tests were done, the police never reported the results.) Although a gun found near Abu-Jamal was positively identified as being legally registered to him, and though it contained five empty bullet casings, the two bullets that hit Faulkner (only one of which was recovered, and it was badly damaged) were never positively identified as having come from that gun, or even from that type of gun.

What is clear is that it did not take police detectives long to realize that the black man collapsed on the curb, whose legally registered handgun, with five spent rounds, they claimed was found only inches from his right hand, and who was immediately picked up as a suspect in the officer's death, was a former Black Panther Party activist and a critic of the city's police and government. Some senior officers who had arrived at the scene within minutes of the shooting had served in the department's Civil Defense Squad, the intelligence unit that had harassed and maintained dossiers on the Panthers for years.[2]

Whether it was because they knew who he was, or just because he was a black man whom they believed had just killed a brother officer, the officers on the scene, in full view of supervisory personnel, treated this suspect brutally. According to the prosecution's own star witness and several other witnesses, the dreadlocked Abu-Jamal was beaten at the scene by several arresting officers, who kicked him and assaulted him with blackjacks.[3] He also had his head rammed into a lamppost and was dropped onto his face while officers were carrying him, handcuffed, to a paddy wagon.[4] Although the dead officer was promptly rushed off to nearby Jefferson Hospital, it would be over half an hour before Abu-Jamal, whose lungs were filling with blood from a bullet to the chest that also pierced his liver, was delivered to the same hospital emergency room by police. By the time he saw a doctor, he was about to go into shock from blood loss.[5]

Abu-Jamal's brother William, who had sustained head injuries at Faulkner's hand, was arrested and jailed, and later tried and convicted of assault. At the time the police arrived on the scene, William Cook told them "I had nothing to do with it." Abu-Jamal's statement to the jury was terse: "I am innocent of the charges against me."[6] In the years since the shooting neither Cook nor Abu-Jamal told anyone, not even their lawyers, what had happened on December 9, 1981.[7]

I

The role of race in the Abu-Jamal case must be understood in terms of a long national history of a legal double standard for African Americans.[8] The existence of white supremacy and black subjection has been an integral part of American life, despite a persistent struggle for racial justice. Slavery existed in all thirteen colonies and states. Although Northern states adopted gradual abolition laws after the American Revolution, Negrophobia was ubiquitous. Before 1865 blacks were allowed to vote in only five states. Segregation in housing, schools, and transportation was the norm; and opportunities for employment were limited. Growing antislavery sentiment after 1830 did not necessarily translate into equal rights under the law for blacks. Although a vocal minority of radical abolitionists called for a color-blind society, most whites interpreted the Republican Party credo of "free labor, free soil, free men" with only themselves in mind. Indeed, during the infamous draft riots in New York City in July 1863, Irish immigrants and other whites vented their social and economic frustration on African American residents with deadly results, a foreboding of explosive ethnic tension mirrored in modern Philadelphia and other American cities.

In the antebellum South slaves had no legal recourse against masters who assaulted/raped them. The paradox of slavery in the republic was resolved only through the Civil War. Emancipation, citizenship, equal rights, and suffrage were given to blacks by three major amendments to the U.S.

Constitution between 1865 and 1870. Notwithstanding the end of slavery (secured by the Thirteenth Amendment) and the grant of new rights by the Fourteenth and Fifteenth Amendments, Reconstruction ended in 1877 with an incomplete revolution for four million freedpeople. The effort to achieve black equality in the postbellum South failed just as it had faltered in the postrevolutionary North. Nineteenth-century notions of restraints on federal power, the tradition of states' rights, the emphasis on self-help, nearly universal white racism, and the lack of any kind of redress (land or cash) for centuries of servitude set the stage by the 1890s for extreme racial bias in the Southern judicial system, legal segregation in public institutions, conveyances, and places throughout the Southern states and for de facto segregation in Northern and Western states.[9]

After 1900 the condition of blacks in the Southern states deteriorated further, as white radicals, alarmed by elite manipulation of dependent black voters to defeat agrarian candidates for public office, supported the systematic disenfranchisement of blacks. Many Southern states enacted debt peonage laws that prevented sharecroppers in debt from moving geographically to rent better land on better terms. White supremacy was sustained by the tradition of white violence against blacks, ranging from innumerable public whippings to brutal torture and death at the end of a rope. Law enforcement authorities in the South looked the other way when whites assaulted blacks. Even after World War II, white-only juries rarely convicted whites who assaulted/murdered blacks.[10]

Fleeing to the North in increasing numbers after 1914 to escape the legal color-caste system in the South and the collapse of the sharecropping economy, blacks encountered powerful institutional forces in the North that created black ghettos and excluded blacks from the skilled and unionized jobs in the industrial economy. Blacks were greatly underrepresented in the police forces of cities that had substantial black populations, such as Chicago and New York. Violent race riots erupted in urban centers during and after both world wars, as whites threatened by black economic advances and by the increasing public criticism blacks made of institutional racism acted to put blacks back into a subordinate position. During these riots white policemen frequently led assaults against blacks and protected white rioters (or looked the other way) as they attacked black people and black homes.[11]

A second Reconstruction was brought about by the civil rights movements, urban uprisings and riots, and black power movements of the 1960s. Civil rights laws in 1964, 1968, and 1972 made it harder for whites to discriminate against people of color (and women) in public accommodations, the labor market, and housing. Certainly these laws and the actions of private sector elites and government officials led to more employment opportunities for blacks (the size of the black middle class tripled between

1960 and 1986), less housing discrimination, and the right to sit in any seat on any public conveyance.

But many blacks remained mired in a condition of poverty. And as more sophisticated work technologies led employers increasingly to seek workers with high school degrees, the poor-quality educational institutions in urban ghettos and the disruption of family life engendered by poverty left many black youth outside of the system, despairing of their ability to obtain decent jobs and inclined to seek quick rewards through the drug culture and other forms of criminal activity. Blacks were thus disproportionally charged and convicted of crimes and swelled the prison populations. While many blacks clearly had been driven to criminal activity by social forces beyond their control, it is also clear, as the pivotal Abu-Jamal case reveals, that the lack of racial justice in the criminal court systems of many cities contributed to the disproportionate number of incarcerated blacks.

II

Founded by Quakers, Philadelphia was a major stop on the Underground Railway for escaping slaves; yet at the same time, slavery was allowed in the city. When George Washington moved into Philadelphia to begin his first term as president of the new nation, he brought seven of his slaves with him from Virginia. (They promptly fled to freedom.)

In the nineteenth century thousands of Irish and German immigrants moved to Philadelphia. After 1880 they were followed by many immigrants from southern Europe, especially Italians. During World War I and thereafter, Philadelphia attracted numerous Southern black and poor white tenant farmers, who moved north in search of jobs. By 1970, the city was 40 percent black, but also heavily ethnic white, especially Irish and Italian. In the 1960s, as Philadelphia's burgeoning black population continued to try to find housing in the long-standing white areas of the city and began to organize, using consumer boycotts and nonviolent civil disobedience to challenge institutional racism in private sector employment and in the public schools, interracial conflict intensified.

It was in this setting that Frank Rizzo, a third-generation Italian American and second-generation policeman, rose to power, first as a ham-fisted, head-banging police chief who proudly accepted the moniker of the "Cisco Kid" and later as mayor, when he played on those racial tensions by campaigning against the construction of low-income (read "black") federal housing projects in white working-class parts of the city. One of Rizzo's first actions as the city's police chief was to order a massive police assault on

November 17, 1967 on 3500 peacefully demonstrating black high school
and junior high school students during a rally at the city's school board
headquarters; he launched their attack with the words, "Get their black
asses!"[12] Two years later, he made the city's recently organized Black Panther Party a special target for harassment and surveillance by his department's
"red squad," the Civil Defense Squad. In a coordinated early morning raid
on August 31, 1970, on several party offices around the city, Rizzo had the
arrested Panthers stripped while local photographers snapped away; afterward, in a press conference, he gloated, "Imagine, the big black Panthers
with their pants down."[13]

Rizzo's rise to power coincided with a wholesale shift in the black
empowerment movement in Philadelphia. As Matthew J. Countryman explains in his landmark work on Philadelphia's black political history, the
1960s and 1970s saw the decline of the old liberal integrationist approach of
the city's black movement and a turn to a more confrontational approach that
stressed black power and black pride. Radical black leaders and black organizations like the Student Nonviolent Coordinating Committee, the Black
People's Unity Movement, and the Revolutionary Action Movement (RAM)
became increasingly active. According to Countryman, as early as 1966, when
he was still just deputy police chief, Rizzo was getting support from then-
mayor James H. J. Tate, who had decided that attacking black militants "was
the key to maintaining his popularity in the city's white working-class neighborhoods."[14] It was a lesson the politically ambitious Rizzo seems to have
taken to heart. With aggressive use of large numbers of heavily armed police,
and with an undercover operation complete with informants and agent pro-
vocateurs, Rizzo virtually destroyed the Philadelphia SNCC operation as well
as RAM, and while the local Panthers operation probably was more a victim
of national attacks and national internal conflicts, Rizzo's attacks on the
Philadelphia chapter certainly helped things along.

At the same time as all this was going on, and indeed in part because
of Rizzo's attacks on militant black organizations and their activities, racial
polarization in the city grew apace. As Countryman writes, "If, in fact, the
turn towards black nationalism was a response to the persistence of whiteness
and the defense of white privilege as a usually unspoken organizing principle
in Philadelphia's politics, labor markets and neighborhoods, then it is ironic,
though not surprising, that it was black activists' efforts to use race as the
explicit basis for political and community organization that became the rationale for the reemergence of an avowedly white racial politics in the city." He
goes on to add, "The central institution in the resurgence of a conservative
politics in Philadelphia was the Philadelphia police department."[15] It was, it
should be noted, from that pool of conservative ethnic voters that most of
Abu-Jamal's jury panelists would be chosen.

Rizzo seemed at times discouraged that he couldn't prod the Panthers into a shoot-out with his police sharpshooters (he once called the group's members "yellow" for failing to use their guns during a police assault on their offices),[16] but a few years later he got a new target on which to focus his racial antipathy: a small but vocal and largely black back-to-nature but militantly antiauthoritarian commune called MOVE. Built around the teachings of a self-styled guru named Vincent Leapheart, and like him assuming the surname of Africa, MOVE's members had occupied a house in the low-income integrated neighborhood of Powelton Village, where they irritated some neighbors by keeping dozens of dogs and by blaring out propaganda and curse-laced invective with amplified megaphones from their porch.

On August 8, 1979, at the direction of Mayor Rizzo, hundreds of police, armed with everything from shotguns to machine guns, staged a military-style assault on the home and headquarters of the group, despite the presence in the house of small children. A number of unarmed MOVE members were brutally beaten and one officer was shot dead, possibly by "friendly fire" from other officers. (A second MOVE house was later firebombed by police in 1985, under the city's first black mayor. It was an action that led to the destruction of sixty-three houses and the killing of eleven people in the house, including five children.)

Ironically, the Panther Party that had been founded in 1969 in Philadelphia was a pretty tame affair. Under the leadership of Vietnam veteran Reggie Schell, a serious rebel without the headline-seeking flamboyance or the penchant for gun-toting bravado of leaders in New York and California, the Philadelphia Panthers primarily worked at organizing children's breakfast programs and protests by students. It was not a violence-prone chapter, nor did it last very long; it fell apart along with the national organization by 1970. In 1970 the Black Panther Party outside Philadelphia had shifted its focus from armed self-defense against police infringements of the civil rights of blacks to community-level antipoverty programs. As Countryman has pointed out, the Black Panthers had concluded that insisting on their First Amendment rights to self-defense had engendered such massive police repression that the Panthers' goal of increasing black pride and black political and economic power could not be met if that strategy continued.

By 1981 Philadelphia's blacks had begun to win political power in the city. They elected city council members and state legislators, and two years later they would elect a black mayor, Wilson Goode. Under pressure from equal opportunity laws and regulations, even the police department had begun to hire black officers, though at that point the 7,500-member police force, composed largely of men trained, hired, and promoted under Rizzo's leadership as police chief and mayor, was still almost entirely white. It was also notoriously corrupt—and notoriously brutal. In 1979, Philadelphia became the first city to be sued by the federal government for police brutality.[17] In the late 1970s and early 1980s, the U.S. Justice Department conducted a probe of corruption in the department's Center City district and eventually indicted and convicted some thirty officers, including high-ranking supervisors and even the deputy chief of police, who was sentenced to eighteen years in prison. Police in the district were convicted of extortion, of bribery, of falsifying evidence, and of paying for false testimony to win convictions.[18] A significant number of those convicted of such crimes turned out to have played key roles in the arrest and trial of Abu-Jamal.[19]

Says Alan Yatvin, a Philadelphia attorney who specializes in civil rights and civil liberties law, "Just visually, it's troubling. . . . They could have been motivated to do something in order to avoid conviction. It's always troubling when you have an environment where people in uniform feel that they can get away with lying, and the level of corruption that they had in Philadelphia in the 1980s and 1990s is staggering."[20] It was against this background that Abu-Jamal's case was investigated, and that he was tried and convicted.

III

In 1935 the Supreme Court had ruled that the Fourteenth Amendment barred the systematic exclusion of blacks from juries (*Norris v. Alabama*). But proving systematic exclusion was difficult. As the civil rights movement erupted after February 1960, Congress responded with a variety of laws that enhanced the civil liberties and civil rights of Americans. Influenced by the movement's ethos of expanding individual rights, which in turn reflected many twentieth-century developments, including the antifascist fight in World War II and the cold war, which prompted efforts to "clean up" America's democratic image, the Supreme Court expanded the rights of persons accused of crimes in 1966 in its famous *Miranda v. Arizona* decision. Congress passed the Jury Selection Act of 1968, which was interpreted by the Supreme Court to mean that the Sixth Amendment right to a trial by jury meant that jury pools had to be "truly representative of the community."[21] But this decision did not deal with the prosecutorial tactic of using peremptory challenges to eliminate nonwhite jurors from an actual jury. The Supreme Court did not try to prevent this tactic until four years after Abu-Jamal's trial was completed.[22]

The transcript of Abu-Jamal's trial shows that the prosecutor Joseph McGill struggled mightily to have the first juror Abu-Jamal had approved, a young black woman, rejected "for cause." After failing in that effort, McGill used his first peremptory challenge to prevent her from being impaneled. He went on to apply ten or eleven (the number remains in dispute) of the fifteen peremptory challenges he used to remove potential black jurors who had met with Abu-Jamal's approval, and who had said they could vote for a death sentence. Abu-Jamal, for his part, peremptorily rejected only one black juror (who had been found acceptable by McGill).

In the end, in a city that at the time was over 40 percent black, there were only three African-Americans (25 percent of the jury) on the twelve-member panel. (The four alternate jurors were also white.) One of the three black jurors impaneled, a feisty older black women, was tossed off the jury right before opening arguments after she ignored the judge's order to remain sequestered and left her hotel briefly to bring a sick cat to the veterinarian's office. At a meeting attended by Judge Albert Sabo, McGill, and the defense attorney, Anthony Jackson, from which Abu-Jamal was excluded by the judge, she was replaced by a white alternate. The initial selection of that juror as an alternate had been opposed by Abu-Jamal, because he had stated during the *voir dire* that he did not think he could be fair to the defendant. Sabo denied a challenge for cause, and as the defense had exhausted its peremptory challenges at that point, the juror had been seated as an alternate.[23] Thus the final jury was $16^2/_3$ percent black, less than one-half the proportion of blacks in Philadelphia.

As is generally the case in capital trials in urban settings, the death-qualifying process itself resulted in blacks being disproportionately removed from consideration. This is because a much higher percentage of blacks than whites tend to oppose capital punishment. As long as death penalty verdicts have to be unanimous (as is the case in most states, including Pennsylvania), and as long as capital juries are death-qualified, African Americans, as well as Catholics, political liberals, and women, all of which groups disproportionately oppose capital punishment, will be disproportionately kept off of jury panels.[24] In Abu-Jamal's case, more than twenty black potential jurors were removed from consideration "for cause" by McGill because they expressed reservations about the death penalty.

Assistant District Attorney McGill, in an interview conducted in the spring of 2000, insisted that he has never rejected anyone as a juror because of his or her race:

> I do not—do not—pick jurors because of race. What kind of fairness do they show. What kind of body language do they have in reference to the defendant. Sometimes it's a question of age or interest. Who would be more likely to listen to his radio show? It's the total package. Whatever the numbers were, it was how they reacted to me, what they said, whether they were the kind of person who'd be mesmerized by his persona. And I would not want to have people who would not like me. If they seemed antagonistic towards me, I would try to get rid of that person. What I wanted was a person who would not be swayed by the parties in the case. I don't remember a

death penalty case in which I didn't have at least three, four, maybe five African Americans. It's absolutely incorrect to say that I didn't chose jurors because they were black.[25]

In saying that he might be concerned about whether a potential juror might "be more likely to listen to [Abu-Jamal's] radio show," McGill could be considered to be demonstrating racial bias. Radio stations are openly and acutely race- and class- and age-conscious in their demographic targeting. In the industry it is quite common to refer to "black radio" as a category. In saying he would be concerned if a potential juror "might be more likely to listen" to the defendant's show, as opposed to saying that a potential juror had actually listened to his show, isn't he really simply saying that that person is black, or young and black? (More to the point legally, his questioning them about what they had heard on the radio was not really "race neutral," since he was not asking this question of white potential jurors.)

In any event, it is evident from a comment made by McGill during the trial that he viewed black jurors as being different in their thinking than whites, raising questions about his real motivations in striking them. During cross-examination by Jackson of Cynthia White, the prosecution's star witness, McGill suddenly noticed a black judge, the late Calvin Wilson, who had entered the courtroom and sat in the spectators' gallery on the side where all of the defendant's supporters and family were seated. It might be reasonable for a prosecutor to be concerned when a judge seats himself in the courtroom near the defendant's family. But McGill's concern was clearly race:

Mr. Jackson: Well—

Mr. McGill: Excuse me? Is that Judge Wilson over there?

Mr. Jackson: [still trying to continue with his cross-examination] It may refresh her recollection.

Mr. McGill: If the court pleases, the two black jurors may know him.

Mr. Jackson: Just because they're black—

Mr. McGill: Or anybody.

The Court: [ignoring McGill's interruption] Let me say this. What is the purpose of this mug shot?[26]

A second element of racial bias in Abu-Jamal's case was the judge, Albert Sabo, who served both as trial judge in 1982 and as Post-Conviction Relief Act (PCRA) fact finder in 1995. Elected to the Philadelphia Court of Common Pleas in 1974, Sabo for the prior sixteen years had been an under-sheriff in the Sheriff's Department. Between 1958 and his election to the bench in 1974, he had been a member of the law enforcement union and lobbying organization, the Fraternal Order of Police. An ardent conservative, on the day that murder defendants' cases went to the jury (including Abu-Jamal's), he routinely wore a tie plastered with the phrase "law and order."[27]

For a number of his years on the bench, Judge Sabo sat only for murder trials. According to a study by Amnesty International, Judge Sabo presided over thirty-one murder cases in which defendants were sentenced to death—a national record. Of those cases, twenty-nine defendents were non-white, including twenty-seven who were black—also a national record.[28] Stuart Taylor, an attorney who edits the conservative-leaning *American Lawyer,* attended Abu-Jamal's postconviction hearing in 1995, which was also presided over by Judge Sabo. Noting Sabo's death penalty trial record and his behavior during the postconviction hearing, Taylor concluded: "The unfairness of Jamal's 1982 trial was almost guaranteed once it was assigned to Judge Albert Sabo."[29]

Jack McMahon, a former assistant district attorney who had experience trying cases before Sabo, put it another way in an interview conducted in June 2000, saying, "Anyone will tell you that Sabo's reputation was that he was just another DA in the courtroom." A veteran of the Philadelphia district attorney's homicide department who was working there during the time of Abu-Jamal's trial, McMahon, now in private practice, said, "The ethics of the prosecutor were the only limits on what went on in Sabo's courtroom."[30]

The prosecutor in the case, selected by then district attorney Ed Rendell, who would become Philadelphia's mayor and is now Pennsylvania's governor, was Joseph McGill, a wily courtroom veteran whose record at jury trials, according to his own recollection, was 147 wins and 3 losses. McGill from the outset clearly planned to play up the defendant's radical past. Only weeks after the shooting, at a January 1982 bail hearing, McGill had tried to introduce a news article from the *Philadelphia Inquirer* dating back to 1970, in which the defendant, then a fifteen-year-old member of the local Black Panther chapter, had been quoted as citing Mao Tse-tung's proverb "Power flows from the barrel of a gun." Though McGill was barred from using that yellowed clipping at the bail hearing, he did return with it at Abu-Jamal's sentencing hearing on July 3, 1982. At that time—thanks to Abu-Jamal's insistence on reading a statement to the jury that opened the door to his being put on the stand—Judge Sabo allowed McGill to read it into the record and to question the defendant about it.[31]

Abu-Jamal responded by insisting that the entire article be read. The article was a report on the new intensity of organizing at the Philadelphia Panther headquarters following the murder by Chicago police of Panther leader Fred Hampton. Abu-Jamal's full quote in that article made it clear that the power he was referring to was police power coming from police guns:

"Since the murders," says West Cook [Panthers rejected the use of pseudonyms or aliases by members], chapter communications secretary, "Black brothers and sisters and organizations which wouldn't commit themselves before are relating to us. Black people are facing the reality that the Black Panther Party has been facing. Political power grows out of the barrel of a gun."[32]

Besides portraying the defendant as an unreconstructed police-hating radical from his childhood Panther days, McGill also used code words to stress to the largely white, middle-class jury that they were dealing with an angry black man. Recalling the frustrated Abu-Jamal's shouted outbursts at the judge as he repeatedly argued to have his right to represent himself restored (it had been removed from him by the judge during jury selection on the grounds that he was being belligerent—a claim that was later rejected by a federal judge [see below]), and to have as an adviser at his table a man of his choice, McGill told the jury during his final summation:

Law and order . . . this is what this trial is all about more than any other trial I have ever seen . . . because you, yourself, have seen, you have heard things that are going on, and you have heard testimony of things that are going on as to what is lawful and what is not lawful, and actions, arrogance, reactions against the law. Law and Order.

So ladies and gentlemen, we then will simply make the response, at least ask yourselves the question, are we going to live in a society with law and order, and are we going to enforce the laws with the intention of law and order, or are we going to decide our own rules and then, act accordingly?[33]

McGill concluded with a hyperbolic statement:

And, if you can at will kill police, ladies and gentlemen, you then make that extra step towards the area which is without law enforcement, which is an outright jungle. We are one step from the jungle.[34]

McGill's characterization of the defendant as a longtime police-hater and a man prone to violence was belied not only by Abu-Jamal's prior history, which included not a single arrest for anything, despite his having been listed on the FBI's so-called Security Index, but also by his FBI file itself, hundreds of pages of which were obtained by the defense through the Freedom of Information Act (Sabo did not permit the FBI file to be submitted as evidence during the 1995 Post-Conviction Relief Act hearing).[35] As one document, describing Abu-Jamal's removal from the Security Index, or ADEX file, stated:

In March, 1973, per bureau instructions, captioned subject was deleted from ADEX and no additional investigation conducted concerning his activities.

Sources, however, have continued to report periodically on COOK and, although he has not displayed a propensity for violence, he has continued to associate himself with individuals and organizations engaged in Extremist activities.[36]

III

While race and politics were certainly central to this case, it was probably testimony concerning a confession allegedly made by Abu-Jamal at the hospital to which he and Officer Faulkner were brought that brought about Abu-Jamal's conviction on July 2, 1982, and his subsequent death sentence on July 3. According to the testimony of both a hospital security guard and a police officer, the defendant, while lying on the floor in the entryway of the hospital, and later while being brought to the resident emergency room physician for treatment of his bullet wound, shouted out, "Yeah, I shot the mother fucker and I hope the mother fucker dies."[37]

Suspiciously, despite the full resources of the police department and the office of the district attorney having been devoted to this case, the confession only came to light two months after the incident, and was discovered, not by police detectives or prosecutors interviewing witnesses at the time, but by investigators from the Philadelphia police department's Internal Affairs (IA) unit, who had initiated an investigation following the filing of a police brutality complaint by Abu-Jamal's attorney. As IA officers interviewed all the police and hospital personnel who had been with the defendant during his arrest and at the hospital, a hospital security guard and two police officers claimed to have heard the confession. At the trial, the security guard, Priscilla Durham, who had been friendly with Faulkner and his partner, testified about having heard Abu-Jamal's statement at the trial. When asked by Jackson, the defense attoryney, why she'd waited two months to report it, Durham claimed, for the first time, that she had reported it within a day to her supervisor, who, she claimed, had written it down. The prosecution immediately sent an officer to the hospital to try and retrieve the statement; he returned to the court within an hour bearing a typed sheet of paper. Although Durham disavowed the document, saying that her supervisor had written, not typed, the account, she testified that the substance of the typed account was substantially the same as what she had told him.[38]

A veteran police officer, Garry Bell, who also testified to having heard the identical statement by the defendant (and who was characterized by the prosecution as Faulkner's best friend on the police force), claimed he had not reported it because he had been in shock.

A second police officer told a strangely contradictory story. But the Abu-Jamal jury never got to hear about his opposing statements. A detective's interview with Garry Wakshul, another veteran officer who had been assigned to stay with Abu-Jamal from the time he was put in the paddy wagon until he was put on an operating table to have the bullet removed from his back, had been conducted within hours of the shooting incident. Wakshul, in that December, 9, 1981, interview, said of his time with Abu-Jamal, "The negro male made no comment."[39] Two months later, Wakshul claimed he had heard Abu-Jamal utter the same words cited by Durham and Bell.

On the last day of the trial, Jackson and Abu-Jamal wanted to call Wakshul in to question him about the contradiction between that claim made to IA unit investigators and his statement to detectives, the morning of the shooting, that Abu-Jamal had made no comment. (Although about a dozen other policemen had been with the suspect at the time of the alleged shouted confession, no one besides Bell, Wakshul, and Durham claimed to have heard it.) McGill vigorously objected to letting the defense bring in Wakshul, whom he claimed was away from town on vacation, and Judge Sabo agreed, saying he would not delay the trial. His final biting comment was to the defense, "Your attorney and you goofed!"[40] Sabo claimed the defense, which had had Wakshul's written statement since the start of the trial, should have called him much earlier, not on the last day of testimony. Jackson countered that he had been so overwhelmed by the task of trying the case that he had simply not noticed the crucial comment until then.

Yet at Abu-Jamal's PCRA hearing in 1995, when the defense finally was able to call Wakshul, he testified that while he was indeed on vacation on July 1, 1982, when the defense was trying to get permission to call him to the stand, he was not out of town. He had been waiting at home, where he had been "instructed" to stay until the end of the trial. It is unclear who had instructed him to keep himself available. It could have been the police department or the district attorney's office.[41] In a May 2002 interview, McGill claimed to have "no recollection" of having asked Wakshul to do so. In any event, he was not called at the trial. Had he been brought in, we can only guess how the jury would have reacted to his explanation as to why he told a detective Abu-Jamal had said nothing, only to state, two months later, that he had overheard him shout out a confession. In 1982 Wakshul had told an Internal Affairs inspector: "I didn't realize it [the alleged confession] had any importance until today."[42] This is certainly an improbable claim, coming from a police officer.

It was also discovered during testimony at Abu-Jamal's 1995 post-conviction hearing that at the time of his arrest and for a day or two following the shooting, police had briefly pursued a theory that there had been another shooter or at least another suspect in the shooting. This was based upon accounts by several witnesses interviewed by detectives immediately following the shooting, but also upon a driver's license replacement application, in the name of one Arnold Howard, that police found in a pocket of Faulkner's shirt. (At the time of the trial, the prosecution had misinformed the defense about where the license document had been discovered, reporting incorrectly that it had been found in the car owned by Abu-Jamal's younger brother William Cook.) What the defense did not know was that police had almost immediately gone to Howard's house and taken him to Homicide to be interrogated about the license application document. He was released when he showed police a receipt from a night market far from the scene with a time stamp of the exact time of the shooting. But Howard, a longtime neighbor and friend of the Cook family, testified in 1995 that he had loaned that license document to another Cook family friend, Kenneth Freeman, who was also a partner with William Cook in a sidewalk trinket stand. There is no record as to whether police ever questioned Freeman, who died under suspicious circumstances in 1985, though in the PCRA hearing Howard testified that the police had also brought in Freeman for questioning at the same time he had been there.[43]

In any event, for reasons that have never been explained, police quickly dropped efforts to locate the "fleeing suspect" reported by a number of witnesses, and the prosecution instead focused exclusively on Abu-Jamal, adopting the theory that the only people at the scene of the shooting had been Abu-Jamal, William Cook, and Faulkner.

IV

On December 18, 2001, after considering Abu-Jamal's habeas corpus petition for over two years, Third Circuit Federal District Judge William Yohn issued a 272-page opinion rejecting all twenty constitutional claims aimed at overturning his conviction. At the same time, he lifted Abu-Jamal's death sentence, claiming that the judge's sentencing instructions to the jury and the design of the jury sentencing form had been flawed. The crucial finding of Judge Yohn was that the jury instruction form and the way the trial judge delivered his instructions to the jury at the sentencing phase of Abu-Jamal's trial, which followed the jury's determination that Abu-Jamal was guilty of the murder of Officer Faulkner, confused the jury about a vital point of law. Under Pennsylvania law, the jury has to weigh those aggravating circumstances it has found against the mitigating circumstances it has found. □If it finds neither, it is supposed to vote for life without parole. □If it finds one aggravating circumstance and no mitigating circumstances, it is supposed to vote for death. □If it finds one ggravating circumstance and one mitigating circumstance, or even one aggravating circumstance and two mitigating circumstances, the jury's deliberations are supposed to proceed as follows: the jury has to decide whether the mitigating circumstance(s) outweigh the aggravating circumstance(s). It is not a matter of simple adding and subtracting. For example, killing a policeman in the line of duty (aggravating) might be considered by the jury to outweigh stable family life (mitigating) or even stable family life and no prior arrests (two mitigating).

In 1988 the U.S. Supreme Court had continued a trend of protecting the civil liberties of persons accused of crimes in general and capital crimes in particular by holding in *Mills v. Maryland* (486 U.S. 367, 384) that jury instructions, both written and verbal, had to clearly indicate to jurors that a mitigating circumstance found by just one juror was sufficient to require that that circumstance be considered by the full jury panel. In short, all the jurors had to consider the mitigating circumstance found by just one juror, whereas no juror could consider an aggravating circumstance unless all twelve agreed that the aggravating circumstance existed. Otherwise the jury decision violated the Eighth Amendment.

Judge Yohn noted that Judge Sabo had told the jurors considering the penalty for Abu-Jamal, "Your verdict must be a sentence of death if you unanimously find at least one aggravating circumstance and no mitigating circumstance. Or if you unanimously find one or more aggravating circumstances which outweigh any mitigating circumstances."[44] Judge Yohn found that "There are numerous aspects of this [Sabo's] charge that created a reasonable likelihood that the jury believed that it was obligated to consider only mitigating circumstances that were found to exist by a unanimous panel."[45]

Abu-Jamal and his attorneys, in their habeas petition, had based their claim concerning the jury sentencing form problems primarily on *Mills v. Maryland*. Although Abu-Jamal was convicted in 1982, the U.S. Supreme Court had made *its Mills* decision apply to all cases currently in their initial appeal at the time of the ruling, which included Abu-Jamal's case. Judge Yohn held that Abu-Jamal's case was subject to the precedent, because his conviction only became finalized on October 1, 1990, when the U.S. Supreme court rejected his writ of certiorari petition.

Regarding the jury sentencing form itself, which consisted of three pages, the third of which had a space to list mitigating circumstances found by the jury, Judge Yohn noted that it was this page which had lines for the twelve jurors to sign:

> I express no opinion regarding the impression created by the appearance of 12 separate signature lines on the same page as the jury is

required to indicate which, if any, mitigating circumstances it finds to exist. However, when articulated verbally in the court's charge, the proximity of these aspects of the verdict sheet do create at least an implicit correlation. . . . Indeed this aspect of the instructions indicates that there is a reasonable likelihood that the jury believed that it was precluded from considering mitigating circumstances that were not unanimously found to exist.[46]

Judge Yohn found a number of instances where he felt mistakes had been made by the prosecution or the judge during the guilt phase of the trial, but, constrained by Supreme Court precedent and the strictures of the Effective Death Penalty Act of 1996, he also found that few of these errors were unreasonable—the standard that must be met before a conviction can be overturned—and even where they were unreasonable, that they would probably not have affected the outcome of the trial.

Judge Yohn wrote that the record of the jury selection process showed that Judge Sabo's characterization of the defendant as belligerent—one of the reasons he had cited for removing Abu-Jamal's pro se right—had been incorrect. As Judge Yohn wrote:

In fact, the record reflects the opposite. Therefore I find that portion of . . . [PCRA] finding 65 concluding that petitioner had been "belligerent" is unreasonable.[47]

But he went on to say that as there were other reasons also cited for removing Abu-Jamal's right to represent himself, it did not matter that Judge Sabo had been wrong on this particular count.

On the crucial matter of the alleged confession by Abu-Jamal, Judge Yohn, in responding to the defense claim that the confession was fabricated, ruled that the PCRA fact finder, Judge Albert Sabo, had not been "unreasonable" in accepting the explanations of Officers Bell and Wakshul as to why they had waited two months to report a confession of murder. As in all his rulings on the habeas petition, Judge Yohn reached his decision based entirely on the written arguments presented by the two sides, and by his reading of the transcripts of the case. He held no evidentiary hearings during the two years he considered the petition. Judge Yohn also placed the blame for not calling Wakshul at the original trial on the defense, arguing that they should have called him earlier. Judge Yohn also ruled that Abu-Jamal, in his habeas petition, had failed to demonstrate that Wakshul's testimony, if it had been heard by the jury, would have established the lack of a confession, "rather than merely creating a credibility issue at best."[48] It is hard to understand this ruling, since raising credibility issues concerning key testimony or evidence is precisely what the defense needed to do at that point in the trial.

Yohn's decision overturning Abu-Jamal's death sentence but upholding his conviction leaves him in a legal limbo. Still incarcerated in a tiny cell on Pennsylvania's death row and held in solitary twenty-three hours a day, both he and the district attorney's office have appealed to the Third Circuit Court of Appeals. If Judge Yohn's ruling is upheld, the district attorney, Lynne Abraham, a staunch advocate of capital punishment, will have to decide whether to leave it at that, in which case Abu-Jamal, having already filed his one federal habeas appeal, would (absent an unlikely overturning of his conviction by the U.S. Supreme Court) be destined to spend the rest of his life in prison, without possibility of parole, but off of death row and in with the general prison population. The district attorney could also decide to request a new sentencing hearing, which would, of course, require the impaneling of a new jury. This would offer the defendant the chance to introduce witnesses, and possibly even to bring in new evidence, depending upon the decision of the court. It would also raise the possibility of his being returned to death row. Sources close to the district attorney's office say that it is not clear which way Abraham is likely to go, should Yohn be upheld.

A second alternative is that the Third Circuit could overturn Yohn's decision on any of the twenty claims regarding the guilt phase of the trial. In fact, Yohn did certify one of those claims to the appeals court, meaning that he urged them to accept legal arguments from the petitioner on that one claim. That was the claim of race-based peremptory challenges by the prosecution.[49] In 1986, in *Batson v. Kentucky,* the Supreme Court ruled that a prima facie case of discrimination existed whenever a prosecutor's use of peremptory challenges created a racial pattern. Whereas earlier, a defendant had to demonstrate a pattern of race-based jury selection to prove intent by the prosecution, in *Batson* the Supreme Court said that simply demonstrating race-based jury selection in the defendant's case would be sufficient.[50]

Yohn had rejected that claim, saying that the defense had failed to develop the basis for the claim during the postconviction hearing. This is true to a certain extent. When the Pennsylvania Supreme Court first considered an appeal of Abu-Jamal's conviction in 1986, it accepted as correct an affidavit submitted by the prosecutor, McGill, that he had peremptorily challenged eight black venire persons out of fifteen total peremptory challenges used. In fact, he seems to have peremptorily challenged eleven blacks (the district attorney in 1995 officially agreed to accept ten). When the state's top court reconsidered Abu-Jamal's appeal in 1999, they used the number 10, and still concluded that though this was two out of three of McGill's peremptory challenges—it did, by itself, not demonstrate a *Batson* violation. Judge Yohn, noting that the defense had subpoenaed McGill as a witness at the PCRA hearing but had chosen not to put him on the stand, said the defense was to blame for not further developing their claim.

Judge Yohn also declined to consider two jury studies submitted by appellate Abu-Jamal, both on the grounds that they covered periods of time after Abu-Jamal's trial. Here it appears that Yohn made significant errors of material fact. In the case of one study, an analysis of prosecutorial peremptory challenges by race during the terms of District Attorney Ed Rendell, Yohn confused the evidence with a second study of race in jury sentencing that had also been submitted by the defense. This second study was for the period 1983-93, and also was appropriate for Abu-Jamal's case, as he was actually sentenced in May 1983 and his case was included in the study.[51] The study he rejected, however, known as the *Hardcastle* study, had been developed by David Baldus, a law professor at the College of Law, University of Iowa, for use in a case known as *Hardcastle v. Horn*. Baldus's study not only covered the period of Abu-Jamal's trial; it included his trial. That study showed that prosecutors under Rendell over the course of his administration, which ran from 1977 to 1985, peremptorily disqualified 61.02 percent of black jurors, compared to 21.4 percent of nonblack jurors.[52]

The second study rejected on grounds of relevance by Yohn was a study conducted by the Federal Defender's Office of the peremptory challenge record of Abu-Jamal's prosecutor, Joseph McGill. A study showed that McGill, over the course of six capital trials, had rejected blacks at a rate of 74.14 percent, compared to 25.3 percent for whites.[53] Yohn, confusing that study with another study of the district attorney's office under Rendell's successor, Ron Castille, said that the study of McGill's record was not relevant to Abu-Jamal's case, since the study covered the period 1987–1991. In fact, McGill left the D.A.'s office in 1986. The study of his peremptory challenge history included Abu-Jamal's trial. As David Zuckerman, the homicide expert at the Philadelphia Public Defenders Office, noted in an interview, "Judge Yohn was confused. He could have avoided making that mistake if he had granted a hearing on the issue, where Jamal's lawyers could have explained things to him."[54]

Likewise, Yohn rejected defense efforts to introduce evidence concerning a 1986 D.A.'s jury selection training tape that openly told young assistant prosecutors how to keep young blacks and educated blacks off a capital jury without getting caught in a *Batson* violation. Although the D.A. who made that tape for the office was at the time a senior prosecutor, and has subsequently stated that he was only articulating what had long been standard practice in the Philadelphia district attorney's office in 1982 and for many years thereafter, Judge Yohn again held that the tape was too new to be relevant to the 1982 Abu-Jamal case.[55]

It is unclear what the significance of Yohn's factual errors regarding the evidentiary submissions on race-based jury selection by the D.A.'s office and by the prosecutor, McGill, might be. Attorneys familiar with capital appeals say that it should lead the Third Circuit to order a hearing on the issue. Bill Goodman, legal director of the Center for Constitutional Rights, said in an interview in July 2002, "These mistakes certainly more than open the door for the [full] Third Circuit to review Judge Yohn's opinion, because there are factual errors that require rectification and a reconsideration of his opinion. If there's real evidence that there was a systemic pattern of racial bias in jury selection in the D.A.'s office and by the prosecutor, a reviewing court has to look at that evidence."[56] In any event, the fact that the judge certified this particular claim for appeal raises the possibility that the Third Circuit could throw the matter back to him for further consideration or a hearing.

There have been a number of ironies in this case. It is ironic that it was the habeas appeal written up and filed by the attorneys Weinglass and Williams that succeeded in getting Abu-Jamal's death sentence overturned, since they were fired by Abu-Jamal while it was being considered by the federal court. His subsequent attorneys, Marlene Kamish and Eliot Grossman neither of whom has had any federal death penalty experience, were unable to get the court to accept any additional claims or amendments to the original habeas petition.[57] It is ironic, too, that Abu-Jamal, who was a moderately well known journalist and critic of the Philadelphia political establishment at the time of his arrest, has become, on death row, an internationally acclaimed writer and social critic. It would be a final irony if, after being convicted and sentenced in part because of appeals to the racial fears of the jury, he were to win a new trial because of the prosecutor's exclusion of blacks from the jury in violation of *Batson*. (In 2003 Abu-Jamal dropped Kamish & Grossman and hired San Francisco death-penalty appellate expert Robert Bryan.)

V

If Abu-Jamal had been tried and sentenced in 1960, he most likely would have already been executed. In the years after 1954, the Supreme Court, applying the Fourteenth Amendment's requirement that states provide citizens with the equal protection of the law to the interpretation of the liberties granted by the Fourth Amendment, the Sixth Amendment, and the Eighth Amendment, vastly expanded civil liberties for all Americans, and especially for nonwhites who had been subjected to systematic discrimination. Accused persons who had competent lawyers (after 1966 many defense lawyers were funded by state and federal dollars) and were tried by judges sympathetic to the Supreme Court's new rights jurisprudence received fairer treatment than they had previously. The historic bias of white-only or racially skewed juries and racist judges and prosecutors was mitigated considerably, but not entirely, as the Abu Jamal case indicates.

The significance of the Abu-Jamal case goes far beyond the question of whether or not he murdered Officer Faulkner. Due process is designed to protect the innocent, even if a guilty person occasionally goes free. The absence of due process in the Abu-Jamal case has been affirmed by Judge Yohn, who overturned Abu-Jamal's death sentence. The Third Circuit might yet order a new trial. It was the irrefutable evidence of the history of gross racial bias in Southern and non-Southern judicial and police systems and in courtrooms throughout the nation, publicized dramatically by the civil rights movement in the 1960s, that convinced the Supreme Court's justices to find mechanisms to give more protection to the civil liberties and rights of racial minorities and to all Americans accused of crimes and convicted of murder. But these new legal rights have not been universally accepted by the police and lower court judges; and often the new safeguards of civil rights have been extended only to those who can meet rigorous standards of proof of rights violations. The tension between court jurisprudence and segments of the public that was so evident in seventeenth- and eighteenth-century murder cases has persisted to the present. The influence on murder jurisprudence of strong racial bias against African Americans, Native Americans, and other peoples of color has also persisted for over four centuries.

Notes

1. *Philadelphia Magazine*, "Eighty-one People to Watch in 1981," January 1981, 107.

2. Dave Lindorff, *Killing Time: An Investigation Into the Death Penalty Case of Mumia Abu-Jamal* (Philadelphia: Common Courage Press, 2002), 33.

3. Trial transcript, *Commonwealth of Pennsylvania v. Mumia Abu-Jamal*, June 21, 1982, 153.

4. Ibid., June 19, 1982, 179.

5. Ibid., June 28, 1982, 77.

6. Ibid., June 19, 1982, 131.

7. On May 4, 2001, Abu-Jamal and his brother William each made public newly signed affidavits in which for the first time since the shooting they gave their accounts of what they said happened on the morning of December 9, 1981. The accounts, which are at variance with the testimony of some defense witnesses and which are at some points in conflict with each other, have never been accepted as evidence in any court of law. Efforts to have them included as part of Abu-Jamal's habeas petition were rejected.

8. Daniel Williams, a lawyer with the New York Capital Defender's Office, was Abu-Jamal's legal strategist during his state postconviction hearing and his state supreme court appeal. Together with Leonard Weinglass, he drafted Abu-Jamal's federal habeas corpus petition (filed in October 1999). The author interviewed Williams on May 18, 2001. Williams was unequivocal about the biases involved in the Abu-Jamal trial: "Race and politics were pervasive in this case. Race affected the jury selection process. And race and politics affected the jury's attitude towards who Mumia was. It also affected the way [prosecutor Joseph] McGill tried to sell the case to the jury. Remember, 1981 was not that long after the sixties, which really ended in about 1975. And what was the most fearful thing to the people on that jury? It was not just a black man, but an angry black man, and that's pretty much what]. McGill portrayed Mumia as. Race and radical politics were an explosive combination for these jurors."

9. Christopher Waldrep, "In a Mississippi County Court," *Journal of American History* 82 (March 1996): 1425–51, suggests the gains that African Americans made in local courts during Reconstruction, gains that eroded quickly when the withdrawal of federal troops deprived blacks of protection of their persons and their right to vote.

10. W. Fitzhugh Brundage, *Lynching in the New South: Georgia and Virginia, 1880–1930* (Urbana: University of Illinois Press, 1993); W. Fitzhugh Brundage, ed., *Under Sentence of Death: Lynching in the South* (Chapel Hill: University of North Carolina Press, 1997).

11. William Tuttle, *Race Riot: Chicago in the Red Summer of 1919* (New York: Atheneum, 1970); Gilbert Osofsky, *Harlem: The Making of a Ghetto* (New York: Harper and Row, 1966).

12. S.A. Paolantonio, *Frank Rizzo: The Last Big Man in Big City America* (Philadelphia: Camino Books, 1993), 92.

13. Frank Donner, *Protectors of Privilege* (Berkeley and Los Angeles: University of California Press, 1990), 215.

14. Matthew J. Countryman, "Civil Rights and Black Power in Philadelphia, 1940–71" (diss., Duke University, 1998), 453.

15. Ibid., 442.

16. Ibid., 215.

17. Paolantonio, 241.

18. Mike Leary, "Corruption Probes against Philadelphia Police Have a Long History," *Philadelphia Inquirer*, May 1, 1983, 11; Tim Weiner, "Focus of Police Probe Shifts to East Division," *Philadelphia Inquirer*, November 30, 1985.

19. Lindorff, 34.

20. Ibid., 35.

21. *Taylor v. Louisiana*, 419 U.S. 522, 527 (1975).

22. In 1986, in *Batson v. Kentucky*, the Supreme Court ruled that a prima facie case of discrimination existed whenever a prosecutor's use of peremptory challenges created a racial pattern. As Alan Rogers indicates in the introduction to this volume, p. [X-REF], the courts did not apply this standard rigorously.

23. Trial transcript, June 16, 1982, 153.

24. Craig Haney, "On the Selection of Capital Juries: The Biasing Effects of the Death-Qualification Process," *Law and Human Behavior* 8 (1984): 244; Craig Haney, Aida Hurtado, and Luis Vega, "'?Modern' Death Qualification: New Data on Its Biasing Effects," *Law and Human Behavior* 18 (1994): 630.

25. Lindorff, 97.

26. Trial transcript, June 21, 1982, 130. While the phrase "law and order" might seem rather prosaic and natural in a courtroom, it should be noted that back in 1981 at the start of the Reagan administration, and only six years after the Nixon administration, the term still carried a far more loaded political meaning, for it was used by both those presidents in their campaigns for office to signify a hard-nosed, anticrime attitude that disdained and derided many constitutional protections such as Miranda warnings and due process, which were deemed "liberal" and "soft on criminals."

27. Lindorff, 86–87.

28. Amnesty International, "A Life in the Balance: The Case of Mumia Abu-Jamal," *Amnesty International*, February, 17, 2000, 4.

29. Stuart Taylor Jr., "Guilty and Framed," *American Lawyer*, December 1975, 81.

30. Lindorff, 86.

31. Trial transcript, July 3, 1982, 22.

32. Ibid., 25.

33. Ibid., 63. It might be asked here whether Judge Sabo, who at this trial as always wore a special sentencing tie emblazoned with the words "law and order," was sending an improper signal to the jury that he agreed with the prosecutor.

34. Ibid., 64.

35. Lindorff, 62. The Security Index was established as a part of the Nixon administration's COINTELPRO program, and was a list of thousands of alleged radicals and subversives who were to be surveilled and, in the event of a national emergency, rounded up by police and federal agents.

36. Lindorff, 79.

37. Trial transcript, June 24, 1982, 29.

38. Ibid., 97.

39. Investigative Interview Record, Philadelphia Police Department Homicide Div., December 9, 1981, 2.

40. Trial transcript, July 1, 1982, 48.

41. Lindorff, 216.

42. PCRA Hearing transcript, *Commonwealth of Pennsylvania v. Mumia Abu-Jamal*, August 1, 1995, 61.

43. Ibid., August 9, 1995, 9.

44. Ibid, 253.

45. Ibid., 254.

46. bid., 259.

47. Memorandum and Order, *Mumia Abu-Jamal v. Martin Horn*, Commissioner, Pennsylvania Department of Corrections et al., Dec. 18, 2001, 119. Note: Since Judge Yohn determined that the removal of Abu-Jamal's pro se right had been based upon more than a determination that he was being belligerent, he offered no relief on this claim, despite a finding of error on the part of the trial and PCRA judge.

48. Memorandum and Order, 84.

49. *Batson v. Kentucky*, 476 U.S. 79, 108 (1986).

50. Ibid. See the discussion of the Batson decision in chapter 1, note (X-REF), of this volume.

51. Baldus, and George Woodworth, "Race Discrimination and the Death Penalty in the Post-Furman Era: An Empirical and Legal Analysis with Recent Findings from Philadelphia," *Cornell Law Review* 83 (1998): 1638.

52. *Hardcastle v. Horn*, no. 98-CV-3028 (E.D. Pa.).

53. Habeas petition, *Mumia Abu-Jamal v. Horn*, 94.

54. Lindorff, 88.

55. Memorandum and Order, 220.

56. Lindorff, 283.

57. One of his new lead attorneys, Eliot Grossman, had no death penalty experience; his other lead attorney, Marlene Kamish, had only been an attorney of counsel in one death penalty appeal, and she was fired from that case by her employer. Dave Lindorff, "Mumia's All-or-Nothing Gamble," *Salon Magazine,* June 15, 2001. www.salon.com/news/feature/2001/06/15/mumia/index.htm. The new attorneys have attempted to introduce evidence, in the form of an affidavit by a self-described mob hit man, Arnold Beverly, who claimed it was he, and not Abu-Jamal, who shot and killed Faulkner, but both the state and federal courts refused to accept the evidence. Both courts have noted that the witness and his story were rejected in 1999 by Abu-Jamal himself.

Mental Competency

5

Murder and Minors: Changing Standards in the
Criminal Law of Connecticut, 1650–1853

Nancy H. Steenburg

From the seventeenth century to the mid-nineteenth century in Connecticut, those few cases in which a minor (a person under the age of twenty-one)
committed murder revealed a society initially committed to biblical retribution with little apparent concern for the societal rehabilitation of a youthful
criminal.[1] At its founding, the legal system of Connecticut melded ecclesiastical law and traditional English law (both statute and common law). The
influence of Puritan religious ideals affected primarily capital laws, many of
which took their authority from quotations from the Bible. But Connecticut's
civil laws, dealing with torts, contracts, and property, drew largely on the
traditional body of English civil law, both statute and common law. Perhaps
this reflected the background of Roger Ludlow, the only trained lawyer in the
colony, who wrote Connecticut's Code of 1650. In Connecticut, the combination of ecclesiastical and secular English legal traditions complicated the
determination of a minor's legal responsibility for criminal action and led to
significant variation in the procedures used in trying minors.[2]

While the code's criminal laws initially made few distinctions between
the legal capability of minors and adults, the code's civil laws relied on
adaptations from the English common law, which regarded children as lacking in the capacity to act as independent beings.[3] Minors were not allowed to
execute contracts without the approval of a parent or adult guardian; minors
could not bring or defend a civil lawsuit without the assistance of a parent or
guardian; and minors inherited real estate conditionally, with full title often
not passing until a child reached the age of twenty-one. If a child had no
parent to assist in civil cases, a justice of the peace, magistrate, or judge
would appoint a temporary guardian. (There were few lawyers in early

Connecticut, so guardians were simply adults who could represent minors.) In criminal cases the courts were inconsistent, occasionally appointing guardians for minors.[4]

Reflecting the belief in the legal incapacity of minors, Connecticut's code contained the common law presumption that children seven years old and under lacked the understanding and thus the intent to commit a crime. Children between the ages of eight and fourteen were in an amorphous category, which the colonists called the "doubtful period." Children in this age range were viewed as incapable of telling the difference between good and evil, a common law doctrine. For most, but not all, crimes, Connecticut jurisprudence presumed that children who had reached the age of fourteen, designated the age of discretion, were as capable as adults of having an evil intent. The colony's early criminal code did not stipulate any differentiation by age in the punishment for most crimes, but, the Code of 1650 recognized differences in age for the punishment for lying and for disobedience to parents. By 1715, under the laws of the colony, arson and sodomy were no longer capital crimes if committed by a youth under the age of sixteen.[5] Nevertheless, because judges and magistrates had considerable discretion over the sentencing, punishments for minors were seldom as severe as those imposed on adults, except in murder cases. Before the nineteenth century, guardians and lawyers representing minors convicted of murder rarely argued for lesser sentences for their charges.[6]

The colony's earliest statute on murder provided no loophole for those underage, ordering the death penalty if "any person shall commit any wilful murder, which is manslaughter committed upon malice, hatred or cruelty." Not only was this language lifted nearly straight from the Bible; it also clearly indicated the murderer had to have the intent to commit the crime. Even in the nineteenth century, on paper children still faced the identical penalty as adults if they committed murder. Despite this blanket condemnation, the almost formulaic language used by the courts in adult murder indictments was at times lacking when children committed heinous crimes, perhaps an early indication that adults viewed child murderers through different eyes.

In the 1790s, the legal authority Zephaniah Swift decried the colony's and then the state's unwillingness to consider the extenuating circumstances of age and criticized the state for continuing the practice of holding youths fully responsible when they committed the crime of murder. Swift asserted that determination of guilt should not depend on age alone: he insisted that if a child between the ages of eight and fourteen "appears to have a mischievous disposition and to have conducted [himself] in such a manner as to show himself possessed of discretion, he may be considered guilty of a crime." Thus, determination of guilt also depended on the strength of the young person's understanding and capacity to discern the difference between good and evil. "Malice," said Swift, "supplies the want of age." Yet Swift was also arguing that if a child between eight and fourteen lacked malice and understanding, authorities should not apply the full penalty of the law. Swift's schema would have given judges great leeway in determining guilt or innocence and in punishing guilty children in the "doubtful period."[7]

By the middle of the nineteenth century, the influence of Enlightenment ideas about the inherent goodness of children led to increasing concern for the fate of underage murderers. The members of the General Assembly began to debate new ideas of society's responsibility toward children who broke the law. The murder cases found in Connecticut's colonial and state legal records provide insight into the change in the way adults viewed minors who committed murder. They also reveal how changes in the idea of the criminal responsibility of minors influenced the way in which the legal system examined, tried, and convicted such children.

I

In 1678, in one of the earliest cases in which a minor was tried for murder, sixteen-year-old Jonathan Stoddard was charged with four murders in the New London area of southeastern Connecticut. Just past sundown on June 6, 1678, thirteen-year-old Deborah Stebings saw Jonathan Stoddard pass by her father's house in New London as her father and Jonathan Lockwood were standing there together. After the boy walked by, Mr. Stebings and Lockwood met Mr. Thomas Bolles by the bridge; and this, according the girl's testimony, made it appear that young Stoddard must have been at Mr. Bolles's house on his way home. Elizabeth Waterhouse also testified that she saw the boy pass by her house a little after sunset that same evening. These seemingly unimportant bits of observation were a key eventually linking the Stoddard with a bloody slaughter at Bolles's house earlier that same evening.[8]

Not long after Jonathan Stoddard had passed by, Kerveebhunt, identified in the legal documents as an Indian, reported that a vicious murder had taken place at Bolles's house. An assailant had smashed Zipporah Bolles's head in with a hatchet, killing her, and had also murdered Mrs. Bolles's daughter, Mary Bolles, and her nephew, Thomas Bolles, by chopping them in their faces with the same hatchet. The only survivor of the bloody massacre was a month-old baby that Mrs. Bolles had been nursing when she died. Kerveebhunt said he suspected another Indian had committed the crime, because he had traded venison with Mrs. Bolles earlier in the day and had seen the Indian Resuekquinek trying to trade venison with the woman for rum. When the justice of the peace questioned the second Indian, he admitted that he had been at the Bolles's house, but claimed he had been unsuccessful in completing a trade. In what seemed to be an incriminating statement, Resuekquinek then asked if Mrs. Bolles and the children were dead.[9] These developments made Resuekquinek suspect in the eyes of the colonists and produced a great deal of unease in the New London area, especially because members of the community still had clear memories of King Philip's War, which had ended in southern New England in May 1676.

Because Deborah Stebing's testimony placed Jonathan Stoddard near the site of the murder, the magistrates Edward Palmer and Daniel Wetherall interviewed the boy to discover what he might know about the crime, yet did not require that Stoddard's mother or stepfather be present during the examination. This failure to notify a responsible adult may have been because the boy himself was not yet a suspect. (Had the magistrates been pursuing a civil action against the minor boy, they would have had to notify his parent or guardian so that he or she could represent him.) The teen admitted that he had passed by the Bolles's house. He claimed that, because it was late, he had decided to ask to stay there for the night. The reason he gave for passing on was that when he came to the house, he found the door open. He told the magistrate he heard no noise nor saw anyone, circumstances that convinced him to continue home to his mother's house that evening. He further testified that he did pass by the Stebings' house but saw no one else going toward Mr. Bolles's house.[10]

As a result of the testimony of both Indians, the boy himself, and the various witnesses, the magistrate initially charged Resuekquinek and a second Indian named Sucquanch with the murder of the Bolles family but did not charge the boy. The charges against Resuekquinek apparently resulted from his being in the wrong place at the wrong time; magistrates provided no additional evidence beyond what Kerveebhunt had provided. The charges Sucquanch depended on additional testimony by Kerveebhunt and by Chachasymus, a "Moheag" Indian. Chachasymus claimed that Sucquanch had said before his arrest that he would spoil one family in New London before authorities transported him. The other witness testified that while they both were in jail, Sucquanch had bragged to him that he had "helped to eat some English flesh." Though James Lathrop and John Latham (who acted as interpreters) and Sucquanch himself claimed he had merely boasted he would do some mischief to the English in the future, the magistrates indicted him for the crime against the Bolleses.[11]

Less than two months later, on July 25, 1678, Jonathan Stoddard himself went to the house of Daniel Wetherall, a magistrate in New London, to report another vicious crime. He said his stepfather, John Sampson, and his mother had gone over the river and left him to keep house and to look after his young brothers, aged six (or seven), and one. The teen's father, also named Jonathan Stoddard, had died about two years before, and his mother had married John

Sampson, a man well known to the magistrate for his quarrelsome disposition. The youth had come to report the violent death of his baby brother in circumstances that seemed to mirror the murders of the Bolleses. Young Jonathan claimed that while he was outside and at some distance from his parents' house with the older of his two brothers, he saw some Indians go into the house and come out shortly after. The sixteen-year-old said that as soon as they had disappeared, he had gone into the house and found his baby brother knocked on the head with a hatchet and lying on the floor. When the magistrate sent some officials to the house with the boy to investigate the crime, they found the baby gravely wounded but still alive. They took the infant away to try to care for it.[12]

When Wetherall questioned Stoddard again the next day about the assault, he found the boy's recollection differed from what he had reported earlier. Apparently the magistrate had some suspicions about Jonathan, because he continued to question him, eventually confronting him with the dying child, who had been taken to Palmer's house. Wetherall, apparently unconcerned about the possibility the lad would incriminate himself, also displayed the bloody murder weapon to him. This triggered a confession by the boy, who admitted he had knocked his half-brother on the head to stop him from crying. Not only did he admit to the crime, but he rather callously asserted that he had no love for the child's father and none for the child himself.[13] Nothing in Wetherall's report of the boy's confession indicated that either parent was present to protect the boy's interests or that he had informed them of his intent to examine Jonathan. Nor did the magistrate seem worried about tricking the lad into admitting his guilt.

Not content with this confession, Wetherall, remembering that the youth had been near the Bolles house on the night of the ax murders, asked the boy about his possible involvement in the prior "horrid murder." Initially the boy stuck to his earlier story that he had never been inside the house, but he eventually broke down and confessed to those crimes as well. He said he had gone to the Bolles house on the night of June 6 and had asked Mrs. Bolles if he could stay the night. Not only had the woman refused him shelter, but, Jonathan complained, she had shoved him out the door and struck him as he left, angering him. The boy related that he went around to the back of the house and entered, taking up an ax inside the house and striking Mrs. Bolles in the head as she sat nursing an infant. After she fell to the floor, he struck her again to make sure she was dead. Jonathan also admitted killing the young girl and boy who were in the house with Mrs. Bolles, because he was afraid they would go into town and tell of the crime. He asserted that he had not thought it necessary to kill the baby, because there was no danger of it telling on him. Jonathan told the magistrate that after committing the crimes, he went calmly back to his mother's house. Apparently as a further test of the boy's guilt, the magistrate had the murder weapon along with several other axes displayed to Stoddard, and the lad correctly identified the weapon and again admitted he had done the murders.[14]

In the face of the boy's confession, Wetherall formally charged him with the murder of Mrs. Bolles, her daughter Mary Bolles, and her nephew Thomas Bolles. Unlike many contemporary murder indictments, this initial indictment did not use the formulaic language that the perpetrator had been in league with the devil; it merely said Stoddard had wickedly risen up against his neighbors and taken their lives. In contrast, the two Indians earlier indicted for the murders had only been accused of rising up against their neighbors. The word "wickedly" was absent from both of their indictments. The New London grand jury found a true bill of charges against the boy and bound him over for trial in Hartford before the Governor's Assistants, who functioned as a court for the entire colony. Because of the youth's confession and lacking any factual evidence linking either Indian to the crime, the grand jury dismissed the indictments against the Indians.[15]

While much of the original investigation had taken place in the homes of the magistrates Daniel Wetherall and Ebenezer Palmer in New London, the murder trial itself took place in Hartford. Authorities carried the boy to Hartford, where William Lester and John Allyn, two of the Governor's Assistants, repeated an examination of the facts of the case on July 27, 1678. Jonathan reiterated his confession, again admitting he had given Mrs. Bolles two blows on "the hinder part of her head" and that he had killed the two children for fear they would go down to the town and tell on him. He also repeated that he had murdered his baby brother because of the child's crying. In the written record of the boy's testimony, there was no notation that his parents or any other adult had accompanied him to Hartford to look out for his defense. He was alone. The Governor's Assistants lodged a formal indictment against the boy that made it clear they considered he had had the requisite intent to commit murder. The document asserted that Jonathan, "not having the feare of God before thine eyes, [had] most wickedly and maliciously" taken the lives of Zipporah Bolles and the two children. The indictment continued by saying that the boy's actions were against both the law of God and the law of the colony, for which he deserved to die.[16]

At the actual trial before the Governor's Assistants in October 1678, the earlier evidence of witnesses that placed the boy near the murder scene and Jonathan's confession provided a clear-cut case of the boy's guilt. Again, noticeably lacking was the standard phrase found in the murder indictments of many adults—namely, that the perpetrator was influenced by the devil. It was a surprising omission, considering the biblical basis for much of the colony's criminal code.

Yet the colonial officials did hear testimony that the boy had always been terribly wicked; he was a child who cursed, lied, and stole, and was in fact a "very vile, stubborn, and rebellious child." No one provided any defense for the youth. Despite colonial law, which required that in any civil lawsuit against a minor the plaintiff had to prosecute through the child's parent or guardian, at no time in the proceedings against Stoddard was there any evidence that his mother or stepfather assisted in his defense or that any other adult served as his legal guardian or advisor. No one presented evidence that the boy's parents had not properly raised or educated him; no one mentioned that his mother and father, and later his stepfather, had previously been guilty of several breaches of the peace. No one found any reason to provide him even minimal legal protection. No one argued for a stay in the teen's execution. On October 9, 1678, the Connecticut authorities executed sixteen-year-old Jonathan Stoddard.[17]

While no one argued that Stoddard's family or even the society as a whole bore any responsibility for his crime, one hundred years later the question of adult responsibility for the moral education of children did play a part in the 1786 murder case against Hannah Occuish, a twelve-year-old, half-black, half-Pequot New London girl. By the 1780s the ideas of John Locke and Jean-Jacques Rousseau had convinced many people in the Western world that education was essential in raising moral, responsible adults. The adults responsible for Hannah would be criticized publicly for their failure to teach the girl proper morals and standards. At age twelve, Hannah was under the age of discretion, age fourteen, when children were judged capable of having evil intent.

According to the inquest following the discovery of the body of Eunice Bolles in July 1786, some unknown person had "wilfully and barbarously" murdered the girl. After an investigation, the magistrate charged that Hannah had lured the younger girl away from her home and crushed her skull with a rock, acting out of revenge because the younger girl had previously stolen some strawberries from her. A newspaper report later claimed that Hannah "had been heard to threaten" the victim and had followed Eunice, waylaying the girl on her way to school. Perhaps adding to the suspicion against Hannah was that authorities had charged her with a prior assault on seven-year-old Mary Fish when she was coming home from school. In that assault young Hannah was alleged to have beaten Mary on the head with a rock, and then stripped the child, stealing her clothes. Because Hannah's mother had concealed her, the state had dropped that earlier prosecution. Yet the prior case suggested Hannah's violent tendencies. In the murder case, the court said that Hannah's actions after she killed Eunice showed she understood the wrongful nature of her act, because she had supposedly hidden the body under some rocks on a stone wall to conceal the crime by making it appear to be an accident. The indictment claimed that Hannah acted with malice aforethought and great violence, striking many mortal blows on Eunice's head and body, so the intent to kill was clear. As in many other eighteenth-century cases against children, especially when the children were black, Native American, or poor, the court did not notify either Hannah's mother nor her master of the charges against her, nor did it provide a court-appointed guardian to assist in her defense at the time of the original hearing. Taken to the site where the authorities had found the body concealed, Hannah supposedly showed that she recognized the location and burst into tears when shown the body, displaying what onlookers decided was a guilty reaction. The magistrate and jury viewed both facts as proof both of her responsibility for Eunice's death and, more importantly, her understanding of the evil nature of her actions. The court found grounds to charge Hannah and jailed her for trial in September.[18]

At the New London County Superior Court trial, Judge Law did finally recognize Hannah's youth and appointed Timothy Larrabe, an attorney, as counsel to advise the girl. When Judge Law summarized the evidence to the jury, he pointed out the depravity of the murderous act, saying Hannah had revealed "such evidence of premeditated malice, and marks of such a mischievous and guileful discretion" in her concealment of the body to make the crime appear to be an accident that the "circumstances have supplied the want of age." She was therefore fully responsible for her evil actions. Law added that to spare Hannah from hanging would be a dangerous precedent, "holding up an idea, that children might commit such atrocious crimes with impunity." Yet the judge did take note of Hannah's youth and ignorance. He said that if the "unhappy prisoner" had been properly taught, she would not have been "so abandoned as to have committed the fatal deed." The trial documents do not record how Larrabe assisted the girl, but whatever he said was useless to shield Hannah. After hearing the evidence, the jury took only one day of deliberation to convict the twelve-year-old of willful murder and sentence her to death.[19]

In October, Hannah petitioned the Connecticut General Assembly for a "reprieve from the sentence of death." The petition, written by Larrabe, tried to play on the sympathies of assembly members. It claimed that Hannah was actually only eleven and a half years old and had descended from "low parents." The girl, wrote Larrabe, had "been totally deprived of a Christian education" and did not even know the difference between her right hand and her left. In the petition he presented a slightly different version of the crime, to support his claim that Hannah had lacked murderous intent. Hannah had intended only to whip the younger child for the earlier theft of strawberries, but when Eunice cried out, the older girl had hit her on the head to silence her. She had not intended murder. Larrabe further claimed that the ineffective hiding of the body displayed the girl's lack of understanding of right and wrong. But he could not offer any other evidence to demonstrate that Hannah lacked an understanding that deadly assault was wrong. Larrabe's petition asked the assembly to find some other suitable punishment for the child. The request evoked no sympathy from the assembly. On October 26, 1786, members rejected Hannah's plea for clemency and reaffirmed the death sentence.[20]

Newspapers noted that Hannah did not seem conscious of her fate until about two weeks before the date scheduled for her execution. The Reverend Mr. Channing "was indefatigable in his attention to her during her confinement" and finally brought the wretched child to an awareness of her impending death. The *Connecticut Courant* reported the girl was in tears the day before the execution and appeared "in distress for her soul." In reporting the death the paper picked up on Larrabe's earlier plea for clemency, noting the girl's inadequate education: "The unhappy fate of this young girl is particularly to be lamented, as it is to be charged principally to a want of early instruction and government."[21]

In an execution sermon delivered on the occasion of the girl's hanging, the Reverend Channing developed a similar theme. Channing, a young Yale tutor who had Unitarian sympathies, drew on the old Puritan concept of innate evil in asserting that the girl's actions were "striking evidence of the depravity of human nature; that we are indeed transgressors from the womb." Yet as Daniel Cohen points out, the young minister focused more attention on "the critical role of upbringing" in creating a moral adult. Thus the real point of Channing's sermon was not to castigate Hannah for her sins but to admonish not just the adults in Hannah's life but the entire community for failing in their responsibility toward her. In Lockean terms, he explained that if responsible adults did not provide the example of "virtuous principles," it would lead to the development of "those which are vicious." He blamed the girl's master and mistress for their failure to teach her proper moral standards, noting that her religious education had been neglected. Because Hannah lacked such guidance, Channing claimed, authorities could not hold the girl responsible for her actions, despite her being within the questionable area of having legal discretion. Failure to provide Hannah with a moral upbringing, Channing claimed, had resulted in her "ignominious end." Instead of blaming evil results on original sin, Channing was saying what later reformers would emphasize: that failure by parents or guardians to set their children's feet on the paths of rectitude was the cause of criminal behavior by children.[22] Legislation that reflected these ideas would not be enacted in Connecticut for another sixty years.

Writing of the child's execution in 1850, the New London historian Frances M. Caulkins lamented that the only alleviating circumstances of the case were Hannah's extreme youth and ignorance. Though Caulkins wrote that those were forcible arguments for mercy in her opinion, neither consideration had swayed the jury that sentenced the girl to death. The child died on December 20, 1786, on a gallows erected behind New London's old meetinghouse.[23] Did racial and religious bias play a role in the way the judge and jury treated pagan, nonwhite Hannah Occuish? We lack explicit evidence about the motivation of the jury, the judge, and the General Assembly. Although she was twelve, the jury and General Court concluded that Hannah understood her actions and intended to kill Esther. They could have reduced her sentence, citing her age, two years short of the age of discretion. They did not.

II

Nineteenth-century cases involving children accused of murder illuminate the influence of racial prejudice on the functioning of the Connecticut legal system. These cases also indicate the way the spreading influence of Enlightenment ideas gradually changed the attitudes of judges and juries, and led to the transformation of statute law.

Although there was no question that eleven-year-old Edward Perkins, a white boy of Norwich, shot Prudence Maples of Norwich to death in 1808, the white males who made up the jury of inquest found the death was by "misadventure or casualty." They readily accepted the "young lad's" explanation that he had "snapped it once without discharging it," so that he assumed the gun was not loaded and then had fired it[24]. Unfortunately, the record of this case is very sparse.

Eight years later the Connecticut Superior Court found twenty-year-old Minor Babcock guilty of murdering his stepfather, London Babcock, by stabbing him with a knife. Despite Minor's being underage, the original indictment identified him as a black man rather than as a youth and charged that he acted feloniously with malice aforethought. Though witnesses testified that Minor was protecting his mother from a murderous assault by London Babcock and acting only to stop the attack, the Court did not examine the question of motive or make any effort to determine whether Minor acted with the requisite malice. The defense presented twenty-three witnesses, including Merry, Thisbe, and Olive Babcock, who may have been relatives of the deceased or half-siblings to Minor, but Babcock's claim of defending his mother was not sufficient to gain him clemency from the jury. The jury found the youth guilty of murder and sentenced him to die on the gallows on June 6, 1815. Fairly late in the legal proceedings, the Superior Court had appointed William Cleaveland, Esq., as the accused's guardian *ad litem*. Unable to forestall the guilty verdict, Cleaveland filed a motion in arrest of the judgment, not on the grounds of his client's age but on the claim that one of the jurors had not been a freeholder in New London County and that the jurors had not remained together to deliberate a verdict but had gone to their own homes. The Court found the matters alleged to support the abatement were insufficient and executed young Minor. The evidence in this case suggests that the jury harshly treated a black youth who had produced significant evidence of justifiable homicide.[25] Thirteen years later, a white minor, in a somewhat comparable case, convinced a jury to reduce a murder charge to manslaughter.

In 1828, Dexter Adams, a transient mariner, assaulted a Stonington resident. (Court records did not specify Adams's exact age, only his status of being under twenty-one. There was no trial transcript, making it impossible to determine if Adams defended himself.) Josiah Isham, serving as a justice of the peace, charged Dexter with assault with intent to commit murder for his knife attack on William Sewall of Stonington. The indictment asserted that Dexter's attack on Sewall with a Spanish jackknife, had left a four-inch-deep wound on Sewall's left side between the fifth and sixth ribs. Sewall lingered from September 9, the day of the assault, until September 12, when he died of his wounds. Although the indictment drawn up by Isham included a minute description of the specific injuries and even of the murder weapon, including its cost at thirty cents, it did not identify Dexter as a minor. On the exterior of the writ, in a different handwriting, someone entered "David C. Smith is appointed guardian to Dexter a minor." Apparently the appointment of a guardian took place after the initial hearing, although Isham, from his earlier experience representing Minor Babcock, ought to have been familiar with state standards for providing representation for underage defendants. Isham summoned Thomas Cogseller and John George as material witnesses in the case, but noted on the file that they could not be found because they had put to sea on the schooner *Harriet* on September 11 to avoid testifying. Because the witnesses were inaccessible, Connecticut State's Attorney J. B. Gurley, representing the state, dropped the charges against Dexter.[26]

The state reopened the case against Dexter Adams as a murder charge at the end of September 1828, because authorities had located and arrested the witnesses Thomas R. Cogseller, George Armour, and Matthew Toole of Stonington, all of whom had fled to avoid giving evidence. At this new hearing, Isham took formal note that Dexter was underage and appointed Coddington Billings as his new guardian for the reopened case. Under Coddington's advice, the youth pleaded not guilty to the charge, but the justice of the peace found sufficient cause to arrest Dexter and commit him to the New London County jail to be held for a hearing before the New London County superior court in October 1828. At the superior court hearing, the judge clearly identified Dexter as a minor and continued Billings's guardianship of the boy. Again Dexter pleaded not guilty. The jury found him guilty of manslaughter rather than murder, but since the witnesses appeared in person, there is no record of their testimony, which must have partially exonerated the defendant. Furthermore, rather than sentencing the youth to the maximum term for manslaughter, the court sent Dexter to the newly opened Connecticut State Prison to serve a three-year punishment. Neither of Dexter's guardians appealed the sentence, though the late appointment of a guardian at the initial hearing could have been grounds for an appeal.[27]

Although John Barnum was eighteen when the state convicted him of murdering his own father, Barnum's trial and sentencing in 1833 raised an important issue of whether a minor over the age of discretion always had sufficient understanding of his actions to be executed for murder. The case for the prosecution charged that the Danbury teen had ambushed his father through an open window of his house, shooting him with a musket loaded with sand and gravel. At the trial, the boy's mother testified that John had been eating dinner with his parents "in harmony" when his father sent him on an errand to the boy's sister, who lived nearby. Moments later, a shot through the window killed the elder Barnum. Although no one witnessed the actual shooting, authorities charged John Barnum with murder.[28]

At the trial, John maintained his innocence, saying he had had no grudge against his father and no recollection of committing the crime. Reflecting this claim, evidence at the trial raised the question of the boy's mental competence. His teacher testified that the teen was "not an idiot," but added that he was "much below mankind in general understanding." The teacher pointed out that the eighteen-year-old John was far behind his peers at the school. When the jury found the lad guilty of murder and imposed a death sentence, even the presiding judge, David Daggett, was surprised, because there was evidence that the boy lacked sufficient understanding of the crime. Daggett was so convinced of the incorrectness of the verdict that he later supported the petitions that pleaded for commutation of the youth's death sentence. John's own petition for clemency revealed that he viewed with terror his impending death by hanging, but that he felt no guilt, because he could not remember shooting his father.[29]

Friends and neighbors petitioned the General Assembly for clemency for the youth, seeking commutation of the death sentence to internment in an asylum or to life in prison. John also filed a clemency petition in his own behalf, pleading for mercy because he had previously been visited by insanity. All of the petitioners stressed the boy's reduced mental capacity, repeating the teacher's claim and adding that the teacher had noted on the day of the murder that the teen's eyes had had "a wild and unusual appearance." A separate memorial from the grand jury that had indicted the boy commended the boy to the mercy of the General Assembly, saying that John had been insane eighteen months before the crime but had seemed to recover. They said that they had not anticipated the youth would receive the death sentence, because they believed his disease had returned by the time of the crime. Though adults had previously used pleas of insanity to escape the death sentence, in this case the combination of pleas concerning the defendant's youth and his questionable mental capacity led the General Assembly to eschew the death penalty.

The General Assembly committee on John's plea for mercy reviewed the facts of the case and interviewed Judge Daggett and other witnesses. It ruled that John had indeed killed his father. Nevertheless, the committee members also agreed that John's insanity had returned at the time he killed his father, and they commuted the teen's sentence to life in prison.[30]

Whether John Barnum was indeed insane or whether insanity rather than his youth had been the reason for clemency became an issue again in 1846 when John, now age thirty-one, petitioned for release from the state prison. In his petition John reviewed the facts of his case but asserted that he was but eighteen when convicted and had acted "without consideration or knowledge." Thus he seemed to allege he had lacked the necessary motive to commit the crime. He further claimed that he acted through excitement caused by the abuses of his father against him and that his father had repeatedly threatened to kill him and had once thrown an ax at him, actually endangering his life. Thus, he seemed to be arguing self-defense as justification of his actions. Notably, he did not raise the claim that he had been insane at the time of the crime. More striking was that the petition lacked any sense of remorse. John seemed to be asking the General Assembly to take into consideration his youth and heedlessness, without his accepting any responsibility for his actions. The language of repentance and reformation was missing, and perhaps in consequence the General Assembly refused to consider the petition.[31]

Five years later John Barnum again sought release from his life sentence. He wrote in his petition to the General Assembly that he had been but eighteen at the time of the crime, "young, ignorant, and very inconsiderate." He again claimed that his father had often threatened his life and had actually made a dangerous assault on him soon before the time of the crime. Differing from the prior plea, this time John admitted that he had killed his father in a fit of fear and anger. In this petition, using the language of rehabilitation, he claimed that he had reformed and been born again. Six prison officials cosigned John's petition, supporting his claim of reformation and seeking his release. Despite John's admission of guilt and his change of language, the General Assembly again refused to agree to a commutation of the life sentence. Apparently neither heedlessness nor self-preservation could work as a defense of the crime of murder.[32]

By the 1830s reform attitudes had led many in Connecticut to question whether society should treat children who broke the law with the same severity as it treated adult criminals. Many reformers now stressed that lack of education and poor moral upbringing rather than innate depravity were responsible for most of the crimes committed by children. This new attitude, reflecting the beliefs of both Judge Law and Rev. Channing in the Hannah Occuish case, had been behind the effort to create an alternative to making children serve their sentences with adults, because the adult prison provided no chance for education and no positive role models. In Newgate Prison, the state's only prison before 1828, all convicts spent every night collected together in the tunnels of the former copper mine. The new state prison in Wethersfield, completed in 1828, had individual cells, making remorse by the criminals and their reformation possible. Yet even isolation did not work to rehabilitate underage criminals. To protect children more fully from the contamination of career criminals, in 1843 the General Assembly passed a discretionary sentencing law. The statute gave judges the discretion to sentence children under sixteen to equivalent terms at the county jails, which ostensibly offered a less venal environment for the young and impressionable.[33]

The campaign to treat child criminals as patients in need of care rather than as felons in need of punishment also led to the creation of the Reform School for Boys in Meriden in 1853. Even murder cases illustrated the transformation of public attitudes about youthful responsibility for crime. A murder case from 1854 revealed how those currents of reform influenced public attitudes toward minors who committed murder.

A crime nearly as horrific as the murder of Zipporah Bolles and the children shocked and horrified New Haven County in 1853. Returning from church in North Haven on July 24, 1853, Barzilla Bradley, "one of the most respectable citizens of North Haven," had found his wife Esther brutally stabbed to death, "horribly mutilated and weltering in blood." Though Mrs. Bradley had been ill and had been too weak to attend church, she had "fought desperately with the fiend who had attacked her." Blood soaked her apron, and wounds on her hands indicated she had tried to use them to shield her face from the knife. Though the inquest determined that the cause of death was loss of blood from over fifty stab wounds, after Mrs. Bradley had fallen to the floor under the rain of blows, her murderous assailant had slit her throat from ear to ear, cutting to the back of the windpipe and sawing back and forth to enlarge the wound. Barzilla Bradley also found that the murderer had ransacked the house and removed all the valuables he could carry away, leaving bloody handprints and footprints to mark his passage.[34]

As reported in the local newspapers, Bradley immediately directed suspicion toward "an Irishman" who had worked for him a few months previously. The grieving widower claimed the man had left without settling for his wages but that his son had seen him in town the day before the murder, though the two had not spoken. More damning was an eyewitness report that three-quarters of an hour prior to the estimated time of the murder, a neighbor had seen "a man answering the description of this Irishman" wearing a straw hat, brown pants, a checked shirt, and a coat going up the road toward Bradley's house. The same witness testified he had seen the man return between 1 and 2 P.M.; no longer was he wearing the coat. Only belatedly did the newspaper reveal that the Irishman was in fact just a teenager, a seventeen-year-old Irish youth named Michael Jennings.[35]

Michael Jennings was an Irish boy who had worked for Bradley in his brickyard earlier in the summer. Michael had contracted to work for Mr. Bradley for a few weeks, but, according to some witnesses, had stayed only fifteen days, supposedly long enough to learn the family's habits. Michael then left without giving notice or any reason for leaving his job other than to claim he had found another job at higher wages. Bradley refused to pay him for his work for the short time he had stayed, but Michael considered that Bradley owed him for his time. Bradley later testified that he, indeed, had not paid the youth, assuming they would settle accounts at a later date. The youth then hired himself out to Amos Harrison of Northford, who lived about six miles from the Bradleys; he agreed to work for him for a period of one and a half months. In what seemed to the suspicious authorities part of a premeditated plan, the boy had lied to Mr. Harrison, telling him that he had just arrived in the area directly from New York, and concealing that he had been working locally for Mr. Bradley. Just a few days later, Michael left the Harrisons' farm saying he was returning to New York City.[36]

More circumstantial evidence mounted against the youth. On July 20, Enos Camp of Durham had given the boy a ride into New Haven, where the youth stayed until Sunday the twenty-fourth. Witnesses claimed that Michael knew the Bradleys' practice of weekly church attendance, and also knew that Mrs. Bradley was a small, weak woman who was too ill to attend church. In the chain of damaging evidence, as reported by the newspapers, witnesses saw Jennings going toward the Bradleys' house on foot the morning of the crime and spotted him returning from the house an hour and a half later.[37]

When authorities arrested Michael the next day in New Haven near the railroad station on the suspicion that he had committed the murder, the teen's clothes were wet, as though recently washed, and blood had soaked into his boots. Michael's explanation of the blood and newly washed clothes was that he had helped some friends slaughter a pig. More incriminating was the discovery of a bloody pocketknife in the youth's pocket, a knife with a broken edge and snapped point that matched pieces of a knife taken from Mrs. Bradley's breastbone. The *Hartford Courant* said this proved the knife had killed the woman, and it fixed the blame on the youth "unless he can show otherwise." Perhaps more damaging to the youth's claim of innocence was that his boot matched a bloody boot print found outside the house, placing him at the site of the murder. Though the arresting officer found no valuables upon the boy, the local newspaper reported he had disposed of the loot with Richard Connor, Connor's wife, and Connor's brother, fellow Irish immigrants.

The police found the three had some of the stolen money and arrested them as well. When confronted with the supposed evidence of his involvement, Michael asserted that he had spent the previous afternoon at the Catholic church in New Haven, but the fact that no one could testify to his being there seemed damning evidence, adding hypocrisy to the murder. In fairly short order the court found Michael guilty of murdering Mrs. Bradley and sentenced him to death.[38]

The reaction among the Irish community was prompt, but Irishmen were not the only people who protested the death penalty for the boy. Nine different petitions for clemency arrived at the Connecticut General Assembly; all sought a commutation of the death sentence to one of life imprisonment. Many of the signers did bear Irish surnames, but the majority did not. Most shared the attitudes found in a separate petition from the boy's father, James Jennings, writing from Brooklyn, New York. Jennings wrote that Michael had just turned eighteen and had always been of good character; according to his father, he was a kind, affectionate brother and a mild, peaceable, and affectionate companion. He mentioned the lad's industrious and steady habits and vowed that he had never committed a crime, having spent nearly all his life "in the country, surrounded by healthy moral influences." Mr. Jennings was adamant that "no felon's blood flowed in his veins." He described the situation between his son and the Bradleys, saying that no unkind feeling existed between them and the boy, and that though Bradley did owe his son money, Michael had had no complaint against Mrs. Bradley. After asserting that all the evidence was circumstantial, he also claimed that if his son had indeed killed Mrs. Bradley, he had not done so with malice or premeditation, but because he was afraid of getting caught. Michael's case, the father said, differed "very widely from that of old and hardened offenders who wind up a long life of crime and infamy with a deliberate murder in cold blood." Yet, complained Jennings, the law made no distinction between such career criminals and his son and punished them equally. Speaking the language of those who sought to reform the criminal justice system for minors, Jennings concluded that reformation was one of the principal objects of punishment and could not be achieved by executing his son.[39]

Clearly influenced by the reform impulse, a majority of the General Assembly members on the Committee on Capital Punishment initially supported the pleas for clemency and recommended commutation of the death sentence to one of life in prison. Reviewing the trial evidence and the various petitions, the members agreed with Mr. Jennings that the evidence was entirely circumstantial. They said there had been no evidence of quarrels between the boy and the Bradleys, nor had there been any problems between Michael and the Harrisons. The Irish youth had even gotten along well with both the Bradley and Harrison children. The committee members clearly accepted the idea that Michael's youth and lack of understanding of the consequences of his actions had been important factors in the events leading up to the crime, if he had actually killed Mrs. Bradley. They said the state claimed that the boy had returned to the Bradleys' home to collect money owed to him for his work for Mr. Bradley. "To a youth of seventeen, this might not appear criminal." They viewed the fact that the boy carried only a pocketknife as evidence of lack of premeditation. They explained the killing of Mrs. Bradley as the reaction of a frightened, trapped youth who saw in her unexpected presence a bar to "reputation, safety, and liberty"; thus, he had no intent to murder, just to escape. They agreed with the boy's father that he was very unlike the old and hardened offenders who normally received the death sentence, and the majority of the committee recommended that a life sentence would better serve the ends of public justice. Testimony from Michael's jailers in the New Haven County jail supported the idea that the boy could be reformed; they said that his behavior had improved in the months he had been in jail awaiting trial and sentencing. In a final plea for mercy, the committee added that it would be more congruent with Christianity not to hurry Michael into "the presence of his Maker" while he was still in his boyhood.[40]

In response to the majority committee's recommendation of clemency, the indignation of the minority report from the Committee on Capital Punishment was palpable. This opposing report built up a damning case against the boy. The hostility was apparent in the opening sentence of the document that called Michael an Irish man. There was no sympathy evident for the boy's youth or inexperience. The first strike against Michael was that he had but lately arrived from Ireland. Second were the alleged lies he told when obtaining work, first from the Bradleys and then from the Harrisons. The members said the fact that the attack took place on a Sunday, when the boy knew the "small, feeble woman" would be home alone, proved premeditation. The report provided as proof of malicious intent the fact that he had ransacked the house and taken all the valuables he could carry. These facts proved that the youth had intended robbery rather than merely collecting what was owed to him. The committee members disposed of the claim that Michael was of good character, saying it was unreliable because the source of that claim was the boy's own father. Furthermore, they rejected the claim that imprisonment could reform the teen. Instead they asserted that, rather than his deportment improving while in jail, the boy's behavior had been worse than that of any other prisoner; he was sullen, uncooperative, obscene, and profane. The minority, which did not cite any specific evidence to contradict the report of the jailors, recommended that the state carry out the death sentence.[41]

Although the recent opening of the State Reform School for Boys in Meriden was ample evidence of strong support for more lenient treatment of underage criminals, the minority report calling for Michael's execution was more influential on the members of the General Assembly as a whole. After first postponing its decision, the General Assembly then rejected the petitions for clemency and refused to commute Michael's sentence.

Though an editorial in the *Hartford Courant* had revealed wide public support for the reform school because prisons lacked any "reformatory or educational" influences, the General Assembly's refusal to mitigate Michael's punishment clearly showed that the desire to maintain law and order and to provide swift and sure punishment was stronger than any desire to redeem unfortunate youths.[42]

III

In the late eighteenth century, a minor murder defendant under the age of discretion (fourteen) accused of murder was treated harshly and executed, perhaps because she was non-white. (Children under fourteen were usually treated less severely than minors between fourteen and twenty-one.) In the nineteenth century, an accused minor in the same age category was treated leniently, but there appear to have been significant extenuating circumstances. In nineteenth-century cases involving mentally sound minors between the ages of fourteen and twenty-one, in one case a jury chose to accept evidence of extenuating circumstances presented by a white minor in this age category, but in another case what appears to have been more extensive mitigating evidence offered by witnesses on behalf of a black minor did not sway the jury. John Barnum, age eighteen, could not plead extenuating circumstances, but his friends, neighbors, and a grand jury sought clemency, because they believed John had reduced mental capacity. The General Assembly concurred. By the 1830s and thereafter, the citizens of Connecticut were softening their attitude toward criminals judged to be mentally deficient and toward children who broke the law. Connecticut jurisprudence had finally accepted some of the ideas of the Enlightenment. But the Enlightenment tradition produced both theories of racial equality and theories of racial stratification. The long-standing bias of Europeans and Americans against nonwhite peoples was rarely challenged in the eighteenth and nineteenth centuries, a sad reality that may have cost Hannah Occuish and Minor Babcock their lives.[43]

Notes

1. The incidence of crimes committed by children was very low. The author examined all records of the Particular Court (a Hartford court that preceded the creation of county courts) and the New London County Court, 1639–1855. Fewer than

3 percent of all the cases found in these court records identified either party to the case as a minor, and most of these minors were involved in civil cases. Murder cases in which the defendant was under the age of twenty-one were very rare. These findings indicate that for low-frequency crimes, sampling is not an effective research methodology. The complete body of relevant records must be examined.

2. Bruce Mann, *Neighbors and Strangers: Law and Community in Early Connecticut* (Chapel Hill: University of North Carolina Press, 1987), 7–9, asserts that early civil cases in Connecticut did not reflect the common law, because few colonists had legal training. But the civil laws in the Code of 1650 provide evidence that the English common law was an integral part of Connecticut's legal system. *The Code of 1650* (Hartford, Conn.: Silus Andrus, 1830), 64. Albert E. Van Dusen, *Connecticut* (New York: Random House, 1961), 65–67, makes a cogent argument for Ludlow's authorship of the Code of 1650. Edgar G. McManus, *Law and Liberty in New England* (Amherst: University of Massachusetts Press, 1993), 4, 10, 12, which focuses primarily on Massachusetts, sees a significant erosion of biblical influence on capital law, 1630–42 and thereafter. This was especially manifest in the significant reduction of the number of crimes categorized as capital crimes. (These crimes were converted to noncapital criminal offenses.)

3. The Code of 1650 invoked the concept of the age of discretion and applied it to lying, setting a penalty of fines and whipping for "every person of the age of discretion, which is accounted fourteen years, who shall wittingly and willingly make a lie." Younger children "such as being under the age of discretion," were to be corrected (in the presence of a magistrate) by their parents. In the colony's so-called stubborn child laws, the death penalty applied to boys over sixteen who refused to obey their parents, and to any child of either gender of over age sixteen who cursed or hit a parent. Ibid., 29, 64. While my research did not turn up a single case in which the colony executed a child for stubbornness or for striking a parent, the existence of the law (based on the Bible) showed that adults recognized that children under sixteen had a lesser capacity to understand the consequences of their actions.

4. See the observations by the eighteenth-century legal expert Zephaniah Swift, *A System of the Laws of the State of Connecticut*, vol. 1 (Windham, Conn.: John Byrne, 1795), 217–18.

5. *Code of 1650*, 335–36; *Acts and Laws of His Majesties Colony of Connecticut in New England* (New London, Conn.: Timothy Green, 1715), 13.

6. If those representing minors argued for leniency, the arguments were not recorded in the legal records. McManus, 117, argues that seventeenth-century courts opted for milder treatment of minors convicted of crimes, except murder, because children were "better candidates for rehabilitation."

7. *Code of 1650*, 64–65; *Acts and Laws of His Majesties Colony of Connecticut*, 68; Zephaniah Swift, *A Digest of the Laws of Connecticut*, vol. 2 (Hartford, Conn.: 1797), 368

8. Crimes and Misdemeanors, ser. 1, vol. 1, part 1, Connecticut Archives, 104–5, Connecticut State Library (hereafter CSL).

9. Ibid.

10. Ibid., 108.

11. Ibid., 107

12. Ibid., 109a; New London County, County Court Records, vol. 3, September 1676. #86.

13. Crimes and Misdemeanors, 109a.

14. Ibid., 109a, 109b, 110.

15. Ibid., 112a.

16. Crimes and Misdemeanors, 110.

17. Ibid., 114; New London County, County Court Records, vol. 1, , #53, #62, CSL; Frances M. Caulkins, *History of New London* (Hartford, Conn.: 1860), 369.

18. Connecticut Superior Court, New London County files, CSL, Box 21, March 1780, case 34; *Connecticut Courant,* July 31, 1786; Connecticut Superior Court New London County files, CSL, Box 25, September 1786, case 74.

19. Connecticut Superior Court New London County files, CSL, Box 25, September 1786, case 74; *Connecticut Courant*, October 9, 1786 and October 30, 1786. Thank you to Denise Grosskopf for directing my attention to the newspaper articles on this case.

20. Connecticut General Assembly Papers, 1786, Petitions, Resolves, 306, CSL.

21. *Connecticut Courant*, December 25, 1786.

22. Daniel Cohen, *Pillars of Salt, Monuments of Grace* (Oxford: Oxford University Press, 1993), 90–93.

23. Ibid.; Frances M. Caulkins, *History of New London, Connecticut* (New London, Conn.: 1895), 576–77.

24. New London County Superior Court, Papers by Subject, Box 134, Inquests, 1711–1870 A–M, May 23, 1810, CSL; Connecticut Superior Court, New London County, "Records of Trial," vol. 3, January 1816, case 50, CSL.

25. *Black Roots in Southeastern Connecticut,* (Detroit: Gail Research Company, 1980), 15; Connecticut Superior Court, New London County files, Box 42, January 1816, case 50, CSL.

26. Connecticut Court Records, Justice Courts, Box 569, New London, Josiah Isham, Justice of the Peace, September 1828, CSL.

27. Connecticut Superior Court, New London County, "Record of Trials," vol. 5, October 1828, case 96, CSL; Connecticut Superior Court, New London County files, Box 50, October 1828, case 96, CSL.

28. Connecticut General Assembly Papers, Box 18, 1833, Continued Petitions and Resolves, 1–45, #5A, 9A, CSL.

29. Ibid. It is notable that at the original trial neither John nor anyone else raised the question of parental abuse to explain or justify John's action.

30. Connecticut General Assembly Papers, Box 18, 1833, Continued Petitions and Resolves, 1–45, #5A, 9A, CSL.

31. Connecticut General Assembly, Rejected Bills, Box 21, folder 131, 1846, #86, CSL.

32. Connecticut General Assembly, Rejected Bills, Box 26, folder 173, 1851, #51, CSL.

33. Connecticut General Assembly Papers, Box 36, 1833, File 1–116, #47, CSL.

34. *Hartford Courant*, July 26, 1853, 2; Connecticut Assembly, Rejected Bills 1853–54, Box 29, folder 195, 1854, # 68 G–H, CSL.

35. *Hartford Courant*, July 26, 1853, 2.

36. Connecticut General Assembly, Rejected Bills 1853–54, Box 29, folder 195, 1854, #68A, CSL.

37. *Hartford Courant*, July 26, 1853, 2

38. Ibid.; Connecticut General Assembly, Rejected Bills 1853–54, Box 29, folder 195, 1854, # 68 G–H, CSL.

39. Connecticut General Assembly, Rejected Bills 1853–54, Box 29, folder 195, 1854, #70 A–C, 71–80, CSL.

40. Ibid., #68 A

41. Ibid., #69 A–D.

42. Ibid., #69 D, CSL; *Hartford Courant*, August 20, 1853, 2. The state executed Michael on July 11, 1854, on a gallows in the yard of the New Haven County Jail.

43. David Brion Davis, *The Problem of Slavery in the Age of Revolution, 1770–1823* (Ithaca, N.Y.: Cornell University Press, 1975).

6

Murder and Madness:
The Ambiguity of Moral Insanity
in Nineteenth-Century Connecticut

Lawrence B. Goodheart

In a presidential address to the Connecticut Medical Society, Dr. Francis Bacon complained in 1888 of that "illogical chimera of American medical jurisprudence—'transitory frenzy,' or 'acute moral insanity.'" State courts, he charged, "share in the general disrepute into which American tribunals have fallen on account of the frequency and confidence with which insanity is pleaded as a defense in criminal cases."[1] Three years earlier, Dr. Patrick Cassidy, a colleague from Norwich, told the same organization that "wily lawyers" abetted by some physicians assume that "all moral depravity is moral insanity." Instead he argued that "the distinction between crime and insanity should be clearly defined. This necessitates a knowledge of what insanity really is, and how we may judge the responsibility of an alleged insane criminal."[2]

Ironically, a half century earlier another generation of physicians, enthusiastic about the new specialty of asylum medicine, had thought they had done just that in broadening the concept of insanity. In response to prior European developments, a wave of asylum building occurred in the United States after 1830. Physicians argued that institutionalization of the insane was more humane and effective than traditional home care or other forms of treatment. Asylum doctors gained professional recognition with the formation of the Association of Medical Superintendents of American Institutions for the Insane in 1844 and publication of the *American Journal of Insanity* in 1845. They also gave expert legal testimony.[3]

Connecticut illustrates in important ways the national discord over forensic psychiatry during the nineteenth century. This essay also provides new knowledge about the moral insanity defense at the state trial level, a neglected subject.[4] The state was a leader in the new asylum medicine and the professional assertion of physicians. Opened in 1824, the Hartford Retreat for the Insane was the only institution of its kind in the United States founded by a state medical society.[5] Dr. Eli Todd, superintendent from 1824 to 1833, gained international recognition for his claim of some of the highest cure rates in the Western world. His application of "a law of kindness" to the insane relied significantly on "moral" or emotional techniques in treatment. The innovation of moral treatment readily translated into the concept of moral insanity; both shared great appreciation for the psychology of behavior, particularly the abnormal.[6]

Todd's protégé, Dr. Amariah Brigham, superintendent of the Hartford Retreat for the Insane from 1840 to 1842, promoted the concept of moral insanity. A resident in Hartford during the 1830s, Brigham had in several major works introduced European neuroscience to America and laid the intellectual foundation for the concept of moral insanity.[7] Theorists, particularly the Austrians Frans Joseph Gall and Johann Kaspar Spurzheim and the Scottish brothers Andrew and George Combe, correlated specific structures of the brain with certain mental functions. The popular form of the theory was phrenology.[8]

Asylum medicine, a harbinger of what would be called psychiatry after 1900, was far from being established. Before and even after the opening of the Hartford Retreat, medical models did not overwhelmingly influence the determination of mental disorder. Nor did physicians play an exclusive role in the care of the mentally ill. Instead, population dispersion and town government in a largely rural setting usually made mental illness a family and community concern governed by informal practices. During the colonial era and later, home care, folk remedies, and religious lore were the norm. Lay opinion was weighed in judgment as well as that of physicians, ministers, and other elite figures.[9]

In contrast, the professionalization of medicine during the late eighteenth century contributed to a medical model of madness. The growing belief that mental illness was a natural phenomenon humanized madness and suggested the relevance of medicine. The founding of the Connecticut State Medical Society in 1792 marked a notable assertion among physicians. Bloodletting, purges, and often ineffective drugs still remained standard. Rather than major technological breakthroughs, a growing sense of professional confidence and humanitarian purpose prompted innovation. Physicians deplored the nontherapeutic sequestration of the insane and pointed to some egregious examples of cruelty. A vanguard of state doctors, as early as 1800, called for hospitalization of the insane. Although the creation of asylums would have consequences diametrically different from what the founders hoped, the institutionalization of the insane during the nineteenth century radically transformed long-standing practice.[10]

An age-old Anglo-American tradition held a defendant not guilty by reason of insanity, because of a lack of mental capacity to appreciate the criminality of the deed. The critical judicial determination of non compos mentis rested not only on legal precedents but on common sense and community standards.[11] Drawing on European thought, the American Isaac Ray in 1838 published his influential *A Treatise on the Medical Jurisprudence of Insanity*, the first text of its kind in English. The young Maine doctor redefined the model of madness to include "moral mania," otherwise known as "moral insanity." He explained that "cerebral organization" and hence mental functioning were liable to disease; therefore "the *affective* as well as *intellectual* faculties are subject to derangement."[12]

The premise that not only rational but emotional judgment might be impaired through disease had vast implications for the law. Regarding one who was morally insane, Ray concluded that "to judge his acts by the standard of sanity and attribute to them the same legal consequences as to those of sane men would be clearly unjust, because their real tendency is not and cannot be perceived by him."[13] Five years later, in England, the McNaughten rule was developed by the courts. It applied the "knowledge of right and wrong" as a test of insanity. Although the McNaughten rule became standard in American courts, it varied in application.[14] For example, in 1841 the Massachusetts courts ruled that moral insanity was characterized by "irresistible impulse," a standard adopted in Connecticut. Thus, in Isaac Ray's formulation, overwhelming emotions might lead an individual to a criminal act without impairing cognition. The legal conundrum was in the determination of culpability. Were the passions emphatically beyond control, or could they have been reasonably expected to have been suppressed? These innovations extended the opportunity for a legal defense based on moral insanity.[15]

The thesis of this essay is that the new psychiatric paradigm did not bring greater precision, but rather more complexity and heightened controversy to medical jurisprudence. Now the emotional as well as the rational had to be weighed on the scales of justice. Addressing the issue of moral insanity in 1858, Justice William Wolcott Ellsworth of the Connecticut Supreme Court pondered, "Whether the person accused had, at the time of the act, sufficient understanding to know the nature and effect of the act for which his is put on trial. . . ."[16] If so, the defendant might be punished; if not, the accused was not criminally responsible.

Although the law was procedurally straightforward, the fundamental problem was philosophical. Even medical specialists differed over whether moral insanity existed ontologically. And epistemologically, how was it to be diagnosed? As with mental disorder in general, the etiology was more speculative than empirical. As a Connecticut court put it in 1876, "Unsoundness of mind is a fact which is not susceptible of direct proof." In addition, the fatalism of moral insanity grated against the free will ethic in a culture in which reformed Protestantism and liberal capitalism stressed individual accountability, personal discipline, and self-control. Controversy escalated over the course of the century; the public, justices, and physicians were at odds. The latter often disputed among themselves. Juries, composed of laymen, had to resolve all these issues.[17]

The first Connecticut case to contribute to the development of medical jurisprudence was the now forgotten 1835 trial of the ax murderer Agostinho Rabello. Brigham thought that the Rabello trial was an important opportunity for asylum doctors to assert their expertise.[18] They nonetheless had to contend during the proceedings not only with diverse professional opinion, but with a citizenry who valued their own intuitive ability to identify who was mad and who was not. The verdict of insanity (see below) first made clear for nineteenth-century America that moral insanity was a medical matter with profound legal implications. The Rabello precedent, however, proved only a momentary triumph for the new model. In Connecticut and elsewhere, the protean quality of moral insanity at best suggested imprecision and at worse a means to evade responsibility. Three subsequent murder trials in the state reviewed by the Connecticut Supreme Court—those of Willard Clark in 1855, John Andersen in 1876, and Edwin Hoyt in 1878—reveal the increasing problematic nature of the moral insanity defense. Over the course of the century, the profession of medicine fell short of the antebellum promise that it would bring clarity and consensus to the complex legal issues raised by mental illness and personal responsibility.[19]

I.

The facts of the homicide committed by Agostinho Rabello were as clear as the murder was grisly, but the apparent motivation was incredible. Rabello, a Portuguese national in his early thirties, had lived for six weeks in the home of Beer and Sally Beardsley, where he was employed as a cobbler in their workshop. The victim was the Beardsley's only son. Why had the perpetrator brutally killed a twelve-year-old boy in New Preston for accidentally stepping on his toes? The case also reveals much about social relations in an antebellum New England village when an impoverished stranger arrived looking for work.[20]

The superior court at Litchfield heard a variety of witnesses with distinct interpretations of the defendant's sanity. The Beardsley family related that Rabello lived with them during the six-week time of his employment, a common arrangement for hired men in the countryside. Ferris, a twelve-year-old, had accidentally bumped Rabello's foot, an elder sister explained, while serving him bread on Saturday. The workman glared and angrily rebuffed the boy, exclaiming, "Is there no other way [to walk]?"[21] Various witnesses offered that Ferris was an amiable boy who had previously had an untroubled relationship with Rabello, with whom he shared sleeping quarters. Now Ferris confided to his sister that he was afraid of the hired man.

The next Monday morning at 6:00 A.M. Ferris fetched kindling for the breakfast fire, and Rabello followed him outside. Beneath a budding apple tree, the hired man pulled an ax from the chopping block. As Ferris stood with his back to him engaged in his chore, Rabello committed a "most barbarous and fiendlike homicide," as a local newspaper put it.[22] With a series of violent blows, the boy's head was split open, body parts were severed, and the torso was mutilated. The gory tool was left with its head buried deep in the ground. Rabello gathered his things and fled. The mother discovered the mangled corpse and cried alarm. Rabello was captured without resistance at a nearby creek where he was washing off the victim's blood. Officials placed him in the local jail.

A number of local people, including Ferris's father, concluded that Rabello was sane and responsible for his actions. The *Litchfield Enquirer* perceptively summed up the quandary of the brutal murder of the boy. "It seems strange indeed," the newspaper editorialized, "that any person in his right mind could be so base and so hardened as to commit such a horrid act; but we understand he shows no symptoms of insanity, or weakness of intellect."[23] Although a "foreigner," Rabello spoke fluent English, wrote well, and conversed with all. In other words, there was no obvious sign that the Portuguese man was a homicidal maniac. He was well known and had lived in the area, albeit under difficult circumstances, for nearly two years.

James Wilson of Fairfield, who had employed Rabello in the early autumn of 1833 for almost two months, found "no indications of insanity."[24] Wilson had first encountered him in August 1833 and learned that he was an itinerant whose journeys had taken him from Portugal to Brazil, Philadelphia, and New York. Homeless and poor, he was living in an abandoned cider mill, and Wilson took him home. A neighbor who hired Rabello for three weeks subsequent to his employment with Wilson "did not consider him insane" but well informed.[25] He had worked side by side with Rabello in the field pulling turnips, and the hired man had walked his son to school without incident.

Rabello's marginal existence, however, had brought him into antagonism with local officials. He had arrived in central Connecticut from New York penniless and hungry. Sometimes he slept alongside the road or in graveyards; other times he boarded for work or stayed in abandoned buildings. During the long New England winter he wore a heavy cloak and stopped at people's doorsteps asking for work. Looking woebegone, he fitfully accepted a handout when no employment beckoned. On occasion the selectmen "warned" him out of town, a procedure in which officials expelled the wandering poor out of their jurisdiction so that undesirable nonresidents would not become a financial burden.[26] Yet on occasion Rabello was also supported by town funds as a charity case who resided with a local family or was placed with a keeper of the poorhouse.[27] He nonetheless remained in the vicinity in various forms of dependency, destitution, and dejection.

One philanthropic couple took pity on him. Schuyler Seely, a Trumbull selectman, and his wife treated Rabello, whom they found living in a graveyard, with "kindness."[28] They brought him food and had him to Sunday breakfast. He complained of tormentors, by whom Seely thought he meant officials who warned him out of town. Seely thought Rabello "crazy."[29]

When riled, Rabello's would often become violent. He also complained of persecution, but in a vague, general sense. Henry Lum dismissed Rabello from Lum's shoe shop because of poor work habits. Rabello responded with excited behavior and threatened his employer, "You will be skinned like the eels."[30] Lum also remembered that Rabello had complained about tormentors who trod on his toes. They "ought to be broken to pieces," he warned.[31] Lum concluded he was "a deranged man."[32] Ezra Morehouse, who kept Rabello on town charity, found him "an ugly tempered fellow."[33] He became enraged at a three-year-old girl who stepped on his toes. On another occasion, he resisted being taken to the poorhouse by pulling a shoe knife on the keeper.[34]

Timothy Risley, who employed Rabello for two weeks in June 1834 as a gardener in Bridgeport, was impressed with his knowledge of viniculture and judged him "a polished man."[35] He had town officials evict him from his property, however, after Rabello and other workmen got into a heated dispute. Risley concluded that Rabello was revengeful but not insane.

In two incidents, Rabello had sparked a dangerous level of violence. Isaac Thorp, who had worked with Rabello in Weston, found that he was short-tempered. One official encouraged him to seek treatment at the Hartford Retreat for the Insane. Meanwhile, at a project where heavy rocks were being removed, another laborer dislodged a stone that struck Rabello's foot. Rabello confronted him with a raised ax. With an uplifted crowbar in his hands, Thorp told Rabello to lay down the ax or he would kill him. Rabello desisted. Thorp surmised that he was "perfectly sane except when angry," an implicit recognition that mental disorder might manifest itself only in specific circumstances.[36]

At the same place, David Patchen warned an incensed Rabello out of town. Rabello swung an ax at the constable's head that came so close that the officer felt a rush of air on his face. Warned sharply, Rabello dropped the tool but was not arrested. Patchen recalled that his assailant "cursed our laws, stamped his feet, grated his teeth, said he could find no peace anywhere, and that our laws [, which] ground men into dust, were worse than in the old countries."[37] The constable characterized Rabello as not insane but as a man with a violent temper.

The officials who apprehended Rabello after the killing saw no clear signs of insanity in Rabello's demeanor. Rabello told two justices of the peace and a constable, "I did the deed, but am not guilty. I was tempted, I was insulted."[38] In other words, the boy had stepped on his toes; therefore, Rabello killed him. Although it was not raised as a motivation, perhaps the tension between honor and shame in antebellum culture predisposed Rabello to meet a purported insult with violence. A perceived affront to his manhood, a violation of personal identity, compelled his disproportionate response.[39]

Physicians were more convinced of Rabello's derangement than was the public. Several doctors examined Rabello sometime after the homicide. Although he had been hospitalized in Brazil and was in ill health, he had received no medical care in Connecticut, because he could not afford treatment. Nonetheless, several physicians in the area, like other citizens, had informally encountered Rabello and formed interpretations of his mental state. Dr. Noah Dyer of Trumbull thought him "malicious, not insane," as did a Salisbury physician.[40] In contrast, two New Preston physicians thought him "crazy," with one identifying Rabello as a "monomaniac," a diagnosis that Isaac Ray included under moral mania.[41]

Indeed, most doctors endorsed the latter diagnosis, which had gained currency with the development of asylum medicine. The attending physician, Dr. J. B. Beckwith of Litchfield, described a "partial alienation of mind." He observed that Rabello was indifferent and withdrawn, but when he considered himself insulted, he responded with a "paroxysm of increased irritability."[42] Dr. Silas Fuller, then superintendent of the Hartford Retreat for the Insane, explained that "it is well settled that one faculty of the mind may be deranged, while the rest are sound." As part of the examination, a local physician, named Dr. Plumb, sitting next to Rabello, placed his foot on the defendant's; the latter's pulse shot up, his face flushed, and he became enraged. This clever experiment confirmed the diagnosis for Fuller. As he put it, "The insane idea is, that all his friends are enemies, and this hostility is shown by stepping on his toes, mocking him, etc." He concluded that "the dominion of monomania is complete over the mind."[43] The jury concurred that the defendant was insane and acquitted him of the crime.

With the Rabello trial in 1835, forensic psychiatry came of age in Connecticut. Brigham was an earnest advocate of the criminally insane, including a mother who killed one of her children with a hatchet. He explained that madness could affect morality as well as intelligence, since they were different faculties of the brain. "Society is still disposed," he admonished his colleagues, "to hold responsible for their actions as rational beings, some who are in fact actually deranged."[44]

The testimony of an asylum doctor and the new nomenclature of madness—the broad nosology of moral mania—enhanced the legal role of the specialist. Physicians and ministers had previously offered statements in court on the issue of insanity. Elite testimony had, however, since colonial times been complemented by lay opinion. Community judgment still played a vital role in this case, but the expert by dint of training and experience had gained enhanced standing. Important social change over the last several decades, including the professionalization of medicine and the creation of the asylum, now transformed the culture of the court.[45]

Yet even as forensic psychiatry mounted the legal battlements, there were premonitions of a pyrrhic victory. Some citizens and a few doctors maintained that the assailant was sane and culpable. They asserted the tradition of citizen judgment in matters of insanity. Three years later, a legislative committee protested "the uniform practice of our courts, to clear criminals . . . where the plea of insanity is proved at the time the act was committed." A county sheriff complained that "it has become very fashionable for rogues to be crazy, especially before trial."[46] Popular perception was that the insanity plea was abused.

Even among specialists in insanity, there was disagreement on important subjects, such as phrenology. For example, Dr. Fuller observed that the shape of Rabello's skull resembled that of many "incurables" at the Hartford Retreat for the Insane.[47] Thus he must be hopelessly disordered. Dr. Brigham dissented; he rejected craniometry as bogus. He saw no causal relationship between head shape, brain function, and personality traits.[48] He judged Rabello morally insane based solely on his abnormal behavior, a result ultimately of a dysfunction of a specific region of the brain.

What became of Rabello? His fate reflected a lack of clear resolution in state policy of where to house the criminally insane. With the exception of Rhode Island, Connecticut was the only state in the Northeast not to confine in some sort of medical facility those acquitted of crime because of insanity. Wary of Rabello's inclination to violence, the Hartford Retreat for the Insane refused to admit him. By a special act of the legislature, Rabello was admitted to the state prison at Wethersfield, not as a convict per se, but for safekeeping. Brigham protested, "He ought to be placed in a Lunatic Asylum."[49] In 1838 Rabello was one of seven criminally insane people held at the state prison in similar circumstances. A legislative committee complained of their detention, "They should be treated as *unfortunate,* not as *criminal*; as objects of *compassion,* not of *punishment.*"[50]

For nearly twenty years Rabello resided in solitary confinement at Wethersfield in a small cell (seven feet long by three feet wide) on the east side of the prison yard. Much of the time he was a "raving maniac," who cried out in Portuguese and grated his teeth. At midcentury he suffered circulatory problems and became emaciated. He complained to the prison doctor of pain shooting through his body. One observer noted in 1854, "He seemed to be worn out, and died in comparative peace."[51]

II.

Twenty years after the Rabello trial, the murder case of Willard Clark in New Haven also garnered national attention over the moral insanity defense. The events of the homicide on April 28, 1855, were clear. At close range and without warning Clark shot Richard Wight in the head with a pistol; the victim died three days later. Clark had been the fiancé of Henrietta Bogart, who in January 1854 broke their engagement and in March 1855 married Wight, a boarder in her mother's house. The deadly assault occurred the day before the newlyweds planned to move from New Haven. The fatal relationship was fraught with sexual tension: Bogart claimed that Clark had demanded "improper liberties" with her during their engagement; and Clark charged that Wight had lured the eighteen-year-old woman into a debauched marriage. Clark explained that he had killed his rival in order to rescue the bride, who he maintained loved him.[52] The state attorney charged that the defendant was guilty of malice aforethought, while the counsel for the defense countered that the accused was not guilty on the sole ground of insanity. Justice William Wadsworth Ellsworth made the charge to the jury explicit, "Everything would seem to turn upon the state of the prisoner's mind. Was he capable of understanding the transaction, or was he not? If he was, you have no alternative but to pronounce him guilty; if he was not, then he is not guilty. . . ."[53]

Forty-five witnesses testified. A score reported a change in Clark's behavior in the months preceding the murder. He ran his grocery store irregularly; he was distracted and depressed. A former landlord remembered that in an another failed love affair, Clark had hung the woman's dress in his room and even slept with it. Another deponent recalled, "His head seemed to be full of women." Clark told the man from whom he borrowed the pistol that he had shot "a two-legged cat." He had been cool and indifferent when arrested in his store. While in the New Haven jail, he told a minister he was pleased to have killed Wight. His actions appeared odd to many, but there was no public consensus that he was "crazy," as one man characterized him.[54]

In contrast, three eminent asylum doctors (Dr. John Butler of the Hartford Retreat for the Insane, Dr. Pliny Earle of the New York City Hospital for the Insane at Blackwell's Island, and Dr. Isaac Ray of the Butler Hospital in Rhode Island) concurred with the defense. After interviewing the prisoner that August, Butler concluded, "In [the] case of general unsoundness of mind, the patient may be conscious of right and wrong, abstractly, and yet so far as he is concerned, not be. I believe he thought it right and his duty to take life in this particular case. I think that, upon this matter, he did not discriminate between right and wrong."[55] Earle and Ray agreed that "insanity produced the homicide." Although there was some difference about what form of moral mania the assailant had, all three professionals agreed with Butler's observation, "A man may know all he is doing, and yet not be responsible."[56]

After five hours of deliberation, the jury acquitted the defendant on the grounds of insanity. A local New Haven physician, Worthington Hooker, penned a protest, claiming "community dissatisfaction" with the verdict.[57] For example, the Reverend J. R. Garfield found infidelity at the heart of the crime. He charged that the murderer was corrupted by reading Voltaire and other free-thought literature that ostensibly led him to devalue human life and disbelieve in eternity. For the minister, the erosion of tradition, especially religious orthodoxy, amid the transformation of midcentury America put individuals at risk of immorality. Willard was a sinner, responsible for his transgressions.[58]

Hooker also inveighed against religious skepticism. "We must look," he instructed, "to his vicious habits of feeling and thought, and his infidel and gross materialism, as the agencies without which he would never have committed this deed." He also lodged a major criticism of medical jurisprudence. First, he noted that the three asylum doctors had not talked with the prisoner until three months after the crime. Unlike in France, where a commission of lunacy would examine the accused right after the event, there was in America no provision for an immediate medical interview. The French plan would be better able to assess the mental state of the defendant at the time of the crime.[59]

Second, Hooker faulted Anglo-American law for not distinguishing to what degree insanity might be involved in the crime. "The bare fact that a man is insane does not furnish a valid excuse for crime," he wrote. "In order to make a verdict of entire acquittal proper, the act must flow wholly, or chiefly at least, from the insanity." Hooker, too, judged Clark insane, but with an important difference. He argued that the motivation for the killing was jealousy and revenge, which dominated his mad delusions at the time. Thus the murderer was culpable and guilty as charged.[60]

Hooker's imperative to determine to what degree insanity, notably moral mania, played in crime called for more precision than forensic medicine could deliver. And for John P. Gray, who had succeeded Brigham as editor of the *American Journal of Insanity*, that was the point. Expanding on Garfield's and Hooker's dissent, Gray emerged as the leading opponent among asylum doctors of the very concept of moral mania. He argued in 1858 that "the general tendency of the doctrine of moral insanity is bad. . . ."[61] Liberty became licentiousness; self-indulgence ran riot; the guilty escaped punishment; and fatalism triumphed over volition. By midcentury, liberal democracy, free market capitalism, and free will theology flourished in the North. The cohesion of this disruptive, dynamic culture rested on an ethic of self-denial and self-control. Gray feared that the elastic concept of moral insanity threatened to dissolve the self-imposed bonds of an individualistic society.[62]

Clark, however, did not escape confinement. He was remanded to the New Haven jail by court order, and there he was housed for some seven years. He was then relocated to the state penitentiary at Wethersfield, because the Connecticut Hospital for the Insane at Middletown that opened in 1868 was not prepared to confine the criminal insane. In 1872 a state commission investigating the condition of insane prisoners noted that he had been incarcerated there almost a decade. In protest of his cramped conditions, he refused to participate in assigned work. Speaking of Clark and other insane inmates, the commissioners protested that it was "inhuman to confine these men in their small cells."[63]

Discord over the insanity defense grew more heated during the Gilded Age. A case in point is that of John Andersen, known as the Wallingford murderer, whom the Superior Court of New Haven sentenced to hang for murder in the first degree on April 20, 1876. The state supreme court heard the case of *John Andersen v. The State* (1876) on appeal, because "where human life is at stake, justice, as well as humanity, requires us to pause and consider."[64] In a narrow three-to-two opinion the justices ordered a new trial, one that "ought to consider moral mania, if satisfied of its existence, in determining the degree of crime, and give it such weight as it is fairly entitled to under the circumstances."[65] For Justice Elisha Carpenter, who wrote the majority ruling, the irrational circumstances of the homicide raised the pressing question whether Andersen "is a proper subject of capital punishment."[66]

Andersen was a Swedish immigrant, a poor workman, and the provider for his family. His sole counsel was young and inexperienced. A number of witnesses testified, as one put it, that "his appearance was not that of an ordinary sane man under like circumstances."[67] Andersen's difficult temperament, quarrelsome and violent, contributed to an imbroglio at his workplace, where he was arrested and charged with assault to kill.

On the morning Andersen was due to appear in court to answer charges of attempted murder, he returned to the shop with a brace of revolvers and shot at four employees, wounding one and killing another. The assault occurred in front of a dozen people; no clear rationale appeared for those he shot; and the possibility of escape was nil. As Carpenter pondered, "The indiscriminate nature of the attack makes the whole matter still more mysterious and incomprehensible."[68] On two subsequent occasions, Anderson attempted suicide, slashing his throat. Citing the celebrated French physician Jean E. D. Esquirol, the justices speculated that an effort at self-destruction, especially by a professed Christian, suggested homicidal mania.

Expert medical opinion at the trial was, however, divided on the issue of insanity, as it was nationally. Two eminent New Haven physicians, including Francis Bacon, a leading critic of the moral mania defense, declared Andersen sane. Another pair of doctors, including John Butler, the state's senior specialist in mental disorder, pronounced him insane. Carpenter himself observed, "Courts have been slow to recognize moral insanity as an excuse for crime; but that it exists and is well understood and in some cases clearly defined by medical and scientific men, can not be denied."[69]

Nevertheless, a new trial in superior court in New Haven resulted in a conviction for murder in the second degree. The verdict still held Andersen criminally responsible rather than not guilty by reason of insanity. The caveat of the Connecticut Supreme Court had, however, stayed the hangman's rope. He was sentenced to life imprisonment at the state prison at Wethersfield. Classified as deranged in 1881 he was transferred to the State Hospital for the Insane at Middletown, where a facility for such convicts had opened.[70]

On the night of May 3 of the next year, Andersen launched a sensational escape. While he was at large for ten days, his wife was placed under police protection, and he threatened to kill two men before he was apprehended in Newark, New Jersey. Abram Shew, superintendent at Middletown, warned that Andersen was a "dangerous homicidal maniac."[71] Returned to his cell at the hospital, a double-locked, wooden crate was placed over his bed so that he had to lie prostrate when asleep. On another occasion, attendants, fearful of grappling with an agitated Andersen, sprayed him for four hours with a hose through the bars of the cell until he collapsed insensible. After almost two hours, he regained consciousness. Sometime later, newspapers reported that "the Swede" had died of tuberculosis at the State Hospital for the Insane.[72]

The case of the parricide Edwin Hoyt was a legal sequel to the Andersen trial. A jury in superior court in Fairfield County found Hoyt guilty of murder in the first degree for the killing of his father and sentenced him to be hanged. The defense claimed that Hoyt was morally insane at the time of the commission of the homicide. Medical testimony on the mental state of the accused offered by both sides negated each other. The counsel for Hoyt sought to read Ray's treatise on moral insanity and the entire state supreme court ruling in *Andersen* in order to make the case for acquittal of his client.[73]

The attorney for the state objected. The prosecution argued that clear malice aforethought of Hoyt toward his father had been persuasively shown and that he clearly knew right from wrong. Ray's treatise and the *Andersen* precedent would confuse and distract the jury from the facts in Hoyt's case. The superior court sustained the states' objection, although limited portions of the Andersen decision were permitted to be read.[74]

On these and other issues in contention, the supreme court agreed to hear the case in 1878. In a narrow three-to-two opinion in favor of a new trial, Justice

Dwight Whitefield Pardee accommodated the defense on the matter of moral mania. He rehearsed the protocol that the law presumes every adult to be of sound mind. "If the defense be insanity, it is to be proved substantially as an independent fact, and the burden of proof is on the accused. Upon this issue he goes forward and the state rebuts."[75] Therefore Pardee thought the superior court was wrong to limit the opportunity for Hoyt's attorney to make the case.

Furthermore, Pardee endorsed Ray as an expert on mental disorder and upheld the rule that medical works could be entered into evidence. "The question is not, shall such reading be now for the first time permitted; it is, shall it now for the first time be forbidden without notice," he emphasized.[76] In addition, he validated moral mania as a legitimate concept in medical jurisprudence and allowed the *Anderson* ruling to be quoted in its entirety. "The jury having statutory power to determine the law of his case," the majority opinion stated, "the accused had the right to read to them the determination of this court upon points affecting him, in such manner as to give the most complete knowledge of its precise scope and meaning. . . ."[77]

The dissent by Justices Dwight Loomis and John Duane Park was consistent with their opposition in *John Andersen v. The State* (1876). They were skeptical of the moral insanity defense. Although they held Ray's *Treatise* in high regard, they noted, "Books may be crazy as well as men, and all sorts of theories relative to responsibility for crime are advocated in books." They added that "the standard works of to-day may not long continue such," observing that the wisdom of one age was the foolishness of another.[78] The court thus had the right to act as arbiter of what was presented to the jury. Finally, to read the *Andersen* opinion with its numerous descriptions of insanity was to confuse the Hoyt case. "I cannot well conceive anything," Loomis complained, "that could be offered to a jury more irrelevant, misleading and mischievous."[79] Jurors were of similar inclination, because a new trial also found Hoyt guilty of murder in the first degree.[80]

During the Gilded Age the insanity plea, especially the argument for moral mania, was highly contentious. Although belatedly recognized in law, the test of whether a defendant emotionally appreciated the wrongfulness of his actions was difficult to determine. New York State instituted a lunacy commission in 1874 to make the decision, and that created additional furor about its power. Furthermore, asylum medicine found itself under siege. The emerging specialty of neurology challenged the lack of scientific rigor among asylum superintendents, who had dominated the field since antebellum times. New studies, such as Robert Dugdale's in 1877 of the notorious Jukes family in New York, explained crime and mental disorder in terms of degenerative, hereditary nature of disease, including the moral faculties.[81]

Deterministic explanations of behavior were, however, at odds with a culture rooted in assumptions of free will. For example, Connecticut's two superintendents of mental hospitals rebutted the plea of Charles J. Guiteau, the assassin in 1881 of President James A. Garfield. Guiteau had pleaded not guilty because of congenital, moral insanity.[82] "There is no such disease known to science as hereditary insanity," Abram Shew of the state hospital declared.[83] And Henry P. Stearns of the Hartford Retreat for the Insane echoed, "His act in shooting the President was not the result of a pathological condition of his brain."[84] In effect, Shew and Stearns argued that not all criminal behavior was moral insanity. The assassin was depraved, not deranged.

Guiteau's conviction and execution were due more to public outrage than to a philosophic consensus on medical jurisprudence. Disagreement and dissent dominated. In Connecticut, the physician Patrick Cassidy in 1885 looked for "some legal test of insanity," but found "conflictions upon conflictions."[85] And three years later his New Haven colleague Francis Bacon upbraided "the keen-eyed pathologist" and "neurological specialist" who, at the behest of a "wily and unscrupulous lawyer," were ready to excuse a crime because of a hereditary, moral insanity. "The evil of the matter," he concluded, "is that the most expert of alienists forms his opinion in any given case just as the unlearned do, on the basis on common sense, by considering the acts of the patient as indications of mental processes."[86]

The celebrated Rabello trial in 1835 did not herald, as Amariah Brigham had hoped, a solid standard for forensic psychiatry, a subject that remains hotly disputed. Perhaps Polonius, the chamberlain in Shakespeare's *Hamlet*, still has the last word—"For, to define true madness, What is't but to be nothing else but mad?"[87]

Notes

1. Francis Bacon, "Some Thoughts Concerning Insanity and the Connecticut Laws," *Proceedings of the Connecticut Medical Society, 1888* (Hartford, Conn.: Case, Lockwood and Brainard, 1888), 34–36.

2. Patrick Cassidy, "Are There Any Symptoms or Criteria by Which We May Diagnose Insanity from Crime When Made as a Plea for Criminal Acts?" *Proceedings of the Connecticut Medical Society 1885* (Hartford, Conn.: Case, Lockwood and Brainard, 1885), 132–33.

3. See "Medical Association," *American Journal of Insanity* 1 (1845): 255–57; and Gerald N. Grob, *Mental Institutions in America: Social Policy to 1875* (New York: Free Press, 1973), who persuasively revises the social control thesis of David J. Rothman, *The Discovery of the Asylum: Social Order and Disorder in the New Republic* (Boston: Little, Brown, 1971).

4. In Lawrence M. Friedman's words, "There is little hard information about how the insanity defense played out at the level of the trial courts." Friedman, *Crime*

and Punishment in American History (New York: Basic Books, 1993), 144. And James C. Mohr adds, "Much work needs to be done on the history of American criminal law and how it was actually administered and experienced by ordinary citizens in the past." Mohr, *Doctors and the Law: Medical Jurisprudence in Nineteenth-Century America* (New York: Oxford University Press, 1993), 143.

5. Francis J. Braceland, *The Institute of Living: The Hartford Retreat, 1822–1972* (Hartford, Conn.: Institute of Living, 1972); Leonard K. Eaton, *New England Hospitals, 1790–1833* (Ann Arbor: University of Michigan Press, 1957); and Lawrence B. Goodheart, *Mad Yankees: The Hartford Retreat for the Insane and Nineteenth-Century Psychiatry* (Amherst: University of Massachusetts Press, 2003).

6. See "Doctor Eli Todd, First Superintendent of the Retreat for the Insane, Hartford, Connecticut" *75th Annual Report of the Hartford Retreat for the Insane* (Hartford, Conn.: Case, Lockwood and Brainard, 1899); Charles W. Page, "Doctor Eli Todd and the Early Days of the Hartford Retreat," *Transactions of the Connecticut State Medical Society* 2 (1913): 158–85; [Amariah Brigham], "The Moral Treatment of Insanity," *American Journal of Insanity* 4 (1847): 1–15; J. S. Bockover, "Moral Treatment in American Psychiatry," *Journal of Nervous and Mental Diseases* 124 (1956): 167–94, 292–321; Eric T. Carlson and Norman Dain, "The Psychotherapy That Was Moral Treatment," *American Journal of Psychiatry* 117 (1960): 519–24; Abraham S. Luchins, "Moral Treatment in Asylums and General Hospitals in Nineteenth-Century America," *Journal of Psychology* 123 (1989): 585–607; and Bruce Clouette and Paul Deslandes, "The Hartford Retreat for the Insane: An Early Example of the Use of 'Moral Treatment' in America," *Connecticut Medicine* 61 (1997): 521–27.

7. Amariah Brigham, *"Remarks on the Influence of Mental Cultivation and Mental Excitement upon Health" (1832) and "Observations on the Influence of Religion upon the Health and Physical Welfare of Mankind" (1835)* (Delmar, N.Y.: Scholars' Facsimiles and Reprints, 1973); idem, "Insanity and Insane Hospitals," *North American Review* 44 (1837): 91–121; and idem, *An Inquiry Concerning the Disease and Functions of the Brain, the Spinal Cord and Nerves* (1840; reprint, New York: Arno Press, 1973).

8. John D. Davies, *Phrenology: Fad and Science; A Nineteenth-Century American Crusade* (New Haven, Conn.: Yale University Press, 1955).

9. See Mary Ann Jimenez, *Changing Faces of Madness: Early American Attitudes and Treatment of the Insane* (Hanover, N.H.: University Press of New England, 1987); Larry D. Eldridge, "Crazy Brained: Mental Illness in Colonial America," *Bulletin of the History of Medicine* 70 (1996): 361–86; Gerald N. Grob, *The Mad among Us: A History of the Care of America's Mentally Ill* (New York: Free Press, 1994), chap. 1; and Lawrence B. Goodheart, "The Distinction between Witchcraft and Madness in Colonial Connecticut," *History of Psychiatry* 13 (2002): 434–44.

10. See David J. Rothman, *The Discovery of the Asylum: Social Order and Disorder in the New Republic* (Boston: Little, Brown, 1971), chap. 5; Grob, *Mad among Us*, chap. 2; and Goodheart, *Mad Yankees*, chap. 1.

11. Thomas Maeder, *Crime and Madness: The Origins and Evolution of the Insanity Defense* (New York: Harper and Row, 1985); Friedman, 143–48; and James C. Mohr, *Doctors and the Law: Medical Jurisprudence in Nineteenth-Century America* (New York: Oxford University Press, 1993), 140–45.

12. Isaac Ray, *A Treatise on the Medical Jurisprudence of Insanity*, ed. by Winfred Overholser (Cambridge, Mass.: Harvard University Press, 1962), 127. On moral mania, see ibid., 127–72. On the development of moral insanity as a concept, see Norman Dain, *Concept of Insanity in the United States, 1789–1865* (New Brunswick, N.J: Rutgers University Press, 1964), 71–77. See John S. Hughes, *In the Law's Darkness: Isaac Ray and the Medical Jurisprudence of Insanity in Nineteenth-Century America* (New York: Oceana Press, 1986).

13. Ray, 189. On the legal consequences of moral mania, see ibid., 188–202.

14. See Joel P. Eigen, *Witnessing Insanity: Madness and Mad Doctors in the English Court* (New Haven, Conn.: Yale University Press, 1995), 58–81; Dain, 197–98; and Mohr, 146.

15. For the ruling, *Commonwealth v. Rogers* (1844) by Chief Justice Lemuel Shaw of the Massachusetts Supreme Judicial Court, see Leonard W. Levy, *The Law of the Commonwealth and Chief Justice Shaw* (Cambridge, Mass.: Harvard University Press, 1957), 211–18.

16. "Cornelius G. Dunham and Another: Appeal from Probate," 27 Conn. Reports 206 (1858).

17. *John Andersen v. The State*, 43 Conn. Reports 515 (1876). Regarding the debate in the medical profession over moral insanity, see Dain, 77–82; S. P. Fullinwider, "Insanity as the Loss of Self: The Moral Insanity Controversy Revisited," *Bulletin of the History of Medicine* 49 (1975): 87–101; and Nancy Tomes, *A Generous Confidence: Thomas Story Kirkbride and the Art of Asylum-Keeping, 1840–1883* (New York: Cambridge University Press, 1984), 120–21. For the broad legal picture in the nineteenth-century United States, see Mohr, 140–53, 164–79; and in England, Roger Smith, *Trial by Medicine: Insanity and Responsibility in Victorian Trials* (Edinburgh: Edinburgh University Press, 1981).

18. Amariah Brigham, "Agostinho Rabello," *American Journal of Insanity* 3 (1846): 41. Isaac Ray thought so too, citing the Rabello case in *Treatise*, 166–67. Modern historiography has neglected the case, except for Dain, 158, 201.

19. As Lawrence M. Friedman observes, "The nineteenth century was an age of rampant science. Science was not unembattled (the fate of Darwinism is an obvious example), but science had prestige and persuasive power nonetheless." Friedman, 143. Yet, the concept of moral insanity was trumped when a defendant violated community standards and dominant norms; then punishment prevailed. An example is the case of the presidential assassin Charles Guiteau. He was hanged in 1882 more out of a national rage for punishment than because rival psychiatric persuasions publicly debated his sanity. See Charles E. Rosenberg, *The Trial of Assassin Guiteau: Psychiatry*

and the Law in the Gilded Age (Chicago: University of Chicago Press, 1968). In addition, the hopes placed in many antebellum reforms, including forensic psychiatry, were overly optimistic, as pointed out by John L. Thomas, "Romantic Reform in America, 1815–1865," *American Quarterly* 17 (1865): 656–81.

20. On the antebellum period in Connecticut, see Jarvis M. Morse, *A Neglected Period of Connecticut's History, 1818–1850* (New Haven, Conn.: Yale University Press, 1933).

21. Brigham, "Rabello," 41–44.

22. *Litchfield Enquirer*, April 30, 1835, quoted in the *Connecticut Courant*, May 4, 1835. See also *The State v. Agostinho Rabello* (1835), Record Group 3, Litchfield County Superior Court, Criminal Files, M–Z, Box 217, #3130, Archives, Connecticut State Library.

23. *Litchfield Enquirer*, April 30, 1885.

24. Brigham, "Rabello," 53.

25. Ibid., 54.

26. See Josiah H. Benton, *Warning Out in New England, 1656–1817* (Boston: W. B. Clark, 1911).

27. See Edward W. Capen, *Historical Development of the Poor Law of Connecticut* (New York: Columbia University Press, 1905).

28. Brigham, "Rabello," 52.

29. Ibid., 53.

30. Ibid., 50–51.

31. Ibid.

32. Ibid., 51.

33. Ibid., 56.

34. Ibid., 57.

35. Ibid.

36. Ibid., 60.

37. Ibid., 60–61.

38. Ibid., 61.

39. On issues of manhood, honor and violence, see E. Anthony Rotundo, *American Manhood: Transformations in Masculinity from the Revolution to the Modern Era* (New York: Basic Books, 1993); and Bertram Wyatt-Brown, *Southern Honor: Ethics and Behavior in the Old South* (New York: Oxford University Press, 1982).

. 40. Brigham, "Rabello," 59, 64. The other physician was Doctor L. Ticknor of Salisbury.

41. Ray wrote, "The last and most important form of moral mania that will be noticed consists in a morbid activity of the *propensity to destroy*; where the individual without provocation or any other rational motive apparently in the full possession of his reason, and oftentimes, in spite of his most strenuous efforts to resist, imbrues his hands in the blood of others; oftener than otherwise of the partner of his bosom, of the children of his affections, of those, in short, who are most dear and cherished around him." Ray, 146.

42. Brigham, "Rabello," 48–49.

43. Ibid., 64.

44. Amariah Brigham, *Eighteenth Annual Report,* (Hartford, Conn.: Hartford Retreat for the Insane, 1842), 17; and idem., "Insanity as a Subject of Medical Jurisprudence," *Proceedings of the Connecticut Medical Society,* May 12, 1842, 7.

45. See Friedman, 143.

46. *Report on the Insane Poor to the General Assembly* 1838, 11.

47. Brigham, "Rabello," 62.

48. See Amariah Brigham, *A Letter from Doctor Brigham to David M. Reese, M.D.* (Hartford, Conn.: n.p., 1835), in which the author distances himself from phrenology.

49. Ibid., 67.

50. *Report on the Insane Poor*, 11.

51. "Death of Rabello," *American Journal of Insanity* 10 (1854): 285–86; and *Report of the Directors of the Connecticut State Prison, 1854*, 29.

52. *Report of the Trial of Willard Clark, Indicted for the Murder of Richard W. Wright, before the Superior Court of Connecticut, Holden at New Haven, on Monday, September 17, 1855* (New Haven, Conn.: Thomas H. Pease, 1855), contains a detailed account that is shortened in "Trial of Willard Clark . . . ," *American Journal of Insanity* (1856): 212–37.

53. *Report of the Trial of Willard Clark,* 214.

54. Ibid., 28–37; and Connecticut State Library, Archives, Criminal Files, New Haven County Superior Court (1851–55), no. 607.

55. "Trial of Willard Clark," 230.

56. Ibid., 229–35.

57. Worthington Hooker, "Insanity and Crime," *New Englander* 14 (1856): 32.

58. Ibid., 39. On the broader controversy over free thought, see Lawrence B. Goodheart, "The Ambiguity of Individualism: The National Liberal League's Chal-

lenge to the Comstock Law," in *American Chameleon: Individualism in Trans-National Context,* ed. Richard O. Curry and Lawrence B. Goodheart, (Kent, Ohio: Kent State University Press, 1991), 133–50.

59. Hooker, 46–49, 51–52.

60. Ibid., 49–51.

61. Dain, 77–82. See Robert J. Waldinger, "Sleep of Reason: John P. Gray and the Challenge of Moral Insanity," *Journal of the History of Medicine and Allied Sciences* 34 (1979): 163–79.

62. See Richard O. Curry and Karl E. Valois, "The Emergence of an Individualistic Ethos in American Society," in Curry and Goodheart; Robert M. Calhoon, "Religion and Individualism in Early America," in Curry and Goodheart; Robert E. Shalhope, "Individualism in the Early Republic," in Curry and Goodheart; James A. Henretta, "The Slow Triumph of Liberal Individualism: Law and Politics in New York, 1780–1860," in Curry and Goodheart; and Richard D. Brown, *Modernization: The Transformation of American Life, 1600–1865* (New York: Hill and Wang, 1976).

63. *Report of the Commissioners on State Prison Matters . . . 1872* 23–24. A. S. Warner, the official physician at the Connecticut State Prison and crusader for better treatment of insane convicts, added, "It is perfectly well known that men, neither morally nor legally accountable, are left to drag out a miserable existence in a solitary cell." *Report of the Directors of the Connecticut State Prison, 1869,* 23.

64. *John Andersen v. The State,* 43 Conn. Reports 517 (1876).

65. Ibid., 526.

66. Ibid.

67. Ibid., 523.

68. Ibid., 520. John Andersen v. The State, no. 119, Record Group 3, Criminal Files, Superior Court, New Haven County, Archives, Connecticut State Library, Hartford. The assault to kill against a Horatio G. Hall in Wallingford occurred on March 7, 1874.

69. *John Andersen v. The State,* 43 *Conn. Reports* 515 (1876).

70. [Undated clippings], James Olmstead Scrapbook, Connecticut Valley Hospital Papers, Box 5, Archives, Connecticut State Library, Hartford; and *Hartford Post,* May 8, 1882. I thank Mark Jones, the Connecticut state archivist, for his knowledgeable assistance with these documents.

71. Connecticut Hospital for the Insane, *Seventeenth Annual Report,* (1883), 10–11.

72. [Undated clippings], James Olmstead Scrapbook, Connecticut Valley Hospital Papers, Box 5, Archives, Connecticut State Library, Hartford.

73. *The State v. Edwin Hoyt*, 46 Conn. Reports 330–35 (1878).

74. Ibid.

75. Ibid., 337.

76. Ibid., 338.

77. Ibid., 339.

78. Ibid., 340–41.

79. Ibid., 344.

80. See *The State v. Edwin Hoyt*, 47 Conn. Reports 518–46 (1880). In this opinion, the state supreme court was unpersuaded by Hoyt's motion for a new trial based on sixteen distinct points. The rejection was unanimous.

81. See Mohr, chap. 12; and Robert Dugdale, *The Jukes: A Study of Crime, Pauperism, Disease, and Heredity* (1877; reprint, New York: Arno Press, 1970).

82. See Rosenberg

83. "The Guiteau Trial," *American Journal of Insanity* 38 (1882): 368.

84. Henry P. Stearns, *Essays on Insanity, Etc., Etc.* (Hartford, Conn.: n.p., 1882), 20.

85. Cassidy, 132–33.

86. Bacon, 40–41.

87. William Shakespeare, *Hamlet*, 2.2.:93–94.

7

Mad Men and Wronged Women: Murder and the Insanity Defense in Massachusetts, 1844–2000

Alan Rogers

The legal defense for murder of not guilty by reason of insanity has a venerable and controversial history. One of the basic assumptions of Anglo-American law is that a defendant must have the capability to exercise free will in order to be held responsible for a criminal act. The legal term *mens rea*—a state of mind that renders the accused and his or her other act culpable—is a reflection of the fundamental belief that it would be morally reprehensible to execute a person who does not know or understand what he or she did was wrong. Although there is little disagreement with this principle, the public occasionally becomes outraged at the prospect that someone committing a heinous crime can be found not guilty by reason of insanity. The controversy over the insanity defense stems from the fact that the concept of mental illness is not static and that the formulation of a legal test to determine criminal responsibility is difficult to frame. For this reason, from the early nineteenth century to the present the public has called for steps to limit or abolish the defense.[1]

Once thought to be a panacea, the mixture of science and law that constitutes the basis for the modern insanity defense often has failed to temper justice with mercy or to curb public outrage when a murderer was found not guilty by reason of insanity. In the intellectual and emotional melee that followed a contentious verdict based on the insanity defense, courts and psychiatrists and politicians competed over who would shape and control the reforms said to be needed. In part, the quarrel between psychiatrists and lawyers was a result of the ferment within psychiatry beginning in the early twentieth century. Increasingly, psychiatrists looked beyond the mental asylum, to which they had been linked in the nineteenth century, to the pathology, diagnosis, and treatment of mental disease. Modern psychiatry was desperate to be a hard science, but it remained reliant upon symptoms as a basis for analysis. Because psychiatry lacked cognitive and professional unity, legislators and courts sought to balance the claims made by science and the demands made by the law with the public's perception of insanity. Understandably, the results were mixed.

Before the advent of modern science—the idea that physical and emotional causes, rather than moral wickedness explained human behavior—courts applied the "wild beast" standard. This test exempted a defendant from punishment only if he were "totally deprived of his understanding and memory, and doth not know what he is doing, no more than an infant, than a brute or a wild beast." As psychiatry's scientific status became established, however, the wild beast standard was denounced as too narrowly drawn and as missing the essence of insanity. In 1843 an English court chased the wild beast from the courtroom, but opened up new avenues of controversy when it found the Scottish woodcutter Daniel McNaughten not guilty by reason of insanity for the murder of Prime Minister Robert Peel's secretary.[2]

The uproar that followed *McNaughten* led to an extraordinary meeting of all fifteen high court judges. They approved the change in the legal definition of insanity from the wild beast symptoms to a more inclusive cognitive test, but the judges amplified the trial court's rules, beginning with the so-called right-from-wrong test. A defendant was required to prove beyond a reasonable doubt that while committing the criminal act he "was laboring under such a defect of reason, from disease of the mind, as not to know the nature and quality of his act; or, if he did know it, that he did not know what he was doing was wrong."[3]

The year following *McNaughten,* the Massachusetts Supreme Judicial Court (SJC) sought to improve upon its insanity rules. Dr. Isaac Ray, the Massachusetts-born American founder of forensic psychiatry whose work was quoted authoritatively in the McNaughten trial, guided Chief Justice Lemuel Shaw's ruling in *Commonwealth v. Rogers* (1844). Ray aggressively advocated legal reform. Before his appearance in *Rogers,* he had charged the legal profession with being woefully ignorant of insanity; such ignorance, he claimed, "led to frightfully numerous cases of judicial homicide." Ray testified that Abner Rogers could tell the difference between right and wrong, but that he was driven by an "irresistible impulse" to murder Charlestown State Prison Warden Charles Lincoln. Rogers had believed Lincoln was part of a conspiracy to persecute him and that the only way he had to protect himself was to murder the warden. Within Rogers's delusional framework, the killing seemed right, Ray argued.[4]

Attorney George Bemis begged a skeptical jury to accept Ray's expert analysis and to put aside the "common opinion" that a plea of not guilty by reason of insanity was nothing more than a clever excuse for getting away with murder. The prosecutor countered Bemis's plea by attacking the medical experts who had testified to the defendant's insanity. "Can mere opinions of medical men, founded on representation of facts not seen by themselves, representations coming through partial, contradictory, suspicious and doubtful channels, be a sure or a safe foundation for a judicial verdict?" he asked. In other words, the methods used by psychiatrists could not lead to the truth.[5]

Coming just eight years after the Massachusetts legislature nearly abolished capital punishment and in the midst of a string of capital jury nullifications, Shaw's charge to the jury grafted Ray's irresistible impulse argument onto the *McNaughten* right-wrong test. Once established that the mind of the accused is diseased, Shaw wrote, the question becomes "whether the disease existed to so high a degree, that for the time being it overwhelmed the reason, conscience and judgment, and whether the prisoner acted from an irresistible impulse." The McNaughten-Shaw test invited jurors to make a link between the alleged existence of a mental disease and a defendant's criminal behavior or between the uncontrollable emotional aspects of a defendant's behavior and his or her ability to form a rational intent. Shaw's carefully crafted instructions to the jury—the first opinion delivered by an American court of last resort on the criminal responsibility of the insane—led the jury to a verdict of not guilty by reason of insanity.[6]

The ink was barely dry on Shaw's opinion, however, before psychiatrists insisted that McNaughten-Shaw failed to reflect accurately the available knowledge about the human mind. Lawyers also were divided about the worth of psychiatric testimony. Prosecutors believed a psychiatrist's testimony was useful only if it focused exclusively on the legal question of whether the defendant knew his or her conduct was wrong. Defense attorneys, on the other hand, wanted to enlarge that focus to include expert testimony about the causes of a defendant's mental state. Politicians and the public also weighed in on the issue. Despite these fissures, the Massachusetts test to determine criminal responsibility remained substantially unchanged well into the twentieth century. As late as 1958, for example, a special Massachusetts committee created to study the death penalty acknowledged there were major problems with the insanity defense. "There can be no doubt," the committee wrote, "but that the psychiatric unsoundness of the present Massachusetts law on legal responsibility for criminal behavior has imposed an almost impossible task upon psychiatrists testifying in court. They are called upon to testify in terms of a completely erroneous conception of mental responsibility." Still, because modern psychiatry "is far from an exact science," the committee announced its intention to stick with McNaughten-Shaw.[7]

Shaw's insanity rules establish the framework for this essay. Focusing on Massachusetts's capital cases in which a defendant pleaded not guilty by reason of insanity, I intend to uncover the neglected legal history of the insanity defense for murder in the twentieth century. The broad questions raised by this historical exploration are how and why the definition, presentation, reception, and legal resolution of a not guilty by reason of insanity plea have changed over time. Although the history of Massachusetts murder trials involving the issue of criminal responsibility is pockmarked with popular bias, I argue the SJC transformed the insanity defense by whittling away at the common law concept of malice, enhancing the jury's deliberative role, and extending greater protection to mentally ill defendants. Beginning with *Rogers* and culminating in a series of rulings from 1967 to 2000, the SJC redefined legal insanity and focused upon the relationship between a criminal defendant's subjective mental state, short of insanity, and the element of malice within the crime of murder.[8]

Shortly after the SJC adopted Ray's 1844 formula for determining if a defendant was sane, Ray identified contradictory psychiatric testimony as the single biggest obstacle to widespread acceptance of McNaughten-Shaw. Professionals and outside observers alike believed scientific truth should point to a single conclusion about a defendant's sanity. Ray argued the problem lay with lawyers, not psychiatrists. He warned his colleagues that a psychiatrist who testified in court should be prepared "to have his sentiments travestied and sneered at, his motives impugned and pit-falls dug in his path by lawyers feigning 'cordiality and fellow-feeling.' " To withstand courtroom assaults, Ray stressed the need for psychiatrists to prepare carefully and to avoid the traps set by lawyers. Don't be drawn into giving an "unqualified reply," but express "modest doubt." Don't go along with a general hypothetical question, but insist on "even the minutest of circumstances" about the homicide and the defendant's state of mind. Don't link insanity to a single factor. And above all, don't try to define insanity, because lawyers will use your answer "to perplex and embarrass." Alas, Ray admitted that even if psychiatrists were to follow his advice, he and his colleagues would still be the butt of a popular joke told in courthouse corridors and taverns: "If you have an uncontrollable impulse to commit crime," the storyteller would say of a murder defendant pleading not guilty by reason of insanity, "we have an uncontrollable impulse to punish you."[9]

Dr. L. Vernon Briggs was Ray's intellectual heir. During the first half of the twentieth century, Briggs made it his goal to end the courtroom spectacle of dueling psychiatrists. Boston-born, he was an active participant in the turn-of-the-century transformation of American psychiatry. Briggs and a handful of others looked beyond the boundaries of medicine to create a mental hygiene movement that aimed to demonstrate the social usefulness of modern psychiatry. Convinced that mental disease was a product of environmental, hereditary, and individual deficiencies, Briggs believed that psychiatry and progressive politics should work together to identify and treat mentally ill people as one step toward creating a new social order. In fact, until society acted "to stop the swelling stream of defectiveness and mental illness," Briggs predicted more crime and murder.[10]

When mentally ill people landed in court, Briggs believed that the law's adversary procedures undermined scientific truth and the legal protection provided a defendant. He wanted to bridge the gulf between law and psychiatry by intervening in the process before a mentally ill defendant appeared in court. He was especially critical of the "spectacle in our courts of two or more physicians . . . pitted against one another, testifying to diametrically opposite opinions as to the mental condition and responsibility" of the defendant. Such a procedure not only humiliated the mentally ill defendant, but it increased the likelihood a mentally ill capital defendant would be executed. Against the opposition of the Massachusetts Psychiatric Association and Attorney General J. Weston Allen, Briggs lobbied for a law that required all capital defendants to undergo a psychiatric exam by neutral experts as soon as he or she was taken into police custody.[11]

Briggs launched his campaign for transforming Massachusetts's criminal insanity laws in his 1921 book, *The Manner of Man That Kills*. One of the book's three case studies focused on Briggs's testimony as an expert witness in the murder trial of Bertram G. Spencer. While confined to jail awaiting trial, three court-appointed psychiatrists had examined Spencer. During their interviews, they learned that mental illness was common within Spencer's extended family, that his father had abused him, and that throughout his life Spencer had suffered fits of uncontrollable rage and bouts of deep depression. Other pieces of Spencer's troubled personal history also emerged during his exam. His erratic behavior had caused him to be expelled from school, to be abruptly discharged from the United States Navy, and to be fired from two jobs. These facts, together with their observations of his behavior, led the examining psychiatrists to conclude that Spencer's "mental deficiency and the obliquity of his moral nature is [*sic*] so great that it constitutes real insanity." Acting on that judgment, the court committed Spencer to Bridgewater Institute for the Criminally Insane "pending the determination of his sanity." The court ordered Dr. Alfred Elliott to submit monthly reports describing Spencer's behavior and treatment.[12]

The people of Springfield were not convinced of Spencer's insanity. The *Springfield Republican* gave voice to the popular belief that Spencer should stand trial so that lawyers and a jury and not psychiatrists might determine the question of his sanity. Democrat Christopher T. Callahan made this argument the centerpiece of his successful campaign against the incumbent district attorney, Stephen Taft, a Republican. Although he insisted he was not criticizing Taft's handling of Spencer's case, Callahan denounced both the law permitting the use of state-paid psychiatrists to buttress a defendant's insanity plea and the way in which the experts reached their conclusion about Spencer's insanity. According to Callahan, echoing prosecutors in *Rogers* more than a half-century earlier, the psychiatrists had not gathered their facts correctly.

> How were these facts brought to the minds of the experts? As facts established by evidence from the witness stand? Not at all. They were furnished by the defendant's family and friends, and accepted by the experts without legal proof. These facts, in my opinion, should have been submitted under oath in open court and should have been subjected to the test of careful cross-examination.[13]

Although there may have been other reasons for Callahan's election as district attorney in 1910, it is clear that voters' dissatisfaction with Taft's handling of Spencer's insanity claim played a major part. "In the public mind the fact that Spencer was allowed to go to the Hospital without a trial," the *Republican* editorialized, "either rightly or wrongly, was a very effective political argument against Mr. Taft." The voice of the people also may have caused Dr. Elliott to change his evaluation of Spencer. Beginning a month after Callahan's election, Elliott no longer used the term "insane," to describe Spencer's mental condition, as he had in his first court report. Rather, from December to May he diagnosed Spencer as a "moral imbecile of a rather low order." Then, following a meeting with Callahan, Elliott told the court he now believed Spencer was sane and that his crimes were "for gain, revenge or to satisfy his passion, or to protect himself when overtaken in criminal deeds, and were not the result of an irresistible impulse or obsession or the reaction of a delusion or hallucination, or the result of some acute mental observation." The court promptly ordered Spencer transferred from Bridgewater to the Springfield jail preparatory to his trial for murder.[14]

Trial began in the Hampden County Superior Court on November 13, 1911. Attorney General James M. Swift and the newly elected district attorney, Callahan, represented the state. Spencer's court-appointed counsel, Richard P. Stapleton, and Charles M. Young asked Judge John Crosby to probe jurors' attitudes about the insanity defense during voir dire. Judge Crosby denied the request, stating he believed his instructions to the jury at the close of the trial would clear up any confusion. Of the 125 men called, nearly one-quarter (24 percent) of the potential jurors stated that their opposition to capital punishment would prevent them from finding Spencer guilty regardless of the evidence, and they were dismissed. A larger number of men admitted they had formed an unshakable opinion as to Spencer's guilt. Not until late afternoon was a jury of twelve men impaneled.[15]

District Attorney Callahan opened for the state. He outlined the details of the murder and defined legal insanity.

> In our Commonwealth simple insanity, a word which can and is stretched to cover a multitude of mental imperfections, does not excuse a criminal. It is not sufficient for the defense to show that he is a moral pervert, or that he is mentally defective. There are few of us who are wholly free from those imperfections. It is not enough that the alienists may pronounce him insane. The evidence must go further and show that he was so far insane that at the time he committed the crime he did not know the difference between right and wrong.

When Callahan began to speak, the *Boston American* noticed that Spencer sat well back in the open-top steel cage where criminal defendants were confined during trial and seemed oblivious. "His head tilted back slightly and a pair of large eyes, almost round, stared fixedly and vacantly ahead." But, according to the *New York World*, Spencer's vacant passivity was exceptional. He "jerks and twists his body, [and] his spasmodic movements of the neck, his ceaseless, crazily rapid teetering of the upper foot of his crossed legs" seem to signal an impending outburst. Several times during the trial Spencer did explode. His "hair flying, his big eyes wild with fury, his mouth dripping," Spencer shouted, flew into a rage, and lunged forward as if to burst out of the defendant's box.[16]

Near the end of the third day of testimony, Col. Young, Spencer's white-haired lead counsel, made his opening statement. "We have but one defense," he acknowledged, "a mental defectiveness, mental incapacity, mental unsoundness." Spencer was not able "to distinguish right from wrong to the extent that the law requires in order to constitute capacity to commit crime; that he is the victim of impulses and desires which he is unable to control." Following testimony from Spencer's relatives and coworkers in which garden-variety terms such as "queer," "wild-eyed," "nervous," "enraged," and "hysterical" were used to describe Spencer's behavior, Stapleton questioned Dr. Elliott. "My opinion," Elliott said of Spencer, "was that he knew right from wrong; he knew his act was wrong. He knew there was a penalty connected; he knew what the penalty was, and he was not governed by an irresistible impulse."[17]

Wearing a tweed suit, a fashionable flat collar and necktie, and a Van Dyke goatee, Briggs walked from the defense table to the witness stand when summoned. He flatly contradicted Elliott. Without hesitation, Briggs, who was testifying in his first capital trial, stated he believed Spencer to be legally insane, that it was not possible for him to distinguish between right and wrong, and that his criminal acts were driven by an irresistible impulse. Under fierce cross-examination by Attorney General Swift, Briggs insisted Spencer's mind "broke up" because of inherited mental defects and a brutal childhood. Briggs could not explain why some people who experienced similar childhood trauma were sane adults. Finally, Swift asked Briggs to explain the apparent conflict between his diagnosis of insanity and Spencer's rational actions on the fatal night. Briggs answered that he did not "understand the question," since it was possible for a person to be both rational and insane. Swift derisively dismissed the doctor.[18]

On the eleventh day of the trial, Stapleton closed for the defense. He reiterated his argument that Spencer should be found not guilty by reason of insanity. To make his point, Stapleton emphasized Spencer's "heredity" and "the veritable hell" of his boyhood home life that created a "diseased and disordered brain that has been defective from birth and twisted toward a criminal life by impulse, training and treatment." Stapleton also highlighted Elliott's early diagnosis of Spencer's insanity and accused Elliott of changing his diagnosis because of political pressure.[19]

Late on Friday afternoon, November 24, 1911, Attorney General Swift made his closing statement to the jury. He poked fun at Spencer's defense of not guilty by reason of insanity. "My father struck me on the head when I was nine years old and that was why I did it," Swift mockingly intoned. Swift insisted there was nothing wrong with Spencer. He had feigned insanity to save his life, and for a time he had fooled the experts. Eventually, however, all but one of the examining psychiatrists concluded Spencer was legally sane. Only Briggs—that "wonderful expert"—clung to the diagnosis that Spencer was insane. But Briggs was "foolish," "deceptive," and "gullible," the attorney general told the jury. There was "nothing the matter with [Spencer] except a quick temper," and Swift urged the jury to use the law to avenge the "foul murder" of Martha Blackstone. In fact, the jury found Spencer guilty of murder in the first degree, and he was sentenced to death. When, several months later, Spencer walked into the execution chamber, he nodded to the witnesses, said "Good night," and smilingly took his seat in the electric chair.[20]

Briggs was appalled. He contended that all of the psychiatrists who examined Spencer knew he was insane at the time of the murder and at the trial. Briggs denounced the distinction between medical insanity and legal insanity as without a difference. The awful result of the confusion between psychiatry and the law was the unnecessary execution of an insane person. "The whole legal machinery of the State," he wrote angrily, "had been put in motion to crush this defective and uphold the Majesty of the Law and so it came about that Bertram G. Spencer, a defective from birth, with the mind of a child, was tried for his life and sentenced to death and executed with a smile upon his lips."[21]

Briggs turned his energies to promoting reform, and in the spring of 1921 he pushed through the legislature a law providing for impartial psychiatrists appointed by the Massachusetts Department of Mental Diseases to examine all persons indicted for a capital crime or for repeated felonies. The court, the prosecutor, and the defense attorney had access to the psychiatrists' report, but it was not admissible as evidence at trial. Briggs believed this procedure would spare the mentally ill defendant the bewildering experience of a trial, or, if a trial occurred, the neutral psychiatric report would eliminate the spectacle of dueling psychiatrists. The reform, he boasted, "practically does away with the necessity of expert testimony or the trial of mentally ill persons in criminal cases." A defendant found to be insane was committed to a state mental hospital until he or she was determined fit to stand trial, and if acquitted at trial by reason of insanity was sentenced for life to a state hospital. The governor might pardon the prisoner only if state psychiatrists certified that he or she was no longer dangerous.[22]

Lawyers were slow to credit the Briggs law with bringing about significant changes, but Boston psychiatrists trumpeted its beneficial effects. The attorney Frank W. Grinnell, secretary of the Massachusetts Bar Association, for example, claimed that the "public and the professions were still ridiculing the absurdities of expert testimony in general and that of alienists in particular." Most lawyers, he wrote in the 1928 *Massachusetts Law Quarterly*, believe that psychiatry "is the study of 'nuts' and that some psychiatrists and their enthusiastic adherents are 'nuts' themselves who need study."[23]

The psychiatrist Winfred Overholser presented a completely different picture of the Briggs law. According to Overholser, codirector of the Massachusetts Department of Mental Diseases, the law not only transformed the legal treatment of mentally ill defendants, but criminal justice in general. It all but ended the possibility that a mentally ill defendant would be put to death or imprisoned. For this reason, "vindictive justice" waned, and the mentally ill defendant received the medical treatment he or she needed. He also noted that the average annual number of capital defendants found insane steadily declined from 1921 to 1934 and suggested this trend reflected the examiner's tendency to avoid speculating about the "exceedingly tenuous and metaphysical topic of 'criminal responsibility.' " Despite this obvious flaw, Overholser concluded on an upbeat note, heralding the Briggs law as the "most significant step yet taken toward a harmonious union of psychiatry with the criminal law."[24]

Overholser's praise for the Briggs law came just as its usefulness began a precipitous decline. A sensational 1934 robbery-murder trial ended the dream of neutral psychiatrists. A bank heist and two machine gun murders committed by the fleeing robbers eventually led to a trial in which the sanity of the three defendants became the central issue. Irving Millen, Murton Millen, and Abraham Faber, the latter a recent graduate of the prestigious Massachusetts Institute of Technology, had burst into a suburban Boston bank and grabbed nearly $15,000 in cash. The fleeing robbers gunned down two men. Captured after a bruising fight in a New York City hotel lobby, the Millen brothers and

Faber were returned to Massachusetts under heavy guard. The defense attorneys William R. Scharton and George S. Harvey announced that all three men would plead not guilty by reason of insanity.[25]

However, according to the results of an exam administered by Briggs and Dr. Earl Holt, each of the three men was sane. At trial, Briggs, whom the *Globe* described as the "picturesque patriarch of the courtroom," testified that the Millen brothers were "perfectly sane." But Briggs astonished the prosecution and the packed courtroom when he stated that the evidence he heard in court about Faber's family tree, his upbringing, and his adult behavior had changed his diagnosis of Faber. He now believed Faber's "judgment as to right and wrong, or his resistance to outside domination[,] might be impaired." Holt stuck by his original diagnosis, insisting that Faber and the Millen brothers were sane and should be held criminally responsible.[26]

The defense challenged the accuracy of the state's psychiatric assessment as well as the Briggs law's constitutionality. Scharton insisted the Briggs law was a violation of the defendants' right against self-incrimination, because information divulged during an exam might be disclosed during the psychiatrist's trial testimony. Judge Nelson Brown overruled the defense motion, and Scharton excepted, hoping to make the trial court's ruling the basis for an appeal to the SJC. To counter the state's psychiatric report, the three capital defendants enlisted their own mental health team, the first time such a move had been made since passage of the Briggs law thirteen years earlier. The three defendants were insane according to Dr. Ely Jellife and Dr. Evelyn G. Mitchell. Jellife contended that "four-fifths of all men who go out with guns to rob and kill are mentally diseased." Using easily understood language, Jellife focused on the Millens' insanity. "Nature handed them both a lemon" and their home environment "increased the difficulties that nature imposed," stated Jellife. Every move the brothers made during and after the bank robbery and murders "was a symptom of the Millen brothers' insanity."[27]

In his closing argument to the jury, District Attorney Edmund Dewing ridiculed the trio's insanity defense. Their defense of not guilty by reason of insanity is "bunk, it is rot," he said. The psychiatrists assigned under the Briggs law found the three men perfectly sane. Remember, the prosecutor shouted, Faber had graduated from M.I.T., and the gang depended on his brains. His actions before, during, and after he had committed robbery and murder were those of a "normal human being." Faber and the Millens wanted money, and they had "worked together, ruthlessly and efficiently" to get it. "So that you can go home and face your neighbors with a clear conscience," Dewing concluded, "find these three murderers guilty."[28]

Leaning comfortably on the mahogany railing framing the jury, Scharton spoke directly and quietly to the jurors. Faber had lived a blameless life for twenty-four years, he began, but Murton "exerted the maniacal force of the diseased mind" upon the impressionable young man, causing him to rob and murder. Murton also psychologically tortured and twisted his younger brother, driving him to the same murderous goal. You should find them not guilty by reason of insanity, Scharton told the jurors. "In a place like Bridgewater, full of insane men, there can be no happiness. The sun seldom shines there," he concluded in a whisper.[29]

After six hours of deliberation the jury returned a verdict of guilty of first degree murder for each man. Murton and Irving Millen and Abraham Faber stood impassive, while their family members wailed or silently wept. Outside the courtroom, a crowd cheered the guilty verdicts. The jurors sat tired and motionless, not knowing what to do next. The district attorney smiled and shook the hand of each juror. The defense attorneys followed. "You don't have to sit there any longer, Mike," a court officer said to the jury foreman. At that the foreman stood. "It's the Red Sox tomorrow afternoon," he said smiling.[30]

Following *Millen-Faber*, the trend identified earlier by Overholser for state psychiatrists to file brief general reports that avoided the specific question of criminal responsibility and, therefore, invited conflicting expert testimony at trial became dominant. Interest in reforming the insanity defense or abolishing the death penalty waned until after World War II. In 1953 in England the Royal Commission on Capital Punishment raised serious questions about the efficacy of capital punishment generally and attacked the norms governing the insanity defense in particular. The commission published testimony from U.S. Supreme Court Justice Felix Frankfurter, among others, labeling the McNaughten rules "in large measure shams." Frankfurter did "not see why the rules of law should be arrested at the state of psychological knowledge of a time when they were formulated." Likewise, the American Committee on Forensic Psychiatry concluded that the right-and-wrong test was "based on an entirely obsolete and misleading conception of the nature of insanity." A 1958 Massachusetts commission came to a similar conclusion, but clung to the McNaughten-Shaw rule simply because it didn't know what else to do.[31]

U.S. District Court Judge David Bazelon took up the challenge of bringing insanity rules into conformity with contemporary psychiatric knowledge. In *Durham v. United States* (1954) he flatly rejected both the right-vs.-wrong and the irresistible impulse tests as outdated and inadequate. Peppering his opinion with citations to psychiatric literature, Bazelon ruled "an accused is not criminally responsible if his unlawful act was the product of mental disease or mental defect." The jury's task is to weigh the facts and the expert opinions to determine if there was a casual connection between the defendant's criminal act and his mental abnormality. Such a test would go far toward upholding the best legal and moral traditions of the western world, Bazelon grandly concluded. He was convinced his new rule was solid and that it would usher in a new era of harmony between psychiatrists and lawyers and also benefit mentally ill criminal defendants.[32]

In fact, the *Durham* rule did not restore peace. Rather, it provoked an acrimonious debate, and its expansiveness tempted defense lawyers everywhere to make use of the so-called product rule, which in turn eventually caused some state courts and the American Law Institute to redefine legal sanity. In 1958, for example, Massachusetts attorney Louis Goldstein used the product rule to frame a defense for Jack Chester, a tactic that pushed the SJC into including *Durham* in its review of the available methodological options for interpreting a defendant's sanity. Chester had murdered his eighteen-year-old girlfriend after their marriage plans had collapsed. Although his personal statements sometimes belied his legal argument, Chester pleaded not guilty by reason of insanity.

Psychiatric evidence offered by the defense at trial highlighted the cumulative effect of Chester's troubled childhood, his adolescent attempts at suicide, and his inability throughout his young life to deal with frustration or to control his anger. Three experts concluded that Chester "had suffered from a serious mental illness since he was twelve years old" and that he was in the grip of that illness when he shot to death his girlfriend as she stood in the doorway of her home. To counter this interpretation, the prosecution relied on the testimony of two psychiatrists who had examined Chester shortly after his arrest. They found him "perfectly sane," "normal," and without "any mental disease or defect which would affect his criminal responsibility." Chester's own impromptu speech deepened the confusion about his sanity. Speaking in staccato bursts, he told the jury, "I am not looking for your sympathy. I am not denying what I did to Beatrice Fishman. It was premeditated. It was cold-blooded murder." Later, Chester made another remarkable statement. "It is my opinion that any decision other than guilty, guilty of murder in the first degree, with no recommendation for leniency, is a miscarriage of justice," he shouted as the jurors filed out of the courtroom.[33]

Were these the words of a mentally disturbed person or a remorseful, guilt-ridden defendant? The jury puzzled over this dilemma. After several hours of deliberation the jury asked the judge about irresistible impulse. Judge Eugene Hudson did his best to describe someone whose illness made him "incapable of resisting and controlling an impulse which leads to the commission of a crime." Apparently satisfied that Chester was not suffering from a mental disease that caused him to be in the grip of an irresistible impulse, the jury found Chester guilty of first-degree murder. He appealed to the SJC, arguing that if allowed to stand, the verdict "would work a miscarriage of justice."[34]

Essentially, Chester asked the SJC to assess a jury verdict based on contradictory psychiatric opinions by plunging into the vast literature focusing on the question of insanity and criminal responsibility. The subject of criminal responsibility "is receiving more attention today than any other subject in the criminal law," the court sighed and reviewed three methodological options for finding legal insanity. First, the SJC joined the chorus of *Durham's* critics, noting that Bazelton's product rule left undefined key words such as "disease," "defect," and "product." Second, the court acknowledged that its own 114-year-old McNaughten-Shaw insanity rule was not perfect. But, at least, the combination of right-wrong and irresistible impulse provided a jury with "a standard." The *Durham* rule provided nothing. Third, a new rule proposed by the American Law Institute (ALI) promised to bring greater clarity to the issue, but "no question touching that rule is before us." In the end, the court stuck by its ancient rule and upheld Chester's death sentence.[35]

Nine years later in *Commonwealth v. McHoul* (1967), the "troublesome" issue of criminal responsibility again was before the SJC. James McHoul was a mental patient at Boston State Hospital. On March 29, 1966, he appeared in the ward without his trousers. He told a male nurse who asked about the whereabouts of his clothing, "I want to tell you something. I did something wrong. I raped a woman." At trial, McHoul pleaded not guilty by reason of insanity, but a jury convicted him of assault with intent to rape, chiefly on the testimony of a state psychiatrist. "According to the M'Naghten [McNaughten] rule," Dr. Malcolm Rosenblatt stated, McHoul "was legally sane." Defense counsel moved to strike the doctor's entire statement, but the trial judge struck only that part about the McNaughten rule, allowing the jury to believe that a qualified expert had decided McHoul was sane according to Massachusetts law. The trial judge also refused a defense request to charge the jury using the ALI's wording on mental disease and criminal responsibility. McHoul appealed.[36]

The SJC reversed McHoul's conviction and adopted the ALI standard, describing it as an "evolutionary restatement of our rule, rather than as a substantially new rule." "A person is not responsible for criminal conduct if at the time of such conduct as a result of mental disease or defect he lacks sufficient capacity either to appreciate the criminality of his conduct or to conform his conduct to the requirement of law." The new statement "will tend to minimize misunderstanding," sustain the "principle of criminal irresponsibility," uphold the "deterrent effect of criminal penalties for wrong conduct," and recognize the "injustice of punishing those lacking the capacity to appreciate the wrongfulness of their behavior." The court also contended the new definition would lessen "semantic dueling between attorneys and experts and [put an] end to the confusing debate on the issue of 'Does he know right from wrong?' "[37]

The architect of McHoul's successful insanity appeal came before the SJC in the fall of 1975 to argue for additional changes in the insanity defense. In the intervening eight years, however, the climate of opinion about the insanity defense had changed drastically. Public skepticism about the value of psychiatric justice had resurfaced, linked chiefly to fear generated by a sharp increase in violent crime and the feeling that criminals were escaping the punishment they deserved, sometimes by falsely claiming insanity.[38]

In *Commonwealth v. Mutina* (1975) Boston's legendary criminal defense attorney William Homans Jr. successfully bucked the national conservative trend. He asked the SJC to reverse Harry J. Mutina's first-degree murder conviction and to make significant changes in the procedural rules for insanity trials. Homans faulted the prosecution's reliance upon the "presumption of sanity" and the trial court's refusal to instruct the jury about what would happen to Mutina if he were found not guilty by reason of insanity. Although the SJC specifically rejected both arguments, it decided unanimously the verdict was "against the weight of the evidence" and reversed Mutina's conviction. Chief Justice G. Joseph Tauro also wrote for a slim majority, arguing that at the option of a defendant who raised the insanity defense a trial judge must instruct the jury regarding the consequences of a verdict of not guilty by reason of insanity.[39]

Just two years after *Mutina* the court revised its insanity defense procedure again. At issue in *Blaisdell v. Commonwealth* (1977) was the constitutionality of the legislature's revisions (1970–1973) of the Briggs law. The Massachusetts legislature had divided the Briggs law into two parts. The first part of the new statute allowed the court to order a psychiatric exam to determine a defendant's competency to stand trial. The new law's second part required a defendant who declared his or her intention to plead not guilty by reason of insanity to undergo a psychiatric examination to shed light on the question of whether the defendant was criminally responsible by reason of mental illness or defect. Charles Blaisdell was indicted for murder, and three Essex County psychiatrists found him competent to stand trial. Blaisdell entered a plea of not guilty by reason of insanity, and the Commonwealth asked that he submit to a psychiatric examination that would provide the court with expert opinion about his criminal responsibility. Blaisdell refused. The trial judge told him if he did not cooperate he would be prohibited from making the defense of not guilty by reason of insanity. Blaisdell asked the SJC to rule on the question, arguing that the statute and the procedure constituted an "impermissible 'chill' " on the exercise of his right to avoid self-incrimination.[40]

A divided court ruled that a court-ordered psychiatric exam was a form of compelled self-incriminatory testimony, because it was likely to result in disclosure of information that would constitute a confession or provide the Commonwealth with leads to other damning evidence. To bring the revised Briggs law into conformity with the privilege against self-incrimination, Justice Paul Liacos outlined detailed procedural steps to prevent the prosecution from having access to the psychiatric report unless the defendant elected to testify himself or to present expert testimony based on his statements to the psychiatrist.[41]

Three years after *Blaisdell* the SJC focused on a mentally ill defendant's ability to premeditate murder. Following a breakup with his girlfriend in the spring of 1973, Dennis L. Gould frequently was confined to a hospital for the mentally ill. On one occasion he was treated with drugs and psychotherapy after he had intentionally placed his right arm under the path of a trolley car. Despite a court order prohibiting any contact with his ex-girlfriend, Gould stalked the young woman for more than two years. He suffered from constant, fixed delusions that led him to believe he was the savior of the Jewish people. In that role Gould believed his divine mission on earth was to kill his girlfriend because she was "impure." On July 17, 1978, he brutally stabbed the young woman to death as she left the nursing home where she worked. After his arrest Gould said he would not go to jail or to a hospital, but he would allow authorities to take him to Israel and there be tortured or nailed to a cross.[42]

Every psychiatrist who examined Gould diagnosed him as a "paranoid schizophrenic." Two doctors testified at trial that his long-standing mental illness made it a clear-cut case of "lack of criminal responsibility." But one doctor stated Gould knew that murder was wrong and that he was capable of controlling his behavior. This testimony, of course, echoed the ALI standard adopted by the SJC in *McHoul* (1967). Using that standard, a jury found Gould guilty of murder in the first degree. Gould appealed the verdict.[43]

The SJC used the opportunity to transform its rule about mental impairment and criminal responsibility. *Gould* expressly overruled long-standing precedent forbidding a jury to consider a defendant's abnormal state, short of insanity, by inviting a jury to consider the effect of mental illness on a defendant's ability to form a plan to commit murder. The court held that psychiatric testimony may properly be offered to distinguish between intent expressed as a conscious desire and premeditation as expressed by a critical evaluation of the pros and cons of a criminal act. In Gould's case experts testified that his intent to murder his girlfriend was the result of a "long-standing, constant delusional belief system," and not a well-thought-out premeditated plan. Because a defendant's diminished capacity bore only on the question of degree of guilt, Justice Ruth Abrams insisted the court's new rule was not tantamount to adopting a doctrine of diminished responsibility, a slippery slope the court wanted to avoid. The court ordered a new trial at which Gould would be permitted to offer evidence on the issue of whether or not his mental impairment prevented him from being able to deliberately premeditate a murder. Because a defendant's diminished capacity bore only on the question of degree of guilt, Justice Ruth Abrams insisted the court's new rule was not tantamount to adopting a doctrine of diminished responsibility, a slippery slope the court wanted to avoid. Five years later, however, the court took a giant stride in just that direction when it decided *Commonwealth v. Henson.*[44]

Albert Henson, Regina DiBlasio, and eighteen-year-old Lori Newton were parked curbside at John's Lounge in Brockton early in the morning of July 21, 1981. DiBlasio was behind the steering wheel and Henson was seated in the front passenger seat. Newton sat alone in the rear. When Ernest Hill walked out of the club, Henson called to him. As Hill approached the car, Henson shot and wounded him, and DiBlasio drove the car away. Four months later Newton made a statement to the police that led to Henson's arrest. At trial Henson was convicted of assault with intent to murder.[45]

On appeal, Henson insisted the trial judge was required to instruct the jury on the element of specific intent to kill. Henson contended the jury should have been allowed to consider the effect of his intoxication—Newton had testified that Henson had been drinking nonstop for nearly twenty-four hours. The SJC agreed with Henson's argument. Speaking for a nearly unanimous court, Justice Herbert Wilkins stated that a jury should be instructed to consider if a defendant's mental state prevented him from forming a specific intent—weighing the pros and cons of action—for assault with intent to murder. *Henson*, like *Gould*, focused upon a necessary state-of-mind element and planted the seed from which the court's subsequent decisions about the relationship between a defendant's mental state and the question of intent flourished.[46]

The SJC's carefully calibrated reforms were threatened by two shocking national events. In November 1978, Dan White, a former member of the San Francisco Board of Supervisors, ran amok in city hall, shooting to death Mayor George Mascone and Supervisor Harvey Milk. White was arrested and charged. He pled diminished capacity, not insanity, but the distinction was lost on the general public. The supposed cause for White's inability to control his actions was the so-called Twinkie defense. White sometimes stuffed himself with junk food, and there was testimony that excessive sugar consumption tended to impair his mental clarity. The jury found White guilty of voluntary manslaughter, not murder. The verdict touched off riots in San Francisco and howls of outrage throughout the state and nation. Reacting quickly, the California legislature abolished the defense of diminished capacity and irresistible impulse.[47]

Additional animus against the insanity defense was stimulated by the trial of John Hinckley Jr. On March 30, 1981, Hinckley stood waiting and alert outside a Washington, D.C., hotel. As President Ronald Reagan left the Hilton Hotel and walked toward his waiting limousine, Hinckley fired six shots, seriously wounding Reagan and his press secretary, James Brady. Hinckley's self-professed goal in shooting Reagan was to impress the actress Jody Foster, a woman Hinckley had never met. At trial in federal district court, his defense was not guilty by reason of insanity. There occurred the predictable battle between psychiatrists. The trial lasted eight weeks, and the jury deliberated for three and a half days before reaching a verdict of not guilty by reason of insanity.

It was a reasonable verdict, but it stirred up a storm of protest. A news poll found 75 percent of the public disapproved of the verdict and 70 percent wanted to get rid of the plea of not guilty by reason of insanity. Driven by these polls, Congress restructured the federal rules regulating an insanity defense. A defendant may use the defense only if "at the time of the commission of the act," he or she "as a result of a severe mental disease or defect" is "unable to appreciate the nature and quality or the wrongfulness of the act." The rule omitted the possibility of "irresistible impulse" and stipulated that insanity did not include psychopathic or sociopathic behavior. Finally, the 1984 Insanity Defense Reform Act placed the burden of proving insanity on the defendant rather than making the prosecution prove sanity.[48]

The SJC did not succumb to popular hysteria. Rather than abolishing or restricting the insanity defense, the Massachusetts court aggressively extended its *Gould* and *Henson* decisions. In *Commonwealth v. Grey* (1987) the SJC ruled that evidence of mental impairment, short of criminal insanity, was relevant to a jury's determination of whether a defendant accused of murder possessed the capacity to act with malice. Four years later, in *Commonwealth v. Sama* (1991), the court held that a defendant's mental impairment also might be part of a jury's assessment of the accused's intent, or his knowledge that his actions likely would cause a death.[49]

Both *Grey* and *Sama* departed markedly from the traditional view of malice as judged by the objective standard of the reasonable person. Malice aforethought is an essential element of both first- and second-degree murder. If the prosecution proves the killing was the result of cool reflection—a process that may take but a few seconds—a jury may find the defendant guilty of murder in the first degree. A conviction of murder in the second degree requires proof that the killing was committed with malice aforethought, but without the aggravating factors of deliberate premeditation, or cool reflection, extreme cruelty, or felony-murder. Malice is the element that separates murder from manslaughter.[50]

Malice "is the requisite mental element" of murder and includes "any unexcused intent to kill, to do grievous bodily harm, or to do an act creating a plain and strong likelihood that death or grievous harm will follow." The first two parts of this tripartite definition of malice focus on a defendant's specific intent and spell out a subjective standard based on proof of a defendant's actual state of mind. This did not mean, the court made plain, that malice aforethought required any actual intent to kill, or any foresight of such consequences by the defendant, "if the jury thought them obvious." In other words, it is not a legitimate excuse for a murder defendant to argue he could not have predicted the fatal consequences of his actions.[51]

In 1983, fifteen-year-old Terry Grey worked for a summer youth program cleaning Franklin Park in the Dorchester area of Boston. He and some of the other teenaged workers were fearful that persons within the group might attempt to steal their paychecks. On August 8, Grey brought to work a switchblade knife that he showed off to his coworkers by flicking the blade in and out. One of Grey's coworkers asked to hold the knife, but Grey refused, saying he believed the coworker intended to steal his paycheck. When the coworker stepped toward Grey, Grey pulled the knife from his pocket, flicked the blade open, and stabbed the boy in the chest, killing him.[52]

Before trial, two psychiatrists examined Grey and later testified that he was of borderline retarded intelligence and suffering from paranoid traits. They also believed Grey's mental impairment might cause him to act impulsively and aggressively when confronted with a stressful situation. Other witnesses contradicted the experts, stating that Grey stabbed the victim with the intention of killing him. The defense asked the trial judge to instruct the jury that Grey's mental state at the time he stabbed the victim was relevant to questions as to the defendant's ability to form a specific intent to kill. The judge denied the request. On appeal, Grey, who had been convicted of murder in the second degree, argued that the denial of the requested instruction was an error. [53]

The SJC reversed Grey's conviction, noting that the trial judge should have instructed the jury on the issue of intent so that it might "consider the defendant's mental status on the day in question." In fact, given Grey's mental condition, he may not have formed a specific intent to kill his coworker. "We reach this conclusion," Justice Herbert Wilkins wrote, "because we do not know on what possible basis the jury concluded that the defendant killed the victim with malice." Wilkins insisted the court's decision did not mean it had embraced a diminished capacity defense.[54]

In *Sama* the SJC turned its attention to the third part of the malice definition. Daniel Sama and his friend were living in a halfway house for recovering alcoholics. On December 20, 1989, the two violated their pledge of sobriety and consumed large quantities of alcohol and Xanax, a prescription drug that affects the central nervous system. The two men ended up in Waltham near the Amtrak railroad tracks, and there Sama slashed and stabbed his friend nearly two dozen times in the face and neck. An Amtrak worker reported the fight to the Waltham police and, acting on a tip from a young boy, they arrested Sama.[55]

Sama was represented by Bill Homans, who sixteen years earlier had won two major victories: the abolition of the death penalty and the right to have a jury instructed as to the consequences of a verdict of not guilty by reason of insanity. At trial, Sama did not contest the murder of his friend, but he claimed his uncontrolled alcohol and drug consumption that day caused him to black out, to lose all memory of the incident. An expert witness testified that Sama might have been hallucinating when he slashed his friend to death. Homans asked the trial judge to tell the jury it could consider the effect of the defendant's mental state on the question of "what he knew." Judge Hiller Zobel refused, and a Middlesex County jury returned a verdict of murder in the first degree against Sama.[56]

The SJC concluded that Zobel's refusal to issue the instruction asked for by the defense constituted reversible error. The court ruled that under the third part of the definition of malice a jury should examine the "nature and extent of the defendant's knowledge of the circumstances at the time he acted" and whether a reasonable person "would have recognized that the defendant's conduct would create a plain and strong likelihood of death." In order to establish the third part of malice the prosecution had to show the defendant knew he was stabbing the victim and that a reasonable person would know that such an act could lead to the death of the victim. In other words, a murder defendant could not be found guilty without the requisite guilty mens rea.[57]

The SJC's innovative and far-reaching decisions in *McHoul, Mutina, Gould, Grey,* and *Sama* seemed to usher in a new era, but the popular turmoil stimulated by the trial of Kenneth Seguin turned back the clock. In the spring of 1992, Seguin, a thirty-five-year-old software designer, lived in suburban Holliston, Massachusetts, with his wife, Mary Ann, and the couple's two children: Daniel, age seven, and Amy, age five. On the morning of April 29, police found Seguin wandering in the Hopkinton State Forest. He said two unidentified men had left him there after assaulting him. He told police the masked men had burst into his home late the previous night and "whacked" his wife in the head with an ax as she lay sleeping next to him and forced his two children to take pills. There were superficial wounds on Seguin's left wrist, left ankle, left temple, and the right side of his neck. A search by police led to the discovery of Mary Ann's body in the Sudbury River and the children's bodies in a Franklin pond. The children's throats had been slashed. The police dismissed Seguin's story about masked intruders and charged him with three counts of murder. At trial Seguin pleaded not guilty by reason of insanity.[58]

After describing the crimes in general terms, Judge Robert Barton asked each prospective juror if he or she would have difficulty returning a verdict of not guilty by reason of insanity. Ten prospective jurors stated they did not believe in the concept of insanity as a defense. "I just think if there's a crime committed someone should pay for what they've committed," said one potential juror. Five potential jurors expressed the opposite view: "Well, as far as I'm concerned he's definitely insane to do something like that to his wife and kids." The jurors who were chosen said they were open to a verdict of not guilty by reason of insanity.[59]

Psychiatric testimony presented by the defense and the district attorney differed sharply. Experts called by Seguin argued that he was not criminally responsible, that his "mental illness made it impossible for him to conform his conduct to the requirement of law." They told the jury Seguin had a history of chronic depression, made worse by work-related stress, and that he had manifested some of the dangerous side effects of the drug Prozac. For these reasons, the psychiatrists testified, Seguin believed the only solution to his problems was "to take his family to a better and safer place, heaven." To counter the defense, Assistant District Attorney Marguerite Grant called three psychiatrists, two of whom had testified for the prosecution in the trial of John Hinckley. They said that on April 28 and 29, Seguin was able to appreciate the wrongfulness of his actions. The state psychiatrist Nancy Gregg added that she examined Seguin within a few days following the murders, and she formed the opinion then that he had the capacity to control his conduct.[60]

Opinions outside the courtroom also were divided sharply. The *Boston Globe* columnist Bella English thought Seguin's insanity defense was nothing more than a cynical attempt to escape punishment for his horrible murders. "If Hitler were tried today, he'd wage an insanity defense," she wrote, adding, "How do the judge and jury keep a straight face?" The *Los Angeles Times* expressed the opposite point of view. "If Kenneth Seguin wasn't mad, what other explanation could there be?" *USA Today* put the case in a larger context. A 1992 study found that nearly 75 percent of female murder victims knew their killer intimately. Twenty-six Massachusetts women were murdered by their husbands or boyfriends, up from fourteen in 1990.[61]

After six days of deliberation, a jury found Seguin guilty of murder in the second degree. That is, applying the court's *Gould* rule, the jury concluded that Seguin's psychosis undercut his ability to premeditate the murders of his wife and children, but that he was not insane. Standing on the courthouse steps following the announcement of the verdict, Seguin's attorney blasted the media for "pandering to people's fears about mental illness." He also lamented "all of the prejudices and biases that are built into people through years of simplistic and ignorant commentary on the nature of mental illness."[62]

Critics of the insanity defense, including Republican governor William Weld, used the public's dissatisfaction with the Seguin verdict to call for reinstating the death penalty and for abolishing the insanity defense. The *Globe*'s Bella English applauded the U.S. Supreme Court's approval of Montana's abolition of the insanity defense. But, she lamented, it was not likely Massachusetts would adopt the Montana scheme, "because many legislators are defense lawyers and others are pretty nutty themselves and some are both." The *Boston Herald* commentator Howie Carr believed the insanity defense was nothing but a way for murderers to avoid the punishment they deserved. "Granted, Seguin didn't beat the rap this time," Carr wrote in September 1995, "but someday, sooner or later, and probably sooner, Seguin will run this jive past a particularly stupid court, or an even dumber-than-usual

Governor's Council or parole board. And he'll walk." Given this "reality," how can the attorney general "still think we don't need a death penalty in Massachusetts?" Both Carr and English cheered when Governor Weld filed a bill calling for the abolition of the insanity defense. The *Globe* editorial page, however, rebuffed the governor's proposed law.

> Weld's bill proposes a solution not to a genuine problem but to a constellation of perceptions that are understandable, perhaps, but false. Abolition of the insanity defense answers no true social need. On the contrary, it deprives society and the criminal justice system of a choice that affirms free will and responsibility as guiding values for the American rule of law.[63]

The Democrat-controlled legislature voted down the governor's bill.

The public furor caused by Seguin's trial and verdict eventually subsided, but the contentious debate about the rules governing the insanity defense continued to be heard in the courtroom. In *Commonwealth v. McLaughlin* (2000) the SJC revisited the insanity defense's fundamental questions. Who should assume the burden of proving whether a capital defendant was sane or insane? What level of proof was required? Could a jury rely on a "presumption of sanity" when weighing a defendant's plea of not guilty by reason of insanity?[64]

George McLaughlin believed that two of his nursing home coworkers and several unidentified residents in the apartment building where he lived were harming him with high-frequency beams. To escape the punishment they were inflicting upon him, McLaughlin murdered his two coworkers and set fire to his apartment building, resulting in the death of one of the residents. McLaughlin told the police he thought the building's fire alarm would alert all the tenants. The only issue at trial was whether McLaughlin was criminally responsible at the time of his acts. McLaughlin was found guilty of involuntary manslaughter and arson and not guilty by reason of insanity of two charges of murder in the first degree.[65]

The SJC granted review and affirmed McLaughlin's convictions, but took the occasion once again to alter the rules governing an insanity defense. The court argued that Chief Justice Shaw's classic charge to the jury in *Commonwealth v. Rogers* (1844) had been modified by the SJC when, without reason, it shifted the burden to the government of proving a defendant's sanity beyond a reasonable doubt. To allay potential confusion, to make it simpler to explain to jurors, the court barred any future mention of the "presumption of sanity." Rather, the new *McLaughlin* rule called for the defendant to show the absence of criminal responsibility by a preponderance of the evidence and for the prosecution to prove all elements of a criminal act, including mens rea, beyond a reasonable doubt.[66]

The rule changes introduced by the SJC in *McLaughlin* mirror the long history of the insanity defense in Massachusetts: the SJC promoted reform by extending its commitment to the principle that in order to be culpable a capital defendant must have the capability to exercise free will. Further, the court consistently enhanced the deliberative role of the jury and extended greater protection to the defendant. Specifically, the court pioneered the nation's first insanity instruction and ushered in a new era in the late twentieth century by allowing a jury to assess a criminal defendant's subjective mental state and the element of malice within the offense of murder. By basing guilt on personal liability rather than dated presumptions of law, the Massachusetts court brought the law into closer conformity with the science of psychiatry and with prevailing moral and legal principles.

But the court's rules could not eliminate popular bias against the insanity defense for murder. The prospect that someone committing a particularly repellent murder may be found not guilty by reason of insanity because a jury determined that a mental defect impaired the defendant's ability to act with malice aforethought or to form a criminal intent continues to stir public anger. Likewise, opposition to the insanity defense also surfaced under the *Gould* rule allowing a jury to find that a defendant's mental impairment short of insanity is a basis for a verdict of murder in the second degree.

During the last quarter of the twentieth century, in the face of public opposition fueled by a cluster of hoary myths, the SJC worked to improve the law in regard to insanity and mental impairment. The defense still must prove beyond a reasonable doubt that the accused was not responsible for his actions or unable to form a clear intent to murder. The question of whether the enlightened reforms enacted by the Massachusetts court finally have succeeded in harnessing psychiatry to the law remains unanswered. It is clear the court's commitment to the fundamental principle that all criminal defendants have a right to a fair trial distinguishes its procedure in insanity trials from other state and federal courts. The SJC's long history shows that it is convinced a jury must find a defendant mentally competent to stand trial and capable of acting with malice and of forming a criminal intent in order to be held responsible for his or her acts. However susceptible to bias or to misunderstanding, the Massachusetts court has ruled there is no other choice in a society whose criminal justice system affirms free will and responsibility as guiding principles for the rule of law.

Notes

1. The quotation in the title is from Justice Arthur Whittemore's opinion in *Commonwealth v. McHoul*, 352 Mass. 544, 546 (1967). The literature on the insanity

defense is enormous. See generally, Sheldon Glueck, *Mental Disorder and the Criminal Law* (Boston, 1927); Norman J. Finkel, *Insanity on Trial* (New York, 1988); idem. *Commonsense Justice: Jurors' Notions of the Law* (Cambridge, Mass., 1995); Committee on the Judiciary, United States Senate, *Insanity Defense* (Washington, D.C., 1982); Rita Simon, *The Jury and the Defense of Insanity* (Boston, 1967); "The Insanity Plea on Trial," *Newsweek*, May 24, 1982, 56. Ralph Slovenko, "The Meaning of Mental Illness in Criminal Responsibility," *Journal of Legal Medicine* 5 (1984): I. Dorothy O. Lewis, *Guilty by Reason of Insanity: A Psychiatrist Explores the Minds of Killers* (New York, 1999). To date two states have abolished the insanity defense and twelve states have adopted a "guilty but mentally ill" option; see Norman J. Finkel, "The Insanity Defense: A Comparison of Verdict Schemas," *Law and Human Behavior* 15 (1991): 533.

2. See, generally, Thomas Maeder, *Crime and Madness: The Origins and Evolution of the Insanity Defense* (New York, 1985). Sir Matthew Hale articulated the "wild beast" theory in *The History of the Pleas of the Crown* (London, 1736), chap. 4, 34–35. For McNaughten's case, see 10 Cl. And Fin. 200, 210, 8 Eng. Rep. 718 (1843). I use the term "psychiatrist" throughout, although Massachusetts courts and newspapers used the term "doctor" until about 1900 and then "alienist" until the 1930s to describe expert witnesses who testified about a defendant's mental condition. The Harvard Medical School established its first chair of psychiatry in 1920, and the American Medico-Psychological Association became the American Psychiatric Association in 1921.

3. Hale, 34–35.

4. *Commonwealth v. Rogers*, 7 Metcalf 500 (1844). Ray, "Criminal Law of Insanity," 28 *American Jurist* 254 (1835); George T. Bigelow and George Bemis, Esqs., *The Trial of Abner Rogers, Jr. for the Murder of Charles Lincoln, Jr.* (Boston, 1844), 43.

5. Bigelow and Bemis, 45.

6. *Commonwealth v. Rogers*, 7 Metcalf 500 (1844). Alan Rogers, " 'Under Sentence of Death': The Movement to Abolish Capital Punishment in Massachusetts, 1835–1849," *New England Quarterly* 26 (1993). Only a handful of states followed Massachusetts and added the "irresistible impulse" rule to their legal definition of insanity: Pennsylvania, Connecticut, Iowa, Kentucky, Minnesota, and Ohio. In 1849 the Massachusetts legislature passed a law that allowed the court to commit to an asylum a criminal defendant found to be insane before trial. See *Acts and Resolves*, 1849 chap. 68 (Boston, 1850). In 1904 the law was changed to permit the court to appoint two experts to determine a defendant's sanity; it also permitted defendants to be committed for observation, *General Laws, 1921*, chap. 123, sec. 100.

7. *Commonwealth v. Rogers*, 7 Metcalf 500 (1844). Bigelow and Bemis, 45, 224. In his 1850 inaugural address Boston's mayor John Bigelow criticized the insanity defense, claiming that criminals escaped punishment by falsely pleading insanity. See *Boston Herald*, Jan. 7, 1850; Henry Weihofen, in *Insanity as a Defense in Crimi-*

nal Law (New York, 1933) ("No branch of the criminal law has been the subject of so much criticism and controversy as the defense of insanity"); and *Report and Recommendations of the Special Commission Established for the Purpose of Investigating and Studying of the Death Penalty in Capital Cases* (Boston, 1958), 83.

8. *Commonwealth v. Rogers*, 7 Metcalf 500 (1844). Legal insanity, as defined by *Commonwealth v. McHoul*, 352 Mass. 544 (1967) is the lack of a substantial capacity, as a result of mental disease or defect, to appreciate the wrongfulness of one's conduct or to conform one's conduct to the requirements of the law. *Commonwealth v. Gould*, 380 Mass. 672 (1980); *Commonwealth v. Grey*, 399 Mass. 469 (1987); and *Commonwealth v. Sama*, 411 Mass. 293 (1991).

9. Only a relative handful of nineteenth-century capital defendants plead not guilty by reason of insanity. Of the 625 indictments for murder from 1832 to 1899, 22 pleaded not guilty by reason of insanity, and 8 were successful. Beginning in 1832 the attorney general published homicide data annually (*Report of the Attorney General*). For a full discussion of the insanity defense in nineteenth-century Massachusetts, see Alan Rogers, "Murders and Madness: Law and Medicine in Nineteenth-Century Massachusetts," *Proceedings of the Massachusetts History Society* 106 (1995): 53.

10. Gerald N. Grob, *Mental Illness and American Society, 1875–1940* (New York, 1983). Clifford Beers's autobiography, *A Mind That Found Itself* (1908) usually is credited with launching the mental hygiene movement, but it should be noted that as early as 1906 Briggs promoted a Boston psychopathic hospital. Briggs, *History of the Psychopathic Hospital* (Boston, 1922). Briggs spells out his views in *The Manner of Man That Kills* (Boston, 1922), 5–16. Briggs's membership in the National Committee for Mental Hygiene is found in L. Vernon Briggs, *History and Genealogy of the Cabot Family, 1475–1927*, 2 vols. (Boston, 1927), 2:776. Richard Child's popular series on American crime summarized popular attitudes about the insanity defense when he wrote that the odds were good that a murderer would not be brought to trial, but if that did happen he or she would likely "go to an insane asylum on the testimony of bought doctors." *Saturday Evening Post*, August 1, 1925, 8.

11. Briggs, "Conditions Leading to the Passage of the Massachusetts Law Commonly called the Briggs Law," *Bulletin of the Massachusetts Department of Mental Diseases*, 12 (1927): 2–5; for the Briggs law, *Acts and Resolves*, 1921, chap. 415; *Annual Report of the Attorney General for the Year 1922* (Boston, 1923), xxix–xxx.

12. Briggs, *Manner of Man That Kills*, 23–28, 47–53, 102–6.

13. Ibid., 99–100, 128–37. As acting district attorney for Norfolk and Plymouth counties in 1902, Attorney General James Swift had applied the same strategy advocated by Taft in, *Attorney General's Report for the Year 1902* (Boston, 1903), xxi.

14. Briggs, *Manner of Man That Kills*, 107–8, Elliott's court reports, 138–44; *Springfield Republican*, August 2, 1911.

15. *Trial of Bertram G. Spencer*, Boston, 1912, 6–18.

16. Ibid.,, 75–76; *Boston American*, November 15, 1911; *New York World*, November 16, 1911. For a discussion of the prisoner's dock, see Alan Rogers, " 'In the Cage': The Prisoner's Dock and the Presumption of Innocence in Massachusetts Criminal Trials," *Massachusetts Legal History* 3 (1997): 89.

17. Trial of Spencer, 503. Briggs claimed that Elliott "hung his head" when he gave testimony at trial. *Manner of Man That Kills*, 148.

18. A picture of Briggs was published in the *Boston Globe*, March 12, 1913. For a contemporary summary of the cross-examination techniques used by lawyers to expose the weaknesses in forensic diagnoses, see John E. Lind, "The Cross-Examination of the Alienist," *Journal of Criminal Law and Criminology* 13 (1922): 228. *Trial of Bertram Spencer,* 673.

19. Trial of Spencer, 854–55, 857, 865. The contemporary psychiatrist Dorothy Lewis makes a roughly parallel argument in *Guilty by Reason of Insanity*.

20. Trial of Spencer, 204–21, 228–29, 894–95, 903, 908–9, 912–18.

21. Ibid., 230.

22. *Acts and Resolves*, 1921, chap. 415. L. Vernon Briggs, "Conditions Leading to the Briggs Law," *Bulletin of the Massachusetts Department of Mental Diseases,* 4 (1927): 11. *General Laws*, chap. 123, sec. 100A; for provisions regarding commitment and release, *General Laws*, chap. 123, secs. 90, 99–105.

23. Frank W. Grinnell, editorial, *Massachusetts Law Quarterly* 13 (1928): 34. Grinnell added, "Most of us are still in doubt as to the correct pronunciation of 'psychiatry' and as to what it means."

24. Winfred Overholser, "The Briggs Law of Massachusetts: A Review and Appraisal," *Journal of Criminal Law and Criminology* 25 (1935): 859, 865, 873, 883. According to Overholser, from 1921 to 1934 only 66 of 429 persons indicted for murder were found insane. Overholser's data may have masked a systemic bias against women murdered by men. Of the 1,253 murder indictments for 1900 to 1940, 49 defendants raised the issue of insanity, 31 of whom were men indicted for murdering their wives or lovers. Of the 31, 18 were found to be insane before trial, and 10 men were found not guilty by reason of insanity at trial, and several pleaded guilty of a lesser crime. This data was compiled from the annual *Reports of the Attorney General*, 1900 to 1940. In the latter year the attorney general ended the practice of reporting homicide statistics to the legislature. By contrast to the post-Briggs era, during the period 1844 to 1899 13 of the homicide defendants who raised the issue of insanity were men indicted for murdering their wives. The thirteen cases were disposed of as follows: the court sent 9 men to an asylum before trial; 1 was found guilty of murder in the first degree and sentenced to death; a jury found another defendant guilty of murder in the second degree; and 2 men who pleaded not guilty by reason of insanity were found not guilty and sent to an asylum. For examples of gender bias, see the following three sources for cases of men who murdered their wives and were declared insane: Christopher Cullen, in *Boston Globe*, February 23 and 26, 1929; Michael J.

Walsh, *Boston Globe*, November 21, 1931; and *Commonwealth v. Soaris*, 275 Mass. 291 (1931).

25. *Boston Globe*, February 3 and 26 1934, March 22, 1934.

26. Ibid., June 5, 1934.

27. Ibid., May 31, 1934. Scharton asserted that Faber was a "victim of overstudy" at M.I.T. and that his "condition" was aggravated by his extraordinary concentration on the development of radio. *Boston Globe*, March 22, 1934. The SJC revisited Scharton's position in *Blaisdell v. Commonwealth*, 372 Mass. 753, 757 (1977).

28. *Boston Globe*, June 8, 1934.

29. Ibid.

30. Ibid.

31. Overholser played a prominent role in promoting psychiatry during World War II. See Frankfurter's testimony, *United States v. Currens*, 290 F. 2nd 751 n. 5 (1961); *Royal Commission on Capital Punishment, 1949–1953* (London, 1953), 80; *Report of Massachusetts Commission*, 83. The United States approved the International Covenant on Civil and Political Rights adopted by the United National General Assembly in 1966, but until 1992 excepted to those articles calling for abolition of the death penalty for juveniles and pregnant women. See Hugh A. Bedau, "International Human Rights Law and the Death Penalty in America," in *The Death Penalty in America: Current Controversies,* ed. Hugh A. Bedau (New York, 1997), 246.

32. *Durham v. U.S.*, 214 F. 2nd 862, 870, 875–76 (1954); Bazelon's product rule was a restatement of *State v. Pike,* 49 New Hampshire 399 (1899), in which the judge instructed the jury that the verdict should be not guilty by reason of insanity "if the killing was the offspring or product of mental disease in the defendant." See A. S. Goldstein, *The Insanity Defense* (New Haven, Conn., 1967), 83. For an early debate about the Durham rule, see Simon E. Sobeloff, "Insanity and the Criminal law: From McNaghten to Durham and Beyond," *ABA Journal* 41 (1955): 793; and Jerome Hall, "Responsibility and Law: In Defense of the McNaghten Rules," *ABA Journal* 42 (1956): 917.

33. *Commonwealth v. Chester*, 337 Mass. 702, 708, 709 (1958).

34. Ibid., 707–8, 703.

35. Ibid., 711, 713–14. In jail awaiting sentencing, Chester committed suicide.

36. *Commonwealth v. McHoul*, 352 Mass. 544, 546–47.

37. Ibid., 544, 547, 551, 554.

38 Thomas Maeder, *Crime and Madness: The Origins and Evolution of the Insanity Defense* (New York, 1985), 92; *U.S. v. Brawner*, 471 F. 2nd 969 (D.C. Cir., 1972). Data generated in the District of Columbia supported the public's suspicion. The year Durham was adopted, only 0.4 percent of all cases tried resulted in a verdict of not guilty by reason of insanity. By 1961, the figure had jumped to 14.4 percent.

39. *Commonwealth v. Mutina*, 366 Mass. 811, 812 (1975). The *Boston Globe* was critical of Tauro's appointment, but upon his death the paper admitted its error in judgment and lauded Tauro; see *Boston Globe,* October 7, 1994. By a vote of 4 to 3, the court decided that at the defendant's option a jury should be informed about the outcome of a verdict of not guilty by reason of insanity. The "presumption of sanity" rule was justified again in *Commonwealth v. Kostka*, 370 Mass. 516 (1976).

40. For revisions of the Briggs law, see *Massachusetts Statutes,* 1970, chap. 888; *Massachusetts Statutes,* 1971, chap. 700; *Massachusetts Statutes,* 1973, chap. 569; *Blaisdell v. Commonwealth*, 372 Mass. 753, 757 (1977).

41. Ibid., 772, 768.

42. *Commonwealth v. Gould*, 380 Mass. 672, 675–76 (1980).

43. Ibid., 677–79; *Commonwealth v. McHoul*, 352 Mass. 544 (1967).

44. *Commonwealth v. Gould*, 380 Mass. 672, 682–83 (1980). *Commonwealth v. Henson*, 394 Mass. 584 (1985). The concept of diminished capacity or diminished responsibility had roots in 19th century cases in which a defendant offered intoxication as a defense even though criminal procedure explicitly prohibited voluntary intoxication as a defense for a criminal act. Joel Bishop, *Commentaries on the Criminal Law* (2nd ed. Boston, 1858), 341. But murder required a specific intent and, therefore, the question of whether the accused could form an intent to murder when intoxicated was often put to a jury. For a discussion of the 20th century use of diminished responsibility, Norman J. Finkel, *Commonsense Justice: Jurors' Notions of the Law* (Cambridge, Mass., 1995), 275–278, 292–295. The Supreme Court of New Mexico pioneered in the adoption of a diminished capacity defense; see *State v. Padilla*, 66 N.M. 289, 347 Pac. 2d 312 (1959).

45. *Commonwealth v. Henson* 394 Mass. 584 (1985).

46. Ibid., 592, 593. Chief Justice Hennessey concurred, but added, "It's not in the public interest to conclude that a defendant's voluntary intoxication is relevant to most crimes of violence."

47. *Laws Cal.,* 1981, chap. 404, 1592, penal code dec. 28 (b). White was paroled after serving five years of his sentence and shortly thereafter committed suicide.

48. William F. Lewis, "Power, Knowledge and Insanity: The Trial of John Hinckley, Jr.," in *Popular Trials: Rhetoric, Mass Media, and the Law,* ed. Robert Hariman (New York, 1990), 114, 117, 127. See also 98 *Stats.* 2057, 18 U.S.C.A. sec. 17.

49. *Commonwealth v. Grey*, 399 Mass. 469 (1987); and *Commonwealth v. Sama*, 411 Mass. 293 (1991).

50. *General Laws of Massachusetts,* chap. 265. Felony murder is the commission of murder in the course of another felony.

51. *Commonwealth v. Huot*, 380 Mass. 403, 408 (1980). *Commonwealth v. Amaral*, 389 Mass. 184, 190 (1983). *Commonwealth v. McGuirk*, 376 Mass. 338, 346 (1978).

52. *Commonwealth v. Grey*, 399 Mass. 469, 472–73 (1987).

53. Ibid., 471, 474.

54. Ibid., 469, 472, 477, 478 (1987).

55. *Commonwealth v. Sama*, 411 Mass. 293, 294 (1991).

56. Ibid, 295, 296. *Commonwealth v. O'Neal*, 367 Mass. 440 (1975); and *Commonwealth v. Mutina*, 366 Mass. 817 (1975).

57. Ibid., 298.

58. *Boston Globe,* May 14, 1992.

59. *Commonwealth v. Seguin*, 421 Mass. 243, 246n (1995).

60. *New York Times*, February 3, 1993; *Boston Globe*, January 27, 1993.

61. Ibid., January 18, 1993; Los Angles Times, April 18, 1993; *USA Today*, January 13, 1993.

62. *Commonwealth v. Gould*, 380 Mass. 672 (1980); *Boston Globe*, February 3, September 28, 1993.

63. Ibid., March 30, 1994, October 13, 1995; *Boston Herald*, September 13, 1995.

64. *Commonwealth v. McLaughlin*, 431 Mass. 506 (2000).

65. Ibid., 507–9.

66. Ibid., 529, 521–22, 534.

Gender and Class Norms

8

Murder by Inches: Shakers, Family, and the Death of Elder Caleb Dyer

Elizabeth A. De Wolfe

It was late afternoon on a July Saturday, 1863. Shaker men had finished their work in the fields and mills and were headed back to their communal dwelling houses. In the Church Family, the section of the Enfield, New Hampshire, Shaker village where the most dedicated Shakers lived, William Perkins, Trueman Johnson, and George Aiken chatted near the town road that passed by their Shaker home. Thomas Wier, a recently returned Civil War soldier, walked by and complimented the men on their attractive and productive communal gardens. A few moments later, a shot rang out, and the Shaker leader Caleb Dyer staggered to the door of the Trustees Office. "I am shot, but not killed," Dyer said, before collapsing. As Sister Mary Fall and Brother Sylvester Russell carried the bleeding Dyer to the infirmary, Wier ran, then stopped and walked, to the town of Enfield, several Shaker men walking alongside him in silence. Two days later, Caleb Dyer died—as some would later suggest, an accomplice in his own murder.

Since the Enfield, New Hampshire, Shaker village was first organized in 1793 the Shakers had frequently found themselves the target of suspicion. Physical abuse, mob attacks, lawsuits, and anti-Shaker writings threatened the community and its members. The Shakers' sectarian religion formed the basis for public fear: it was a female-founded sect, and its practices of celibacy, communal ownership of property, and confession of sin were practices that challenged the cultural norm of patriarchal Protestantism and the conjugal, reproducing family. But although the Shakers were suspect in the first decades of the nineteenth century, by 1863 most of that fear had turned to admiration for the Shakers' superior agricultural products, for their neat and productive villages, and for the savvy leadership of Caleb Dyer, who brought prosperity not only to the Shakers, but to the surrounding communities of Enfield and Canaan, New Hampshire.[1] The murder of Caleb Dyer and the subsequent extensive newspaper coverage of Wier's trial reinvigorated anti-Shaker sentiment, which aimed not so much at Shaker belief as at Shaker practice, specifically, their version of "family." During Wier's court appearances, and especially during pardon hearings, what was on trial was not a murderer per se, but the limits of variation on the American family.

The issue of family and children had been at the center of debate between Shakers and nonbelievers for decades. The Shakers, who disavowed the marriage bond and attempted to suppress special ties between parents and children, challenged popular conceptions of the family. Shaker children were raised by the entire community and urged to develop bonds of brotherly and sisterly love to all the community members. Since the Shakers were celibate and produced no offspring of their own, all new members came through conversion. A frequent pattern was for an entire family to join the Shakers; such as had been the case with Caleb Dyer and his family. The difficulty arose when one member of the family, usually the mother or father, decided to leave Shakerism; then custody of the children became an issue. In the early nineteenth century, non-Shaker family members of Shaker-held children often resorted to mob violence in their attempts to "rescue" the children. The Shakers appeared in numerous court contests over child custody. The Shakers' active and successful participation in the legal system, defending their right to raise children indentured by parents and/or willingly living with Shakers, helped legitimate the Shakers' reorganization of the family unit.[2] The disagreement between Wier and Caleb Dyer would have struck a chord with Caleb: fifty years earlier, his mother, former Shaker Mary Marshall Dyer, had used mobs, lawyers, the legislature, and the courts in an ultimately unsuccessful attempt to retrieve Caleb and his four siblings from the Enfield Shakers.[3]

Born in Stratford, New Hampshire, in 1800, Caleb Dyer had come to the Enfield Shakers with his parents and siblings in 1813. The Dyers were one of many families caught up in the religious revivals sweeping northern New England, and for them Shakerism seemed to be the path to salvation. At the Shakers the young Dyer showed considerable potential and was taken under the wing of the Shaker trustee Nathaniel Draper. In 1821, Caleb became assistant trustee, one of the leaders of the community who handled business transactions and interacted with non-Shakers or, as the Shakers referred to nonbelievers, the "World." In 1838 Dyer became first trustee, a position he would hold for life. Under his guidance the Enfield Shakers prospered. Dyer planned and oversaw the building of the six-story Great Stone Dwelling, the largest dwelling house among the nineteen Shaker communities. Dyer traveled to many of the Shakers' communities, which in the 1840s and 1850s reached a peak population of some four thousand members.[4] Dyer constructed mills and developed industry; he was instrumental in bringing the railroad into Enfield and built a bridge across Mascoma Lake, facilitating travel for residents on both sides. It is said that at one time residents of Enfield moved to change the town's name to "Dyersville," an honor Caleb Dyer refused.[5]

Thomas Wier was born in Grafton, Vermont, around 1813. As a young man, for a short time he worked for the Enfield Shakers. Later in life he married, had five children, and struggled to make ends meet. In Canaan, New Hampshire, he was warned out as a pauper, and forced to take up residence with his widowed sister. In the 1860s, Wier faced both economic and personal hardship. Still poor, his family reeled from the death of two of their children within days of each other. When the Civil War broke out, Wier enlisted in the Fifth New Hampshire. His wife, Mahala, was very ill. Fearing that she might die while he was away and certain that he would not survive the war, Wier placed his two youngest daughters, Ellen and Sarah, with the Shakers, signing a standard indenture that bound the children to the sect until they reached adulthood. In return, the Shakers would care for the children, provide an education, and train them in a gender-appropriate trade.[6] As trustee of the Enfield Shaker community, Caleb Dyer signed the indenture agreement and became the Wier girls' guardian.

But Mahala regained her health and Wier, though debilitated by chronic diarrhea, survived the war and returned to Enfield in the summer of 1862. Wier set about to reunite his family, but was stunned when Caleb Dyer refused to release twelve-year-old Sarah and ten-year-old Ellen. Wier argued, pleaded, and threatened, and when that did not work he sent Mahala to the Shaker village under the pretense of a visit, but with the plan of stealing their children away from the Shakers. In late October 1862, Mahala arranged to see Ellen and Sarah, accompanied by the Wiers' adult daughter, Martha Follansbee. During the visit, Mahala suddenly grabbed one child and Martha grabbed the other child, but the frightened children struggled and screamed, alerting nearby Shakers, and Wier's self-styled "raid" was aborted.[7] Wier then turned to local lawyers, who offered to speak to Dyer on Wier's behalf, but could offer little else. As the months turned into a year, Wier's anger at Dyer reached its peak. On Saturday evening, July 18, Wier asked to visit his daughters. Dyer, as trustee responsible for managing non-Shaker visits to the community, cited the lateness of the day and thus refused Wier the opportunity to visit his daughters. Thomas Wier then shot Caleb Dyer.

The news of the shooting traveled rapidly. Shaker John Bradford hurried down the road to fetch the physician Benjamin Skinner and, seeing the grave nature of Dyer's wound, then telegraphed the neighboring villages of Lebanon and Hanover for two more local doctors. Bradford sent a message to the Canterbury, New Hampshire, Shaker village, calling home the Enfield Ministry leaders who were visiting the nearby community.[8] Shakers took turns sitting with Caleb, and for a short time it appeared he might recover. But after enduring surgery to remove the bullet and an agonizing decline, early in the morning of July 21 "he ceased to breathe, and his spirit took its departure to a better, brighter world than this."[9] The funeral, attended by five hundred people, was the next day. Dyer's body was carried from the meetinghouse to the burial ground, his Shaker family following in a solemn procession.[10] The Shakers were voluminous writers, and news of his tragic death was carried in intercommunity correspondence: Enfield brother Sylvester Russell sent the news to South Union, Kentucky, who in turn informed the Shakers at Pleasant Hill, Kentucky, who passed the news to Union Village, Ohio. The Parent Ministry at New Lebanon, who had received the news by letter on July 22, also wrote letters to each Shaker community, enclosing clippings from local newspapers. Correspondence and journals described the "distressing occurrence," "outrageous, brutal and fiendish murder," "horrid and lamentable occurrence," "murderous assault," and the "most heinous & diabolical deed ever committed."[11] Shakers were stunned by the brutal crime, the only murder in Shaker history. Public interest prompted the publication of a pamphlet on Caleb Dyer's life, death, and funeral. Dyer's "tragical death" was understood to be a tremendous blow to the Enfield Shakers. Not only had the Shakers lost a member of their community, but they had lost a talented leader—at the beginning of a period of decline of the quality of Shaker leaders as well as quantity of Shakers, the loss was doubly felt.[12] Abraham Perkins wrote that Dyer's death gave him forebodings of trouble. His intuition was accurate. The Enfield Shakers were about to be plunged into a nightmare of trials and debt.[13]

The Trial: *State v. Wier*

The development of the handgun facilitated murder. Invented by Samuel Colt in 1832, the handgun replaced larger dueling pistols and heavy military weapons. Revolvers were small and easy to load, and could fire several shots. As it was easier to shoot someone than to physically assault that person, a handgun (convenient to carry and hide on one's person) permitted death at a distance.[14] Having served in the military, Wier was no stranger to weapons. On that fateful day, Wier had pointed his gun at Dyer, shot, and attempted to shoot again. When he realized his revolver had jammed, Wier ran but then slowed to a walk, traveling to the center of town accompanied by six Shakers, and walked to the village of Enfield.[15] Wier made no attempt to flee; he walked to the home of the county sheriff, Wyman Pattee, who came out his front door and arrested Wier, placing him in the tavern with local residents assigned as "watchers." An inquest was held immediately, presided over by the local coroner, who determined not only the cause of death but also the likely perpetrator. A few days after the murder, Wier was moved to the Grafton County jail in Haverhill, where he awaited indictment and trial. In October, the grand jury indicted Wier for murder. Wier's trial was set for April 1864.[16]

The trial outcome seemed obvious. Several witnesses had seen Wier shoot Dyer, and numerous local residents had heard Wier threaten to kill Dyer, blow up the Great Stone Dwelling, and sink the Shakers with a stone fleet. Wier had given himself up and said that he expected to "pull hemp" (hang) for his crime. Yet Wier pleaded not guilty, and his lawyers, appointed by the court for the indigent accused, offered his defense: insanity.

Following jury selection, the trial began on April 11, 1864, with the prosecution's case. Several Shakers testified to Wier's appearance at the village, the shooting, and his walk to Enfield. They commented on the indenture, producing the document signed by Thomas Wier and Shakers Caleb Dyer and Mary Fall in which Wier bound his children to the Enfield Shakers. Prior to the murder, Wier had told townspeople that he had never indentured his children to the Shakers and that their stay there was to be only temporary. He accused Caleb Dyer of secretly altering the written agreement Wier had signed, changing a temporary stay into a permanent indenture. Despite Wier's claims of Shaker forgery, the court (as it had in many prior Shaker cases) accepted the proffered document as a legal and valid contract. Testimony also revealed that Caleb Dyer had permitted frequent visits with the children to Wier and his wife, despite Wier's angry manner and Mahala's October 1862 attempt at kidnapping the children. In fact, when an attorney visited Dyer on Wier's behalf, Dyer, with a nod to the best interests of the children (and recognition that children had interests and individual rights) insisted that the attorney meet alone with the Wier girls and ask them if they wished to leave, promising to release them if they so desired. They requested to stay.[17]

The witnesses for the defense did not deny the shooting and did not challenge the legality of the indenture. The Shakers anticipated that evidence would "be presented to show up our institution in as unfavorable light as possible, to elicit sympathy for Wier, and justify him in his foul act."[18] But the defense did not attack the Shaker way of life, a strategy used by many plaintiffs in earlier custody cases. Testimony instead focused on Wier's odd behavior from the time he returned home from the war. Residents remarked how Wier often broke out suddenly and for no reason with a "boisterous and unearthly laugh" and how he sang loudly as he walked around town, sometimes pulling an empty hand sled.[19] Wier was said to have worn his full army uniform, including heavy topcoat and blanket, even in the heat of summer. Neighbors reported that Wier was jovial one moment, then sullen and morose the next, and that Wier would perform impromptu military marches carrying a hoe. Most damning were town residents' statements of Wier's growing obsession with Caleb Dyer, and his repeated threats, plans, and assertions that if he could not have his children, then neither would Dyer. One witness told the court how he warned Caleb of the impending confrontation, but, as the Shakers later recorded, "no notice was taken of these threats, and no one believed Wier would attempt any thing of the kind."[20]

Wier was obviously guilty of murder, but was he responsible for his crime? To establish insanity Wier's lawyers needed to demonstrate that their client suffered from a "defect of reason from disease of the mind" that prevented him from realizing the horrific nature of his crime and from realizing that murder was wrong.[21] If Wier was insane, what would have made him so? The state called three witnesses to speak to the issue of insanity: Dr. John E. Tyler and Dr. Jesse Bancroft (the current and former superintendents of the New Hampshire Asylum for the Insane) and Dr. Dixi Crosby (a Dartmouth College professor and surgeon who had worked with returned soldiers). Lawyers for the state and the defense asked two days of "what if" questions, covering every aspect of Wier's odd behavior. Great care was taken to establish the doctors' medical credentials and experience working with the insane, an example of the growing professionalization of the psychological disciplines and the legal use of expert witnesses. In fact, when the defense asked various Enfield residents to comment on Wier's insanity, the state objected to the amateur opinions that would be offered. The defense countered by citing a long list of legal precedents permitting such opinions to be voiced.[22] The judge waived the question for later consideration, and testimony, both expert and amateur, continued, elucidating Wier's behavior and the potential causes for his alleged insanity.

Perhaps his alcoholism was to blame for his mental state; numerous witnesses testified to Wier's habits of drinking to excess, or at least drinking more than necessary for the medicinal purpose Wier claimed. Perhaps he was overly excitable, especially in matters of religion. The defense attempted to show that Wier's previous religious experiences contributed to his questionable state of mind. James Barber (Wier's widowed son-in-law) testified that Wier had been religiously enthusiastic, even claiming "with a peculiar expression of the eye" to be perfect. Testimony revealed that Wier had once been a Millerite, that is, a follower of William Miller, who offered immediate salvation to those who would wait with him for the imminent return of Christ. In 1843 Wier and several neighbors left their homes and traveled for six or eight weeks with Miller, returning when the world did not end as promised. At that time and in the next two decades to follow, Millerites were linked in the popular press and the medical community with "religious insanity." Wound up with anticipation, then disappointed with the failure of prophecy, confused Millerites were sent to insane asylums and provided interesting cases for physicians, who debated whether Millerism was the cause or the effect of religious insanity.[23] Other sectarian faiths were linked to religious insanity as well. Earlier in the nineteenth century, Amariah Brigham, superintendent of the

Utica, New York, insane asylum, detailed the effects of religious overstimulation, citing cases of suicide and murder as the unfortunate results.[24] In the 1850s, spiritualism replaced Millerism as a cause of insanity, and participation in groups as varied as the Mormons and the Oneida Perfectionists was identified as a possible instigator of insanity. Shaker records include mentions of insanity, including the case of Betsy Scott, who committed suicide by slitting her own throat; the Shakers were careful to note, however, that although "considered somewhat insane" and having attempted suicide previously, Scott was in that condition "before uniting with Believers."[25]

The defense's portrayal of Wier as an excitable man built on a long tradition of religious excitement leading to insanity, which could then lead to murder. In addition to the link between insanity and espousing a particular sectarian belief, a connection was made between insanity and fighting against a particular faith.[26] Wier was clearly agitated by the Shakers' refusal to release his children. Witness after witness described how when Wier spoke of his Shaker-held children he became excited and talked loudly with wild gesticulations. While in the 1840s Wier had been excited by religious belief, perhaps in the 1860s he was excited by fighting against a particular belief. But perhaps the Civil War was to blame. Much of the testimony concerned how Wier returned home from the service a changed man. Intemperance, excitability, the Civil War—the defense approach was scattershot, offering as evidence a variety of Wier's personal practices and life experiences, any one of which may have led him to insanity. But despite the various possibilities of what might have made Wier insane, all three expert witnesses agreed that Wier appeared sane. He had considered the crime beforehand, knew murder was wrong, and realized the consequences for it—several witnesses had reported how Wier claimed that the day Dyer died would be a happy day, and that he expected to hang for it. Wier may have been delusional, angry, overwrought, or excited, but he was not insane.

The jury took just fifteen minutes to find Wier guilty, but struggled over the definition of the crime: first- or second-degree murder? Had Wier acted with deliberate premeditation, or had the murder been prompted by the heat of the moment? The following morning the jury reached a verdict and the judge handed down his sentence: guilty of murder in the first degree. Following New Hampshire murder law, the judge ordered that Wier be imprisoned in the Grafton County jail for one year and one day. At the end of the 366-day period, Wier would "be taken to the place of execution and between the hours of nine and twelve o'clock in the forenoon of that day, . . . be hanged by the neck until [he was] dead." The judge offered Wier a note of sympathy: "and may the God of infinite grace have mercy on your soul."[27]

Public hangings were intended to deter potential criminals with a visual, and gruesome, warning of what fate awaited those who broke the law. Yet, in the nineteenth century, instead of a solemn edifying occasion, public hangings became a spectacle for hundreds of onlookers. Pickpockets, entertainers, and vendors lent their services to the festive day.[28] By the 1830s and 1840s, several states passed laws that made hangings more private affairs. In New Hampshire, public hangings were banned in 1837. Wier would be executed in the yard of the state prison, accompanied by the county sheriff, a physician, a minister, and witnesses selected by the sheriff. Despite the move to a "private" execution, onlookers could peer over fences or watch from adjacent rooftops. Should Wier hang, he would not die alone.[29]

Despite the violence of his crime, Wier was not without supporters. Family and friends petitioned the New Hampshire legislature in June 1864 asking that Wier's death sentence be commuted to life in prison.[30] Mahala Wier's petition contained 175 signatures; 4 additional petitions were signed by another 139 citizens of Grantham, Goffstown, Plainfield, and other nearby New Hampshire communities, a total of 315 petitioners. The legislature appointed a special committee to consider the request. After much discussion, the House passed a bill entitled "An Act Authorizing the Governor and Council to Commute Punishment in Capital Cases," but the bill died in the Senate. Some saw Wier's trial as an opportunity to voice anti-Shaker sentiment. Sarah Crosby blamed the Shakers (and particularly Caleb Dyer as "foreman in the game") for a friend's early death and wrote an angry letter to the Shakers asking that if Wier was hung for Dyer's death, "what sentence in justice awaits your whole Shaker fraternity at the High Court of Heaven, for murdering by inches . . . a valuable wife & mother, because she could not embrace your sentiments & abandon all her children. . . ."[31] Questioning the competency of expert witnesses (a common complaint in insanity pleas), Wier's lawyers filed an appeal. The superior court judges returned to the question raised during the trial regarding expert and nonexpert witnesses opining on Wier's sanity and agreed with Wier's attorney that some of the testimony may have unduly harmed his client's case. Fifteen months later, a second trial was undertaken. The prosecution began their case, but Wier had a sudden change of heart and pleaded guilty to second-degree murder. He was sentenced to thirty years, the maximum for his crime, and was sent to the state prison in Concord.[32]

New Hampshire's state prison reflected changing attitudes toward crime and punishment in nineteenth-century America. In the first decades of the nineteenth century, American legal codes, particularly as they related to the punishment of criminals, became increasingly less harsh, moving away from the more severe British penal code from which the American codes had emerged. Instead of physical penalties, incarceration became the norm. And instead of secluding criminals in a household arrangement, states moved to incarceration in state-run prisons. New Hampshire revised its laws in 1810, and completed the building of its first prison two years later in 1812. By the

1830s, two systems of prisons had developed nationally. New Hampshire followed the Auburn or congregate system, where prisoners slept alone in cells but worked together during the day in a workshop. No talking or eye contact was allowed, thus lessening even further any degree of contact with bad influences found within the prison. As the historian David Rothman has noted, "The thick walls that surrounded the penitentiary were not only to keep the inmates in, but the rest of the world out."[33] By removing the criminals from society, from inadequate families, and from the world's temptations (not the least of which was alcohol), prisons would reform the criminal, and "train the most notable victims of social disorder to discipline."[34]

New Hampshire's prison, located on State Street just north of the State House, had a four-story administrative building, with an attached wing three stories high, eighty feet long, and thirty-six feet wide, with thirty-six cells. By 1833, overcrowding prompted a block stone addition, two stories high.[35] One hundred twenty-seven feet long and thirty-seven feet wide, the new addition had cells for 120 prisoners. The cells were small, just six and a half feet high, six and a half feet long, and three and half feet wide. At five feet six and a quarter inches in height, Thomas Wier would have just fit inside the cramped space.[36] Made of brick with iron doors, the cells were lighted by gas and heated by steam. When first opened, the prison received considerable attention, and well-known individuals of the day visited what one noted visitor described as "a noble edifice of beautiful granite."[37] But by 1873, Alonzo Fogg, writing a gazetteer of New Hampshire, described the prison in much dimmer terms. "The dark, heavy, stone walls, together with the antique architecture of this building, do not present a very imposing appearance from the street, and . . . remind one of an old French Bastile [sic]. . . ."[38] Within these forbidding walls, the prisoners avoided idleness (which led to crime) and worked at daily labor. In the New Hampshire prison, convicts, under contract to an outside firm, manufactured bedsteads. Fogg reported that "10,000 feet of lumber of various kinds are cut up daily for bedsteads."[39] The prison labor turned a profit, and the money was put toward improvements in the prison. When Wier arrived in 1865, the prison held just seventy convicts, but by 1877 the prison population had risen to 212, and the legislature approved a plan to build a larger, more modern prison.

While Wier began his sentence and a life of silent labor, the Shakers struggled to keep their community afloat. Immediately following Caleb's July 1863 funeral, necessity called the leading Shakers to work. A replacement trustee had to be found for Caleb, business accounts settled, and his estate probated. Canterbury Shaker David Parker traveled to New York to investigate business accounts and found "Caleb's business in a sorrowfully bad state."[40] The Shakers discovered the distressing fact that Caleb had kept the community financial records in his head, and his accounts of monies owed the Shakers, and amounts the Shakers owed, died with him. The assistant trustee was ill, and there were so few capable men who were not already placed in another leadership position. The local sheriff, Wyman Pattee, was appointed as agent to settle Dyer's local business accounts "as no one in the Society is adequate to the task."[41] In the fall of 1863, Caleb's brother Orville was appointed lead trustee with the unenviable task of straightening out the fiscal chaos, one of a number of leadership changes that fall.[42] The worst was yet to come. Sensing an opportunity to make a quick profit, a local company turned a bill owed to the Shakers into a bill due them and sued the Shakers for money not actually owed. What came to be called the "Shaker Case" dragged on for twenty years, wearing down the Enfield Shakers spiritually and financially.

Amid these challenges were problems of the Civil War. Despite their pacifist stance, Shaker men were added to a list of local conscripts, and Shaker leaders were consumed with fighting conscription in several states.[43] Within the Enfield community, morale dropped and apostasy rose with more and more men leaving the already strapped community. Of the eight Shaker witnesses for the prosecution in Wier's trial, half would secede from the Shakers, three within months of the trial.[44] Ellen and Sarah Wier remained at the Shaker village and, the New Lebanon Ministry journal recorded, "cling closely."[45] Mahala Wier's brother "threatened violence" if the girls were not released, but the attorney general asked the Shakers to continue to hold them, at least until the case was decided. The Shakers had reluctantly accepted the girls from Wier in 1862, but did so to be "neighborly." That neighborly spirit had cost them their leader. Thinking both of the safety of the Shakers and of the traumatized girls, one Shaker asked himself in his journal, "Is it right to hold them?"[46]

The Shakers' troubles were well recognized, perhaps even beyond the grave. The *Granite State Free Press* reprinted a message received in an 1863 spiritualist's meeting. Caleb Dyer spoke from that "better, brighter world" and told his Shaker brethren that the religion of Shakerism was in its infancy, and was imperfect, and that the Society was "in some respects, at fault." Yet Dyer beseeched his fellow Shakers to "continue to live in the holy way of truth and righteousness which their religion has marked out for them."[47] Reflecting continued internal and external problems for the Shakers, in 1874 Caleb Dyer again spoke, warning his brethren of startling new changes that would soon be revealed. He urged them not to have fear, "for [the changes] will lead them out into clearer light, give them greater strength and far more happiness than at present."[48] In the next century historians would look back to this period and point to it as the beginning of the Enfield Shakers' decline.

Pardon

Wier had his supporters throughout the trial and in the following years. Following his incarceration in the state prison, petitions were circulated and sent to the governor asking for Wier's pardon. With each new governor, Wier's supporters would file a petition. In 1872, "Thomas Muzzy and others" filed a petition requesting Wier's pardon, but the Governor's Council took no action. In December 1876, a new petition was presented, and the council ordered that Enfield Shaker leader Abraham Perkins be notified. By February 1877, the petition was withdrawn. A year later, the petitioners returned, represented by Charles P. Sanborn. Sanborn brought several witnesses to "explain the circumstances of the homicide, the origins of the petition, and the conduct and character of the prisoner since he has been in the State prison." The attorney Herman Greene represented those opposed to Wier's release and brought several witnesses of his own to testify. Abraham Perkins expressed the Shakers' view of Christian forgiveness mixed with concern for community safety. "[N]otwithstanding our sufferings by the hands of the murderer, we bear him no ill will, yet for the protecting of our lives and property, we consider a person of his strong passions, impulsive nature, and criminal character should be taken care of and not allowed the liberty of running at large. . . ."[49] Once again the council denied the petitioners' request, voting four to one against recommending Wier's pardon.[50]

In June 1880, yet another attempt was made to secure Wier's release.[51] During March 1880, family and friends of Thomas Wier fanned out across New Hampshire, gathering signatures on multiple copies of an identically worded petition. An estimated 1,424 individuals signed petitions for Wier's pardon, asserting that Wier had paid his debt to society, that at age sixty-eight he was an old and ill man, that he was fully penitent, and that he presented no threat to society. Petition signers included Civil War veterans, members of Wier's family, and local residents who supported Wier or found the petition a good opportunity to rally against the Shakers. Forty-six individuals signed a petition in Concord; twenty-five soldiers and one "citizen" signed a petition in Gilford, New Hampshire. Along with the 420 signatures on one petition was a brief note from A. H. Randlett, who explained that he had served with Wier in the Fifth New Hampshire and found Wier to be a "good soldier and . . . not a man to commit a crime, except under some strong provocation." There was a general sympathy for Civil War veterans who had committed crime. An 1878 petition to the governor requested the commutation of the death sentence of John Pinkham, another Civil War veteran who had committed murder. The petition claimed that at the time of the murder Pinkham "was in such a frame of mind occasioned by disease, exposure and imprisonment in southern military prisons . . . and by the excessive use of intoxicating liquor, as to render him partially irresponsible for the commission of the crime. . . ."[52] Like Pinkham, Wier's experiences in the Civil War had had a dramatic effect on his mental stability.

In June 1880 Abraham Perkins wrote to Governor Natt Head asking that Wier be kept in jail, as the Shakers feared Wier would make good on alleged threats of revenge. Reflecting nineteenth-century ideas about the reformatory nature of prisons, Perkins added that the Shakers thought Wier "best conditioned where he is, being well cared for and away from temptation of ardent spirit &c."[53] But this time, the council was moved by the petitioners' claims. While Wier's insanity was denied in 1865, in 1880 the petitioners offered a unique twist on the argument that Wier was not responsible for Dyer's murder: they said that Wier had been temporarily overcome with parental affection, "maddened to a sort of frenzy at the many and oft-repeated ineffectual attempts to obtain possession of or even to see his much loved children," and in that aberrant moment (what today we might call temporary insanity), "by a father's love," shot Dyer.[54]

Here was the crux of so many nineteenth-century complaints against the Shakers: that Shaker life and practice broke up the biological family. Mary Marshall Dyer (Caleb's mother) wrote that she was so upset by the loss of her children in 1815 that her "trouble was more than I could bare [*sic*] and at times I lost my reason."[55] Fighting her husband-turned-Shaker for custody of their children in New York State, Eunice Chapman compared the loss of her Shaker-held children to their captivity by Indians. In New Hampshire, friends of Mary Cummings charged that she "came to a premature grave years ago from the cold inhuman treatment she received from the Shakers and her lordly husband."[56] Opposing Shakerism for the sake of their children's safety, Dyer, Chapman, and Cummings each struggled with unhappiness, uncertainty, and illness as they fought to reunite their broken families. And as in the case of Thomas Wier, anti-Shakerism led to sickness, insanity, and death.

While only a few violently opposed the Shakers, many non-Shakers wondered just how satisfying a celibate life could be. Newspaper accounts penned by visitors to Shaker villages and the published short stories of several writers provided the answer to the public's question about celibate lives. In the 1830s and 1840s numerous visitors' accounts described Shaker women as gaunt, a physical effect of the absence of romantic love and maternal bonds. In Nathaniel Hawthorne's short story "The Shaker Bridal," a young Shakeress gives up the man she loves for the faith she practices and dies. As Hawthorne and other authors suggested in popular periodicals of the day, the practice of Shakerism—specifically, the disruption of the biological family— led its members to take on a ghastly, ghostly presence.[57] Whether supporting or opposing the faith, those individuals whose paths crossed with Shakerism thus had a grim fate, indeed.

The 1880 petition campaign added new evidence to help make the case for Wier's pardon: a statement from Wier's daughter Sarah Dillingham, and a letter from two former Shakers urging Wier's release. Both letters asserted the importance of the biological family. Sarah Wier Dillingham, one of the two Wier girls placed at the Shakers, recanted her previous testimony in which she expressed fear of her father, saying, "but now I know my father is harmless." Dillingham (and others) claimed she had been misled by the Shakers, who at the time of the trial had told the young girl that she was in danger, a frequent complaint of an earlier generation of anti-Shaker activists who claimed the Shakers controlled young members with false information about the outside world. The 1880 petitions emphasized Dillingham's new support of her father; underlining the word *daughter* three times in the text, it said "that a daughter previously opposed . . . now believes [her previous] statement untrue. . . ."[58] In addition to Dillingham's statement, her signature and that of her mother Mahala, husband Edward, and sisters Martha Follansbee and Ellen Wier headed the long list of supporters. Thomas Wier's family wanted his presence to make their family complete.

Enoch Cummings and George Aiken, former Shakers who had lived with Caleb Dyer, explained that while they were living as Shakers they had been stunned by Wier's crime, but now that they were no longer Shakers and were parents themselves and "knowing now what we did not know then," understood the bonds of "parental affection" and urged that Wier be forgiven.[59] In the last half of the nineteenth century, middle-class society believed that carrying out faithfully one's domestic duties was a sign of manhood. Hand in hand with "mother's love," "father's care" helped to raise good, moral children who would strengthen the nation. The upheaval of the Civil War reinforced this domestic paradigm and the critical role fathers played.[60] The petitioners argued that it was only natural that Wier felt overwhelming feelings of father's care. The crime, they argued, was not motivated by "any love of gain or hope of riches," but by protection for "bone of his bone and flesh of his flesh."[61] Wier had placed his children among the Shakers in order to protect them in his absence, but once he returned from the war he sought to reclaim his rightful role as guardian of his children's moral development—a role Caleb Dyer usurped. The tragic murder, by the petitioners' logic, was at least in part the Shakers' fault. In challenging the social norm with their aberrant version of "family," the Shakers became accomplices in their own leader's murder. If, as Mary Dyer had written a decade before her son's murder, the Shakers would "replenish their society with their own children . . . [t]hey would then have parental affections, not cruel hate. They would be fathers and mothers, sons and daughters, instead of task-masters, task-mistresses, servants and slaves."[62] Wier's supporters suggested that if the Shakers had understood parental affection, the murder would not have occurred. While Wier was not of the middle class, those who could release him were, and they were well steeped in the beliefs surrounding the importance of a father's care. The letters from Wier's daughter and the former Shakers tipped the balance; Wier received his pardon.

Wier was released in July 1880 at the age of sixty-eight.[63] In a new suit of clothes provided by the warden, and carrying a diary he had kept daily while imprisoned, Thomas Wier traveled to Enfield by train accompanied by his daughter Ellen, who had left the Shakers a few years after the murder and was the force behind the numerous petition drives for his release. At Enfield he was met by his wife, Mahala, and his now married daughter Sarah Dillingham, who had remained with the Shakers until just one year before her father's pardon, leaving to marry a former Shaker. The local press interviewed Wier upon his return to Enfield. Of the murder, Wier said that on that day "it seemed to him that he could skate right across Mascoma Lake on the water." Wier credited the prison library with his rehabilitation and reflected how it was only six years ago, prompted by reading a book, that he fully realized "the condition in which he was at the time he committed the deed, and for years after. . . ."[64] While it is not known what specific book Wier read, a survey of the library collection reveals some likely arenas for prisoner rehabilitation. A good number of books concerned alcoholism and included *The Inebriate's Hut, The Anatomy of Drunkenness, Temperance Tales,* and *Essay on Drunkenness.* Character guides formed another prevalent grouping: *The Young Man's Guide, Mental Discipline, Manly Character,* and *The Young Man's Friend* are a few examples.

The local paper reported that "public opinion hereabouts is divided in regard to the case," yet toward the Shakers, Wier said he held no malice or grudges.[65] Shortly after his return to Enfield, Wier received his military pension of four dollars a month, calculated from the date of his discharge in May 1862. With the $952.57 he received, Wier bought a farm. He watched his daughter Ellen marry and ran a business grafting trees. His obituary suggests he even worked briefly for the Enfield Shakers. Perhaps the Shakers forgave him, or perhaps under the pressure of too few Shaker men for too much communal work, the Shakers were willing to use the grafting skills the now elderly Wier o ffered. Wier died at the age of eighty-nine in 1898.[66] Three years after Wier's release, the endless "Shaker Case" was decided against the Shakers, and the community was assessed $14,000 to pay alleged debts. A Shaker brother reflected how "the Enfield [Shakers] of today are to be pitied as they are made to suffer for the transgressions of others."[67]

Conclusion

The murder of Caleb Dyer and the subsequent trials and release of Thomas Wier highlight the tension between intentional communities and the surrounding dominant culture in the nineteenth century. By the midpoint of the nineteenth century, the public had come to accept Shakerism as part of the American landscape. Far from fearing what in 1780 was a new and strange religion, in the 1860s the public looked to Shakers as a model for rural, agricultural life. Yet while the public praised Shaker products, and felt no threat from Shaker theology, Shaker practice still caused the world some concern. In his closing comments the trial judge had commended Wier for the strength of his parental feelings, indicating his support of Wier's attempt to retrieve his children, though not the method Wier ultimately employed. At what the anthropologist Donald Janzen has called the "interface" between the Shakers' intentional community and the dominant national culture, tension arose between conflicting definitions of family.[68] Shaker practice, emphasizing community-wide bonds over individual biological bonds, enhanced commitment to Shaker communal life. But non-Shakers saw this behavior as destructive of the family, the foundation unit of American society. The world worried about the best interests of the children. Were they being shaped to carry out their role as the bearers of morality and culture of the next generation? Or was that future being murdered inch by inch by Shaker practice that erased biological bonds, maternal love, and a father's care? When Sarah and Ellen stated their preference for the mainstream family, despite their father's crime, and when the former Shakers illustrated how the Shakers were unable to defend what they could not understand, the Governor's Council was reluctant to disagree.

Shakers were not the only group to endure the clash between the dominant culture and intentional communities over differing visions of family. Nineteenth-century Mormons and Oneida Perfectionists faced the wrath of those dismayed and alarmed by their alternative family arrangements. In the twentieth century—specifically in 1935, 1944, and again in 1953—Arizona state officials and police raided the Short Creek fundamentalist Mormon community. In their zeal to protect women and children living in polygamous households, officials separated men from their families, arrested plural wives, and took children into state custody, breaking apart the family unit officials claimed they were there to protect. Allegations of child abuse led Vermont officials to raid the Messianic Community at Island Pond, Vermont, in 1984, which resulted in the removal of 112 children from their homes and family.[69] These are but a few of many examples of the clash between communities that continue to provide grist for the mills of public debate over the definition of a "proper" family.

The clash between the Shaker vision of family and that of the dominant mainstream family fueled public interest in Wier's story and provided the rationale for his release. Murder could be forgiven. Decades earlier, when Caleb's mother raised a public outcry about her Shaker-held children, the Shakers ruefully remarked how she had stimulated both "the sympathy and malice of mankind."[70] Likewise, months before Dyer was killed, lawyers had warned Caleb that there would be a great degree of public support for Wier's attempt to reunite his family, despite the legal indenture. This sympathy for the sanctity of the biological family illustrates how, under certain circumstances, a murderer could be forgiven and the circumstances of murder mitigated. Social norms could repaint a black-and-white portrait of murder into shades of gray. Wier had irreparably damaged the Shaker family, yet his family could still be saved. With the passage of time and through the sympathy of mankind, Thomas Wier had been transformed from a murderer into a loyal father, and his crime of murder into an unfortunate, but pardonable, homicide.

Notes

The research for this paper was supported by a grant from the University of New England faculty research fund. The author is also grateful to Walter Brumm, Mary Ann Haagen, and the staff of the New Hampshire Bureau of Records Management and Archives for their help in locating materials related to Wier's case.

1. For a history of Shakerism, see Priscilla Brewer, *Shaker Communities, Shaker Lives* (Hanover, N.H. : University Press of New England, 1986); and Stephen J. Stein, *The Shaker Experience in America* (New Haven, Conn.: Yale University Press, 1992). For insight on the changing public perceptions of Shakerism, see Elizabeth A. De Wolfe, "A Very Deep Design at the Bottom: The Shaker Threat, 1780–1860," in *Fear Itself: Enemies Real and Imagined in American Culture*, ed. Nancy Lusignan Schultz (West Lafayette, Ind.: Purdue University Press, 1999), 105–18.

2. On Shaker custody disputes, see Barbara Taback Schneider, "Prayers for Our Protection and Prosperity at Court: Shakers, Children, and the Law," *Yale Journal of Law and the Humanities* 4 (1992): 33–78. On additional legal challenges, see Carol Weisbrod, *The Boundaries of Utopia* (New York: Pantheon, 1980).

3. On Mary Marshall Dyer's anti-Shaker campaign, see Elizabeth A. De Wolfe, *Shaking the Faith: Women, Family, and Mary Marshall Dyer's Anti-Shaker Campaign, 1815–1867* (New York: Palgrave, 2002).

4. In the 1860s, Shaker communities were located in Maine, New Hampshire, Massachusetts, Connecticut, New York, Ohio, Indiana, and Kentucky. In the late nineteenth century, two Southern communities, White Oak, Georgia, and Narcoossee, Florida, were established. One active Shaker community remains today in Sabbathday

Lake, Maine. See the map of community locations and table of community longevity in Brewer, [xx].

5. On the life of Caleb Dyer, see Carl Irving Bell, "The Noble Life and Sad Death of Brother Dyer," *New Hampshire Profiles* 13 (June 1964): 36–37, 47; Henry Cummings, "Caleb Dyer," *The Enfield Advocate*, December 30, 1904; Enfield Membership Data Records (hereafter EMDR), Enfield Shaker Museum, Enfield, N.H.; Wendell Hess, *The Enfield (N.H.) Shakers: A Brief History* ([Enfield, N.H.]: for the author, 1993), 32–36; and *A Biography of the Life and Tragical Death of Elder Caleb M. Dyer* (Manchester, N.H.: American Steam Printing Works of Gage, Moore & Co., 1863).

6. Thomas Wier appears in the historical record as Wiers, Ware, Weir, and Wier. For consistency, I use the latter, which appears to be the most frequent spelling. Mary Wier (born 1841) died October 13, 1861; her sister Ella (born 1848) died October 17. Sarah was born December 6, 1850; her sister Ellen was born in December 1852. Wier's third surviving child, Martha (born 1843) married Joseph Follansbee in 1858. Information on the Wier family is found in EMDR; George McKenzie Roberts, "The Vital and Cemetery Records of the Town of Enfield, Grafton County, New Hampshire," part 2, 1957, typescript in the Enfield Public Library; Census Records, 1860–80, town of Enfield, typescript compilation in the Enfield Public Library. On Wier's military service, see Augustus D. Ayling, *Revised Register of the Soldiers and Sailors of New Hampshire in the War of the Rebellion, 1861–1866* (Concord, N.H.: Ira C. Evans, 1895).

7. The Wiers' attempt at kidnapping their own children occurred on October 22, 1862. Caleb's mother, Mary Marshall Dyer, used the same strategy in May 1818 in an unsuccessful attempt to retrieve her five Shaker children. See Elizabeth A. De Wolfe, "The Mob at Enfield: Community, Gender, and Violence against the Shakers," in *Intentional Community: An Anthropological Perspective,* ed. Susan Love Brown, (Albany: State University of New York Press, 2002), 107–30.

8. Canterbury sister Asenah Stickney forwarded the early news to Lydia Dole of the Groveland, New York, Shaker village. She concluded her letter with the prayer that "beloved Elder Caleb will recover. It would be a serious loss to Enfield people to have him die." Letter of Asenah Stickney, Canterbury, to Eldress Lydia Dole, Groveland, July 19, 1863, Western Reserve Historical Society Shaker Collection, IV:A–7 (hereafter WRHS).

9. New Lebanon Ministry Journal, 3 (July 22, 1863): 168. In the collection of the Emma B. King Library, Old Chatham Shaker Museum (hereafter NLMJ).

10. A description Dyer's funeral is found in the *Granite State Free Press*, July 25, 1863 (hereafter *GSFP*). On Shaker funerals, see Etta Madden, *Bodies of Life: Shaker Literature and Literacies* (Westport, Conn.: Greenwood Press, 1998): 125–59; and Barbara Rotundo, "Crossing the Dark River: Shaker Funerals and Cemeteries," *Communal Societies* 7 (1997): 36–46.

11. "A Register of Incidents and Events Kept by Giles B. Avery, October 20, 1859–December 21, 1874" [Mount Lebanon, Church Family], entry dated July 23, 1863, New York Public Library Manuscript Division, Shaker Collection (hereafter NYPL), transcript in EMDR; Letter Ministry West Gloucester to Ministry New Lebanon, August 2, 1863, Sabbathday Lake Ministry Correspondence, vol. 1, Sabbathday Lake Shaker Library, Maine; *GSFP*, July 25, 1863; Pleasant Hill Journal of Events, vol. 7, August 2 and 16, 1863, Filson Historical Society, Louisville, Kentucky.

12. See the discussion in Brewer, 204.

13. Information on the trials is found in *State v. Wier*, Fall Term 1865, records of the New Hampshire Superior Court, New Hampshire Bureau of Records Management and Archives (hereafter N. H. Archives) and in detailed court reports published in the *Daily Mirror and American*, Manchester, N. H., April 13–26, 1865, and October 9, 1865.

14. Roger Lane, *Murder in America: A History* (Columbus: Ohio State University Press, 1997), 109.

15. Trueman Johnson, Edward Babcock, George Aiken, William Perkins, Frances Bradford, and Samuel Keniston accompanied Wier on his walk, an 1863 version of a "slow-speed chase."

16. On nineteenth-century inquests and homicide procedures, see Lane, 112–14.

17. This incident mirrors an 1818 visit to the Enfield Shakers by Caleb's mother, Mary Marshall Dyer. When she met with her five children and asked if they wished to leave, they responded no. In the 1820s, sons Caleb and Orville published affidavits to that effect in an attempt to stop public agitation for their "release." Orville Dyer wrote, "[A]s there is no law to compel me to live with the Shakers, contrary to my choice, I do not wish to have one made to compel me to leave them contrary to my choice." *A Review of Mary M. Dyer's Publication, Entitled "A Portraiture of Shakerism," Together with Sundry Affidavits, Disproving the Truth of Her Assertions* (Concord, [N.H.]: Jacob B. Moore for the United Society, 1824): 18–19.

18. NLMJ, November 30, 1863, 189.

19. "Trial of Thomas Wier," *Daily Mirror and American*, April 16, 1864.

20. NLMJ, July 22, 1863, 167.

21. Lawrence Z. Freedman, ed. *By Reason of Insanity: Essays on Psychiatry and the Law* (Wilmington, Del.: Scholarly Resources, 1983), xii.

22. See the list in "Trial of Thomas Wier."

23. See Ronald L. Numbers and Janet S. Numbers, "Millerism and Madness: A Study of 'Religious Insanity' in Nineteenth-Century America," in *The Disappointed: Millerism and Millenarianism in the Nineteenth Century*, ed. Ronald L. Numbers and Jonathan M. Butler (Bloomington: Indiana University Press, 1987), 92–117.

24. Ibid., 95.

25. NLMJ, August 21, 1863, 174.

26. Numbers and Numbers, 100. See also Charles E. Rosenberg, *The Trial of the Assassin Guiteau: Psychiatry and the Law in the Gilded Age* (Chicago: University of Chicago Press, 1968). Guiteau, a one-time member and later violent opponent of the Oneida Perfectionists, assassinated President Garfield in 1881.

27. *State v. Wier*, N.H. Archives.

28. On public hangings as spectacle, see Negley K. Teeters, *". . . Hang By the Neck . . .": The Legal Use of Scaffold and Noose, Gibbet, Stake, and Firing Squad from Colonial Times to the Present* (Springfield, Ill.: Charles C. Thomas, 1967), 39–46. See also the description of a late eighteenth-century public execution in Deborah Navas, *Murdered By His Wife: A History with Documentation of the Joshua Spooner Murder and Execution of His Wife, Bathsheba, . . . 2 July 1778* (Amherst: University of Massachusetts Press, 1999), 95–104. On crime literature, including execution sermons, see Daniel A. Cohen, *Pillars of Salt, Monuments of Grace: New England Crime Literature and the Origins of American Popular Culture, 1674–1860* (New York: Oxford University Press, 1993); and Karen Halttunen, *Murder Most Foul: The Killer and the American Gothic Imagination* (Cambridge, Mass.: Harvard University Press, 1998).

29. Teeters, 152–53. See also Frank E. Hartung, "Trends in the Use of Capital Punishment," in *Murder and the Penalty of Death*, ed. Thorstein Sellin (Philadelphia: American Academy of Political and Social Science, 1952), 8–19.

30. *Journals of the Honorable Senate and House of Representatives, June Session, 1864* (Concord, N.H.: Amos Hadley, Printer, 1864), 55, 64–65, 71, 94, 112,124, 245, 262, 291, 296, 366.

31. Sarah Crosby to the Enfield Shakers, April 28, 1864, author's personal collection.

32. Wier arrived at the prison on October 9, 1865, with five additional new inmates. Wier, at age fifty-two, was the oldest of the group. Four of the five were between seventeen and twenty-six years old, the fifth man was forty-five (and from Finland). Wier's new companions had been convicted of horse stealing and breaking and stealing, and were each sentenced to three years. State Prison Register of Convicts, 1812–1912, page 83, N. H. Archives.

33. David Rothman, *The Discovery of the Asylum: Social Order and Disorder in the New Republic* (Boston: Little, Brown, 1971), 96.

34. Ibid., 107.

35. Joseph Walker, "State Prison," in *History of Concord*, ed. James O. Lyford, (Concord, N.H.: Rumford Press, 1903), 1157–58.

36. Wier's height is provided in the State Prison Register of Convicts, 1812–1912, 83, N. H. Archives. The entry also provides his hair color (gray), eye color (gray), and complexion (light).

37. Walker, "State Prison," 1157.

38. Alonzo J. Fogg, *The Statistics and Gazetteer of New Hampshire* (Concord, N.H.: D. L. Guernsey, 1874), 537.

39. Ibid., 538.

40. NLMJ, November 30, 1863, 190.

41. Ibid., August 25, 1863, 174.

42. Orville Dyer, First Elder of the Church Family, was appointed trustee on September 26, 1863 and would hold the post until October 27, 1867. See Henry C. Blinn, "Historical Notes Having Reference to Believers at Enfield," 1, 72, typescript (photocopy), Shaker Library, United Society of Shakers, Sabbathday Lake, Maine; and NLMJ, November 10, 1863, 187. Enfield was not alone in its financial crisis. An October 1863 entry in Giles Avery's "Register of Incidents" (NYPL) indicated enormous debt and inaccurate record keeping at several Shaker communities. By 1880, all communities kept detailed written financial records that were forwarded to the New Lebanon Shaker leaders.

43. On the Shakers' pacifist stance, see James M. Upton, "The Shakers as Pacifists in the Period between 1812 and the Civil War," *Filson Club History Quarterly* 47 (1973): 267–83.

44. EMDR; see also demographic characteristics of Enfield, N. H. in Brewer, appendix B, 215–27.

45. NLMJ, November 25, 1863, 188.

46. Ibid.

47. "A Communication from the Spirit of Caleb M. Dyer," *GSFP*, January 16, 1864. The letter "from the disembodied spirit of the late Caleb M. Dyer" originally appeared in the spiritualist publication *Banner of Light*, dated November 17, 1863.

48. *Banner of Light*, December 19, 1874, 6.

49. Abraham Perkins to Giles Avery, January 13, 1878, WRHS IV:A–15.

50. Council Records, 1812–1900, vol. 12, 504, and vol. 14, 42, 50, 206, and 225, N.H. Archives.

51. See Petitions for the Pardon of Thomas Weir, 1880, Box 42, Folder 9, N.H. Archives; Council Records, 1812–1900, vol. 14, 488, 507–9, N.H. Archives.

52. Petitions to the Legislature, December 18, 1878, N.H. Archives.

53. Abraham Perkins to Natt Head, June 15, 1880, in Petitions for the Pardon of Thomas Wier, N.H. Archives.

54. Petitions for the Pardon of Thomas Weir, 1880, Box 42, Folder 9, N.H. Archives.

55. Petition for Divorce, Dyer v. Dyer, Grafton County Superior Court, November Term, 1830, N.H. Archives.

56. Sarah Crosby to the Enfield Shakers, April 28, 1864, author's personal collection.

57. On popular representations of the Shakers, see Flo Morse, *The Shakers and the World's People* (New York: Dodd, Mead, 1980).

58. Petitions for the Pardon of Thomas Weir, 1880, Box 42, Folder 9, N.H. Archives.

59. Enoch Cummings, Juliet Cummings, and George W. Aiken to the Governor of New Hampshire, May 16, 1880, in Petitions for the Pardon of Thomas Wier, N.H. Archives.

60. Stephen M. Frank, *Life With Father: Parenthood and Masculinity in the Nineteenth-Century American North* (Baltimore: Johns Hopkins University Press, 1998), 22, 178–81. See also Robert L. Griswold, *Fatherhood in America: A History* (New York: Basic Books, 1993); Mary Ann Mason, *From Father's Property to Children's Rights: The History of Child Custody in the United States* (New York: Columbia University Press, 1994); and E. Anthony Rotundo, "American Fatherhood: A Historical Perspective." *American Behavioral Scientist* 29, no. 1 (Sept./Oct. 1985): 7–25.

61. Petitions for the Pardon of Thomas Weir, 1880, Box 42, Folder 9, N.H. Archives.

62. Mary Marshall Dyer, *Shakerism Exposed* (Hanover, N.H.: Dartmouth Press, ca. 1852), 27–28.

63. Four months later, the remaining 149 prisoners were transferred to the newly completed new prison. Manuscript note dated Tuesday, November 30, 1880, on the frontispiece of the State Prison Register of Convicts, 1812–1912, N.H. Archives.

64. *GSFP*, July 30, 1880. An 1867 prison library catalogue shows a collection of works on biography, travel, theology, history, and the natural world. There were no Shaker or anti-Shaker books in the prison collection, but there were books on Mormonism and on William Miller and the Millerites, two sectarian religious movements that had, like Shakerism earlier in the century, endured antagonistic relationships with the public. For a complete listing of the library collection, see *Catalogue of the N.H. State Prison Library* (Concord, N.H.: George E. Jenks, 1867).

65. *GSFP*, July 23, 1880.

66. On Wier's pension, see *GSFP*, March 31, 1882; on the purchase of his farm, "Montcalm News," *GSFP* February 16, 1883; on his grafting business "Montcalm News," *GSFP*, May 16, 1884. Wier's obituary is found in "Lebanon," *Independent Statesman* (Concord), May 19, 1998. There is an interesting parallel here to Mary Dyer's life. Despite being a lifelong vociferous opponent of the Enfield Shakers, in her elderly years Dyer received gifts of wood and supplies from Shakers passing by her home.

67. Letter to Benjamin from Henry, January 15, 1883, transcribed in EMDR. On the conclusion of the Shaker case (*Davis v. Dyer*), see *GSFP*, January 12, 1883.

68. Donald E. Janzen, "The Intentional Community–National Community Interface: An Approach to Communal Studies," *Communal Societies* 1 (Autumn 1981): 37–42.

69. On the removal of children from polygamous Mormons, see Martha Sonntag Bradley, *Kidnapped from That Land: The Government Raids on the Short Creek Polygamists* (Salt Lake City: University of Utah Press, 1993). On messianic communities, see Jean Swantko and Ed Wiseman, "Taking Our Children, Part I: Messianic Communities, Sociologists, and the Law," *Communities: Journal of Cooperative Living,* Fall 1995, 34–35; and Isaac Dawson, "Taking Our Children, Part II: My Son Michael," *Communities: Journal of Cooperative Living,* Fall 1995, 36–38.

70. Ministry New Hampshire to Ministry New Lebanon, December 14, 1818, WRHS IV:A–3.

9

"He Has Ravished my Poor, Simple, Innocent Wife!": Exploring the Meaning of Honor in the Murder Trials of George W. Cole

Laura-Eve Moss

The social and political position of the parties, the peculiar circumstances that led to the homicide, the manner in which it was accomplished, and the eminent ability of the counsel engaged, all tend to invest the case with features that will make it one of the most celebrated causes in the criminal annals of this country.

—*Albany Argus*[1]

On the night of Tuesday, June 4, 1867, George W. Cole of Syracuse walked into the crowded common room at the Stanwix Hall hotel in Albany, New York. Cole approached Syracuse lawyer L. Harris Hiscock, raised a pistol, and, with no warning, shot Hiscock in the head. Hiscock died within the hour as Cole waited for the police, all the while exclaiming that Hiscock had dishonored Cole's wife, Mary. There was no doubt as to who committed the deadly act, no great mystery to be unraveled in that regard. Yet the shooting and its aftermath held the attention of New Yorkers for more than a year, through two murder trials, the first ending in a hung jury. In part the episode remained so significant because it engaged questions about important social issues, including criminal insanity, gender roles, and the nature of honor. The latter subject will receive the most attention here. Differences of opinion between legal interpretations, especially as reflected by lawyers' arguments and jury verdicts, and social interpretations, as seen mainly in the editorial expressions of newspapers, indicate different understandings of the meaning

207

and significance of honor. This debate also reflects an intriguing social dynamic, in which the traditional male concept of honor is attached to women.

The Cole-Hiscock case is one of a series of high-profile murder trials of the mid-nineteenth century connected with crimes of passion,[2] particularly "outraged husbands who killed their wives' alleged paramours."[3] On June 5, the day after the homicide, newspapers statewide carried extensive descriptions of the shooting and key figures involved.[4] Hiscock, age forty-three, had been raised on a farm in Pompey (near Syracuse) in central New York State. Admitted to the bar in 1840, Hiscock served as justice of the peace and town supervisor in nearby Tully, where he practiced law. During the 1850s he extended his law practice to Syracuse, and beginning in 1861 worked exclusively from that city.[5] During the Civil War, Hiscock worked to promote enlistments, and in 1865 he was elected as a Republican to the state assembly. His election as delegate to the state's constitutional convention had taken him to Albany.[6] Hiscock's wife, Lucy, had died in 1861, and he was survived by a daughter and a son.[7] He had been a cousin of U.S. Senator Ira Harris.

Early biographies of Cole indicated that he served in the U.S. Army during the Civil War, rising to the rank of brevet brigadier (and later, major) general, and afterward worked for the U.S. Revenue Service. He was politically connected; one brother was a U.S. Senator from California, and another brother was acting as American consul in Mexico.[8] Additional details of Cole's background became known in ensuing months and during his first trial, by which time he was forty-one years old. Born in Lodi, New York, in 1827, he attended the Medical College at Geneva in central New York and received his degree as a physician around 1850. Cole wed Mary Barto of Trumansburg, New York, soon thereafter. The couple moved around the state while rearing two daughters and in 1857 settled in Syracuse, where Cole invested in a lumber business. He volunteered for military service in 1861,[9] and throughout the Civil War Syracuse newspapers printed stories about Cole's military activities, injuries, and occasional visits home.[10]

These early newspaper reports described Cole's activities on the day of the shooting, including his train trip from Syracuse to Albany with Mary, his arrival at Stanwix Hall around 8:30 P.M., his comments after the shooting that Hiscock had "raped" his wife, and Cole's claim that "I have the evidence now in my pocket." Accounts of the police taking Cole to Albany's Third District station house, testimony taken at the coroner's jury after the shooting, and Cole's lengthy statement made at the jail also appeared. [11]

According to Cole's statement, his wife, Mary, had been "as pure as snow" before Hiscock's pursuit began in 1864. But while Cole was in the army, Hiscock, who Cole had considered his best friend, took advantage of Mary, kissing her while she was ill in bed and continuing after her recovery. On one occasion, Hiscock embraced Mary "and endeavored by all means in

his power to have criminal intercourse with her, she remonstrating and praying him to desist, which he finally did, but not until after shamefully exposing
her." The event left Mary feeling ashamed, but also afraid of the consequences if Cole found out. "All this time," Cole explained, "I as a husband
felt that there was something wrong in regard to my wife, because she seldom
smiled, and seemed broken-hearted during all these three years."[12]

Cole's suspicions were piqued the week before the shooting when Hiscock
met Cole on a street in Syracuse and asked when Cole would be going away
again. Hiscock's "guilty manner" led Cole to ask a friend, Montgomery Pelton,
about "improprieties" between Mary and Hiscock, and he learned there had
been some "suspicious circumstances."[13] Cole confronted Mary on Sunday,
June 2, "and learned the above facts from the lips of my wife herself; when
I found that he had betrayed the love of my wife, and defiled her person, and
when I found her utter broken hearted and my home desolated, I felt distracted, and as if I should be obliged to kill her destroyer." Mary urged Cole
to remain calm, and two days later they were traveling to Brooklyn so Mary
could stay there with her sister. They stopped in Albany, where Cole wanted
to speak with Mary's brother, Henry D. Barto, also a convention delegate.
Cole planned to deliver Mary to Brooklyn, then return to Albany to confront
Hiscock and "force him at the mouth of a pistol on his knees to beg forgiveness for the great injury he had done me, and then to compel him to leave
the country in ten days. . . ." But when Cole saw Hiscock at Stanwix Hall,
"The fall of my poor heart-broken wife and the disgrace of my children rose
up before me, and I could not restrain myself. . . ." A moment later, Hiscock
lay dying.[14]

Testimony taken at the coroner's jury after the shooting vividly depicted
the incident. One witness, Moses Summers, an editor and publisher of the
Syracuse Standard, immediately afterward asked Cole "What does all this
mean?" Cole replied, according to various accounts, "He has dishonored my
simple, innocent wife"[15] and "He has ravished my poor, simple, innocent
wife!"[16] At the police station, Cole wrote a letter to Mary, who visited her
husband the next morning at the jail, where "Both evinced deep agitation. . . ."[17]
According to newspapers, Cole explained in the letter that he had met the
person who had "so grossly wronged her"[18] and "that he had been impelled
to the act by the insults and outrages offered to her, and by a sense of the
shame cast upon his own honor."[19]

Though often a trait especially associated with the American South,[20] the
desire to defend personal honor is well entrenched in the broader American
culture. Most familiar is the use of dueling as a mechanism for defending a
man's honor in the era of the American Revolution and subsequent decades,
when duels were a facet of life in both North and South. Though dueling was
illegal and participants when deaths occurred could be charged with murder,

the law was often ignored, and the military, in which dueling was popular, never court-martialed any of its members for the act.[21] Heavily condemned and prosecuted after the 1804 death of Alexander Hamilton from dueling, the practice died out in Northern states.[22] But the code of honor extended beyond dueling to encompass "the entire cult of killing to avenge wounded sensibilities."[23] This type of killing as a response for personal slights, real or perceived, became a central feature of cases like Cole's in the mid-nineteenth century.

Though Cole maintained that the shooting was not premeditated, he insisted that his actions were justified and expressed no remorse for killing Hiscock. By Cole's interpretation, his act restored honor to himself and his family by removing the transgressor Hiscock. Other men, most notably Daniel Sickles in 1859, had been acquitted for similar actions as juries decided, based on an "unwritten law," that husbands had the right to shoot a wife's paramour, if he caught them in the act.[24] According to Hendrik Hartog, this right "was part of the privileged identity of a husband" in defending an invasion of his property, and the unwritten law was very real when invoked in American courts.[25]

In theory, the unwritten law should have been irrelevant in situations like Cole's where the husband had days to calm down, but juries had shown that was not always the case.[26] The *Buffalo Daily Courier* was one of the few major New York State newspapers to support at least the theory captured by the unwritten law, explaining, "It is well for the libertine to feel that the vengeance of the one he wrongs is liable to overtake him, and that the law will overlook its violation by the avenger." The problem Cole faced, from the perspective of the Buffalo editors, was convincing people to believe his story.[27] Most of the response to Cole's shooting of Hiscock was emphatically negative, and indicated that Cole had not acted honorably. In these initial responses, denunciations of Cole's conduct focused on his actions toward Hiscock on the night of June 4, for which few commentators could fathom there was any defense. Most editors pointed to the social threat implicit in acts like Cole's, and few newspapers hesitated to label the shooting a murder. In Syracuse, Cole was an "assassin."[28] In Rochester, the press deemed the shooting a "deliberate, atrocious and cowardly murder."[29] In New York City, the *New York Times'* editors insisted that "If his act was not murder, then it is impossible for murder to be committed."[30]

The *New York Tribune* denounced labeling Cole a murderer before it had been proven that the shooting was premeditated—by definition, necessary for murder—because the press had an obligation "in the interests of justice and humanity" to avoid pronouncing guilt before it could be so judged in a court.[31] While the *New York Times* readily admitted that Cole remained innocent "In the eyes of the law . . . it is not so in the eye of the Press or of the Public."[32] This continuing difference in the interpretation of Cole's actions and the character of his behavior would be reflected in lawyers' arguments and newspaper commentaries over the course of two trials in 1868. Cole remained newsworthy in the months before going to trial, with occasional reports about the books he read to pass the time, his "excellent treatment"[33] at the jail, and the status of his case,[34] including speculation that Cole's lawyers would present a defense based on the grounds of temporary insanity.[35] Cole's trial was twice postponed from being heard before the court of oyer and terminer (the criminal branch of the state supreme court)—once in November 1867 and once in January 1868—because key witnesses were unavailable.[36]

The trial finally convened on April 20, 1868, and ran through May 6, taking up an extensive amount of time and money in the estimation of one Albany newspaper.[37] Judge Daniel P. Ingraham presided. Prosecutors included Henry Smith, the district attorney for Albany County; Lyman Tremain, the former attorney general of New York State; and the Albany lawyer Charles B. Sedgwick. Cole's primary counsel were Amasa J. Parker, formerly a judge of the state supreme court, and the prominent attorneys William J. Hadley of Albany and James T. Brady of New York City.[38] The *Syracuse Standard* planned to devote extensive space to covering the trial, even though it meant limiting coverage of other news, because community interest was so great "that our columns cannot be better occupied than in giving the fullest details of it. . . ."[39] Newspapers in Albany and Syracuse printed almost full testimony, with coverage in other papers around the state ranging from full accounts to brief summaries. The trial generated so much interest in Albany that the courtroom could not accommodate all the spectators who sought to attend.[40]

The trial opened with the prosecution outlining its case, and prosecution lawyers indicated that the jury's duty was to decide if Cole intentionally killed Hiscock. For Henry Smith, the evidence was clear: while Hiscock was standing and talking with two gentlemen, "Cole, coming in from the Maiden Lane door, entered the rear part of this public room, advancing with a pretty rapid step; and when he got near enough, holding his Derringer pistol almost against the ear of his victim, discharged it into his face and head, producing death." The prosecution's case developed quickly, with testimony from the doctor who examined Hiscock after the shooting, a Syracuse merchant who sold Cole a pistol, the police officer who arrested Cole, and a handful of eyewitnesses to the shooting, including the constitutional convention delegate Cornelius Allen.[41] The prosecution would later add testimony by medical experts and a letter implying premeditation that Cole had left in Syracuse with his cousin, Mary Cuyler, on June 4.[42]

Most of the trial was taken up with defense testimony. The real question for the jury, William Hadley asserted, was if George W. Cole "shall be restored not to home . . . (for home, alas, he has none); not to wife (for wife though living, is dead to him as though the cold grave enclosed her once

loved form), but whether he shall be restored to liberty, and to the compan-
ionship and affection of his loved children, and be permitted to endure the
remainder of his wretched and heart-broken existence. . . ."[43] Defense attorneys developed two contradictory lines of argument: that Cole had a right,
based on biblical imperatives and human nature, to kill Hiscock and restore
his honor, and that Cole had been insane at the time of the shooting and
therefore was not legally responsible for his actions. While the legal decision
in the case turned on this question of temporary insanity, debate along the
first line of defense reflected serious questions about social dynamics and the
changing status of women that were engaging the broader society.

The defense emphasized throughout the trial that social dictates as much
as legal guidelines were relevant to the case. In particular, counsel depicted
a paternalistic image of society in which the husband and father was responsible for defending his family from both physical and moral threats, and they
appealed to jurors on those grounds. Hadley explained that "The question is
to be submitted to you as husbands, as fathers, as moral minded men, to
decide what was the character and nature of the act which George W. Cole
committed, when with reason temporarily dethroned, he took the life of this
destroyer of his domestic peace." The prosecution, Hadley continued, would
try to convince the jurors "that there is no distinction in guilt between the
man who slays in order to commit a crime and the man who slays in order
to prevent one, that crime being the continuance of an adulterous intercourse
with his own wife."[44] Indeed, Hadley queried the jury why a man should
"defend his country if he is to be hung for defending his own family?"[45]

The image of Cole as a staunch defender was developed in early testimony that established Cole's distinguished service during the Civil War.
Witnesses testified about an injury Cole suffered on campaign in 1862 when
his horse fell on him, causing injuries to his bowels and, as the defense
argued, the beginnings of melancholia. Several men who served with Cole
described changes in his disposition after the accident and his sometimes odd
behavior.[46] These included the Philadelphia physician Marcus M. Manley,
who met Cole in the army in 1863. Manley explained that problems from
Cole's injury extended through the time of Cole's discharge in 1866, and that
while in Texas that year Cole's "mind [was] very desponding when he had
these spells; sometimes not speaking for half a day; frequently heard him
groaning . . . I think he inclined towards dementia."[47] Frank B. Garrett, a
Syracuse businessman, had served in Cole's unit in 1862, but found after the
war that Cole "had lost that jovial hearty disposition that he had in the
service; he would sit still in my store and not speak, and I would have to
arouse him; he would walk out abruptly. . . ."[48]

The defense called nearly a dozen men to testify as medical experts
about Cole's state of mind.[49] These witnesses emphasized a history of insan-

ity in Cole's family and Cole's "melancholia," described in the words of the
Ovid physician Alfred Boker as "a depression of spirits" that is "generally
accompanied with delusion."[50] According to Boker, if a person experiencing
melancholia "should suffer an injury and should meet the author of the injury,
he might slay him; I should regard that as an insane act."[51] The prosecution
countered with its own medical witnesses, including the state surgeon-general
James E. Pomfret, who testified that Cole's subdued behavior did not
sufficiently prove insanity, which could only be concluded "If there was an
entire change in character and disposition, and in all his conduct. . . ."[52] Defense attorneys challenged the testimony of prosecution witnesses on the
grounds that they had never seen or examined Cole.[53] The jurors were left to
decide which set of doctors they found more convincing, a problem complicated, as Judge Ingraham later pointed out, by contradictory testimony that
even he had not fully clarified in his own mind. The jury also needed to
determine if Cole's mental condition fit the legal definition of insanity provided by the judge, namely: "It is the law that an insane man is not responsible for his acts. I mean by insanity such a state of mind as that the party
does not know what he is doing; does not know the difference between right
and wrong, and does not know the consequences of his acts."[54] As the jurors
contemplated these issues, the lawyers moved on to other questions.

Having established Cole as a war hero who had suffered in service to his
country, attention then turned to the purported relationship between Mary
Cole and L. Harris Hiscock. John L. Cuyler, a twenty-five-year-old book-
keeper who in 1866 had married Cole's cousin, the aforementioned Mary
Cuyler, testified about Cole's behavior in the days before the shooting. On
Sunday, June 2, a distraught Cole had summoned Cuyler to Jervis House,
where the Cole family resided.[55] Cuyler told Cole he had seen Hiscock at
Cole's house frequently, and Cole then told John Cuyler that Mary had confessed, and Cole sobbed about his poor children. According to Cuyler's testimony, Cole "believed his poor wife was more sinned against than sinning,"
but Cole did not know what to do and said he did not want to live.[56] It was
that Sunday that Cole showed John Cuyler what became known at the trial
as Mary Cole's "first confession"—Exhibit A, a letter in Mary's handwriting.
When Cuyler returned to see Cole the following day, Cole gave him an
envelope and asked Cuyler to keep it; it held Mary's "second confession,"
introduced as Exhibit B.[57]

These two "confessions" contributed to ongoing speculation about Mary's
relationship with Hiscock and her culpability in Hiscock's death, and sparked
new discussion about Mary's behavior, which is hardly surprising. Scholars
have identified changing family and gender roles of the Victorian era as a
crucial factor in the rise of these crimes of passion, as the development of
capitalism, industrialization, and urbanization led to a decline in patriarchy

and an increase in wives' authority.[58] The model of the pure and passionless woman developed as an outgrowth of this change, giving men a means of social control while spending the workday away from their wives. As Americans during the nineteenth century came to value "sexual virtue" at a higher level than at any other time,[59] threats or perceived threats to virtue were taken quite seriously.[60] In this context, the unwritten law had flourished. The applause often heard when acquittals were announced in such cases demonstrates some public support for it,[61] despite the warning of many commentators about the threat of acquittals to a secure and stable society. According to Robert Ireland, defenders of this "unwritten law were arguing that women were morally weak and in need of the constant and vigilant protection of their husbands and brothers."[62]

Was Mary Cole morally weak and in need of vigilant protection? Public speculation and lawyers' arguments suggest yes, though in complex ways. In the weeks following the homicide, newspaper articles contemplated Mary's most private behavior. Mary Cole is portrayed as being morally weak, but in some ways she is also seen as a woman who can wield significant power.[63] In reviewing events that led to the homicide at the start of the trial, Hadley explained that George Cole had returned from the war to find Mary "a changed woman," her "affection" had been replaced "with cold indifference," while "her lips gave no utterance of her former love" and she denied Cole "marital privileges." This change occurred after "A libidinous scoundrel had polluted her being; had stolen away her affections, and by the magical sorcery of the adulterer's spell, had transformed her former love into settled hatred and aversion."[64]

But this explanation of events, following Cole's account the night of the shooting, had drawn heavy skepticism. Especially questionable was the idea that Mary Cole had suffered Hiscock's forced attentions for three years. This speculation was critical of Mary's conduct, but it also implied her ability to direct the actions of men around her. Mary's influence was revealed, at least implicitly, in assorted newspaper commentaries. According to the *Buffalo Morning Express,* "An indignant and outraged wife, whose purity was the bulwark of her defence, would scarcely have tolerated a shameless offender within the sanctity of her home after his first attempt upon her honor."[65] The *Utica Herald* questioned Cole's assertion that Mary was an "unwilling victim" for three years, because "Women usually have devices enough to get rid of suitors when they wish to do so." [66] So Mary, like other women, had the power to control the happenings within her household; the fact the she continued to receive Hiscock suggested that any relations between them were mutual. Thus, while Mary's virtue and moral fortitude were subject to question—as the *Syracuse Standard* queried, "Is a perfectly virtuous woman ever approached improperly the second time?"[67]—Mary was generally acknowledged as having actively shaped whatever relationship had developed with Hiscock. Further, one of the prosecutors, Sedgwick, reminded the court that "Man is not always the seducer" and suggested "that more women by their wiles and lascivious conduct have led more men astray than ever fell victims to the arts of the seducer. . . ." [68]

Within this climate came the trial's consideration of Mary Cole's role in leading up to the homicide. Prevented by law from testifying, the two confessions were the only representations of Mary's voice in the proceedings. The letters were admitted to show how their contents might have contributed to Cole's frenzied state of mind, but they were not considered evidence that adultery had occurred. [69] The first confession, Exhibit A, is the "proof" Cole spoke of having on the night of the shooting:

> Dear husband: — In answer to your inquiries I acknowledge that, about the summer of 1864, L. H. Hiscock, having frequently called at my house on business, one evening in the absence of other persons, first by force, prevailed upon me to submit to his desires, and partly succeeded in his efforts. At various times afterwards, from shame and fear of exposure, he obliged me to in part submit to his caresses, only desisting from his persecutions at last on your return. Those assaults were always made while standing. I have refrained from exposure heretofore from fear of consequences. [70]

This confession indicates, at least initially, the act of ravishment Cole indicated in his statement. Penciled in at the top of the paper was a comment not present when John Cuyler first saw the letter on Sunday, June 2. The comment, further clarifying the extent of relations between Mary Cole and L. Harris Hiscock, while not initially entered as evidence at the trial, was later admitted. Smith read the comment to the court, but it was not reprinted in the 1882 version of the trial transcript, the editors noting, "It is of a character not proper for publication." [71] Newspapers gave varying reports of this postscript, and the complete statement appeared in the *Syracuse Standard:* "But upon my soul, he never had an entire connection with me, nor did he ever enter me entirely." [72] More common treatment was that of the *Syracuse Courier & Union,* which indicated the sentence was not read at the trial, but printed it as "But upon my soul he never had an entire * * * with me, nor did he ever * *." [73] The *Syracuse Journal* simply noted there was a handwritten "addenda" but gave no indication as to the content. [74] Public reaction to this addition clearly fits with contemporary attitudes about the idealistic purity of women. Commentators were scandalized that a woman could make such a statement, and most newspapers did not acknowledge the comment. The published trial transcript even omitted the entire sentence about all the incidents occurring while standing. [75]

The *Syracuse Standard* came under attack from other newspapers for printing the statement; it defended the action on the grounds that it was important to see all the evidence "to be impartial." Still, the editors admitted that some of the testimony might have "been of a revolting character," though it "was understood that some of it would be so before the trial commenced."[76] The entire confession actually drew condemnation of Mary Cole's behavior. The *Rochester Union & Advertiser,* for example, considered Mary's "written confession of criminal intercourse . . . nearly as disgusting as the confession" of Daniel Sickles's wife in 1859.[77] Prompting just as strong a reaction was Mary's second confession, Exhibit B, which was admitted as evidence despite the prosecution's questions about its authenticity:[78]

> I acknowledge of my own free will I have had criminal intercourse at Syracuse, with Mr. L. H. Hiscock at various times, and first about the fall of 1864.
>
> I make this acknowledgment of guilt to my husband, hoping by truth and frankness to obtain forgiveness. I acknowledge that since that time I have, when my husband was at home, seldom permitted him those favors due in married life more than once a month, though he has never refused my slightest solicitations to such favor. I acknowledge he has often asked me the cause of such coolness, and complained of its injustice.
>
> Mary B. Cole

> My criminal connections with Mr. Hiscock were at my own house, and only took place after repeated calls, and at first against my remonstrance.
>
> Mary B. Cole[79]

This second confession was another blow to the reputation of Mary Cole. Most obviously damaging was Mary's admission that she had freely committed adultery. If the second confession were true, according to Sedgwick, Mary "ha[d] prostituted herself for years." But the prosecution also theorized that the second confession involved Mary in a scheme to free her husband, because the document justified invocation of the unwritten law. If Hiscock had, in fact, ravished Mary, prosecutors explained, then he was guilty of a crime punishable under existing law, so there was no need for personal retribution. But by admitting a case of adultery, which was not an act subject to criminal prosecution, it would justify Cole's taking action because the legal system could not.[80] Lyman Tremain suggested that Mary could have easily

written the letter after the homicide, and asked, "Why should she have confessed to him a fact which he himself knew before as well as she in regard
to gratifying his desires? Did any woman on the face of the earth ever make
such disgusting revelations of her own accord?"[81] Whatever the motive or
truth behind the second confession, Mary lied in one of the statements and,
according to Sedgwick, "By the rules of law if she had lied in one instance,
she is not worthy of credit in any."[82]

As jurors considered the merits of the two confessions and their effects
on Cole, the trial closed with extended summations by lawyers for both sides.
On top of the dubious character of Mary Cole's confessions, Sedgwick, in his
concluding comments, insisted that Cole's words of defense after the shooting showed his premeditation and sanity, and were consistent with the message he left in Syracuse,[83] Exhibit C, in which he explained "that L. Harris
Hiscock has forcibly endeavored to dishonor my wife" and his intent that
Hiscock "shall abase himself to her and to me, and beg his miserable life of
me."[84] To the prosecution, this evidence proved that Cole had deliberately
planned Hiscock's execution.

Defense lawyers denied that the shooting was premeditated, but argued
the appropriateness of Cole's actions. As James Brady summarized the situation, Hiscock "fell in Stanwix Hall, not as Caesar did in the Capitol; but as
a man whose base conduct had brought the tragedy upon himself, and under
circumstances which is justified by the laws of God and which he hoped will
be by man."[85] Amasa Parker also invoked the unwritten law to justify Cole's
behavior, suggesting it made no difference, in terms of its effects on Cole,
whether the adulterer was caught in the act or whether the fact was revealed
by Mary: "Does it not in either case bring the same agony to his mind?"[86]
However defensible the homicide may have been, though, Cole's attorneys
also emphasized his insanity at the time of the shooting. Parker explained the
impact of Mary's statements: "She writes the first paper; she had been ruined
by Hiscock. The next confession was more full; and there he stands a ruined
man. What was the effect of piling this mountain of misery upon the prisoner,
with his already shattered mind? It is insanity itself."[87] As Parker summarized,
Cole had gone out to get air, wandered into Stanwix Hall, suddenly came
upon Hiscock, and, unable to control himself, shot Hiscock, an act to be
condemned by "no pure man."[88]

Faced with the prosecution's certainty of Cole's premeditation and the dual
lines of the defense argument, jurors received detailed instructions from the court.
Judge Ingraham told the jury that the law defined murder as "the killing of a
human being with premeditation, except under circumstances of justification or
excuse, as laid down in the law."[89] But what did this exception mean? Judge
Ingraham was candid with the jury about the difficulty in defining insanity when
physicians and "the law" disagreed about the meaning of the concept:

You must be satisfied that he was so unsound of mind as not to be responsible for his acts. The law looks upon insanity in one way and the medical profession in another. The doctors regard anything as insanity that disorders the mind. The law does not so regard it, but holds the man accountable if he knows right from wrong.

When the mind is so destroyed as to overcome the will, and deprives him of not [*sic*] knowing what he is doing, then he is not responsible.[90]

With the jury divided after initial deliberations, the foreman asked Ingraham to add any other necessary information. Ingraham explained that Cole could also be found guilty of manslaughter—a possibility never raised during the course of the trial—if the jury found him sane but that the homicide was not premeditated.[91] Despite that additional option, the jurors still could not agree and were discharged.[92]

The jurors' failure to reach a consensus, and particularly their failure to convict Cole, was heavily criticized. Newspapers statewide printed scathing editorials about the jury system, and especially the reason why no verdict was reached, many pointing to contemporary social attitudes. The *Syracuse Standard,* for example, took issue not with the fact that the jurors were unable to agree, "but with the public sentiment which rendered it possible."[93] The *New York Times* chastised jurors who "set aside the law, and decide the case according to their own pleasure,"[94] and the *Albany Argus* rejected the "theory of the right to murder" for being "as repugnant to civilization as to christianity."[95] Few newspapers had been convinced that Cole was innocent, even under the terms of the "unwritten law."

The commentary emerging in response to the jury verdict (in both this first and the second trial) included a renewed and more complex examination of whether Cole's actions could be considered honorable. One facet of that analysis involved the very nature of the unwritten law. From a legal standpoint, the crux of the problem with the simple story of an honorable man who acted in self-defense by doing what all—including the seducers—knew husbands had a right to do, Hendrik Hartog notes, is that it was against the law.[96] Juries had gotten around that obstacle in the past by ruling that the defendant had been insane at the time of the homicide. But questions were being raised as to whether broader social attitudes would continue to condone such a justification. Social opinion in New York was clearly divided as to the appropriateness of personal retaliation to restore honor and the necessarily public nature of any such action. As the *Syracuse Standard* explained, "The honor of a man's wife is his most sacred possession, and ample atonement should be made by him who rifles it—but it is not for unregulated passion to constitute itself a retributory agent."[97]

In part, the call for restraint rests on a change in the meaning and significance of the traditional code of honor that was linked with the unwritten law. By the mid-nineteenth century, that code was being challenged in the northern United States by the concept of dignity. Rooted in New England Puritan beliefs, the idea of dignity was absorbed into middle-class culture, and was particularly embraced by populations that had experienced the reform fervor of the Second Great Awakening.[98] Where as honor was an external value, under which the broad community judged a person's worth, dignity dictated that a person's worth was an internal matter. As Roger Lane explains, an insult to a man of honor would require a public response, while a man of dignity could ignore the insult.[99]

For George W. Cole, honor in its traditional meaning, with its emphasis on external judgments, was paramount. From the time he learned that there was some form of intimate relationship between his wife and Hiscock, Cole was frantic about the honor, or public reputation, of his family name, his children, and himself. These concerns are evident from the statement he gave the night of the shooting, from the letter he left with Mary Cuyler (Exhibit C), from his horror at learning from Montgomery Pelton that Mary's behavior had become a topic of gossip in Syracuse, and from his continued insistence that he had acted appropriately in killing Hiscock. Cole's letter to Mary from the Albany jail also implied that his honor had been trampled upon. As Hadley explained at the trial, Cole worried about the "disgrace brought upon his name" as the whole world learned of it, and he even contemplated suicide.[100]

The defense tried to bolster the image of Cole as an honorable man by undercutting any sense of Hiscock's honor. According to Hadley, "Before a man can deliberately debauch the wife of the friend who confides in him, he must have become utterly abandoned to every principle of virtue and be lost to every sentiment of manly honor."[101] Thus, it was Hiscock's behavior, not Cole's, that truly deserved condemnation. The defense repeatedly stressed the rightness of Cole's actions as a response to wounds inflicted by Hiscock. Parker also defended Cole's killing of Hiscock by explaining that adultery was not punished with death in the United States, "because it is supposed that the husband shall be the protector of his own family, and shall vindicate his own honor."[102] To develop this argument, the defense sought to introduce evidence that adultery had, in fact, been committed. But the judge, abiding by the written law, ruled testimony along these lines inadmissible because alleged adultery was no ground for homicide, independent of the question of insanity.[103]

Most commentators remained unconvinced by these arguments in the Cole case. That is not to say they completely dismissed the traditional code of honor, as clearly reflected in the columns of the *Buffalo Daily Courier* and in the *Albany Argus,* which urged, "Let the extreme intervention of personal vengeance be reserved for those cases in which the innocence of youth is betrayed, or the physical weakness of the sex trampled upon."[104] Neither applied in this instance. Particularly offensive in the minds of commentators was that Cole had executed Hiscock without giving him a chance to defend himself. Immediately after the homicide, the *Albany Evening Journal* questioned if this was honor or "a glaring, damning outrage, culpable baseness, sneaking cowardice?"[105] The shooting had been considered especially cowardly because Cole did not meet Hiscock "upon anything like equal terms. . . ."[106] Prosecutors had also denounced Cole's attitude toward the shooting. According to Tremain, if Cole had been insane, one would expect him to show remorse after killing Hiscock. Instead, Cole "declares that the deceased had violated his honor, and that he (the prisoner) was justified in what he did."[107]

In the aftermath of the hung jury, though, the issue that drew the most attention was not Cole's treatment of Hiscock, but rather whether Cole had acted honorably in dealing with his wife. While newspapers had been highly critical of Mary Cole's conduct with Hiscock—she was presumed, at best, to have been an equal partner with him in violation of her marriage vows—Cole was condemned for dishonoring his wife in the quest to save himself and his own reputation. By first killing Hiscock, and then by defending himself in the trial using Mary's two confessions, he had made her most intimate behavior a topic of public discussion and left her open to public ridicule. According to the *New York Times,* Cole might truly be "sorry that he has brought his wife into such unpleasant notoriety." But if Cole's care for his wife's reputation "had been a genuine regard for her honor and her welfare, he would not have taken the most effectual means he could possibly imagine to fasten upon her, in the eyes of all the world, the ineffaceable brand of disgrace and infamy."[108]

Also critical of Cole was the *Ithaca Journal,* which explained, "Mrs. Cole may be an abandoned and worthless woman—but what must we think of Mr. Cole, whose cowardice and love of his own miserable life, could induce him to blast the character of his wife before the world and drag her name through the mire in this manner to save his own worthless neck."[109] For the *Albany Evening Journal,* if Mary is guilty of adultery, but Cole "has dragged her offence into the daylight. . . . He has made her the subject of comment for a thousand journals and a million busy tongues. He has conferred upon her a notoriety that will follow her to the grave and beyond it." If Mary is innocent, Cole "has inflicted upon her a fearful wrong, deeper and more dreadful than even that which is alleged against the murdered man."[110]

None of these accounts portray Mary Cole in a particularly flattering way. She may have initiated a seduction of Hiscock, or if not the initiator, she at least became an equal partner by keeping the relationship hidden from her husband. Whatever the circumstances of that relationship, the *Syracuse Courier*

& *Union* asked the public for "forbearance and charity," because Mary "Even if innocent, as we are inclined to think, the burden to be borne by this unfortunate woman and her more unfortunate children, as well as that of the children of the deceased, is already too heavy to be borne, without the aggravation of baseless rumors and a hasty imputation of unproven crime."[111] The enmity was directed at her husband. If, in fact, women were weak and in need of vigilant protection, George Cole had failed to provide it for his wife by making their private matters public and subjecting Mary to widespread speculation and scorn.

As a writer for *Harper's Weekly* concluded, "It is an entirely false sense of honor which drives a man to murder even the known paramour of his wife. If there has been an offense it is by mutual consent. That knowledge cannot sully the honor of a true soul. It may break a faithful heart, but it will not inspire in a really generous man the desire of revenge."[112] Though the editors reference a sense of honor, they are describing what scholars have come to call a sense of dignity, with its emphasis on internal rather than external judgment. These responses to the homicide reflect the ongoing struggle to define the nature of honor. Honor still clearly has relevance. But it is more than the honor of the man that matters. Not only are women considered people of honor (or dishonor), but if a wife's honor is a man's greatest possession, as the *Syracuse Standard* claimed, it should supersede even the husband's personal honor. Despite some lingering sentiments for personal retribution, the bulk of opinion seems to indicate that the eighteenth-century notion of externally defined and defended honor can be more harmful than helpful, both to the direct participants and to society as a whole.

As furor over the hung jury calmed, Cole, who was denied bail, remained in jail awaiting his second trial.[113] It was begun in November 1868. Judge Henry Hogeboom presided, with the same counsel appearing on both sides. Testimony from the first trial was generally read into evidence without oral examination of witnesses "except as to any points on which counsel desired to make farther inquiry."[114] The defense produced a few new witnesses and tried again to introduce evidence of adultery. This evidence included a series of gifts between Mary Cole and Hiscock that suggested a mutual relationship: Hiscock had given Mary an expensive ring; Mary had given Hiscock a silver tobacco box and a shirt stud that Cole had initially given her. Further, on the night he was killed, Hiscock purportedly was carrying a photograph of Mary Cole. Most of this evidence was disallowed by the judge, though mention of the ring and tobacco box were admitted in the testimony of Mary Cuyler.[115] As the *Syracuse Journal* commented skeptically of the second trial, a bolder defense policy had led to the introduction of new evidence—evidence that witnesses remembered in time for this trial, but not for the first trial or for the grand jury hearings. "Not less remarkable," the editors concluded, "is the fact that the new developments are exactly the things needed to extricate the accused from unexplained and difficult dilemmas attaching to his crime."[116]

But that conclusion was not so easily reached by the jury. Hogeboom explained that the prosecution had to prove Cole's sanity beyond a reasonable doubt, but "that the ordinary condition of man is sanity. . . ."[117] While the charge that Hiscock seduced Mary Cole might spark sympathy, the judge cautioned "we are not here to administer sympathy—but to execute justice. . . ."[118] The possibility of manslaughter was also raised in the charge to the jury, which Brady for the defense opposed, believing there was no way the act could have been manslaughter. After deliberating for several hours, jurors asked for clarification about the insanity defense. Upon a third clarification from Judge Hogeboom, the jury found Cole not guilty; they believed him to be sane just before and just after the homicide, but were uncertain about his sanity at the moment of the shooting, a situation in which the benefit of the doubt had to favor the defendant.[119]

The verdict earned "very loud applause," and Cole thanked the court for a fair trial.[120] Afterward, Cole, his friends, and the jury went to the Delevan House, "where a bounteous entertainment was spread."[121] But formal response to the acquittal from the state's newspapers was just as critical as it had been of the hung jury the previous spring. According to the *Syracuse Journal,* the jury decision in no way changed its opinion of the case. It said the editors would continue to "adhere to our views, through a deep-seated conviction, formed on mature reflection, with the advantages of an intimate acquaintance with the parties to the homicide, a close watching of the legal investigations, and a knowledge of facts and circumstances not admissible as legal proofs on [*sic*] the trials. We believe that the great body of intelligent, reflecting persons, having the same means of judging the case, agree with the views we have expressed."[122]

More common was the opinion seen in the *New York Times,* which commented on Cole's acquittal on the grounds that he was sane just before and after the shooting, but possibly not at the exact moment of the shot. "Probably this is the most extraordinary verdict ever returned by a jury made up of men supposed to be sane themselves," it said.[123] Indeed, editors of the *Rochester Union & Advertiser* reported a few days later that they had intended "to give extracts from various leading journals on the outrageous verdict in the Cole murder case to show the tone of the press on the subject. But as there is only one view expressed—one unanimous expression in denunciation of the finding as against law, evidence and common sense, it is unnecessary to quote."[124]

The verdict was one that technically met the dictates of the law under which, if the jury had reasonable doubt based on the evidence about Cole's sanity at the time of the shooting, it was obligated to lean in his favor.[125] And there was surely some genuine support for points raised by defense counsel in these cases concerning crimes of passion. In Cole's second trial, the jurors asked for clarification on points of law three times, suggesting a real concern with those issues. To some contemporaries, acquittals really came in such cases because "Juries bought defense arguments."[126] Still, the legal judgment was not always satisfactory to the broader society. The *Albany Evening Journal,* for example, said, that "Public opinion, as expressed by the leading newspapers of this and other States, brands Cole with the mark of Cain, and from that verdict there is no appeal."[127]

Shortly after the trial, newspapers reported that Cole would travel with his brother, Senator Cornelius Cole, to Washington, D.C., and then "visit Syracuse during the holidays."[128] In 1869, Cole took a job in the Register's Office of the New York City Post Office. Newspapers continued to report on his activities, still with a watchful eye.[129] Rumors that Senator Cole had been pushing for his brother George to be named secretary of the United States Senate drew criticism.[130] As the *Syracuse Standard* explained, while Cole was "at liberty" to seek a position with the Senate, "An acquittal by a local jury, however, is not so grave a matter as an endorsement by the Senate would be. Public sentiment is too prone to make martyrs of murderers. The Senate should check the tendency."[131]

Mary Cole and the couple's two daughters continued to live with her brother, Henry Barto, in Trumansburg after the second trial. George Cole visited his children there in January 1869. During his stay, Cole had a chance encounter with a correspondent of the *Seneca Falls Reveille* with whom Cole was acquainted. According to a newspaper account of the meeting, Cole indicated that he had seen his daughters but not Mary, and the reporter "inferred from this consultation that he would no longer live with her." Cole continued to justify killing Hiscock "and feels that he did no more than his duty; although at the time too much excited to be conscious of what he did."[132]

This explanation by Cole is similar to the attitude of other acquitted defendants in celebrated crimes of passion of the time, and in many ways the Cole-Hiscock trial adheres to the pattern that scholars like Robert Ireland and Hendrik Hartog have described.[133] That is, in a case where one prominent man killed another, a defense was sought on grounds of temporary insanity, but heavily buttressed by appeal to the unwritten law that the killer was acting in a way that was not only acceptable but that was necessary for preservation of his honor. While defense arguments emphasized the clash of wronged husband and wrongful seducer under the unwritten law, the wives' roles, as Hartog notes, "were barely relevant."[134] Despite the dominance of the unwritten law argument, though, the Cole-Hiscock case points to the need to move beyond its parameters, for our understanding of the period can be furthered by examining the role of and reaction to the wives more closely.

Though Mary Cole could not testify at the trial, her voice was heard through her two confessions; she was the subject of much prosecutorial attention, and public commentary was strongly focused on Mary's actions and how they may have affected those of her husband. Opinions expressed about Mary are particularly illuminating, given the social currents of the time. Just a few years earlier, in 1865, nineteen-year-old Mary Harris had been on trial in Washington, D.C., for the shooting death of Adoniram J. Burroughs. Harris had believed she was engaged to Burroughs, but killed him after learning Burroughs married another woman a few months after he delayed his wedding to Harris. At her trial, which included a claim of temporary insanity, the defense portrayed Harris as weak and helpless, which drew sympathy and resonated with expected notions of womanhood. The acquittal of Harris drew widespread public approval.[135] In the Cole-Hiscock case, though, public discussions about Mary Cole, and about the nature of women in general, present a much more powerful image of women as the societal norm. While Mary Cole's behavior was sharply criticized, commentators believed she had been in a position to turn away Hiscock if she had chosen to do so. A closer examination of the role of the women involved in these incidents not only helps trace changing ideas about family and gender roles, but also about broader societal trends, such as the changing notion of honor.

George Cole's belief that he was acting honorably was challenged, based on new understandings of what comprised honorable behavior that reflected significant shifts in his social world. Those developments also allowed for a broad spectrum of opinion in contemporary interpretations of the homicide. In killing Hiscock, Cole sought, in his words, to protect the virtue of his once innocent wife. This view was very much in keeping with the era's dominant social attitudes about women, including women's propensity for moral weakness. And it did not matter, within the code of honor, what Mary's role had been. If Mary's second confession was indeed authentic, Cole knew the extent of the criminal intercourse a day before getting on the train to Albany. If "the heart of honor was the respect of others," as Edward Ayers defines it for the antebellum period, George Cole could be considered honorable in his efforts to restore his good name.[136]

The problem for Cole was that the nature of honor and its role in Northern society were undergoing a transformation. Honor traditionally had been reserved as a male trait, only affecting women as a consequence of the honor of their male relatives.[137] But as the status of women was changing over the course of the nineteenth century—with evangelical religion and industrial society giving women more opportunities to behave and be treated as individuals—women also were being perceived as people relevant to the trait of honor. Commentators during this episode frequently referenced the honor of Mary Cole, and George Cole agonized over the loss of honor of his wife and daughters. Yet his actions were widely condemned by public opinion, if not by the judgment of a jury, for placing his honor above that of his wife. Cole's behavior was particularly problematic in a society where honor, even broadly defined, was being challenged by the internally focused notion of dignity.

Still, Cole's legacy is mixed, reflecting the social dynamism of his time. George W. Cole died of pneumonia in Mora, New Mexico, on December 9, 1875.[138] A concluding note to the trial transcript, published in 1882, indicates that Cole was not a murderer, but that "Cole's name is still well remembered as the hero of a domestic tragedy" in which he killed L. Harris Hiscock.[139] This interpretation must be weighed against the opinion of the *Albany Evening Journal* on learning of Cole's acquittal: "life is as sacred as honor."[140]

Notes

1. "The Cole-Hiscock Case," *Albany Argus*, 15 April 1868.

2. This term only became commonplace toward the end of the nineteenth century, but it is appropriate as a general descriptor for this type of case. See Ed Hatton, "He Murdered Her Because He Loved Her," in *Over the Threshold: Intimate Violence in Early America,* ed. Christine Daniels and Michael V. Kennedy (New York: Routledge, 1999), 113.

3. Robert M. Ireland, "Insanity and the Unwritten Law," *American Journal of Legal History* 32 (April 1988): 157. Ireland analyzes ten such cases that occurred between 1843 and 1885.

4. See "Murder at Albany," *New York Times*, 5 June 1867; "Terrible Tragedy in Albany," *Syracuse Standard*, 5 June 1867; "Awful Tragedy?" *Syracuse Courier & Union*, 5 June 1867; "Terrible Tragedy," *Syracuse Journal*, 5 June 1867; "Startling Murder in Albany," *New York Tribune*, 5 June 1867; "Bloody Tragedy at Stanwix Hall Last Night," *Buffalo Morning Express*, 5 June 1867; "Murder in Albany," *Buffalo Daily Courier,* 5 June 1867; "Assassination of Mr. Hiscock," *Rochester Daily Democrat*, 5 June 1867; "Terrible Tragedy at Albany," *Rochester Union & Advertiser*, 5 June 1867; "The Murder of L. Harris Hiscock," *Ithaca Journal*, 11 June 1867. Near-verbatim reports of the events of June 4 appeared in newspapers statewide in the days following the shooting. For ease of reference, this essay will generally cite only the *New York Times* coverage of these early accounts.

5. "Terrible Tragedy," *Syracuse Journal*, 5 June 1867.

6. "Murder at Albany," *New York Times*, 5 June 1867; "The Assassination at Albany," *Harper's Weekly*, 22 June 1867, 389.

7. "The Albany Murder," *New York Tribune*, 6 June 1867. The *Tribune* reported that Hiscock's wife, Lucy, had died eight years earlier, but that is incorrect; obituaries announcing her death appeared in 1861. See *Syracuse Journal*, 25 February

1861; *Syracuse Standard*, 26 February 1861. The *Albany Argus* included a similar misstatement. See "The Stanwix Hall Tragedy," *Albany Argus*, 6 June 1867.

8. "Murder at Albany," *New York Times*, 5 June 1867.

9. Cole's military career was discussed at the trial. For details, see Thomas Dunphy, ed., *Remarkable Trials of All Countries*, vol. 2 (New York: S. S. Peloubet & Co., 1882), 212–15.

10. See, for example, *Syracuse Standard*, 30 July 1862; *Syracuse Journal*, 1 August 1862; *Syracuse Journal*, 21 April 1863; *Syracuse Journal*, 26 February 1864; and *Syracuse Journal*, 6 June 1865. Notice of Cole's return to Syracuse after the war was reported in "Personal Mention," *Syracuse Journal*, 19 March 1866.

11. "Murder at Albany," *New York Times*, 5 June 1867.

12. Ibid.; "The Tragedy at Stanwix Hall," *Albany Argus*, 5 June 1867.

13. Illness prevented Montgomery Pelton from testifying at the first trial. He did appear at the second trial and produced the letter Cole had sent him, dated May 30, 1867. Pelton's letter responding to Cole had been lost. Dunphy, 379.

14. "Murder at Albany," *New York Times*, 5 June 1867. Other newspapers carried the same statement, with slight modifications in wording. See, for example, "Awful Tragedy?" *Syracuse Courier & Union*, 5 June 1867.

15. "Murder at Albany," *New York Times*, 5 June 1867; "The Tragedy at Stanwix Hall," *Albany Argus*, 5 June 1867.

16. "The Stanwix Hall Tragedy," *Albany Evening Journal*, 5 June 1867.

17. "The Tragedy," *Syracuse Courier & Union*, 6 June 1867.

18. "Murder at Albany," *New York Times*, 5 June 1867.

19. "The Albany Murder," *Rochester Union & Advertiser*, 6 June 1867.

20. On Southern honor, see especially the writings of Bertram Wyatt-Brown, such as his *The Shaping of Southern Culture: Honor, Grace, and War, 1760s–1880s* (Chapel Hill: University of North Carolina Press, 2001).

21. Roger Lane, *Murder in America: A History* (Columbus: Ohio State University Press, 1997), 84–85.

22. Joanne Freeman's analysis of political culture in the early national period indicates the relevance of honor nationwide. She traces the decline of personal honor as a significant trait in the political realm to the growth of formal political party organizations and their accompanying anonymity for individuals. See Joanne B. Freeman, *Affairs of Honor: National Politics in the New Republic* (New Haven, Conn.: Yale University Press, 2001).

23. William Oliver Stevens, *Pistols at Ten Paces: The Story of the Code of Honor in America* (Boston: Houghton Mifflin, 1940), 272.

24. On the Sickles case, see W. A. Swanberg, *Sickles the Incredible* (New York: Scribner, 1956); Nat Brandt, *The Congressman Who Got Away with Murder* (Syracuse, N.Y.: Syracuse University Press, 1991); Thomas Keneally, *American Scoundrel: The Life of the Notorious Civil War General Daniel Sickles* (New York: Doubleday, 2002).

25. Hendrik Hartog, "Lawyering, Husbands' Rights, and 'the Unwritten Law' in Nineteenth-Century America," *Journal of American History* 84 (June 1997): 67–68; quotation at 67. Hartog notes that the husband could be convicted of manslaughter, as in other acts of self-defense like shooting a trespasser.

26. Ibid., 69.

27. "The Albany Murder," *Buffalo Daily Courier*, 6 June 1867.

28. "Albany Letter," *Syracuse Standard*, 6 June 1867.

29. "The Murder of Mr. Hiscock," *Rochester Daily Democrat*, 6 June 1867.

30. "The Albany Murder," *New York Times*, 12 June 1867.

31. "The Press and Public Justice," *New York Tribune*, 13 June 1867. To do otherwise, whatever the evidence, would threaten an impartial trial: "The assassin taken red-handed, with his weapon in his hand, or his knife still at the victim's throat, is entitled to a fair trial before he is punished, and no man may sit on the jury who has already made up his mind about the prisoner's guilt. The law recognizes the sacredness and grave importance of the duty before it, and wisely provides that man shall sit in judgment upon the life of his fellow man only with passions calmed and mind unwarped by prejudice. How is such a trial to be obtained if the press is to treat the accusation all as proved, to pooh-pooh at the defense before it has been heard, and to put the verdict into the jury's mouths before the accused has been arraigned?"

32. "The Albany Murder," *New York Times*, 12 June 1867. See similar comments in "The Stanwix Hall Tragedy," *Albany Evening Journal*, 5 June 1867.

33. "The Cole Hiscock Murder," *New York Tribune*, 22 January 1868.

34. See, for example, ibid., as well as "General Cole in Prison," *Syracuse Journal*, 7 August 1867; "The Cole-Hiscock Case," *Syracuse Standard*, 8 November 1867.

35. "The Cole Hiscock Murder," *New York Tribune*, 22 January 1868.

36. Among the key witnesses, one was ill and another was pregnant. For a summary of the reasons for the delay, see ibid.; "The Albany Homicide," *New York Times*, 31 January 1868.

37. "The Cole Murder Trial," *Albany Evening Journal*, 7 May 1868.

38 Dunphy, 194–95.

39. "The Cole Trial," *Syracuse Standard*, 22 April 1868.

40. "The Cole Trial," *Syracuse Journal*, 28 April 1868.

41. Dunphy, 203–10; quotation at 204.

42. Ibid., 292. Mary Cuyler testified that Cole gave her the folded letter, introduced in the trial as Exhibit C, and "told me that if I heard of any fuss, that he was going to see Hiscock, and was going to make him get on his knees, and wished to be thus represented, and that I should have it published if I heard of any disturbance. . . ."

43. Ibid., 212.

44. Ibid., 229–30.

45. Ibid., 225.

46. Ibid., 238–50.

47. Ibid., 238–40. Manley also testified that at one time for several weeks, Cole seemed quite childish. According to his testimony, Mary visited Cole in January 1864 and stayed until May; she also returned around the time of Robert E. Lee's surrender in 1865 and traveled with them to Texas.

48. Ibid., 244.

49. Ibid., 249–89.

50. Ibid., 276. Some of the witnesses disagreed whether Cole suffered from melancholia or melancholy, which Boker described as depression of spirits but without delusions.

51. Ibid., 276–77. Boker knew Cole from Cole's days as a medical student.

52. Ibid., 303–11; quotation at 308.

53. Ibid., 316. Tremain later countered, saying the defense medical witnesses had never seen Cole when he was insane. Ibid., 358–59.

54. Ibid., 364. That difficulty would arise over interpretation of the insanity defense is hardly surprising. The 1843 McNaughton (or M'Naghten) decision defined insanity for American practice as being in a state of mind in which the defendant could not distinguish between right and wrong. The temporary insanity plea was even newer, having first been prominently used in the 1859 Sickles case, though it built on a doctrine of "irresistible impulse" that dated to the 1830s. See Ireland, "Insanity and the Unwritten Law," 165; Lee Chambers-Schiller, "Seduced, Betrayed, and Revenged: The Murder Trial of Mary Harris," in *Lethal Imagination: Violence and Brutality in American History,* ed. Michael A. Bellesiles (New York: New York University Press, 1999), 189.

55. Dunphy, 278. Cuyler testified that Cole "appeared to have been weeping; his eyes were bloodshot; had wild appearance; hair seemed uncombed; think he had no coat; he shook hands with me and at once asked if I had ever seen Mr. Hiscock at his house; I said I had. . . ." Defense questions about how frequently Hiscock had

appeared there led to a lengthy debate among the lawyers and judge about admissibility of evidence intended to show communications to Cole by a third party.

56. Ibid., 280–81. On that visit, Cole asked Cuyler to take a telegram to be delivered to Mary Cole's brother, Henry D. Barto. When Cuyler returned to see Cole after dinner, Cole was in the same condition.

57. Ibid., 281. There was much contention about the authenticity of the second confession, reportedly given to Cuyler that day. Cuyler testified: "I placed it in my safe at the office Monday afternoon; I took it out of there on the 7th of June and gave it to Mr. Hadley, sealed; was present when it was opened, I think on Wednesday evening last, at Mr. Hadley's house; it was in the same condition; it had not been opened. . . ."

58. Robert M. Ireland, "The Libertine Must Die: Sexual Dishonor and the Unwritten Law in the Nineteenth-Century United States," *Journal of Social History* 23 (Fall 1989): 28.

59. Ibid., 29.

60. For more on evolution of family relationships, see Michael Grossberg, *Governing the Hearth: Law and Family in Nineteenth-Century America* (Chapel Hill: University of North Carolina Press, 1985).

61. Ireland, "Libertine Must Die," 37.

62. Ibid., 32.

63. Notable is how little we hear from or about Mary Cole. She was usually mentioned in newspaper articles about the shooting amid descriptions of her husband. The *Syracuse Journal*, for example, in a brief sketch of George Cole on June 5 indicated that "His wife possesses unusual attractions of person and mind, and has been a highly esteemed and admired member of the society in which she moved. She is related to some of the most respectable families in the State." "Terrible Tragedy," *Syracuse Journal*, 5 June 1867. Less flattering was the *New York Tribune,* which reported that "Mrs. Cole is small, plain-featured, and rather sickly in appearance." "The Albany Murder," *New York Tribune*, 10 June 1867.

64. Dunphy, 219.

65. "The Albany Tragedy," *Buffalo Morning Express*, 7 June 1867. The editors asked, why should Hiscock have forfeited his life for conduct that had long been permitted (since Mary had allowed Cole to continue visiting the residence) "and only revealed months afterwards under the pressing importunities of a husband, whose suspicions had been aroused by a mischief-maker and tale-bearer?" Mary had allowed Hiscock repeated visits and did not tell her husband of the episodes, and the *Buffalo Morning Express* opined, "Under these circumstances we cannot see the culpability all on one side. It strikes us that the woman who has tolerated, if she has not encouraged, the victim, has no higher title to life than he who is dead."

66. Excerpt from the *Utica Herald* in "Albany Tragedy: Opinions of the Press," *Rochester Daily Democrat*, 8 June 1867.

67. "The Albany Tragedy," *Syracuse Standard*, 7 June 1867.

68. Dunphy, 326, 330.

69. This point was made several times. See, for example, ibid., 362–63.

70. "Letter of Mrs. Cole," *Syracuse Standard*, 30 April 1868. The wording was slightly different as printed in various newspapers. Most papers removed all or part of the sentence indicating that the "assaults" took place while standing. See, for example, "The Trial of Gen. Cole," *Syracuse Courier & Union*, 30 April 1868; "The Cole-Hiscock Case," *Rochester Union & Advertiser,* 30 April 1868; *Albany Evening Journal*, 29 April 1868; "The Trial of George W. Cole for the Murder of L. Harris Hiscock," *Albany Argus*, 30 April 1868. The reprinted letter in the commercially published trial record also omits this sentence. Wording there indicates Mary was prevailed upon to "yield" (rather than "submit") to Hiscock's desires. Dunphy, 289. The *New York Tribune* observed that Mary's letter "was drawn up in the form of a statement, and its brevity and wording indicate that it might have been written from dictation. Certainly it bears no resemblance to the confession of a heart-broken, penitent wife." See "The Albany Murder," *New York Tribune*, 10 June 1867.

71. Dunphy, 299.

72. "Letter of Mrs. Cole," *Syracuse Standard*, 30 April 1868. A somewhat different version of the letter and postscript had been printed in reports of the grand jury proceedings in June 1867. The *Albany Argus* then reported the contents as: "According to your request, my dear husband, I write the particulars of what has occurred between Mr. Hiscock and myself. The improper conduct commenced in 1864, and has continued at intervals ever since until a recent date. The first time was when I was sick in bed, when he came to my bedside and endeavored to have connection with me. The next time was in the hall, when I was seeing him to the door. I was standing up. He used force, and I always resisted him as well as I was able. He never succeeded in entirely * * * There was no * * * I did not tell of it because I was ashamed and afraid to do so." The editors indicated that "The portions omitted are said to be unfit for publication." See "The Cole-Hiscock Tragedy," *Albany Argus*, 10 June 1867.

73. "The Trial of Gen. Cole," *Syracuse Courier & Union*, 30 April 1868.

74. "The Cole-Hiscock Case," *Syracuse Journal*, 30 April 1868.

75. One must make this latter point about the omission in the trial record with caution. There are some errors in the transcript, though generally they are in referencing dates. But given the acknowledged objection to printing the postscript, it is quite possible that this was also a deliberate omission.

76. *Syracuse Standard*, 6 May 1868.

77. "Mrs. Cole's Confession," *Rochester Union & Advertiser*, 1 May 1868.

78. Dunphy, 286–87.

79. Ibid., 296–97.

80. Ibid., 329–31; quotation at 330. Sedgwick would again emphasize this charge at the second trial. See ibid., 388.

81. Ibid., 352.

82. Ibid., 331.

83. Ibid., 326.

84. Ibid., 296. The letter was reprinted in various newspaper accounts, including "The Cole-Hiscock Case," *Rochester Union & Advertiser*, 30 April 1868.

85. Dunphy, 336.

86. Ibid., 322–23. Parker also reminded the court that the law does not prescribe a specific cooling-off period and suggested that if the jurors "find that at the moment of his so killing him [Hiscock] the reason and mental powers of the accused were so affected from any cause that he had not at the moment sufficient mental power to control his own action, he is not in law guilty of murder or any other crime." See ibid., 333.

87. Ibid., 317.

88. Ibid., 319.

89. Ibid., 363–64.

90. Ibid., 364.

91. Ibid., 365. Cole's lawyers objected to the manslaughter option because it was never put forward in the case and not covered in their defense. Ibid., 366.

92. Ibid., 367. Different newspapers reported various divisions among the jurors. See, for example, "The Albany Letter," *Syracuse Standard*, 7 May 1868; "The Cole Murder Trial," *Syracuse Standard*, 8 May 1868; "The Case of Gen. Cole," *New York Times*, 12 August 1868.

93. "The Cole Trial," *Syracuse Standard*, 8 May 1868.

94. "When Murder Is Lawful," *New York Times*, 8 May 1868.

95. "The Trial of Cole—Disagreement of the Jury," *Albany Argus*, 8 May 1868. The article was reprinted as "The Cole-Hiscock Tragedy," *Syracuse Courier & Union*, 13 May 1868.

96. Hartog, "Lawyering," 80–81.

97. "The Albany Tragedy," *Syracuse Standard*, 7 June 1867.

98. Edward L. Ayers, *Vengeance and Justice: Crime and Punishment in the 19th-Century American South* (New York: Oxford University Press, 1984), 23–29.

Ayers notes that dignity originated in Puritanism and grew up alongside societal and personality changes that were brought by the development of capitalism. Southern evangelical Christianity provided an internal challenge to the Southern code of honor. The same challenge was likely posed by evangelical Christianity in the North, particularly in the heart of the Burned-Over District.

99. See ibid., chap. 1; Lane, 85–86.

100. Dunphy, 222–23.

101. Ibid., 220.

102. Ibid., 323. As Brady explained at the conclusion of Cole's second trial, "Whatever may be the law, the dictates of humanity, as impressed by the Creator upon his creatures, teach that Hiscock deserved the death he met. If, said the counsel, my sister had been the victim of the seducer, and I had not shot him down for his crime, I should consider myself unfit to live among men." See ibid., 389–90.

103. Ibid., 293–95.

104. "The Trial of Cole—Disagreement of the Jury," *Albany Argus*, 8 May 1868.

105. "The Stanwix Hall Tragedy," *Albany Evening Journal*, 5 June 1867.

106. "Is It a Proof of Honor?" *Albany Evening Journal*, 7 June 1867.

107. Dunphy, 354.

108. "Minor Topics," *New York Times*, 7 June 1867.

109. "Cole-Hiscock Murder Trial," *Ithaca Journal*, 5 May 1868.

110. "Preserving Honor," *Albany Evening Journal*, 6 June 1867.

111. "The Cole-Hiscock Tragedy," *Syracuse Courier & Union*, 14 June 1867.

112. "The Murder at Albany," *Harper's Weekly*, 22 June 1867, 389.

113. "The Case of Gen. Cole," *New York Times*, 15 August 1868.

114. Dunphy, 372.

115. Ibid., 372–79.

116. "Progress of the Cole Trial," *Syracuse Journal*, 30 November 1868.

117. Dunphy, 399.

118. Ibid., 404.

119. Ibid., 413–20.

120. "The Acquittal of Gen. Cole," *Syracuse Courier & Union*, 9 December 1868.

121. "George W. Cole," *Syracuse Courier & Union,* 9 December 1868; "The End of the Cole Trial," *Syracuse Journal,* 8 December 1868. The Rochester press was especially critical of such celebration, explaining that the verdict and aftermath showed the "farcical finale of a bloody tragedy." See "An Assassin Acquitted and Feasted," *Rochester Union & Advertiser,* 8 December 1868.

122. "The Cole-Hiscock Case," *Syracuse Journal,* 8 December 1868.

123. "The Cole-Hiscock Murder," *New York Times,* 9 December 1868.

124. "The Verdict in the Cole Case," *Rochester Union & Advertiser,* 10 December 1868.

125. Dunphy, 419.

126. Hartog, 87. The Bible also presented a foundation for the actions of the husbands.

127. "The Mark of Cain," *Albany Evening Journal,* 9 December 1868.

128. "George W. Cole," *Syracuse Courier & Union,* 9 December 1868; *Syracuse Journal,* 9 December 1868.

129. *Syracuse Standard,* 2 December 1869.

130. *Syracuse Journal,* 11 November 1869.

131. *Syracuse Standard,* 15 November 1869.

132. "The Homicide Cole and Family," *Syracuse Journal,* 18 January 1869.

133. See also Robert M. Ireland, "Death to the Libertine: The McFarland-Richardson Case," *New York History* 68 (April 1987): 191–217.

134. Hartog, 79.

135. Chambers-Schiller, 194–99.

136. Ayers, 16.

137. Ibid., 29.

138. Roger D. Hunt and Jack R. Brown, *Brevet Brigadier Generals in Blue,* rev. ed. (Gaithersburg, Md.: Olde Soldier Books, 1997), 122. The published trial record, explaining the cause of death, indicates that Cole died on December 11, 1875, which is likely the date of his burial. That record also incorrectly identifies the place of death as Mara rather than Mora. See Dunphy, 420.

139. Dunphy, 420.

140. "Cole Acquitted," *Albany Evening Journal,* 7 December 1868.

10

Bodies of Evidence:
Inquest Photography in the Trial of Lizzie Borden

Tiffany Johnson Bidler

Evidence, like *clue* or *proof*, is a crucial word for the historian and the judge.[1]

I

At 11:10 A.M., Thursday, August 4, 1892, Andrew J. Borden, seventy, and Abby D. Borden, sixty-four, were discovered brutally murdered in their home at no. 92 Second Street, Fall River, Massachusetts. A hatchet found in the Borden residence later that day was the presumed weapon. Circumstantial evidence implicated the now notorious Lizzie Andrew Borden, the daughter of Andrew and the stepdaughter of Abby.

The murder of Andrew and Abby gave rise to a sensation in the United States.[2] National newspapers published lavishly illustrated front-page stories describing the events in exacting, and often gruesome, detail. (The exhaustive description of crimes had begun with the emergence of the "penny press" in the 1840s. Mass-circulation newspapers sensationalized antebellum crimes like the 1845 murder of Maria A. Bickford.[3] The trend continued in the years following the Civil War.)

The press and the public were captivated from June 5 to June 20, 1893, as Lizzie stood trial. The courtroom drama monopolized the gossip of visitors to the Columbian Exposition in Chicago. Strolling on the streets of the White City, children chanted the newly coined rhyme: "Lizzie Borden took an axe / And gave her mother forty whacks / And when she saw what she had done / She gave her father forty-one."[4]

In the 1890s a new medium, photography, also entered into the press coverage of crime and was employed in the courtroom; both prosecutors and defense attorneys presented photographs of crime scenes to juries and a broader audience, as they tried to prove the guilt or innocence of the accused. Police departments began to hire photographers to record images of crime scenes, and prints of the images taken by police photographers were presented as evidence during trials. Thereafter, photographs, and illustrations based on photographs, played a central role in the "reading" of the criminal and the criminal act.[5]

Throughout the Borden trial, photographs were used in numerous ways. Because the photographs carried evidential weight, the court swore in James A. Walsh, the Fall River photographer who had photographed the crime scene. He identified the five photographs he produced of the Borden premises, verifying that they were "accurately taken from their respective points of view."[6] He further verified that he had not moved the bodies, that the views had been taken in the presence of Fall River police officers, and that all the photographs had been taken the same afternoon.

Witnesses on the stand, and subsequently the jury, saw photographs of the scene of the crime, the autopsies of Andrew and Abby, and other material forms of evidence. The photographs added credence to a witness's statements or served to sway (or call into question) a witness's memory of specific events. In addition, the court frequently used photographs in the place of detailed verbal descriptions, or when the court called a witness' memory or spatial description into question. For example, Thomas Keiran, the Fall River city engineer, provided lengthy and detailed verbal descriptions of the Borden premises. C. J. Mason, one of three sitting judges, barked, "Have they not photographs of it from which they can tell in one second more than you can get from the witness in half an hour?"[7]

The court also used the autopsy photographs of the Bordens when Dr. Seabury W. Bowen, the physician and surgeon who first arrived at the scene of the crime, testified. The court asked him to compare his own observation of the scene of the crime with the photographs taken from it.[8] Photographs carried authority because they were thought to be an empirical record of reality—a literal emanation of the referent.[9] Nevertheless, the court did not think photographs were impervious to manipulation. This resulted in the necessity to legitimize or authenticate photographs by way of traditional courtroom procedures.

The initial rise in the use of photography as trial evidence corresponded to a cultural interest in phrenology,[10] which, like physiognomy, was a science that sought to articulate the links between the outward physical appearance and the inner character traits of criminals.[11] Lizzie Borden did not escape the phrenologists' efforts. Photography and phrenology allowed middle-class society to imagine a "knowable social sphere in which their own positions and the positions of others would remain quite literally apparent."[12] Although the science of phrenology claimed to be empirical, its conclusions were based on a reading of physiognomy filtered through well-established stereotypes about race, nationality, and gender. In her study of nineteenth-century photographic archives, the historian Shawn Michelle Smith traces the history of the desire to join gendered, classed, and racialized interior essences to codified physical exteriors. Phrenological studies answered to a desire to obtain knowledge about the "essences" residing in others by way of the reading of the surfaces of their bodies. "Studies of the criminal body," according to Smith, "answered to middle-class concerns about the essences some bodies might mask and hide, and attempted to make those bodies transparent to the technologically aided, professional middle-class eye."[13] The turn-of-the-century understanding of the photograph offered a model for an understanding of the body—just as there was a naturalized relationship between the photograph's denotation and its connotation, there was a naturalized relationship between inner character and outer appearance.

Henry Wood's essay "The Psychology of Crime," written in 1893 and referring obliquely to the Borden murders, presents the reader with a "physiognomic" procedure for reading the criminal act. The essay adds to an understanding of how jurors and other viewers may have interpreted representations of crimes such as the Borden murders, and establishes an implicit theory of representation by attempting to articulate the relationship between exteriors and interiors. Wood characterizes crime as "The Without" expressing "The Within" hidden away from the "popular" gaze.[14] By arguing that crime is a form of *representation*,[15] the criminal act functions as a picture or "snapshot" of an underlying collective psychology:

> Every outward manifestation is a harvest. No full-fledged or overt act takes place that is not the lawful sequence of previous incubation, nourishment, and growth. When a criminal offense "happens," the usual concern is only with the event, its details, and the adequate punishment of the offender. The act is vividly outlined, its heinous features are analyzed, the guilt of its supposed author is passed upon, and a demand is made for the enforcement of the proper penalty. This comprises all that society feels called upon to do in the premises. A blow has been dealt to the community, in one of its parts, and the community deals a proportionate one in return, and thus the transaction is closed and the books are balanced. Possibly some "motive" may be discovered, which forms the last or immediate step behind the act, but no further special investigation is thought necessary.[16]

Figure 10.1: *Sitting Room, body of Andrew Borden, 92 Second Street,* August 4, 1892, Fall River Historical Society.

The process of interpreting a criminal act correlates here with the traditional process of interpreting a work of art. Wood's description could be altered as follows: A work of art "happens" and the usual concern is only with the depicted event, its details, and the status of the artist. The work of art is vividly described, its negative features are analyzed, and the triumph or failure of the artist is determined. The community is given an image, the community views it, and the transaction is closed. It is possible that some kind of deeper "motive" for creating the work of art may be discovered, but usually a special investigation of the way in which society has nourished a particular mode of expression is thought unnecessary. If the turn-of-the-century public deciphered criminal acts in a manner similar to the way in which they deciphered pictures, it follows that an interpretation of a picture of a crime was tantamount to an interpretation of the criminal act.

According to Wood's implicit theory of representation, art is representative of the "inwardness" of the artist and the zeitgeist of the age or place in which the artistic act was accomplished. The twentieth-century British art historian E. H. Gombrich would consider this a mode of "physiognomic perception."[17] "Physiognomic perception" buttresses the "physiognomic fallacy," which is the belief that "the system of signs, the style [of the work of art], is not a language but an utterance of the collective, in which a nation or an age speaks to us."[18] Gombrich's discussion of formalist art analysis as "physiognomic" implicates it in the kind of essentialism the science of physiognomy engages in when hypothesizing that the formal aspects of one's appearance reveal the essence of one's race, nationality, class, or gender. Lizzie's acquittal resulted from a turn-of-the-century desire to maintain a belief in the trustworthiness of appearances, representations and, more specifically, the "physiognomic fallacy."

In his essay "The Photographic Message," Roland Barthes, like Gombrich, discusses "style" as a system of signs or connotations. As a result, the consumption of inquest photographs by the turn-of-the-century public can be usefully analyzed using the critical terms outlined in his essay. Barthes counters the traditional view of the photograph as empirical record by contending that it is comprised of *two* messages, one *denotive* and one *connotative*. A photograph is considered "a message without a code," but it also contains within it a supplementary cultural message—*style*. Style, according to Barthes, is the " 'treatment' of the image . . . whose signified, whether aesthetic or ideological, refers to a certain 'culture' of the society receiving the message."[19] A photograph is an object that has been "worked on, chosen, composed, constructed, treated according to professional, aesthetic, or ideological norms which are so many factors of connotation."[20] The photograph is not merely "perceived" and "received," it is actively "read" by the viewer. It is connected to a "traditional stock of signs," and since every sign supposes a code, it is this "code of connotation" that Barthes feels writers on photography should try to establish.[21] The reading of a photograph is always historical: "it depends on the reader's 'knowledge' just as though it were a matter of real language [*langue*], intelligible only if one has learned the signs."[22] Examined in light of turn-of-the-century pictorial conventions, or codes, the inquest photographs seem to provide "evidence" of Lizzie's innocence. These representational codes allowed the jury to construct an intelligible narrative of feminine passivity, which perhaps led to the desire to indict a male murderer, whom turn-of-the-century society would have seen as having the "agency" to act upon the "passive" victims captured in the photographs.

The inquest photographs of the Borden murders were taken between 11:15 A.M. and 3:00 P.M. on August 4, 1892. One inquest photograph is of Andrew's body (figure 10.1). It captures him in repose on the parlor sofa. A chair sits in the foreground, and the image of a small round table embellishes the left side of the photograph. His face, butchered beyond recognition, evidences the eleven blows it received with a hatchet. His bisected eye hangs out of its socket. When Andrew was found, blood was still seeping from his wounds, and spots of blood decorated the floor and the wall above the sofa— eighty-six spots of blood described the arc of a circle, within a radius of eighteen inches. Forty blood spots, the highest one being fifty-eight inches from the floor, clung to the frame and glass covering the print of the Arc de Triomphe that hung over the sofa.[23] Dr. Seabury W. Bowen stated: "[H]e was on his right side apparently at ease, as any one would if they were lying asleep." When asked if there were significant differences between his memory of the scene and the photograph, he stated, "I don't think the photograph shows the ease that is natural to a person that is asleep or lying down. I think the form has sunk down a little from what it was when I first saw it . . . I think his head is lower here than it was."[24] Another witness, George W. Allen, a police officer, noticed his "shoes were on, and how small the ankles was [*sic*] for the shoes."[25] Andrew's head was resting on a small sofa cushion covered with a "little white tidy," and Andrew's body rested upon an "afghan or sofa cover, a knitted affair."[26]

The sofa on which Andrew was murdered would have been recognized as an example of the rococo revival style, which had originated in France during the reign of Louis-Philippe (1830-48). This style had been popular in the United States in the 1850s and 1860s, but in the late 1860s the Renaissance revival style replaced the rococo revival style in popularity. The S-curve of the sofa is characteristic of the rococo revival style of furniture, and the print of the Arc de Triomphe above the sofa is appropriate to the decorative scheme.[27] The rococo revival-style furniture featured in the Borden parlor was one of the first styles produced in the United States that utilized the manufacturing techniques of the Industrial Revolution.[28]

Andrew was killed on a "Borden" sofa—an intimate symbol of his rise to wealth and prestige in the Fall River community. He had begun his career in the 1840s as a dealer in "rich and common" furniture, and as an undertaker for the company Borden & Almy's. In the 1850s, the *Fall River Weekly News* carried advertisements for Borden & Almy's furniture that included chamber sets, cabinet furniture, chairs, and other decorative household items. Factory-produced versions of revival furniture styles were still widely available to the middle class in the 1890s. In the August 1892 editions of the *Boston Daily Globe*, the furniture sellers W. H. Hervey and Co. advertised the "affordability" of a "Parlor Suit" that featured a sofa much like the Borden's. At the time of the murders, however, the elite Fall River community would have considered rococo and Renaissance revival styles, long since replaced by the Eastlake mode and eclecticism, quite unfashionable. [29]

A detail of an additional inquest photograph captures Abby, who was murdered first in the second-floor guest room of the Borden home, but was discovered shortly after Andrew (figure 10.2). The photograph agonizingly

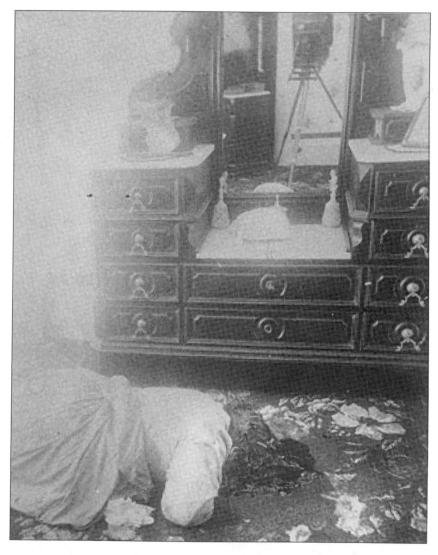

Figure 10.2: Detail, *Guest room, body of Abby Borden, 92 Second Street,* August 4, 1892, Fall River Historical Society.

records the extent of her fatal wounds, later quantified by an autopsy as having been caused by the nineteen distinct hatchet blows. Congealed blood pools around her head and seeps into the fibers of the floral carpet. Abby's legs are cropped out of the picture, yet the neatness and orderliness of the

Figure 10.3: John Singer Sargent, *Repose,* 1911, National Gallery of Art, Washington D.C.

knickknacks arranged on the Renaissance revival dressing case are clearly evident. According to the trial transcript, the bed was in perfect condition and was covered with a white bedspread and pillow shams.[30] Abby is not positioned at the center of the photograph recording her murder. This framing of the photograph is out of step with the rigorous symmetry of the room's furniture, and perhaps serves to reinforce the assumption that a force from outside this domestic order fractured her skull. The officers found the face board of the bed toward the dressing case "besmeared" with matted hair and blood—so many blood spots covered the face board that they did not attempt to count them.[31] One observer remarked that Abby must have had the "natural" amount of hair, "naturally" thickest where it was knotted over the back portion and top of the head (the portion that was caved in).[32] Charles Carroll took a photograph of the fragment of braid found near Abby's body. George W. Allen noticed a fallen handkerchief soaked in blood at Abby's feet. When Dr. Bowen was asked to compare a photograph of the crime scene to his memory of it, he testified, "Mrs. Borden is lying nearer the bed in this picture than the dressing case, which is not a fact."[33] When asked about a photograph in which the bed had been drawn away, he stated, "I think her arms were a little lower down than are represented here, slightly lower, below the breast."[34] Another witness recalled that her hands were up around her head.[35]

In the inquest photographs described above, the police and photographic apparatuses recorded by the photographer discipline the space of the photographs and buttress one's belief in their objectivity. The whole, intact, mechanical eye of the camera peers back at us in the form of a reflection in the guest room's dressing-case mirror; an investigator's bodily movements are rendered intangible as he watches over Andrew's mournfully all-too-substantial body in the parlor. According to Barthes, when an artist wants to be neutral or objective he or she "strives to copy reality meticulously, as though the analogical were a factor of resistance against the investment of values."[36] In the case of photographic evidence, the photographer attempts to rid the image of "artistry" in order to heighten the effect of neutrality and objectivity. The documentary photographer, however, is ultimately not able to rid an image of freely circulating social and historical connotations. The codes of connotation of which Barthes writes are neither natural nor artificial. Rather, they are historical and cultural—"gestures, attitudes, expressions, colours or effects, endowed with certain meanings by virtue of the practice of a certain society."[37] One particular connotation procedure outlined by Barthes is "pose."

> Consider a press photograph of President Kennedy widely distributed at the time of the 1960 election: a half-length profile shot, eyes looking upwards, hands joined together. Here it is the very pose of the subject which prepares the reading of the signifieds of connotation: youthfulness, spirituality, purity. The photograph clearly only signifies because of the existence of a store of stereotyped attitudes which form ready-made elements of signification (eyes raised heavenwards, hands clasped).[38]

Although the court determined that the Borden inquest photographs were objective objects of evidence, they are haunted by stereotyped attitudes, or poses, garnered from painting and photography, that allow for the formation of ready-made elements of signification.

The photograph of Andrew Borden depicts him collapsed on the parlor sofa in much the same fashion as turn-of-the-century representations of women such as Sargent's *Repose* (figure 10.3), which depicts Sargent's niece, Rose-Marie Ormond Michel, languishing on the sofa in a private apartment. *Repose* emphasizes the weight and materiality of the figure's body, which seems to overburden her spirit, strength, and stamina. Her garments harmonize with the green, peach, and gold tonalities of the painting's background, resulting in her disappearance into the domestic environment. Likewise, Andrew's body is barely visible against the tonalities of gray that constitute the black-and-white photograph. The art historian Linda Nochlin has equated these images of repose with an eroticized and feminized mental and physical passivity.[39]

> Repose, the domain of the Aesthetic Woman . . . implies a kind of pensive self-absorption, a dreamy but highly self-conscious interiorization of sensibility. . . . There is something more than a little erotic, then, about these images of reposing women. Their enclosed intimacy, their flower-like passivity[,] recall the hothouse visions of earlier Orientalist paintings—Delacroix's Women of Algiers, Ingres's Odalisques—Westernized, updated, and naturalized, but harem creatures nevertheless. In the enforced, perpetual leisure suggested by the harem captive, the white of repose shades into the more ominous Stygian darkness of Baudelaire's *ennui*.[40]

Andrew's "pose" among "white tidies" and "knitted affairs" can also be compared to that of Sarah Bernhardt in Napoleon Sarony's melodramatic *carte de visite* of the actress (figure 10.4).[41] Bernhardt toured the United States in the fall of 1880 playing the role of Camille in Alexandre Dumas's *La dame aux camélias*. Sarony's image of Bernhardt captures her as Camille in the emotionally charged final scenes of the play, in which she melodramatically "expires." Her drooping body recalls the repose of Andrew and Sargent's Ormond Michel, while a macabre undertone collapses the accouterments of turn-of-the-century femininity—flowing unbound hair, pale skin, delicate lace, and floral motifs—with death.

Illustrations of Lizzie produced during the trial also follow the convention of depicting muscular passivity as an assurance of emotional passivity and femininity. In the June 7, 1893, edition of the *Boston Globe*, and in an image from the *Police Gazette*, Lizzie is depicted as fainting while listening to the closing remarks of the plaintiff's plea. The heavy curvilinear lines describing her drooping body serve to formally emphasize her passivity (figure 10.5). The fan, behind which she would normally hide her face, has fallen into her lap—its handle points toward her womb. Lizzie's fainting spell is framed by the activity of the men who rush to aid her. On the last day of the trial, the *New Bedford Evening Journal* published an illustration of Lizzie collapsed against the rail of the courthouse in response to hearing the "not guilty" verdict from the jury.[42] The suspicion that this is a visual convention of the period is encouraged by the fact that another newspaper depicted her as responding to the verdict while sitting erect in her chair.[43]

Two additional codes of connotation discussed by Barthes are color and effect. At the turn of the century the "painterly" effect of camouflage was

Figure 10.4: Napoleon Sarony, Sarah Bernhardt, c. 1880. Photograph. International Museum of Photography, George Eastman House, Rochester, New York.

Figure 10.5: Bert Poole, *The Fainting of Miss Borden At The Close of Mr. Moody's Plea, The Boston Daily Globe,* June 7, 1893.

endowed with gendered meanings. In an analysis of the turn-of-the-century debate on camouflage and its relationship to attitudes regarding femininity and masculinity, the art historian Alexander Nemerov examines the artist Abbott Thayer's treatise *Concealing-Collaboration in the Animal Kingdom* (1909). The treatise featured illustrations supporting Thayer's theory that all animal markings, even the most vibrant, were intended to render the animal in question invisible against the background of its natural habitat. Nemerov argues that Thayer's theories on camouflage provide a framework for an understanding of Thayer's prototypical representations of angelic women who transcend the materiality of the female body.[44] Although Thayer's paintings are not of primary concern here, Nemerov's essay convincingly points out the turn-of-the-century equation drawn between women's public visibility, on the one hand, and dirtiness, lowness, evolutionary baseness, immorality, brazenness, and prostitution, on the other. Images of women camouflaged against natural and domestic settings were symptomatic of the dualism involved in the description of women.

John Singer Sargent's watercolor, for example, *The Brook* provides for the visibility of the female figure, while it illustrates a communion of the dematerialized female body and nature. The painterly image depicts two women beside a stream; their garments and bodies, depicted in delicate blues, greens, and yellows, are nearly indistinguishable from the surrounding flora and fauna. The curve of the central figure's body echoes the curve of the stream, while the patterns on her gown leave her camouflaged in much the same way as Thayer's *Peacock in the Woods* (1907), which served as the frontispiece for *Concealing-Collaboration in the Animal Kingdom* (figure 10.6). *The Brook* encourages a reading similar to Martha Banta's reading of Sargent's *The Hermit*. In this image, according to Banta, Sargent depicted a hermit camouflaged against the dense forest glade in order to illustrate his transcendence of the body. She states, "The hermit has, for his religious beliefs, given up worldly identity in order to merge with God. Flesh assimilated into spirit is the equivalent of disappearing into Sargent's colors."[45] *Ideal* women transcended nature via invisibility or spiritual oneness with nature and domestic surroundings.

Lizzie's manipulation and recognition of the politics of visibility and invisibility stood as evidence of her good breeding.[46] According to one writer, "it was *plain to see* that she had complete mastery of herself and could make her sensations and emotions *invisible* to an important public [my emphasis]."[47] The movement between visibility and invisibility characterizes the act of disappearance. Andrew's act of disappearance into the tonalities of gray describing his domestic environment may have been seen as "feminine" to turn-of-the-century viewers. One can draw out similar readings of the inquest photograph of Abby (figure 10.7). As a result of its

Figure 10.6: Abbott Handerson Thayer and Richard Meryman,
*Peacock in the Woods, study for book Concealing Coloration
in the Animal Kingdom.* Smithsonian American Art Museum.

Figure 10.7: *Guest room, body of Abby Borden, 92 Second Street,* August 4,
1892, Fall River Historical Society.

black-and-white tonality, the details of Abby's body escape our vision. The blood we know has seeped from her head appears an inky black, barely distinguishable from the carpet on which she lies. Her dress, made from perhaps a pale cotton cloth, decorates the florid carpet much as the pale flower petals that comprise its pattern.

Barthes also writes of the connotative importance of the posing of objects in photographs. As already discussed, Abby's violent death perhaps represented the "chaos" of the outside world that invaded the "order" of the middle-class domestic interior.[48] The order of the middle-class domestic interior was signified by the presence of particular objects. Thus, the middle-class environment in which the crime took place functioned as important evidence in its own right. This environment contained objects that were "accepted inducers of associations of ideas."[49] The art historian John Davis states that the exterior appearance of the Victorian parlor and the objects in it were "a constructed 'portrait' of the taste, morals, and character of the family who created it."[50] This understanding of the parlor's external appearance as indicative of familial morality is a form of "physiognomic perception."[51] The objects and visual images collected in the parlor, in addition to serving as a constructed "portrait," were intended to instruct and shape the moral character of the family's still-impressionable children. Lizzie's murderous act, according to Wood and others, would have been considered an expression of the negative influences of the surroundings that had shaped her in youth. However, the "instructional" objects that surrounded her in the Borden parlor—a settee, armchairs, tables, books, prints—were not unusual. They were those typically seen in the homes of "refined" families.[52]

Davis's essay focuses on Eastman Johnson's *The Brown Family* (1869), which depicts James and Eliza Brown in their elaborate New York City parlor with their grandson, William. The parlor was "designed to nurture the entrepreneurial or combative urge as much as the social or familial."[53] The inclusion of the Brown's grandchild in *The Brown Family* shows the hereditary continuity of the Brown's moral character, power, and property. Artists often represented the parlor as the site of *masculine* control: "The luxurious interiors of the elite, unlike middle-class homes, were more often associated with the men of the family (and their spending power)." These sites were "filled with visible symbols of status and success in the world of business."[54] While it displayed a certain level of comfort, there was nothing particularly extravagant about the Borden parlor decor. In fact, its modesty evidenced a frugality and shrewdness underlying Andrew Borden's entrepreneurial skill. In his opening statement, William H. Moody noted that Andrew was, at the time of his death, "a man of considerable property."[55] In this same statement, Moody emphasizes that Andrew obtained his fortune by "earning and saving" and "retained the habit of saving up to the time of his death."[56] During the trial, a gendered contrast was drawn between Andrew's economy of saving and Lizzie's rumored economy of consumption.[57]

In Davis's discussion of *The Brown Family*, he describes the New York City art world's reception of the Brown portrait. The Browns were attacked for their "gaudy," "garish," and "painfully elaborated" furnishings, or for what we would call in the twenty-first century "conspicuous consumption."[58] In 1869 the decorative scheme of the Brown family parlor was no longer fashionable. The modest and frugal interior of the Borden home captured in the inquest photographs was likewise read as unfashionable, and was viewed by some as the impetus of Lizzie's murderous rage. There was a discontinuity between the Bordens' pattern of consumption and their economic status, between their private wealth and their public display of class signifiers. The prosecution argued that the decor was so incapable of properly signifying Lizzie's class status that the incongruity drove her mad and induced the killing spree.[59] In their closing statements Lizzie's defense argued vehemently against this presumption:

> They [the prosecution] start off on another tack, and they say she killed her stepmother and her father because that was a house without any comforts in it. Well, gentlemen, I hope you all live in a better way than the Borden family lived, so far as having good furniture and conveniences. Are your houses all warmed with steam? Do you have carpets on every one of your floors, stairs, and all? Do you have pictures and pianos and a library, and all conveniences and luxury? Here was a young woman with property of her own. Starved to death, they say; pinched so she could not live, wrought up to frenzy and madness, so that she would murder her own father for the want of things, and yet, as has been shown here, worth, in her own right, of money and personal property.[60]

In addition to pointing out the gendered contrast between the economy of saving and the economy of consumption, and the presumed importance of external display aligning correctly with one's class status, these arguments indicate that the notion of a woman driven mad by her interior surroundings was not foreign to U.S. society at the turn of the century. In January 1892, the *New England Magazine* published Charlotte Perkins Gilman's "The Yellow Wallpaper," a fictional account of a woman's decline into an insanity brought about by a prescribed "rest cure" for neurasthenia. In "The Yellow Wallpaper" the protagonist projects her own feelings of claustrophobia onto the nauseating yellow wallpaper, described as "a florid arabesque, reminding one of a fungus," that covers the walls of the nursery in which she stays.[61] Within the wallpaper pattern, the protagonist sees images of crawling women:

At night in any kind of light, the twilight, candlelight, lamplight, and worst of all by moonlight, it becomes bars! The outside pattern I mean, and the woman behind it is as plain as can be. I didn't realize for a long time what the thing was that showed behind, that dim sub-pattern, but now I am quite sure it is a woman. By daylight she is subdued, quiet. I fancy it's the pattern that keeps her so still.[62]

An anonymous 1899 response to "The Yellow Wallpaper" indicates the way in which the merely unattractive decor described in "The Yellow Wallpaper" was read (perhaps tongue-in-cheek) as unfashionable decor. "After reading ["The Yellow Wallpaper"] the model husband will be inclined seriously to consider the subject of repapering his wife's bed chamber according to the ethics of William Morris."[63] The writer's reference to William Morris is per-haps mordant, given the presence of arsenic pigments in Morris wallpapers that were known to cause chronic illness.[64] We can easily imagine Gilman's wallpaper—a "nauseating yellow reminding one of a fungus"—featuring a yellow tinged with a bit of arsenic green. Charles Dana Gibson's *Design for Wall Paper Suitable for a Bachelor Apartment* (figure 10.8), published in *Life* magazine, didactically and humorously illustrates the way in which women were associated with the floral and the decorative. Interpreted in a more morose manner, the work illustrates the vision seen by Gilman's protagonist in "The Yellow Wallpaper." Placed in front of this background, a corporeal woman disappears.

"The Yellow Wallpaper" and Eastman Johnson's *Not at Home* are de-scriptive of the narrative of feminine "breakdown" encouraged by the mise-en-scène of the turn-of-the-century domestic interior (figure 10.9). *Not at Home* illustrates a woman overwhelmed by her domestic and social duties, and serves as an example of the way in which women were pictorially con-sumed or camouflaged by their domestic surroundings. An absent child who haunts the empty buggy placed in the corner of the composition is, like the nursery's child in "The Yellow Wallpaper," a peculiarly absent but perpetual concern. The presence of the men of the household is indicated by represen-tations within representations—the bust on top of the grandfather clock and the portrait hanging on the wall in the stairwell. The canvas is divided spa-tially into a brightly sunlit parlor and a dimly lit foyer that consumes the fleeing woman who, like Abby Borden in the inquest photograph, does not even occupy the center of her own picture. Abby disappears into the carpet's floral pattern in a manner similar to that of the "creeping" woman who disappears into the yellow wallpaper in Gilman's story. Yet Abby's body is irrefutably *present*. Her inquest photograph performs a complex "movement" between presence and absence, visibility and invisibility, that characterizes photography, and, I would add, historical writing. According to Roland Barthes,

Figure 10.8: Charles Dana Gibson, *Design for Wall Paper Suitable for a Bachelor Apartment, Life Magazine,* September 18, 1902. Image can be found in Martha Banta, "Looking for the Best Type," *Imaging American Women: Idea and Ideals in Cultural History.* New York: Columbia University Press, 1987, 90.

Figure 10.9: Eastman Johnson, *Not at Home,* c. 1873, Brooklyn Museum of Art.

Figure 10.10: Nelson Sizer, "Lizzie Borden," *Phrenological Journal of Science and Health* (December, 1892): 287.

"a photograph is always invisible: it is not it that we see."[65] Like Barthes, the art historian Carol Mavor has focused on the simultaneous presence and absence represented in photography: "For only with photography (as opposed to painting or sculpture) is one assured of the fact that what was once before the artist/camera—its referent—was there and is no longer there. Yet the photograph (fictitiously) registers it as right before your eyes: as simulacrum."[66] *Not at Home* makes use of the photographic framing or "snapshot" effect often reproduced in nineteenth-century impressionistic painting. Photography haunts *Not at Home,* just as photography is "tormented by the ghost of painting."[67] Christian Metz writes that "the snapshot, like death, is an instantaneous abduction of the object out of the world into another world, into another kind of time. . . . In all photographs we have this same act of cutting off a piece of space and time, of keeping it unchanged while the world around continues to change, of making a compromise between conservation and death."[68] This same movement characterizes the writing of history.

II

Although the inquest photographs of the Borden murders support the gendered assumptions utilized throughout the Borden trial, it follows that in order for Lizzie Borden to be acquitted she had to present herself as belonging to the middle-class domestic sphere invaded by the crimes. Lizzie's acquittal was the result of the jury placing steadfast faith in the idea that her outward appearance of femininity and "good breeding" corresponded to internal innocence and moral virtue. It rested on the idea that the lack of stain on Lizzie's dress indicated a lack of stain on her character.[69] Throughout the trial, Lizzie's outward appearance of femininity was used both to support and to contest her innocence.[70] For example, on August 7, 1892, the *Boston Daily Globe* provided a lengthy description of Lizzie that arrives at conclusions regarding her innocence based entirely on her outward appearance:

> The impression [the reporter] had obtained from her published portraits was utterly upset. . . . She makes an exceedingly favorable impression. . . . It was a trying ordeal to pass before the eyes of a crowd of 1500 morbidly curious spectators. She wore a tightly fitting black lace dress with a plain skirt and waist of equally modest cut and finish, while a dark hat, trimmed with a similar material, rested upon her head. Of medium height, she is possessed of a symmetrical figure . . . and a carriage which would dignifiedly repel the attention her personal charms might attract. A wealth of black hair is revealed under the hat which, arranged about her forehead in short curls, parted in the centre and thrown over to the sides. Her dark lustrous eyes, ordinarily flashing, were dimmed, and her pale face was evidence of the physical suffering she was undergoing and had experienced. To sum up, Miss Lizzie Borden, without a word from herself in her own defense, is a strong argument in her own favor. [71]

The phrenologists, however, provided a more ambiguous reading of Lizzie's internal character than the *Boston Daily Globe*. On November 4, 1892, the *Chicago Evening News* published "Lizzie Borden's Head/A Phrenologist Gives His Verdict upon the Accused Woman without Knowing Her Name/The Science Applied to Many Things." The phrenologist was Nelson Sizer, president of the American Institute of Phrenology. The December 1892 issue of the *Phrenological Journal of Science and Health* featured his analysis of Lizzie Borden first printed in the *Chicago Evening News*. After calling the case the "melancholy marvel of the season," Sizer goes on to state that "lawyers and others who have an interest in criminal jurisprudence, as well as writers historical or sensational, bring to our office photos, or send us woodcuts, smooth or rough, from every part of the country for our opinion on the character. . . . On the 27th of October last, a photo was sent to our office with a request for a brief estimate of the character."[72] A "cut" made of this photograph of Lizzie was then included in the *Chicago Evening News* along with Sizer's analysis (figure 10.10).

Sizer took fifteen minutes with the photograph, and then delivered his "analysis and criticism":

> Oct. 27, 1892—Lady: We see in this portrait practical talent. The fullness across the lower part of the forehead evinces large perceptive faculties as a group, making her bright, quick to see, to know and to remember, giving the talents necessary for practical education, for art, mechanism and for business. The head seems to be broad in the sides above and about the ears, showing bravery, energy, severity, and a strong desire for ownership, and laying the foundation for good business talent and the tendency to push the cause which has business involved in it to a successful termination. The face indicates power. The broad cheek bones and the prominence of them, the massiveness of the lower jaw, as it makes an angle to get up toward the ear, show vital power and the tendency to be thorough and severe. The mouth indicates determination and resolution. The breadth of the head above and about the ears shows courage, selfishness and executive ability. She appears to have large firmness that is shown in the height of the head, on a line from the opening of one ear to that of the other over the top. We think she has a pretty good share of self-esteem. She is self-willed, courageous, high tempered, secretive, fond of property. She is not a thinker and reasoner; she is a critic, but she is rather light in the reasoning power, though amply developed in the abilities which relate to practical knowledge and the ability to be ingenious and artistic. If the back and top of the head were available it would be an aid to the full estimate of her character. She appears to have more courage than prudence, more determination than pliability, more force than restraint of mind.[73]

While Sizer's analysis could be read as positive—Lizzie has "executive" ability and a sound mind for business—it comes close to portraying her as "unfeminine" and leads the reader to draw connections between positive qualities associated with U.S. capitalists and capitalism and the way in which these qualities could be put to untoward ends. Both the popular press and the prosecution emphasized Lizzie's desire for "sensuous gratification" in the form of property and luxury goods in order to paint her as a woman of questionable character. This view would seem to be reinforced by Sizer's description of Lizzie as practical, courageous, selfish, resolute, high-tempered, and fond of property. The word "executive" in this context brings to mind the executioner's ax, and Sizer's call for the absent "back and top of the head" provides an unwelcome reminder of Andrew and Abby's fractured skulls.

Alongside these suspicions regarding Lizzie's character, early reports blamed the murders on "outside" forces, such as foreigners, immigrants, and horse traders. Some, like the members of the Fall River Women's Union, were induced to search for a criminal whose external appearance of deviance indicated an internal criminal deviance.[74] An anonymous letter sent to the prosecution on September 1, 1892, stated: "Is it not now about time to look up the Chinaman whom Lizzie Borden is said to have had so much interest in as a pupil? If Lizzie had a hand in the murders it is pretty clear another hand committed the deed, and an Effeminate one."[75] On August 6, 1892, the *Boston Daily Globe*'s headlines read that the murders had been "Traced to [a] Camp of Horse-Traders" and "Westerners."[76] The paper reported that "[the Westerners] have the characteristics of men leading a roving life, not unlike that of the gypsies. They dress in coarse, heavy garments and live in tents in the woods."[77] This same "Western" suspect was conveniently endowed with an adept and powerful swing, as he was said to be wearing "Base-Ball Shoes on His Feet."[78] Lizzie's appearance, unlike that of horse-traders or immigrants, and despite Sizer's ambiguous report, conformed to the standards of middle-class respectability.

A brief evaluation of the murder of Bertha Manchester of Fall River, which occurred on May 31, 1893, is informative when considering the importance of outward appearances and their relation to internal characteristics at the turn of the century.[79] Despite the odd behavior of Manchester's father, a Portuguese immigrant named José Correiro was arrested for the brutal crime on June 5, 1893.[80] For $50.00 in jewelry, he supposedly hacked off Bertha Manchester's head with an ax. Correiro was described in the *Boston Daily Globe* as "lazy," "rather small, of wiry build, black hair, a small dark mustache, dark eyes, and with the sallow complexion peculiar to the Portuguese." This attempt at detailed visual description continues the turn-of-the-century photographic project to collect physiognomic data to document the appearance of criminals.[81] Correiro's clothing was repeatedly described as "old and dark" or "very much worn and not very clean." The police considered his "dusty" shoes evidence of his guilt. His tattered clothing served to "mark" him as "other" than middle-class. Remarkably, during the search and arrest of Correiro the police abstained from releasing information concerning the evidence against him, arguing that they needed to protect their witnesses from the "vengeful Portuguese."[82]

Lizzie's actions and appearances associated with "good breeding" were read as *visible* signs of her innocence and "American blood." The *New Bedford Mercury* stated: "She behaved like a self-possessed girl, with all the grit that comes of American blood, which had flowed pure in her family during centuries."[83] Set within this discourse of purity, the defense's argument that "blood speaks out, although it is voiceless," certainly rings true.[84] At the turn of the century, "blood" served as a signifier of very specific racialized and gendered meanings. Smith writes that in the nineteenth century the discourses of gender and race were intertwined in the articulation of the middle class.[85] White women

Figure 10.11: Charles Baude, engraving after A. Agache,
The Annunciation, c. 1892. Image can be found in
Harper's Bazaar, XXV (March 26, 1892): 249.

were seen as the "guardians" of racialized nationhood, and were expected to
fulfill a reproductive duty for the race by passing on the "gifts" of the biological
stock to progeny.[86] Nineteenth-century eugenicists transformed "blood" into
inherited "property," and transformed intellectual ability and moral character
into "heirlooms." It was reasoned that "good" or "American" blood should be
rewarded with the monetary properties and social standing once held by aris-
tocratic bloodlines.[87] Photography played a pivotal role in the science of biological racialism, because it helped to establish social typologies, which allowed for the systematic reading of physical signs as markers of interior character. "The daguerreotype," Smith writes, "poses a visual map of interior
essence . . . both genealogies and visual technologies trace the bloodlines that
direct the circulation of soon-to-be racialized ancestral 'properties.' "[88] Photographs served as visual evidence that "traced inherited moral characteristics in
the curves and expressions of the face."[89]

Moral characteristics were also tied to outward signs of middle-class cultural refinement. A passage in Wood's *The Psychology of Crime* emphasized
the deterministic role art played in the establishment of character: "The human
consciousness is like an endless corridor in a picture gallery," he wrote, "each
visitor executing and hanging his own works of art. His preference is determined by the character of those before which he lingers."[90] The *Boston Daily*

Globe's August 7, 1892, report on Lizzie's trip to Europe and her "cultivated taste" for the art of European masters thus depicted Lizzie as the "right" kind of woman: "Lizzie brought home a large collection of photographs of buildings and copies of works of the great masters. She was particularly fond of Raphael's *Sistine Madonna*, and brought home several large copies of it."[91] Lizzie lingering before the *Sistine Madonna*, which depicts the paragon of white middle-class motherly virtue, was coded. It signified, to the readers of the *Globe*, something about Lizzie's character. Her "taste" for the *Sistine Madonna* was indicative of her moral superiority and compliance with turn-of-the-century constructions of women as "angels of the household."[92] It also perhaps served to offset the negative impressions left by Lizzie's unmarried and childless status. The *Globe*'s narrative was framed by other sections on topics such as Lizzie's "Christian Home Influence" and her "Personal Charms"—sections that likewise served as evidence of her good character.

The March 1892 edition of *Harper's Bazar* featured a poem by Margaret E. Sagster, titled "The Annunciation," which explicitly drew parallels between the Madonna and turn-of-the-century motherhood.[93] Sagster's poem describes the ideal mother as a "divine" figure "alone within the room":

> With grave eyes rapt in dreams of prayer,
> She sits alone within the room,
> Be golden ray or deepening gloom.
> Her heart uplifted, silent, sweet,
> Her thought goes forth her Lord to greet.
>
> .   .   .   .
>
> Oh, sacred grace of motherhood!
> Divinest thing beneath the sky,
> Which yet the heavens overbrood,
> The watching angels hovering nigh.
> Unending rite of sacrifice,
> Costly beyond earth's utmost price.
>
> "Hail Mary!" thrills each mother soul;
> Ere yet the life-beat faint and sweet,
> That shall not cease while ages roll,
> Each mother hears the glad repeat,
> And thenceforth, hollowed, dwells apart,
> Heaven's matchless lily in her heart.[94]

The illustration for the poem, an engraving by Charles Baude, was based on Alfred-Pierre Agache's painting exhibited at the World's Columbian Exposition in 1893 (figure 10.11).[95] Both the engraving and the illustration cite the

Figure 10.12: *Miss Borden Appeared in the Morning with a Bunch of Flowers, Boston Hearld,* June, 1893.

visual conventions of femininity seen in Raphael's *Sistine Madonna*—conventions such as delicately turned heads and heavy drapery placed over rounded and voluptuous bodies. In fact, the pose of the Madonna in the *Harper's Bazar* illustration is a citation of the pose of the angel who appears to the right of Raphael's Madonna. Both also follow the convention of depicting the Virgin within an interior, or "alone within the room."

Ultimately, however, society was unable to control that which occurred while a woman was "alone within the room." The prosecution recognized this and made the accusation that Lizzie's presence in the home on the day of the murders caused her to appear suspect. The defense responded with an essentialist argument that naturalized Lizzie's presence in the home, and evoked the photograph as a metaphor in order to buttress the "reality" of the "picture" of domesticity presented to the jury as evidence:

> Lizzie was about the house as usual. She was in the house and about the house. What was she doing? Doing just the same as any decent woman does, attending to her work, ironing handkerchiefs, going up and down stairs, going down to the cellar, to the closet. You say those things are not all proved. No; but I am taking you into the house just as I would go into your house, for instance, and say, What are your wives doing now? Well, doing the ordinary work around the house, getting the dinner. Well, where do they go? Undoubtedly they are going down cellar for potatoes, going out into the kitchen, to the sink room, here and there. You can see the whole thing. It is photographed in your mind.[96]

The prosecution used the fact that the rooms of the Borden house were locked to argue that the murderer would be unable to maneuver successfully within the house without intimate knowledge of its intricate interior layout.[97] The Bordens kept their home securely locked against outside intruders at all times, and this, in effect, emphasized the delineation between private interior space and public exterior space and the subsequent invasion of the former.[98] However, it was noted that even within the home doors were intentionally locked to limit access to any given room.[99] "Although they occupied the same household," the prosecution argued, "there was built up between them by locks and bolts and bars, almost an impassable wall."[100] In a pre-trial interview with Lizzie Borden published in the *Woman's Journal*, Lizzie displays intimate knowledge of the house's interior:

> How can they think me guilty? What a fool must I have been if I committed a crime like that in broad day-light, with the certainty of detection, with people going to and fro on the street, with Bridget washing windows and likely to come in for water at any minute; with my uncle visiting us and likely to be back at any time, with the curtains up and the neighbors astir? I knew every foot of that house. I could have walked all over it in the dark, sure of my way. Why, if I contemplated that crime, should I not have done it at night? Two blows as they lay asleep, no noise, no stir; I could have opened wide the street door, made evidence of a struggle in the room, and then with plenty of time to remove from myself all traces of blood, gone quietly to bed. But they say that I committed both crimes at noonday and removed from myself all evidence of the horrible work. How can they believe that?[101]

Though this display of detailed knowledge of the home perhaps helped to exonerate Lizzie in the eyes of *Woman's Journal* readers, it would have served to further implicate Lizzie in the eyes of the prosecution. Her statement indicates that she had the understanding of the complex interior layout necessary to commit the crimes. The prosecution argued that the intimate knowledge of the interior of the Borden home exhibited by Lizzie was "womanly," but their arguments frequently cast the "womanly" in negative terms.[102] "How could she have avoided the spattering of her dress with blood if she was the author of these crimes?" asked one of the prosecutors. "I cannot answer it. You cannot answer it. You are neither murderers nor women. You have neither the craft of the assassin or the cunning and deftness of the sex."[103]

An additional way in which Lizzie coded herself as feminine and aligned herself with the domestic was by way of the display of flowers in the courtroom. It was necessary for Lizzie to offset the statement made by the *Brockton Enterprise*: women who "decorate the land like the floral beauties of June do not become habitual attendants in court rooms."[104] Floral iconography is traditionally used to indicate a woman's fertility and beauty. Moreover, each species and variety of flower was coded, holding a specific meaning to the turn-of-the-century public. In the photograph analyzed by Sizer, Lizzie wears an enamel pin in the shape of a pansy at her neck. She also sometimes carried a bouquet of pansies to the trial (figure 10.12). In the June 4, 1893, edition

Figure 10.13: Sir John Everett Millais, *Ophelia,* 1851, Tate Gallery, London.

of the *Boston Daily Globe* Lizzie is described wearing a "dress of blue serge and a black toque," while in her hands "she carried a bunch of pansies."[105] The *Fall River Daily Herald*'s declaration that the pansy was Lizzie's favorite flower surely sent readers rushing to decipher its meaning and Lizzie's message.

On May 21, 1892, two months before the murders, *Harper's Bazar*, a widely read women's magazine, published a detailed article elaborating on the meanings associated with the pansy. Here pansies are associated not only with thoughts (*pensées*), but with death and remembrance. *Harper's* begins by describing the lines of *Hamlet*'s Ophelia: "There is pansies, that's for thoughts." Pansies are also associated with death, *Harper's* writes: "Milton calls for it, with 'every flower that sad embroidery wears,' to strew the hearse of Lycidas." To further underscore the pansy's association with death, *Harper's* includes lines from Shelley: "Pansies let my flowers be / On the living grave I hear / Scatter them without a tear / Let no friend, however dear / Waste one hope, one fear, for me."[106] Sir John Everett Millais's *Ophelia* (figure 10.13) is called to mind as a result of the description offered by *Harper's*, and, indeed, tiny violet and yellow pansies are among the flowers floating above her body as she slowly drifts downstream.

The image of the deceased Ophelia has something in common with the inquest photograph of Abby (see figure 10.7). The photograph, taken from an odd angle, gives the illusion that the floor is uneven and the carpet pattern mobile. The floor streams toward the viewer and carries Abby in its current. In both *Ophelia* and the photograph of Abby, the dead women lie horizontally and are consumed by their florid and watery surroundings—they are passive riders of its relentless current. The overexposure caused by the sunlight streaming through the guest room window dematerializes the interior walls. The edges of Abby's pale dress disappear as they become indistinct from this light. The photograph provides an accidental illustration of how in death Abby is assumed as a "transcendental" body, vanished and assimilated into spirit. Yet the photograph also makes it apparent that half of her body remains anchored to the base, earthly, material world of furniture, objects, and florid carpets—she has been both metaphorically and literally cleaved down the middle. The photograph itself performs this split. It provides the viewer with the illusion of presence, but it also points to what *was*, but no longer *is*.[107]

Although by bringing pansies to her trial and declaring them her favorite flower, Lizzie indicated that she had "thoughts" of her parents, the message is ambiguous—for, in addition to discussing the pansy's association with thoughts and death, *Harper's* indicates the way in which in German pansies are referred to as stepmothers (*Stiefmütterchen*):

> In their fairy stories the cruel stepmother plays a conspicuous part, and the beautiful heroine suffers grievously from her machinations. Why, then, should the name of this obnoxious personage be given to the delicate blossoms, the flowers of thought and love? Lacking definite, or rather say, any information upon the subject, it is suggested that it may be a bit of poetic justice, a recognition of the noble qualities of the step-mother of real life. For rarely indeed is found a harsh step-dame who figures in fairy literature, but countless are the noble women who, often as mere girls, assume the burden of bringing up a family of children, and who, by their devoted affection, fill lives and homes with heart's-ease.[108]

The ambiguity of Lizzie's message is aided by the ambiguity and confusion of the writer. Despite the writer's attempts to reconcile the negative association between the archetypal German stepmother and the delicate blossoms of the pansy, she has no evidence on which to base her reconciliation. Although Lizzie's admiration for the pansy can be interpreted as a statement intended to honor the selfless devotion of Abby, it can also be read as an indication of Lizzie's conflicted feelings. For lying beneath the surface of the "poetic justice" offered by the writer there lurks the pansy's repressed association with the stepmother of German fairy literature, who is often killed or otherwise eliminated by the beautiful heroine of the story. Lizzie's admiration for the pansy would therefore send to the female readers of *Harper's Bazar* a highly suspect message. Although as women they had no right to register an official verdict as part of a jury, public opinion never quite vindicated Lizzie of the crimes. However, by reinforcing the jury's faith that her outward appearance of femininity corresponded to an inward passivity and innocence, Lizzie's display of feminine attributes perhaps swayed them in her favor. Lizzie Borden's acquittal preserved the turn-of-the-century middle-class conception of women as "the angel in the household," and allowed for a continued faith in the "physiognomic fallacy."

Notes

1. Carlo Ginzburg, "The Judge and the Historian," *Critical Inquiry* 18 (Autumn 1991): 79.

2. Leonard Rebello, *Lizzie Borden: Past and Present* (Fall River, Mass.: Al-Zach Press, 1999), 161. Twenty-six out-of-town reporters and artists and at least ten local newspaper reporters covered the trial. Lucy Stone's 1893 article, "A Flaw in the Jury System," illustrates the way in which the circumstances surrounding the Borden case facilitated arguments in favor of the modification of women's civic duties. To support women's participation on juries, for example, Stone asserts that the Borden case was itself "womanly." Stone is concerned primarily with women's *representation*. She lamented that women lacked representation by their "true" peers, just as she lamented that women lacked representation in the democratic process. Stone is also concerned, however, with representation as *evidence*—a material fragment, such as a hatchet, a photograph, or a description or statement offered by a witness. She argues that female jurors are better able to judge or read the representations put forth by female witnesses as evidence.

3. Daniel A. Cohen, "The Murder of Maria Bickford: Fashion, Passion, and the Birth of a Consumer Culture," *American Studies* 31 (Fall 1990): 5–6.

4. Thomas J. Schlereth, *Victorian America: Transformations in Everyday Life, 1876–1915* (New York: Harper Collins, 1991), 174.

5. Most of the illustrations of Lizzie Borden that appeared in the press were not based on photographs. Portraits of Lizzie, however, were often based on photographs such as that analyzed by the phrenologist Nelson Sizer. An illustration made after the only photograph taken of Lizzie after her arrest appeared in the *Boston Daily Globe* on June 12, 1893. However, I have not been able to locate the actual photograph on which this illustration is based. The illustrations of the crime scene that appeared in the press were based on the inquest photographs.

6. Frank H. Burt, *The Trial of Lizzie A. Borden: Upon an Indictment Charging her with the Murders of Abby Durfee Borden and Andrew Jackson Borden; Before the Superior Court for the County of Bristol; Presiding, C. J. Mason, J. J. Blodgett, and*

J. J. Dewey; Official Stenographic Report by Frank H. Burt, 2 vols. (New Bedford, Mass., np 1893). From the list of exhibits shown at the trial the following were photographs: exhibits 10–14; photographs of Borden house; exhibits 15–19; photographs of bodies; exhibits 24–43; small photographs of Borden premises.

7. Ibid., 105.

8. Ibid., 302. For other uses of the photographic images during the trial, see ibid., 2, 1303, 1609, 1679, 1722. Newspapers published drawings that were based on the photographs shown in the courtroom during Lizzie Borden's trial. In the newspaper illustrations the interior furnishings of the Borden home were visible.

9. Sandra S. Phillips, "Identifying the Criminal," in *Police Pictures: The Photograph as Evidence,* ed. Sandra S. Phillips, Mark Haworth-Booth, Carol Squiers, (San Francisco: Chronicle Books, 1997), 7.

10. According to the science of phrenology, the shape and protuberances of one's skull revealed one's character and mental capacity.

11. Phillips, 7. See also Martha Banta, "Looking for the Best Type," in *Imaging American Women: Idea and Ideals in Cultural History* (New York: Columbia University Press, 1987). In this chapter, Banta argues that phrenology's renewed popularity in the United States was the result of the increasing population of immigrants in the 1880s. This new diverse population called into question traditional understandings of American identity based on the collapse of taking the northern European "type" as identified with the American "type." Phrenology offered to those already established in America sets of clear signs by which to "identify and make known" those who were different.

12. Shawn Michelle Smith, *American Archives: Gender, Race, and Class in Visual Culture* (Princeton, N.J.: Princeton University Press, 1999), 93.

13. Ibid., 69.

14. Henry Wood, "The Psychology of Crime," *Arena* 47 (October 1893): 530–31.

15. Ibid., 529.

16. Ibid.

17. See the discussion of "physiognomic perception" in E. H. Gombrich's essays "On Physiognomic Perception" and "Art and Scholarship" in *his "Meditations on a Hobby Horse" and Other Essays on the Theory of Art* (Chicago: Phaidon Press, University of Chicago Press, 1963).

18. Ibid., 112.

19. Roland Barthes, "The Photographic Message," in *Image-Music-Text* (New York: Hill and Wang, 1977), 17.

20. Ibid., 19.

21. Ibid.

22. Ibid., 28.

23. Burt, 1, 747–48.

24. Ibid., 302.

25. Ibid., 438.

26. Ibid., 854–55.

27. Hanging over the Borden parlor sofa is what appears to be an image of the Arc de Triomphe located on the Champs-Elysées in Paris. The Arc de Triomphe was commissioned by Napoleon to commemorate the victorious armies of the French Revolution and was completed in 1836 during the reign of Louis-Philippe.

28. See Celia Jackson Otto, *American Furniture of the Nineteenth Century* (New York: Viking Press, 1965), 122.

29. See Marvin D. Schwartz, Edward J. Stanek, and Douglas K. True, *The Furniture of John Henry Belter and the Rococo Revival* (New York: E. P. Dutton, 1981), 2–4. See also Otto, 122–60.

30. Burt, 1, 869–70.

31. Ibid., 751–52.

32. Ibid., 951.

33. Ibid., 309.

34. Ibid.

35. Ibid., 869.

36. Ibid., 19–20.

37. Barthes, 27.

38. Ibid., 22.

39. Linda Nochlin, "Visions of Languor," *House and Garden,* April 1983: 172.

40. Ibid.

41. *A Carte de visite* was a small, collectible albumen print, usually of a famous person. It was about the size of a calling card, and was popularized in the 1850s by the Parisian photographer André Adolphe Eugène Disdéri.

42. Image from the *New Bedford Evening Journal,* June 20, 1893, and reproduced in Rebello, 222.

43. Image from the *Fall River Daily Herald,* June 20, 1893, and reproduced in Rebello, 222.

44. Alexander Nemerov, "Vanishing Americans: Abbott Thayer, Theodore Roosevelt, and the Attraction of Camouflage," *American Art* 11 (Summer 1997): 60.

45. Banta, 223.

46. On the complex politics of visibility and invisibility, see Peggy Phelan, *Unmarked: The Politics of Performance* (New York: Routledge, 1993).

47. Julian Ralph, in the *New Bedford Mercury*, June 7, 1893. Cited in Rebello, 233.

48. The Borden interior represents a "middle-class" interior, despite the fact that technically the Bordens were not by any means "middle-class."

49. Barthes, 22.

50. Ibid., 54.

51. See also Clifford E. Clark Jr., "Domestic Architecture as an Index to Social History: The Romantic Revival and the Cult of Domesticity in America, 1840–1870," reprinted in *Material Life in America, 1600–1860,* ed. Robert Blair St. George (Boston: Northeastern Universiy Press 1988).

52. On the history of "refinement" in the United States, see Richard L. Bushman, *The Refinement of America: Persons, Houses, Cities* (New York: Knopf, 1992).

53. John Davis, "Children in the Parlor: Eastman Johnson's Brown Family and the Post–Civil War Luxury Interior," *American Art* 10 (Summer 1996): 73.

54. Ibid.

55. Andrew was worth between $250,000 and $300,000. See Edmund Pearson, *The Trial of Lizzie Borden* (New York: Doubleday, Doran & Company, 1937), 104.

56. Ibid.

57. It is worth noting that the emphasis on Lizzie's modes of consumption finds parallels in the coverage of the murder of Maria A. Bickford. In his study of the murder of Maria Bickford, Daniel A. Cohen points out that the "penny press" depicted Bickford as either a *sentimental victim* or a *depraved seductress*. These divergent views, he argues, were associated with correspondingly divergent depictions of an emerging consumer culture. Descriptions of Bickford's dress and home interior were used to characterize her as either a tasteful and sensitive middle-class consumer of genteel taste, or a wasteful and undisciplined spendthrift. The reading of Bickford's consumer habits was, according to Cohen, a "new semiotics of material consumption." Dress was seen as a reliable "index" of character, and "the pursuit of fashion" was transformed into "a form of moral self-improvement." Cohen, 6–7.

58. Ibid., 64.

59. This conclusion was further solidified in the popular mind after the trial, when Lizzie moved from the modest home on Second Street to the "mansion" she pretentiously named Maplecroft. Unlike her previous home, Maplecroft was located in the elite French Street neighborhood of Fall River, also referred to as "The Hill."

60. Pearson, 304.

61. Charlotte Perkins Gilman, "The Yellow Wallpaper," *New England Magazine*, January 1892, 653.

62. Ibid.

63. Julie Bates Dock, ed., *Charlotte Perkins Gilman's "The Yellow Wall-paper" and the History of Its Publication and Reception: A Critical Edition and Documentary Casebook* (State College: Pennsylvania State University Press, 1998), 106.

64. Between 1871 and 1875 Morris served as the director of his father's mining company, Devon Great Consols (DGC), in its day the largest producer of arsenic in the world. DGC was the main supplier of arsenic for use in green pigments, many of which were used in Morris papers. For example, the green pigment in Morris's famous *Trellis* (1864) wallpaper has been shown to contain the arsenic-based pigments. In damp rooms, fungi living in the wallpaper turned the arsenic salts into the highly poisonous trimethylarcine. The turn-of-the-century popular press concluded that these pigments were responsible for untold numbers of chronic illnesses and deaths, and an analysis featured in the June 2003 issue of *Nature* confirms these fears. The Morris papers literally reiterate the turn-of-the-century belief in an interior's ability to make one seriously ill. See Andy Meharg, "The Arsenic Green," *Nature* 423 (12 June, 2003): 688; and Philip Ball, "William Morris Made Poisonous Wallpaper: Arts and Crafts Traditionalist Manufactured and Used Arsenic-based Greens," *Nature News Service/Macmillan Magazines,* 12 June 2003. http://www.nature.com/nsu/030609/030609-11.html

65. Roland Barthes, *Camera Lucida: Reflections on Photography*. (New York: Hill and Wang, 1981), 6.

66. Carol Mavor, *Pleasures Taken: Performances of Sexuality and Loss in Victorian Photographs* (Durham, N.C.: Duke University Press, 1995), 4.

67. Barthes, *Camera Lucida,* 30.

68. Christian Metz, "Photography and Fetish," *October* 34 (Fall 1985): 81–90.

69. Note the prosecution's statement: "It will appear that about the two rooms in which the homicides were committed, there was blood spattering in various directions, so that it would make it probable that one or more spatters of blood would be upon the person or upon the clothing of the assailant. And there has been produced for the inspection of the Commonwealth—it was produced a good many days after the homicide—the clothing said to have been worn by the prisoner on the morning of August 4—the shoes, stockings, dress, skirt. The most rigid examination by the most competent expert in this country fails to disclose any marks of blood upon the dress which is produced as the one which she wore on the morning of the homicide, and the skirt which she is said to have worn upon that morning produces one minute spot of blood, which I do not think it worth while to call to your attention at the present time." Pearson, 121.

70. I would like to thank Elizabeth Carlson for pointing out that the emphasis the press placed on Lizzie's physical appearance was typical of turn-of-the-century writing on female public figures.

71. "Spot of Blood/Said to Have Been Found on Lizzie's Skirt/Axe Found by Mayor Coughlin/It Seems to Have Been Recently Washed/Mayor and Marshal Ask Girls Questions/Lizzie, as Girl and Woman, Described by Friends/Retiring in Manner, Pure, Modest, and Gentle/Exhaustive Search of Police Reveals Practically Nothing," *Boston Daily Globe*, August 7, 1892.

72. Nelson Sizer, "Lizzie Borden," *Phrenological Journal of Science and Health* 45 December 1892, 287.

73. Ibid., 287–88.

74. In addition to causing a popular sensation, Lizzie Borden's arrest sent shock waves through a feminist community that feared her guilt would tarnish a suffragist movement premised on the moral superiority of women.

75. Quoted in Michael Martins and Dennis A. Binette, eds., *The Commonwealth of Massachusetts vs. Lizzie A. Borden: The Knowlton Papers, 1892–1893* (Fall River, Mass.: Fall River Historical Society, 1994), 59. Also note, in relation to the remark regarding the murders and effeminacy, the comment in "Startling Parallelisms, Many Points of Resemblance Found between the Manchester and Borden Murders," *Boston Daily Globe*, June 1, 1893. The author states: "At the time of the Borden murder, the theory was advanced by many, noticeably by women, that none but a woman would have so hacked and mutilated the body. They argued at the time, and it was one of the strongest arguments advanced in their minds, that Lizzie Borden is guilty of the crime, that if a man had done the deed he would have struck but one blow."

76. See "Stranger/Stood on Borden's Doorstep/Base-Ball Shoes on His Feet/ Man Like Him Has Been Seen Since/Jumped the Fence Day of the Murder/Traced to Camp of Horse-Traders/Morse Is Said to Know These Westerners/Hatchet Was Bought Wednesday in New Bedford/Funeral Scenes in Fall River Today/How Lizzie Borden Bluffed Police When Searching," *Boston Globe*, August 6, 1892.

77. Ibid.

78. Ibid.

79 See "Startling Parallelisms."

80. Newspapers cast suspicion on Bertha's father by implying that he was not showing sufficient outward signs of grievance. For example, "Startling Parallelisms" accuses Manchester's young son (Bertha's brother) as being "happy as a lark," and appearing no more troubled than his father over Bertha's murder. Manchester supposedly drove his milk wagon down the street past the undertakers' establishment in which his daughter was lying and never let his gaze wander across the street to the building. In "Again the Axe," *Boston Daily Globe*, May 31, 1893, the reporter notes that when Manchester's son found the body, Manchester did not rush into the house, but "proceeded to unharness his horse, which he had driven into the yard attached to the milk wagon, and did not go into the house until he had put his horse up." In Machester's defense, these articles also make it clear that the Manchester family was one of rigorous routine.

81. Smith, 73.

82. See "Live Chasers/Running Down Clue from Bridgewater," *Boston Daily Globe*, June 5, 1893. The above behavior contrasts markedly with the free release of witness testimony and incriminating evidence associated with the Borden case. The contrast leads one to suspect that the Fall River police did not have much evidence against Correiro—other than the fact that he was a recent immigrant who did not speak English. In fact, contemporary newspapers commented on the discriminatory behavior. See "Why This Discrimination?" *Fall River Daily Globe*, June 13, 1893; and "A Strong Protest/A Friend of Correiro Says He Has Been Treated Harshly," *Fall River Daily Herald*, June 13, 1893. For additional bibliographic entries on the Manchester Murder, see Rebello, 188–90.

83. Julian Ralph, *New Bedford Mercury*, June 7, 1893. Cited in Rebello, 233.

84. Note the defense's argument: "There was no blood on her, and blood speaks out, although it is voiceless. It speaks out against the criminal. Not a spot from her hair to her feet, on dress or person anywhere. Think of it! Think of it for an instant! Yes, there was one drop of blood on the white skirt, as big as the head of the smallest pin, says Professor Wood; less a sixteenth of an inch in diameter; and that is every particle of blood that was found upon her clothing. I forebear to allude to what is proved in this case, Miss Borden's illness, monthly illness, at that time, and to tell you or remind you that Professor Wood said he would not undertake that that blood was not the menstrual blood." Pearson, 291.

85. Smith, 31.

86. Ibid., 139.

87. Ibid., 44.

88. Ibid., 48.

89. Ibid., 49.

90. Wood, 535.

91. See "Spot of Blood, (n. 71 above).

92. See Martha Banta, "Images of the Ideal" and "Angels at the Threshold," in *Imaging American Women*, (n. 11 above). Also see Bailey Van Hook, *Angels of Art: Women and Art in American Society, 1876–1914* (State College: Pennsylvania State University Press, 1996).

93. Throughout the text, when referring to the periodical *Harper's Bazar*, I remain faithful to the turn-of-the-century spelling of "bazaar."

94. Margaret E. Sagster, "The Annunciation," *Harper's Bazar*, March 26, 1892, 242.

95. Ibid., 249. Alfred-Pierre Agache was a French artist born in Lille. He was a pupil of Colas and Pluchard and a member of the Society of French Artists. See

Charles M. Kurtz, ed., *Official Illustrations from the Art Gallery of the World's Columbian Exposition, Three Hundred and Thirty-Six Engravings* [on-line] (Philadelphia: George Barrie, 1883), 83. *World's Columbian Exposition of 1893: Paul B. Galvin Library Digital History Collection*, Illinois Institute of Technology. Available from the World Wide Web: http://columbus.gl.iit.edu/art gallery/index.html.

96. Burt, 2, 1722.

97. Ibid., 127.

98. See Pearson, 112. The prosecution notes: "Upon that front door were three fastenings: a spring latch, a bolt and a lock which operated by key."

99. For the prosecution's emphasis on the Borden home's odd layout and the locking of its rooms, see ibid., 110–12.

100 For the description of the locked front door see ibid., 106.

101. Mary A. Livermore, "A Talk with Lizzie Borden," *Woman's Journal,* May 27, 1893.

102. See Catherine Ross Nickerson, " 'The Deftness of Her Sex': Innocence, Guilt, and Gender in the Trial of Lizzie Borden," in *Lethal Imagination: Violence and Brutality in American History,* ed. Michael A. Bellesiles (New York: New York University Press, 1999), 275.

103. Livermore, "Talk with Lizze Borden."

104. Rebello, 227.

105. "Lizzie Borden at New Bedford," *Boston Daily Globe,* June 4, 1893.

106. "Pansies," *Harper's Bazar,* vol. XXV (May 21, 1892): 412.

107. Barthes writes that the presence of the referent in the photograph is never metaphoric. If in the photographing of corpses the photograph becomes horrible, it is because it certifies that the corpse is "alive, *as corpse.*" It is, he writes, "the living image of a dead thing." Someone has seen the referent *in flesh and blood.* Barthes, *Camera Lucida,* 78–79.

108. "Pansies," *Harper's Bazar,* vol. XXV (May 21, 1892): 412.

Contributors

Robert Asher is professor of history, emeritus, at the University of Connecticut. He has published *Connecticut Workers and Technological Change* (1983) and *Concepts in American History* (1996). He edited *Connecticut History* from 1997 to 2003.

Tiffany Johnson Bidler is a graduate student in art history at the University of Minnesota. She has taught at the Minneapolis College of Art and Design.

Elizabeth A. De Wolfe is associate professor of history at the University of New England. She has published *Shaking the Faith: Women, Family, and Mary Marshall Dyer"s Anti-Shaker campaign, 1815–1867* (2002) and has coedited *Such News of the Land: U.S. Women Nature Writers* (2001).

Lawrence B. Goodheart, professor of history at the University of Connecticut/Hartford, has written *Mad Yankees: The Hartford Retreat for the Insane and Nineteenth-Century Psychiatry* (2003). His recent essays have appeared in *Connecticut History, History of Psychiatry,* and the *Journal of the History of Medicine and Allied Sciences.*

Dave Lindorff, a two-time Fulbright Scholar and award-winning freelance journalist, writes regularly for *Salon, Counterpunch, Business Week* and other publications. He is the author of *Killing Time: An Investigation into the Death Penalty Case of Mumia Abu-Jamal* (2003), *Marketplace Medicine: The Rise of the For-Profit Hospital Chains* (1992), *and This Can't Be Happening! Resisting The Disintegration of American Democracy* (2004).

Laura-Eve Moss received her doctorate in history from the University of Connecticut in 1999. Her dissertation was "Democracy, Citizenship, and Constitution-Making in New York 1777–1894." She was the managing editor of *The Encyclopedia of New York State.* She is now assistant editor of The Andrea Jackson Papers, University of Tennessee.

John J. Navin, assistant professor of history and associate dean of humanities and fine arts at Coastal Carolina University, specializes in colonial New England history. He is writing a book about Plymouth Plantation.

Alan Rogers, professor of history and chair of the Department of History at Boston College, is the author of *Empire and Liberty: American Resistance to British Authority, 1755–1763* (1974) and numerous articles on American legal history. He will shortly be publishing a book entitled *Murder and the Death Penalty in Massachusetts.*

Nancy H. Steenburg, an assistant professor in residence at the University of Connecticut/Avery Point, earned her doctorate in history from the University of Connecticut (2003) and has published articles in *Connecticut History.* Her book, *Children and the Criminal Law in Connecticut, 1635–1855,* will be published by Routledge in 2004.

Michael A. Trotti received his doctorate in history from the University of North Carolina, Chapel Hill. He is assistant professor of history at Ithaca College and is currently working on a book-length manuscript on crime and culture in the late nineteenth and early twentieth centuries. He has published articles in the *Journal of Social History* and the *Virginia Magazine of History and Biography.*

Index

Index of Cases Cited in Text